Autism: Mind and Brain

Edited by

UTA FRITH

Institute of Cognitive Neuroscience,
University College London, London

and

ELISABETH L. HILL

Department of Psychology,
Goldsmiths College,
University of London, London

Originating from a Theme Issue first published by Philosophical
Transactions of the Royal Society, Series B.

**THE ROYAL
SOCIETY**

OXFORD
UNIVERSITY PRESS

OXFORD

UNIVERSITY PRESS

Great Clarendon Street, Oxford OX2 6DP

Oxford University Press is a department of the University of Oxford.
It furthers the University's objective of excellence in research, scholarship,
and education by publishing worldwide in

Oxford New York

Auckland Bangkok Buenos Aires Cape Town Chennai
Dar es Salaam Delhi Hong Kong Istanbul Karachi Kolkata
Kuala Lumpur Madrid Melbourne Mexico City Mumbai Nairobi
São Paulo Shanghai Taipei Tokyo Toronto

Oxford is a registered trade mark of Oxford University Press
in the UK and in certain other countries

Published in the United States
by Oxford University Press Inc., New York

First published by the Royal Society 2003
First published by Oxford University Press 2004

A Catalogue record for this title is available
from the British Library

ISBN 0 19 852923 6 (Hbk)
0 19 852924 4 (Pbk)

10 9 8 7 6 5 4 3 2 1

Typeset by Newgen Imaging Systems (P) Ltd., Chennai, India
Printed in Great Britain
on acid-free paper by
Biddles Ltd, Guildford and King's Lynn

Preface

Autism is probably the most fascinating and puzzling of all developmental disorders. It is characterised by a profound, yet subtle, impairment in social communication, a strong preference for routines, and an uneven profile of cognitive abilities. The more we find out about autism, the more questions arise. Two major issues are currently debated: What abnormalities in the brain give rise to the core features of autism? And to what extent is the dramatic increase in cases of autism due to changes in the diagnostic criteria? In this book a collection of new studies is presented, which cover a remarkably large range of research interests, and which address some of the questions that arise from these two major issues. Here we pick out just a few of them.

Asperger syndrome is a variant of autism that is increasingly diagnosed, but remains controversial. Chapter two, which is of some historical importance, explores whether the cases seen by Hans Asperger between 1940 and 1970 would meet the criteria used today. All chapters explore links between brain and mind in autism, and do this in a number of different ways. A recent finding, which is in urgent need of further research, is that the brains of individuals with autism tend to be larger than normal. How might brain size relate to intelligence and language in individual cases? Another recently confirmed finding, which is still not entirely understood, is that people with autism have difficulties in recognizing faces. Can these difficulties be explained as part and parcel of impaired functioning of the social brain? An enduring question concerns the problems of impaired planning and flexibility in autism, thought to reflect poor functioning of the frontal lobes. How do these problems distinguish children with autism from those with attention deficits? Do the brain regions, which are known to be critical for some of the skills that are impaired in autism, show anatomical abnormalities?

These and other questions are amenable to answers, because of the ingenious and rigorous experiments carried out and described by the contributors to this volume. Their investigations present a varied and colourful picture of autism research at the cutting edge. They give an insight into the nature and high quality of current research programmes across the world. Common to all is the desire to expose the core problems beneath the superficial layer of behavioural signs and to identify the brain basis of these problems.

This book was originally published as an issue of the Philosophical Transactions of the Royal Society, Series B, *Phil. Trans. R. Soc. Lond. B* (2003) **358**, 275–427.

Uta Frith   *London*
Elisabeth L. Hill   *August 2003*

Contents

List of Contributors ix

Introduction xiii
U. Frith and E. L. Hill

1. Understanding autism: insights from mind and brain 1
   E. L. Hill and U. Frith

2. A retrospective analysis of the clinical case records of
   'autistic psychopaths' diagnosed by Hans Asperger and
   his team at the University Children's Hospital, Vienna 21
   K. Hippler and C. Klicpera

3. Identifying neurocognitive phenotypes in autism 43
   H. Tager-Flusberg and R. M. Joseph

4. Why is joint attention a pivotal skill in autism? 67
   T. Charman

5. Does the perception of moving eyes trigger reflexive
   visual orienting in autism? 89
   *J. Swettenham, S. Condie, R. Campbell,
   E. Milne, and M. Coleman*

6. The pathogenesis of autism: insights from
   congenital blindness 109
   R. P. Hobson and M. Bishop

7. The enactive mind, or from actions to cognition:
   lessons from autism 127
   A. Klin, W. Jones, R. Schultz, and F. Volkmar

8. The systemizing quotient: an investigation of adults
   with Asperger syndrome or high-functioning autism,
   and normal sex differences 161
   *S. Baron-Cohen, J. Richler, D. Bisarya,
   N. Gurunathan, and S. Wheelwright*

9. Towards an understanding of the mechanisms of weak
   central coherence effects: experiments in visual
   configural learning and auditory perception 187
   K. Plaisted, L. Saksida, J. Alcántara, and E. Weisblatt

10. Disentangling weak coherence and executive dysfunction:
     planning drawing in autism and attention-deficit/
     hyperactivity disorder   211
     R. Booth, R. Charlton, C. Hughes, and F. Happé

11. Autism and movement disturbance   225
     M. Mari, D. Marks, C. Marraffa, M. Prior, and U. Castiello

12. Investigating individual differences in brain
     abnormalities in autism   247
     C. H. Salmond, M. de Haan, K. J. Friston,
     D. G. Gadian, and F. Vargha-Khadem

13. The role of the fusiform face area in social cognition:
     implications for the pathobiology of autism   267
     R. T. Schultz, D. J. Grelotti, A. Klin, J. Kleinman,
     C. Van der Gaag, R. Marois, and P. Skudlarski

     Index   295

List of Contributors

José Alcántara Department of Experimental Psychology, University of Cambridge, Downing Street, Cambridge CB2 3EB, UK

Simon Baron-Cohen Autism Research Centre, Departments of Experimental Psychology and Psychiatry, University of Cambridge, Douglas House, 18b Trumpington Road, Cambridge CB2 2AH, UK

Dheraj Bisarya Autism Research Centre, Departments of Experimental Psychology and Psychiatry, University of Cambridge, Douglas House, 18b Trumpington Road, Cambridge CB2 2AH, UK

Martin Bishop Developmental Psychopathology Research Unit, Tavistock Clinic and Department of Psychiatry and Behavioural Sciences, University College London, 120 Belsize Lane, London NW3 5BA, UK

Rhonda Booth Social, Genetic and Developmental Psychiatry Research Centre, Institute of Psychiatry, King's College London, De Crespigny Park, Denmark Hill, London SE5 8AF, UK

Ruth Campbell Department of Human Communication Science, University College London, 2 Wakefield Street, London WC1N 1PG, UK

Umberto Castiello Department of Psychology, Royal Holloway University of London, Egham, Surrey TW20 0EX, UK

Tony Charman Behavioural and Brain Sciences Unit, Institute of Child Health, 30 Guilford Street, London WC1N 1EH, UK

Rebecca Charlton Social, Genetic and Developmental Psychiatry Research Centre, Institute of Psychiatry, King's College London, De Crespigny Park, Denmark Hill, London SE5 8AF, UK

Mike Coleman Department of Human Communication Science, University College London, 2 Wakefield Street, London WC1N 1PG, UK

Samantha Condie Department of Human Communication Science, University College London, 2 Wakefield Street, London WC1N 1PG, UK

Uta Frith   Institute of Cognitive Neuroscience, University College London, 17 Queen Square, London WC1N 3AR, UK

K. J. Friston   The Wellcome Department of Imaging Neuroscience, 12 Queen Square, London WC1N 3BG, UK

D. G. Gadian   Radiology and Physics Unit, Institute of Child Health, 30 Guilford Street, London, WC1N 1EH, UK and Great Ormond Street Hospital for Children NHS Trust, Great Ormond Street, London, WC1N 3JH, UK

David J. Grelotti   Child Study Center, Yale University School of Medicine, 230 South Frontage Road, New Haven, CT 06520-7900, USA

Nhishanth Gurunathan   Autism Research Centre, Departments of Experimental Psychology and Psychiatry, University of Cambridge, Douglas House, 18b Trumpington Road, Cambridge CB2 2AH, UK

M. de Haan   Developmental Cognitive Neuroscience Unit, Institute of Child Health, Mecklenburgh Square, London, WC1N 2AP, UK

Francesca Happé   Social, Genetic and Developmental Psychiatry Research Centre, Institute of Psychiatry, King's College London, De Crespigny Park, Denmark Hill, London SE5 8AF, UK

Elisabeth L. Hill   Department of Psychology, Goldsmiths College, University of London, New Cross, London SE14 6NW, UK

Kathrin Hippler   Station für Heilpädagogik und Psychosomatik, Universitätsklinik für Kinder- und Jugendheilkunde, Währinger Gürtel 18–20, 1090, Vienna, Austria

R. Peter Hobson   Developmental Psychopathology Research Unit, Tavistock Clinic and Department of Psychiatry and Behavioural Sciences, University College London, 120 Belsize Lane, London NW3 5BA, UK

Claire Hughes   Department of Social and Political Sciences, University of Cambridge, Free School Lane, Cambridge CB2 3RQ, UK

Warren Jones   Yale Child Study Center, Yale University School of Medicine, 230 South Frontage Road, New Haven, CT 06520, USA

Robert M. Joseph   Laboratory of Developmental Cognitive Neuroscience, Department of Anatomy and Neurobiology, Boston University School of Medicine, 715 Albany Street L-814, Boston, MA 02118, USA

Jamie Kleinman   Department of Psychology, University of Connecticut, Unit 1020, Storrs, CT 06269-1020 USA

Christian Klicpera   Abtelung für Angewandte und Klinische Psychologie, Neues Institutsgebäude, Universitätsstrasse 7, 1010 Vienna, Austria

Ami Klin   Child Study Center, Yale University School of Medicine, 230 South Frontage Road, New Haven, CT 06520, USA

Morena Mari   Department of Psychology, Royal Holloway University of London, Egham, Surrey TW20 0EX, UK

René Marois   Department of Psychology, Vanderbilt University, 111 21st Avenue, Nashville, TN 37203, USA

Deborah Marks   Royal Children's Hospital, 3052 Parkville, VIC, Australia

Catherine Marraffa   Royal Children's Hospital, 3052 Parkville, VIC, Australia

Elizabeth Milne   Department of Human Communication Science, University College London, 2 Wakefield Street, London WC1N 1PG, UK

Kate Plaisted   Department of Experimental Psychology, University of Cambridge, Downing Street, Cambridge CB2 3EB, UK

Margot Prior   Royal Children's Hospital, 3052 Parkville, VIC, Australia

Jennifer Richler   Autism Research Centre, Departments of Experimental Psychology and Psychiatry, University of Cambridge, Douglas House, 18b Trumpington Road, Cambridge CB2 2AH, UK

Lisa Saksida   Department of Experimental Psychology, University of Cambridge, Downing Street, Cambridge CB2 3EB, UK

C. H. Salmond   Wolfson Brain Imaging Centre, University of Cambridge, Box 65, Addenbrooke's Hospital, Cambridge CB2 2QQ, UK

Robert T. Schultz   Yale Child Study Center, Yale University School of Medicine, 230 South Frontage Road, New Haven, CT 06520-7900, USA and Department of Diagnostic Radiology, Yale University School of Medicine, 333 Cedar Street, New Haven, CT 06510, USA

Pawel Skudlarski   Department of Diagnostic Radiology, Yale University School of Medicine, 333 Cedar Street, New Haven, CT 06510, USA

John Swettenham   Department of Human Communication Science, University College London, 2 Wakefield Street, London WC1N 1PG, UK

Helen Tager-Flusberg   Laboratory of Developmental Cognitive Neuroscience, Department of Anatomy and Neurobiology, Boston University School of Medicine, 715 Albany Street L-814, Boston, MA 02118, USA

Christiaan Van der Gaag   Academic Centre for Child and Adolescent Psychiatry, PO Box 660, 9700 AR Groningen, The Netherlands

F. Vargha-Khadem   Developmental Cognitive Neuroscience Unit, Institute of Child Health, Mecklenburgh Square, London, WC1N 2AP, UK and Great Ormond Street Hospital for Children NHS Trust, Great Ormond Street, London, WC1N 3JH, UK

Fred Volkmar   Yale Child Study Center, Yale University School of Medicine, 230 South Frontage Road, New Haven, CT 06520, USA

Emma Weisblatt   Department of Psychiatry, Developmental Psychiatry Section, University of Cambridge, Douglas House, 18b Trumpington Road, Cambridge CB2 2AH, UK

Sally Wheelwright   Autism Research Centre, Departments of Experimental Psychology and Psychiatry, University of Cambridge, Douglas House, 18b Trumpington Road, Cambridge CB2 2AH, UK

Introduction

Uta Frith and Elisabeth L. Hill

Although we know much more now than we did 50 years ago about autism, the nature, origin and even the definition of the condition are still debated and remain largely unknown. This special volume begins with a review of the facts about autistic disorders, as they are known at present. In this introduction and in Chapter 1, Elisabeth Hill and Uta Frith remind the reader that autism is no longer regarded as a rare disease. They provide examples of genetic and brain research that targets the biological causes of autism and they review the three major cognitive theories that are currently used to explain the core signs and symptoms of autism. Much more is known now about autism than was known only a few years ago, and there is justified hope that our understanding of autism will continue to accelerate at a fast pace. This issue contains examples of the cutting edge of research and highlights some of the most burning questions. Some of these relate to the diagnosis of Asperger syndrome (AS), the identification of subgroups in the autism spectrum and early signs of autistic disorder. Other questions relate to the brain abnormalities that underlie the putative cognitive deficits and whether these can be made visible through magnetic resonance imaging. The shared assumption among the contributors is that autism is a neurodevelopmental disorder that gives us a unique window on the relationship between mind and brain. The research reported elaborates the key theories that have been put forward to explain the signs and symptoms of autism. These theories try to explain the selective impact of brain abnormality on some of the most high-level mental functions, such as social insight, empathy and information processing style.

One of the puzzles presented by the autistic disorders (which we will term 'autism' for short) is that the inability to communicate with others can coexist with high intellectual function. This puzzle has been part of the core description of autism since the beginning, and particularly so in Hans Asperger's early descriptions. When he first described a handful of cases of what he termed 'autistic psychopathy', little could he have imagined the impact on theory and practice. The criteria for AS are currently the subject of hot debate. It is ironic that the present definition of AS, as an autism spectrum disorder without early language and cognitive delay, may be based on a misunderstanding of Asperger's own definitions. However, Asperger's own definitions have been shrouded in obscurity. Kathrin Hippler and Christian Klicpera (Chapter 2) retraced the clinical case records of 74 of Asperger's original cases. For the first time, we have available the catalogued information detailed in these case reports. One finding is that while many of the cases that Asperger diagnosed would still be classified in the same way, a quarter of his cases would now be diagnosed with autism, according to the criteria adopted by both the World Health Organization and the American Psychiatric Association. Furthermore, Hippler and Klicpera's findings suggest that it may be the high verbal abilities of those with AS that allow them to achieve an apparently greater degree of social awareness than is achieved by those diagnosed with autism. However, then, as now, it is clear that high intelligence does not preclude severe impairment in everyday social adaptation, and that the social impairment typical of autism is largely independent of intelligence and surprisingly independent of language ability.

How productive is it to continue with research aimed at explaining the whole of the autism spectrum? Given the enormous heterogeneity of the spectrum, perhaps the time is ripe to reconsider the possibility of new subgroups. Ideally, such groups do not just capture relatively superficial distinctions in terms of overt behaviour, but distinctions that relate to distinct neurological causes. Whether new subgroups confirm historical distinctions is another question. Helen Tager-Flusberg and Robert Joseph (Chapter 3) use the profile of performance on cognitive tests to establish neurocognitive phenotypes, which, in turn, they have related to brain size and organization. They show how it is now possible to strengthen our understanding of autism by integrating the use of several sensitive neuropsychological techniques at our disposal. By drawing on similarities with children with specific language impairment, which is diagnosed in the presence of significant language difficulty and in the absence of other cognitive impairments, Tager-Flusberg and Joseph identified one autistic subgroup with overlapping specific language impairment. Furthermore, a group of boys with autism had reversed brain asymmetry similar to that reported previously in boys with specific language impairment. The other distinct subgroups identified by Tager-Flusberg and Joseph showed a large discrepancy between verbal and non-verbal IQ. In cases where the discrepancy was in favour of verbal IQ, the condition tended to be milder. In cases where it was in favour of non-verbal IQ, autism was more severe, and only this group was characterized by larger head size. Larger head size in autism has recently emerged as an important finding, and correlates with brain size and weight. This difference suggests that different aetiologies may be revealed in the two subgroups.

Impairments in the domain of social communication are the most striking feature of autism, and language impairments would be expected to aggravate these difficulties. However, impairments in gaze-following could be even more fundamental and provide the common denominator between children with both high and low language abilities. It is already known that children with autism do not necessarily look towards the same direction that another person is looking. Normal children tend to do this because they seem to wish to share another person's attention. This behaviour is referred to as 'joint attention' and develops rapidly from 6 to 12 months of age. Joint attention involves the triadic coordination, or sharing, of attention between the infant, another person and an object or event. Looking at another person and pointing to a cup to request a drink, or looking at another person and pointing to a toy to share enjoyment, are examples of this skill. Lack of joint attention is one of the earliest signs of autism. In Chapter 4, Tony Charman highlights the crucial role that joint attention plays in autism, delineating its component parts further in the youngest longitudinal cohort yet studied. He discusses the psychological and neurological processes that might underlie the impaired development of joint attention and confirms that it is one of the earliest manifestations of mentalizing failure. One of Charman's most important findings is that impaired joint attention does not predict repetitive behaviour at later ages. By contrast, individual differences in joint attention ability are associated with language gains and social and communication skills at later ages. Thus, it may be futile to search for a unifying account for all of the currently specified behavioural criteria of autism, which include repetitive behaviour as well as social and communication impairments.

Following another person's direction of gaze is a voluntary action, but there is also an involuntary tendency to follow eye gaze, a kind of reflex. One highly interesting hypothesis is that this reflex is absent in autism. This hypothesis has been tested by John Swettenham *et al.* in Chapter 5, with clear and negative results. These authors investigated whether an observer would be affected by the direction of moving eye gaze of a face. Would the observer be induced to look into the same direction as the face when this gaze did, in fact, give no useful information as to the location of a target that the observer was instructed to look at? The direction of seen eye movement provided an involuntary cue even for children with autism. This new finding suggests that a missing attentional reflex is not the reason why individuals with autism fail to follow eye gaze voluntarily and fail to engage in joint attention.

In blind children, the absence of the visual modality would certainly preclude the use of eye gaze to monitor another person's direction of attention. The importance of the visual channel for developing this ability is shown by the fact that congenital blindness is associated with a raised incidence of autism, and tends to produce some social impairments that are reminiscent of autism. Peter Hobson and Martin Bishop (Chapter 6) report on their longstanding investigations of a group of children with congenital blindness but without the diagnosis of autism. They pose the question of whether visual impairment is a source of the social difficulties and to what extent these difficulties (however they originate) have an intrinsic connection with other autistic features in these children. Intriguingly, autistic features are much more pronounced in some children than in others, and it is the comparison between these groups that is the major concern of Hobson and Bishop's paper. By directly observing the social interactions of blind children, Hobson and Bishop suggest that one reason why congenital blindness may predispose an individual to autism lies in the nature of the experience of two-way interactions.

However, there is another low-level perceptual process that could be at fault: the normally innate preference for faces and eyes may be missing in autism. This hypothesis is developed and tested in the paper by Ami Klin *et al.* in Chapter 7. There is good evidence that even well-compensated individuals with autism experience difficulty with everyday social interactions in a variety of ways, even when their performance on laboratory tests of social cognition appears flawless. These individuals still experience difficulties in peer interaction and are unlikely to have close friends. Klin *et al.* (2003) ask what it is about social situations that high-functioning individuals with autism find difficult to process. They answer this question in a novel attempt to investigate naturalistic performance. Klin *et al.* synthesize the findings of their recent studies in which they have adopted a new technique—eye tracking—to monitor the approach of individuals with autism to finding meaning in naturalistic social scenes. While being able to produce, verbally, the rules of social interaction (such as explaining what a pointing gesture means), the individuals with autism studied in this paper were unable to translate this information into spontaneous social interaction. Such findings lead the authors to propose an alternative way of viewing social cognition, which they term 'embodied cognition', an emerging neuroscience approach to cognitive development.

Possible deficits in very high-level cognitive processes are considered by Simon Baron-Cohen *et al.* in Chapter 8. Successful social interaction involves a need to empathize (the term 'empathizing' is here used to include mentalizing) and this is contrasted to an ability to 'systemize'—a drive to analyse or construct systems. Having developed two scales to assess empathizing and systemizing, Baron-Cohen *et al.* contrast the performance of adults with high-functioning autism or AS and a normal population on these two measures. Not only does a male–female difference exist on these measures in their normal sample (favouring males on their systemizing quotient and females on their empathizing quotient), but individuals with autism also showed an unusually strong drive to systemize. These findings reflect the different pattern of interests of individuals with autism. Could these different interests arise because the normal preference for social stimuli in the environment cannot be presumed? This would correlate well with Klin *et al.*'s hypothesis. The approach provided by Baron-Cohen *et al.* starts to provide methods for the much-neglected area of adult assessment and, with further development, these questionnaires could be useful tools for wide population screening. Furthermore, the systemizing and empathizing quotient instruments could have potential importance for the broader phenotype. It is still an empirical question whether empathy and mentalizing ability correlate strongly with the degree of social interest and whether low social interest is a necessary, if not sufficient, prerequisite for a diagnosis of autism.

Of course, it is not just areas of social interaction that are unusual in the individual with autism. Aside from a cognitive explanation of autism relating to these difficulties, two further cognitive theories of autism—central coherence and executive function—are also widely acknowledged. Clinically, children and adults with autism often show a preoccupation with details and parts, while failing to extract gist or configuration. This cognitive style of weak central coherence has been used to refer to a number of processes including perception, attention, semantic and linguistic processes. In an original and methodologically rigorous attempt to elucidate the mechanisms that can give rise to weak central coherence effects, Kate Plaisted *et al.* (Chapter 9) postulate that these mechanisms may be perceptual and examine these through the use of visual configural and feature discrimination tasks as well as an auditory filter task. Their findings of enhanced feature discrimination and abnormally broad auditory filter widths in autistic children suggest that while perceptual processing in autism is abnormal, this abnormality does not impact on the post-perceptual processes responsible for integrating perceptual information to form a configural representation. Their work identifies areas in which the central coherence account requires modification, and suggests the potential for integrative studies of peripheral perceptual processes, central cortical processes and computational studies to identify the mechanisms underlying the abnormalities of stimulus processing associated with autism.

The relationship between weak central coherence and a third cognitive theory of autism, executive dysfunction, remains unclear. Rhonda Booth *et al.* In Chapter 10, provide an incisive investigation of their relationship by comparing boys with autism with boys from another clinical condition that is also believed to be associated with executive dysfunction: attention deficit hyperactivity disorder. Participants were asked to draw objects with specific items included (e.g. a house with four windows). These drawings were analysed in such a way that it was possible to see whether they focused on a small detail, and whether they showed lack of planning. Booth *et al.* found evidence that both groups of boys showed planning impairments in comparison with a normally developing control group. However, only the boys with autism showed a detailfocused drawing style, as predicted by the theory of weak central coherence. These results indicate that weak coherence may be a cognitive style that is specific to autism and not secondary to deficits in frontal functions.

A new and valuable approach to the neuropsychological impairments in autism may be through the study of motor coordination. Individuals with autism show delays in achieving motor milestones, soft neurological signs and difficulties with motor imitation, among other motor difficulties. Very little is known about the extent of such difficulties within the autistic population. Having developed an innovative reach-to-grasp movement paradigm, Morena Mari *et al.*, in Chapter 11, show differences in movement planning and execution in what they term low-ability children with autism in comparison with normally developing control children. Their paradigm provides evidence that movement disturbances may play an intrinsic part in abnormal neurophysiological processes in at least a subgroup of individuals with autism. The movement abnormalities that these authors found show striking parallels to Parkinsonism. Given the apparent heterogeneity of the ʼtistic condition and the difficulties that this presents for unifying explaiᴎ ɪs of the disorder,

Mari *et al.*'s paradigm may make it possible to identify a particular neurocognitive subtype of the disorder in the future.

Research on the brain in autism is currently undergoing a rapid phase of development and very little is currently known about brain development in autism. One of the more prominent theories about the brain in autism is the amygdala theory, although the evidence to date is equivocal. In Chapter 12, Claire Salmond *et al.* have investigated this theory by comparing the presence of structural neuroanatomical abnormalities in the amygdala with behavioural evidence for amygdala dysfunction. They tested the emotional modulation of the startle response in children, a response known to be dependent on the amygdala in adults, but found no significant group differences. Surprisingly, only half of the children with autism showed structural abnormalities in the amygdala, whereas, in all children, abnormalities in a variety of other brain regions were identified. This highlights the heterogeneity of the disorder and may pave the way to subtyping at the brain level.

In the final chapter of this volume, Robert Schultz *et al.* (2003) provide a vital contribution to an understanding of the network known as the social brain. In a study in which they focus on the fusiform face area (FFA)—an area of the brain that has previously been shown to be involved in the processing and discrimination of faces—Schultz *et al.* show that this is not the only role of the FFA. Rather, it is engaged in social processing in general and is part of a well-established set of brain regions that are specific to social cognition. These include the amygdala, superior temporal sulcus and medial prefrontal cortex. Critically, in their study, the strength of activity across normal participants in the region of the FFA during social attribution was related to the accuracy with which they performed the task. This suggests that hypoactivity of the FFA in autism may be a reflection of a core social brain network underlying the disorder. Clearly, in the future we can look forward to further studies correlating structural and functional brain activity with the behavioural signs and symptoms of autism.

In the past ten years, research on autism has undergone a period of consolidation, with empirical work guided by the three major cognitive theories—theory of mind, central coherence and executive function—and with cognitive explanations of the core features of autism providing a vital interface between brain and behaviour. The varied papers in this issue demonstrate that new ideas on how to link mental dysfunctions and brain abnormalities are emerging, facilitated by the use of new techniques. More is becoming known about the brain basis of autism and the nature and variability of its behavioural symptoms. We are also becoming more aware of the earliest signs of autism and about persistent difficulties, even in well-compensated adults. Last, but not least, the cognitive strengths of individuals with autism are finally being recognized and seriously examined.

We are very grateful for the support of the following for reviewing papers in this issue: Truett Allison, Simon Baron-Cohen, James Blair, Sarah-Jayne Blakemore, Dermot Bowler, Tony Charman, Hugo Critchley, Emily Farran, Chris Frith, György Gergely, Patrick Haggard, Paul Harris, Claire Hughes, Charles Hulme, Knut Kampe, Simon Kilcross, Ami Klin, Sue Leekam, John Morton, Laurent Mottron, Sally Ozonoff, Josef Perner, Trevor Robbins, Michael Rutter, Rebecca Saxe, Jim Stevenson, Michael Thomas, Michael Tomasello, Patrik Vuilleumier, and Lorna Wing.

1

Understanding autism: insights from mind and brain

Elisabeth L. Hill and Uta Frith

Autism is a developmental disorder characterized by impaired social interaction and communication as well as repetitive behaviours and restricted interests. The consequences of this disorder for everyday life adaptation are extremely variable. The general public is now more aware of the high prevalence of this life-long disorder, with *around* 0.6% of the population being affected. However, the signs and symptoms of autism are still puzzling. Since a biological basis of autism was accepted, approaches from developmental cognitive neuroscience have been applied to further our understanding of the autism spectrum. The study of the behavioural and underlying cognitive deficits in autism has advanced ahead of the study of the underlying brain abnormalities and of the putative genetic mechanisms. However, advances in these fields are expected as methodological difficulties are overcome. In this paper, recent developments in the field of autism are outlined. In particular, we review the findings of the three main neuro-cognitive theories of autism: theory-of-mind deficit, weak central coherence and executive dysfunction.

Keywords: autism; Asperger syndrome; theory of mind; weak central coherence; executive dysfunction; phenotype

1.1 Introduction

Only a few decades ago very few people had heard of autism, but now it is widely known that autism entails an inability to engage in ordinary social interactions. Thanks to the film 'Rainman', everyone knows that not only are there children with autism but that these children grow up into adults and that apart from their communication difficulties they have strange obsessions and incredible talents. Of course, these impressions that are nurtured by fiction are far too sweeping, but they do convey something of the fascination of this disorder. Autism is a developmental disorder that is lifelong. It has a neurological basis in the brain and genetic causes play a major role. However, the precise causes are still not known, nor is the true prevalence. Hence, speculations abound and fears of an epidemic have been voiced. One of the difficulties facing genetic studies and studies of prevalence is the definition of autism.

Autism is defined using behavioural criteria because, so far, no specific biological markers are known. The clinical picture of autism varies in severity and is modified by many factors, including education, ability and temperament. Furthermore, the clinical picture changes over the course of development within one and the same individual. In addition, autism is frequently associated with other disorders such as attention deficit disorder, motor incoordination and psychiatric symptoms such as anxiety and depression. For these reasons the behavioural criteria have to be very wide. In line with the clinical recognition of the variability, there is now general agreement that there is a spectrum of autistic disorders, which includes individuals at all levels of intelligence and language ability and spanning all degrees of severity. This widening of the criteria has inevitably led to a dramatic increase in identified cases. Autism is no longer a rare disorder.

Part of the autism spectrum, but considered a special subgroup, is Asperger syndrome. This label, hardly known before 1980, is now widely used to refer to individuals with the typical social communication impairments of autism, but who nevertheless have fluent language and good academic ability alongside obsessions and narrow interests. Some confusion exists between the labels Asperger syndrome and high-functioning autism. By current criteria, the diagnosis of Asperger syndrome requires that there has been no delay in language and cognitive development. This requirement seems somewhat arbitrary, as it is not clear that there are significant differences in the core features of autism between such cases and those who showed significant language delay early on, but later acquired fluent language and a social interest (Prior *et al.* 1998; Gilchrist *et al.* 2001). Indeed, many an autistic adult who is now a fluent talker and is earnestly trying to make friends, was mute and socially withdrawn at preschool age.

What are the core features of autism? The chief criteria for autistic disorder, as set out in the diagnostic handbooks, such as ICD-10 (World Health Organization 1992) and DSM-IV (American Psychiatric Association 1994), are abnormalities of social interaction, impairments in verbal and non-verbal communication and a restricted repertoire of interests and activities, all present from early childhood. These criteria have been agreed worldwide and appear to be working well, to the benefit of clinical practice as well as research. Using these criteria, population studies have shown that autism in a wide range of manifestations affects at least 0.6% of people at a male : female ratio of around 3 : 1. They have also shown that mental retardation, which means an IQ under 70, is strongly associated with autism and is present in between 25% and 40% of cases of autism spectrum disorders (Baird *et al.* 2000; Chakrabarti and Fombonne 2001). Furthermore, additional medical conditions involving the brain are seen in around 10% of the population (Gillberg and Coleman 2000). Asperger syndrome is estimated to affect 0.3%, at an even higher male : female ratio, estimated as ranging from 4 : 1 to 10 : 1.

Not part of the diagnostic criteria, but part of the popular notion of autism are the savant skills. This is justified, as these skills are found to be present in at least 10% of the autistic population. Indeed, almost all savants are diagnosed as suffering from autistic disorder (Rimland and Fein 1988). The savant is an individual with an islet of outstanding skill in one area, which can include calendar calculation, musical or artistic competence, often in the presence of modest or even low general intellectual ability (Mottron and Belleville 1993; Hermelin 2002). We cannot ignore these special abilities when trying to understand the nature of autism, even if they are not present in all cases. We also cannot ignore the common reports of sensory abnormalities, which suggest heightened sensitivity to minute differences between stimuli, be they in sound, sight, taste or touch. These phenomena are little explored but give clues to the unusual mind of the individual with autism. For one thing, they indicate that there are cognitive strengths as well as weaknesses in autism.

In this paper, the term 'autism' is used to describe all individuals on the autistic spectrum, but the research evidence on cognitive and neurological findings is most robust for those without severe mental retardation. This is because, in this subgroup, the effects of mental retardation that lead to generally depressed test performance can be avoided, and also because individuals who suffer from additional mental retardation and other co-occurring disorders have a more limited range and repertoire of observable behaviour. This is why most of the currently available behavioural findings are based on able or high-functioning individuals. Unfortunately, many of the anatomical studies of the brain in autism are based on low-functioning individuals and this makes it difficult to establish links between brain and behaviour. As regards many behavioural and also some of the more recent brain imaging findings, the question remains whether we can generalize these to low-functioning individuals. We have no idea why some individuals are high-functioning and others not, or why some have fluent language and others do not.

1.2 Studies trying to explain the causes of autism

Since autism was first described by the American psychiatrist Leo Kanner (1943) and by the Austrian paediatrician Hans Asperger (1944), many theories about its origin have been proposed. These have progressed from psychogenic ideas of the 'refrigerator mother' (Bettelheim 1967)—the idea that children become autistic in response to a threatening and unloving parent—through greater understanding of the behavioural characteristics of the disorder to a more detailed understanding at both cognitive and biological levels. Research has become focused gradually on genes, brain and mind and their interplay with environmental factors.

The heritability of autism has been one of the most important changes in our conception of the condition since the first pioneering descriptions. Twin studies provide particularly strong evidence. Taking a narrow definition of autism, if one member of a pair of MZ twins has the disorder, then in 36% of cases the other twin, who is genetically identical, also has it. By contrast, such concordance is hardly ever seen in DZ twin pairs. Furthermore, when a wider definition of autism is used the concordance rate more than doubles, with 90% for MZ versus 10% for DZ pairs (Bailey *et al.* 1995). The rate of autism in singleton siblings is 2–6%, around 10 times the prevalence rate found in the general population. It is assumed that multiple genes are involved (see Maestrini *et al.* (2000) for a review of susceptibility genes), and locations on several chromosomes, in particular 7 as well as 2, 16 and 17, have been replicated (International Molecular Genetic Study of Autism Consortium 1998). Some non-genetic factors are also considered, such as viral illness and immunological deficiency, originating either before birth or within the first two years of life. Many of the heated debates that occur in the public domain relate to putative environmental triggers, among them the so far unsubstantiated claim that the measles, mumps and rubella vaccination is a contributory cause. Similar claims relate to the measles virus in conjunction with gastric inflammatory disease. The balance of the evidence at present does not favour these hypotheses (Taylor *et al.* 1999; Farrington *et al.* 2001; Halsey and Hyman 2001).

How much is known about brain structure and function in autism? Post-mortem brains are scarce and cumber-some to analyse. Nevertheless, painstaking studies have provided firm evidence that structural abnormalities exist in the brains of people with autism (Bauman and Kemper 1994; Kemper and Bauman 1998). Of particular interest are the findings of reduced neuronal cell size and increased cell packing density in regions of the limbic system known to be critical to emotional and social behaviour. Outside the limbic system, abnormalities have also been found in the cerebellum and in various cortical regions (Bailey *et al.* 1998*a*). One concern about these studies is not only the scarcity of the material, but also the fact that it is difficult to relate the observed brain abnormalities to mental functions because good behavioural data on the individual cases are not usually available.

Brain imaging studies of blood flow in the living brain are still rather few but are steadily increasing. Two recent, well-controlled studies have revealed reduced blood flow in the medial temporal cortex in both brain hemispheres when at rest (Ohnishi *et al.* 2000; Zilbovicius *et al.* 2000). Unfortunately, it is hard to interpret this finding at present. A handful of studies have reported distinct functional abnormalities in a number of cortical (focusing on frontal and temporal lobes and the cerebellum) and subcortical regions (focusing on the amygdala and hippocampus), but the results are inconsistent (e.g. Courchesne *et al.* 1988; Abell *et al.* 1999; Aylward *et al.* 1999; Haznedar *et al.* 2001; Pierce *et al.* 2001). A useful review has been provided by Cody *et al.* (2002).

The most consistent finding about the autistic brain to have emerged in recent years is that it is on average larger and heavier than the normal brain. Importantly, the increased size is not evident from birth, but from around 2–4 years (Lainhart *et al.* 1997; Courchesne *et al.* 2001). In a recent review, Frith (2003) speculated that a reason for this increase could be a failure of the normal pruning process that occurs several times during development after an initial wave of proliferation of synapses (Huttenlocher and Dabholkar 1997). Pruning eliminates faulty connections and optimizes coordinated neural functioning. Experience is important here but pruning will also show a genetic basis. Lack of pruning in autism might therefore lead to an increase in brain size and be associated with poor functioning of certain neural circuits. The following scenario can be envisaged: the synapses of the so-called feedback (top-down) systems fail to be pruned, while feed-forward (bottom-up) systems are normal. This possibility is suggested by analogy to the development of the visual system. Here, feed-forward systems are laid down at an early stage of brain maturation but feedback connections take much longer to develop and undergo a proliferation and pruning cycle (Burkhalter 1993).

If this is the case for other systems of the brain, then one and the same physiological failure could lead to several of the prominent non-social features of autism. Feedback-dependent control mechanisms might be dysfunctional and hence unable to act as top-down control on basic perceptual processes. One consequence could be executive function problems that are well documented in autism (see Section 1.3c). Another consequence might be perceptual overload. In autism, such perceptual overload is often suspected, for instance, to explain the phenomenon of heightened sensitivity experienced by many individuals (e.g. Gerland 1997). Special talents that are based on apparently enhanced discrimination might also be explained in terms of a relative failure of top-down control. It is conceivable that failure of pruning might occur in different regions of the brain and at different times during development. This would result in a heterogeneous clinical picture with effects on diverse mental functions across individuals.

1.3 Studies trying to explain the causes of the signs and symptoms of autism

To explain the causes of specific behavioural signs in autistic individuals, their changes with age and their modification through remedial programmes, cognitive theories are needed. Cognitive explanations of the core features of autism have provided a vital interface between brain and behaviour. They attempt to provide explanations in terms of faults in basic mechanisms of the mind that normally underlie specific mental functions and facilitate learning in specific domains. The so-called 'theory of mind' deficit hypothesis proposes that a fault in just one of the many components of the social brain can lead to an inability to understand certain basic aspects of communication.

(a) A failure to acquire an intuitive 'theory of mind'

The assumption is that a neurologically based deficit in the understanding of minds lies at the origin of the specific social communication impairment of autism and can explain both aloofness and indiscriminate social approach. This assumption led to the testable claim that autistic children are impaired in their intuitive understanding of mental states, such as beliefs, and a lack of the attribution of mental states to themselves and to others that is automatic in normally developing children. This theory, sometimes referred to as 'mind-blindness' or 'mentalizing failure', has been tested extensively (see chapters in Baron-Cohen *et al.* (1993, 2000)), and has proved fairly robust.

In the first study testing the hypothesis, Baron-Cohen *et al.* (1985) showed children two dolls, one named Sally and the other Ann. Children were shown that Sally had a basket and Ann a box. Sally puts a marble in her basket and goes outside. While she is outside, naughty Ann moves Sally's marble to her own basket. Sally then comes back in and wants to play with her marble. Children were asked, 'where will Sally look for her marble?' To a normally developing 4-year-old child, the answer is clear: Sally will look for her marble where she *thinks* it is and not where it *really* is now. Furthermore, the normally developing child can reason that Sally will look in her basket because this is where she put it and she does not know that it has been moved. However, in Baron-Cohen *et al.*'s study, 80% of children with autism, with a mental age equivalent to a 4-year-old or above, failed to answer this question correctly. They stated that Sally would look for her marble in the box, despite saying that Sally had put the marble in her basket and that she did not know that the marble had been moved. By contrast, 86% of children with Down syndrome, with generally lower ability levels than the children with autism, passed the test question.

Theory of mind involves mental states other than false beliefs. Children and adults with autism have also been shown to have deficits in their understanding of pretence, irony, non-literal language (e.g. double bluff) and deception (e.g. white lies). Such concepts have been assessed in the laboratory using story understanding. In one task, a participant reads a passage and is asked to make a judgement about the normality of a character's behaviour in that story. For example, assessing the 'normality' of asking to borrow a stranger's comb (Dewey 1991). In another task, a participant reads a series of stories and must answer a question about why something happened. In order to respond appropriately, a participant must reason either about cause and effect or about a character's mental state in the story. For example, understanding that a burglar alarm was set off by an animal breaking the electronic detector beam versus understanding that a burglar gave himself up to the police because he *believed* that they knew he had committed a crime (Happé 1994). On this second set of stories, individuals with autism have been shown to lack an intuitive understanding of the motives of a character in a story in parallel to intact cause-and-effect reasoning about the stories (e.g. Happé *et al.* 1996). For these reasons it is now widely accepted that individuals with autism are impaired in the intuitive understanding that people have mental states. Furthermore, some highly able individuals with autistic disorder who have written insightful autobiographical accounts acknowledge this problem, even when they themselves have gained knowledge of mental states and how this can be used to predict and explain behaviour. They have acquired a conscious 'theory of mind', but still apparently lack the intuitive mentalizing ability that is abundant in normal everyday communication.

Recently, a handful of studies have been published investigating the neurophysiological substrate of mentalizing through the use of neuroimaging studies in both normal volunteers and in able individuals with autism. In this way relationships between specific brain function and behaviour have been investigated (for a review, see Frith 2001). The neuroimaging studies of mentalizing in normal individuals have identified a network of brain regions that is consistently active during mentalizing over and above the other task demands. This network involves the medial prefrontal cortex (especially anterior paracingulate cortex), the temporal–parietal junction and the temporal poles (Fletcher *et al.* 1995; Brunet *et al.* 2000; Castelli *et al.* 2000; Gallagher *et al.* 2000; Vogeley *et al.* 2001).

Only a small handful of studies so far have compared individuals with autism with normal individuals on mentalizing tasks while being scanned. Happé *et al.* (1996) conducted a PET study that revealed that individuals with Asperger syndrome showed less activation in the medial prefrontal region than did normal individuals. Baron-Cohen *et al.* (1999*a*) conducted a fMRI study in which participants were asked to judge a person's emotional states from photographs of the eye region, deciding which two words best described their mental state. When reading the language of the eyes, individuals with autism, in contrast to the control group, showed less extensive activation in frontal regions and no activation in the amygdala. Castelli *et al.* (2002) conducted a PET study in which they showed silent animations of geometric shapes to high-functioning individuals with autism and controls. Contrasts were made between brain activation when watching two triangles moving randomly versus moving in a goal-directed fashion (e.g. chasing, fighting) versus moving interactively with implied intentions (e.g. coaxing, tricking). During mentalizing (the latter condition), the individuals with autism showed less activation than the controls in the three brain regions critical to mentalizing in normal individuals (medial prefrontal cortex, temporal–parietal junction and the temporal poles).

Interestingly, both groups in the study by Castelli *et al.* (2002) showed similar activation levels in the occipital gyrus, indicating that all participants devoted more intensive visual analysis to the mentalizing animations. However, there was less connectivity between occipital (V3) and temporal regions (superior temporal sulcus) in the autistic brains than in the normal brains. These findings support the notion of a dysfunction in the specific neural substrate for mentalizing in autism, although the reason for the dysfunction remains to be identified. In summary, there is both behavioural and physiological evidence for a deficit in mentalizing in autism and this cognitive theory can be said to account fairly well for the core social communication impairment in autism, whether these behavioural impairments manifest themselves as withdrawal from other people, or as indiscriminate approach.

The mentalizing deficit theory of autism can account less well for deficits in other aspects of social behaviour in autism, for instance a well-documented impairment in the recognition of faces. This has recently been confirmed also at the physiological level (Critchley *et al.* 2000; Schultz *et al.* 2000; Pierce *et al.* 2001). Individuals with autism do not activate the face area of the fusiform gyrus that is reliably activated by normal individuals when looking at faces as opposed to objects. One interpretation of this finding is that children with autism are not equipped with the normal preference for social stimuli, which is assumed to rest on dedicated brain circuits. An inability to regulate emotions or to respond to emotions in others has also been postulated as a primary deficit in autism (Hobson 1993). Such problems may be related to anatomical abnormalities of the limbic system. Other theories are being offered that revolve around further potentially primary neuro-cognitive deficits, for instance, documented impairments in imitation in autism that have been speculatively related to an abnormal functioning of mirror neurons (Williams *et al.* 2001). Another hypothesis postulates that the innate preferences for attending to social stimuli may be absent in autism (Klin *et al.* 2002). The face/affect recognition abnormalities in autism can also be explained within a developmental perspective on theory of mind (Tager-Flusberg 2001). All of these hypotheses are currently being explored. The results should lead to a better definition of the extent and nature of the social impairments in autism.

(b) Weak central coherence and its variants

The non-social features of autism are a varied and puzzling collection raising more questions than answers. They include repetitive and obsessive behaviour, which Kanner labelled 'insistence of sameness' and others variously describe as a restricted repertoire of behaviours, rigidity and perseveration. They also include a markedly uneven pattern of intelligence, such that tests tapping factual knowledge, rote memory and focused attention to detail can lead to peak performances, while tests tapping 'common sense' comprehension and working memory or strategic task planning can be surprisingly poor.

Non-social features of autism, then, comprise strengths as well as weaknesses and are still less well understood and researched than the social impairments seen in autistic disorder. These non-social features are currently explained by two major cognitive theories and their variants. One theory, labelled 'central coherence', is as yet non-specific as to the underlying neuro-physiological processes, but alludes to poor connectivity throughout the brain between more basic perceptual processes and top-down modulating processes, perhaps owing to failure of pruning. Central coherence refers to an information-processing style, specifically the tendency to process incoming information in its context: that is pulling information together for higher-level meaning. In the case of strong central coherence, this tendency would work at the expense of attention to and memory for details (Happé 1999; Frith 2003). In the case of weak central coherence this tendency would work at the expense of contextual meaning and in favour of piecemeal processing. Why is this relevant to features of autism? An illustration is given in Bartlett's (1932) now classic study of story recall. When retelling a story, individuals find it easier to recall accurately the gist of the story rather than its specific details. People with autism show the opposite profile, recalling the exact words of the story rather than its gist.

By this theory, individuals with autism are described as exhibiting 'weak central coherence'. A tendency to focus on the local, rather than global aspects of an object of interest may explain the uneven profile of assets and deficits in intelligence test performance, regardless of whether the tests are verbal or non-verbal. An example is the block design test found in both the child and adult versions of the Wechsler intelligence scale (Shah and Frith 1993). Another example of the advantage of this processing style is the embedded figures test (Witkin et al. 1971) where a participant must locate a small part within a global picture. Here, people with autism have been shown to be superior to non-autistic controls (Shah and Frith 1983, 1993; Jolliffe and Baron-Cohen 1997). An explanation for such superior ability may be that individuals with autism are less influenced by the global shape (gestalt) and find the local parts of the gestalt more salient. An example where weak central coherence would be detrimental is a task in which one and the same stimulus has to be interpreted differently according to context. One test used homographs (words with one spelling but two meanings, such as 'tear' in the eye or in a piece of fabric), which individuals were asked to read aloud in the context of sentences. Frith and Snowling (1983), Happé (1997) and Jolliffe and Baron-Cohen (1999) all found that individuals with autism did not appear to integrate the sentence context when performing this task, being less likely than controls to pronounce the homograph correctly depending on the context of the sentence.

An important extension of the central coherence account postulates not poor integration of information in a gestalt, but rather enhanced discrimination of the individual elements (Mottron et al. 2000; Plaisted 2001). This variant explains savant abilities as being a result of highly developed abilities that often start with an obsessive interest in small details. Thus, focusing on the day and date of a birthday can lead to interest in other days and dates and eventually result in a phenomenal knowledge of calendar facts. Baron-Cohen's proposal of systemizing as a typical preference in autism can also be characterized as an activity that essentially starts with an interest in single facts, or single objects (Baron-Cohen 2002).

The brain basis of the processing bias identified as central coherence has been little explored. In a fMRI study, Fink et al. (1997) required normal individuals to attend to the global or local aspects of complex visual figures. Brain activation when attending to these different features differed. Processing of the global features of a figure was associated with right lingual gyrus activation while processing of the local features was associated with activation of left inferior occipital cortex. Electrophysiological evidence also indicates increased right hemisphere activity during the processing of global versus local features (Heinze *et al.* 1998).

Central coherence in autistic individuals has yet to be studied at the neurological level, with the exception of one brain imaging study. Ring *et al.* (1999) conducted a fMRI study in which adults with and without autism were scanned while undertaking the embedded figures test. Although several brain regions were similarly activated in the two groups, there were some intriguing differences. Specifically, the autistic individuals showed relatively greater activation of extra-striate regions of visual cortex, while the controls demonstrated relatively greater activation in the prefrontal cortex. These findings are consistent with the idea that the early stages of sensory processing (where emphasis is paid to the local features of a stimulus) are intact in autism while the top-down modulation of these early processing stages (requiring the extraction of the global features of a stimulus) is not functioning appropriately. Thus this study showed that an islet of preserved performance in individuals with autism may be subserved by neural systems that are qualitatively different from those activated in normal control subjects. In this way, a difference has been highlighted in the functional anatomy of autistic individuals in relation to the differential use of local and global cognitive strategies. The main problem of the central coherence theory of autism, and its variants, is a lack of plausible neuroanatomical mechanisms in which the nature of the abnormal activation could illuminate the observed behavioural features. Clearly, a great deal of neuroanatomical work must be done to investigate this.

How far can a weak central coherence account or its variants go in explaining some of the everyday behaviours that we see in individuals with autism? The attention of the autistic individual is often captured by fragments or surface features of objects and sensations that are usually of little interest to normal people within the 'real world' in a way that is demonstrated by the performance peaks observed in laboratory-based testing on tasks such as block design and embedded figures. However, there are other characteristics of autistic behaviour that are best explained by a third cognitive theory, that of executive dysfunction.

(c) Executive dysfunction

A widely accepted cognitive explanation for at least some of the behavioural problems in autism is a theory of executive dysfunction. This theory makes an explicit link to frontal lobe failure in analogy with neuropsychological patients who have suffered damage in the frontal lobes. The behavioural problems addressed by this theory are rigidity and perseveration, being explained by a poverty in the initiation of new actions and the tendency to be stuck in a given task set. At the same time, the ability to carry out routine actions can be excellent and is manifested in a strong liking for routines, repetitious behaviour and sometimes elaborate rituals. These problems are clear in the poor daily life management of people with autism, who benefit from prompts and externally provided structures to initiate well-learned routines.

Executive function is an umbrella term for functions such as planning working memory, impulse control, shifting set and the initiation and monitoring of action as well as for the inhibition of prepotent responses. All are thought to depend on systems that involve prefrontal activity in the brain in normal individuals. Furthermore, these functions are typically impaired in patients with acquired damage to the frontal lobes (e.g. Shallice 1988) as well as in a range of disorders that are likely to involve deficits in the frontal lobes. Such clinical disorders include attention deficit disorder, obsessive compulsive disorder, Tourette's syndrome, phenylketonuria and schizophrenia.

Poor performance on many tasks of executive function has been documented in autism (see papers in Russell 1997). Using a variety of tasks, children with autism have been shown to have deficits in planning. One typical task is the Tower of Hanoi, or the related Tower of London, in which individuals must move discs from a prearranged sequence on three different pegs to match a goal state determined by the examiner in as few moves as possible and following a number of specific rules. Children with autism have been found to be impaired on such tasks (Ozonoff et al. 1991; Hughes et al. 1994; Ozonoff and McEvoy 1994; Ozonoff and Jensen 1999).

The inhibition of a prepotent response has been reported in a number of studies. One illustration of this is given by Hughes and Russell's (1993) 'detour reaching task'. In the original task, participants could obtain a marble visible in a box, but only by turning a knob or flicking a switch at the side of the box, and not by reaching immediately into the box. Individuals with autism found it much more difficult to throw a switch in order to perform an object retrieval than children with moderate learning difficulties with whom they were matched for verbal mental age. Children with autism were less able to inhibit their prepotent response to reach immediately for the marble on this task. Further work manipulating this paradigm reported by Bíro and Russell (2001) indicates that it may be the apparently arbitrary nature of the rules involved that cause particular difficulty in this area of executive functioning for learning-disabled children with autism (see Russell 2002).

Perseveration is another aspect of executive functioning that appears to be a characteristic of autistic individuals. One example of this is seen when performing the Wisconsin card sorting task (Heaton et al. 1993) In this task, an individual must sort cards on one of three possible dimensi (colour, number, shape) according to a non-spoken rule and then shift to ৣ.. cards along a different dimension. On this task, the experimenter tells the participant whether she/he has placed the card correctly (i.e. followed the correct rule), but does not give the participant the rule explicitly. Several studies have reported that autistic individuals are highly perseverative in their response to the Wisconsin card sorting task compared with controls. That is, autistic individuals have difficulty in shifting to sort using the second of two rules, instead continuing to sort using the first rule (Rumsey and Hamburger 1988; Szatmari *et al.* 1989; Prior and Hoffmann 1990; Ozonoff *et al.* 1991; Ozonoff and McEvoy 1994; Ozonoff 1995; Bennetto *et al.* 1996). Such difficulties could be seen to reflect a deficit in mental flexibility. Poor performance on such tests of executive function is related directly to stereotyped and rigid behaviour in everyday life as shown in highly repetitive thought and action. Interestingly, it has proved difficult to identify executive dysfunction in preschool-aged children with autism (Griffith *et al.* 1999; Dawson *et al.* 2002). It remains to be seen whether more sensitive tasks would highlight an autism-specific impairment at a young age.

There is thus at least some evidence that individuals with autism experience deficits in areas of executive functioning, and this cognitive theory has gained much ground in recent years. However, there are some problems with this account. One difficulty arises from a lack of consensus as to which aspects of executive function are typical of autism. A more striking difficulty arises from the fact that executive dysfunction is found in clinical conditions other than autism (e.g. attention deficit disorder). Certainly this problem limits the potential to use executive dysfunction as a diagnostic marker for autism. It may be that this difficulty will be resolved in the light of future detailed work investigating executive functions in autism. A final difficulty with the executive dysfunction account of autism is that while such difficulties appear to be common, they may not be a universal feature of autism. Certain studies have found that the tests of executive function that they have employed have not been problematic for all autistic individuals with normal IQ levels (Baron-Cohen *et al.* 1999*b*; Russell and Hill 2001). However, the executive dysfunction account of autism should not be dismissed because remediation of autistic individuals' difficulties in the executive domain can help to improve the independent living skills of adults with autistic disorders.

We are aware of no studies where the brains of individuals with autism have been scanned while performing tasks of executive function. However, an integration of the behavioural findings in autism and the known brain abnormalities underlying similar behaviours in patients with acquired damage to the frontal lobes of the brain and other disorders that lead to executive dysfunction accords well with the notion of abnormalities in the prefrontal cortex and its connections with other brain structures such as the basal ganglia, striatum and cerebellum in individuals with autism (Robbins 1997). It remains to be seen whether structural magnetic resonance imaging and other neuroanatomical studies of the brains of autistic individuals will support this notion. Diffusion tensor imaging will be particularly suited to the assessment of abnormalities in connectivity.

1.4 The broader phenotype of autism

In many ways, the greatest hope for elucidating the causes of autism lies in genetic studies. However, in our view, these studies are hampered by a lack of definition at the cognitive level. Given the current diagnostic criteria, ideas of the phenotype in autism are based on unsatisfactory behavioural criteria that change with age and the precision of parental report. A small, but increasing number of studies are highlighting the existence of a broader cognitive phenotype of autism (see Bailey *et al.* 1998*b* for a review). In essence, a broader cognitive phenotype exists when close relatives of an individual with autism show a raised incidence of cognitive performance associated with the diagnosis of autism, but to a mild degree that does not put them into the category of being diagnosed with autism themselves. Aspects of the three main cognitive theories of autism have been investigated in relation to the broader phenotype providing good evidence for its existence across broad areas of its features. Baron-Cohen and Hammer (1997) reported that the parents of children with autism showed a similar profile to those with autism on a task claimed to involve mentalizing (inferior to controls)—the language of the eyes test—as well as on a test of weak central coherence—the embedded figures test— (superior to controls).

Happé *et al.* (2001) assessed the parents and brothers of boys with either autism, dyslexia or no developmental disorder on a series of tests of weak central coherence, block design, the embedded figures test and a visual illusion (the Ebbinghaus circles). Like the Baron-Cohen and Hammer (1997) study, the findings from the four tasks were similar: the performance of the fathers of boys with autism was significantly different from that of all other groups, showing a bias towards detail-focus across all tasks administered. Furthermore, a similar profile has been found in studies that have investigated performance on tests of executive function and their relationship to the broader autism phenotype. Hughes *et al.* (1997) reported that the parents, and especially fathers, of children with autism showed relatively poor planning skills and attentional flexibility in comparison with the parents of children with learning disability and children with no disorder. Difficulties in executive function have also been identified in the non-autistic siblings of children with autism (Hughes *et al.* 1999). Thus, evidence of a broader autism phenotype is provided in the domains of each of the three key cognitive theories of autism.

At this stage in our understanding of autism, we have focused on the three cognitive theories—mentalizing deficit, weak central coherence and executive dysfunction. It would be wrong to consider these as rival theories and they certainly do not have to be seen to be mutually exclusive. While each cognitive theory has been tested in the broader phenotype—with positive findings— large-scale studies assessing all three theories in the same sample are still needed. The relationship between the cognitive phenotype (or endophenotype) and the broader phenotype remains to be investigated. Furthermore, this work needs to be widened to include the neuro-cognitive deficits that have as yet received insufficient attention. Such an approach may help us to pinpoint both diagnostic signs and genetic markers of the condition.

This work was supported by MRC Programme grant no. G9716841 awarded to U.F.

References

Abell, F., Krams, M., Ashburner, J., Passingham, R., Friston, K., Frakowiak, R., *et al.* (1999). The neuroanatomy of autism: a voxel-based whole brain analysis of structural scans. *Neuroreport* **10**, 1647–51.

American Psychiatric Association (1994). *Diagnostic and statistical manual of mental disorders*. American Psychiatric Association,Washington, DC.

Asperger, H. (1944). 'Autistic psychopathy' in childhood. In *Autism and Asperger syndrome* (ed. U. Frith), pp. 37–92. Cambridge University Press, Cambridge.

Aylward, E. H., Minshew, N. J., Goldstein, G., Honeycutt, N. A., Augustine, A. M., Yates, K. O., *et al.* (1999). MRI volumes of amygdala and hippo-campus in non-mentally retarded autistic adolescents and adults. *Neurology* **53**, 2145–50.

Bailey, A., Le Couteur, A., Gottesman, I., Bolton, P., Simonoff, E., Yuzda, E., *et al.* (1995). Autism as a strongly genetic disorder: evidence from a British twin study. *Psychol. Med.* **25**, 63–77.

Bailey, A., Luthert, P., Dean, A., Harding, B., Janota, I., Montgomery, M., *et al.* (1998*a*). A clinico-pathological study of autism. *Brain* **121**, 889–905.

Bailey, A., Palferman, S., Heavey, L. and Le Couteur, A. (1998*b*). Autism: the phenotype in relatives. *J. Autism Devl Disorders* **28**, 369–92.

Baird, G., Charman, T., Baron-Cohen, S., Cox, A., Swettenham, J., Wheelwright, S., *et al.* (2000). A screening instrument for autism at 18 months of age: a 6 year follow-up study. *J. Am. Acad. Child Adolescent Psychiatry* **39**, 694–702.

Baron-Cohen, S. (2002). The extreme male brain theory of autism. *Trends Cogn. Sci.* **6**, 248–54.

Baron-Cohen, S. and Hammer, J. (1997). Parents of children with Asperger syndrome: what is the cognitive phenotype? *J. Cogn. Neurosci.* **9**, 548–54.

Baron-Cohen, S., Leslie, A. and Frith, U. (1985). Does the autistic child have a 'theory of mind'? *Cognition* **21**, 37–46.

Baron-Cohen, S. T., Tager-Flusberg, H. and Cohen, D. J. (1993). *Understanding other minds. Perspectives from autism*. Oxford University Press, Oxford.

Baron-Cohen, S.,Tager-Flusberg, H. and Cohen, D. J. (2000). *Understanding other minds. Perspectives from developmental cognitive neuroscience*. Oxford University Press, Oxford.

Baron-Cohen, S., Ring, H., Williams, S., Wheelwright, S., Bullmore, E., Brammer, M., *et al.* (1999*a*). Social intelligence in the normal and autistic brain: a fMRI study. *Eur. J. Psychiatry* **11**, 1891–98.

Baron-Cohen, S., Wheelwright, S., Stone, V. and Rutherford, M. (1999*b*). A mathematician, a physicist and a computer scientist with Asperger syndrome: performance on psychology and folk physics tests. *Neurocase* **5**, 475–83.

Bartlett, F. C. (1932). *Remembering: a study in experimental social psychology*. Cambridge University Press.

Bauman, M. L. and Kemper, K. L. (1994). Neuroanatomical observations of the brain in autism. In *The neurobiology of autism* (ed. M. L. Bauman and K. L. Kemper), pp. 119–145. Baltimore, MA: The Johns Hopkins University Press.

Bennetto, L., Pennington, B. F. and Rogers, S. J. (1996). Intact and impaired memory functions in autism. *Child Devl* 67, 1816–35.

Bettelheim, B. (1967). *The empty fortress: infantile autism and the birth of the self.* New York: The Free Press.

Bíro, S. and Russell, J. (2001). The execution of arbitrary procedures by children with autism. *Devl Psychopathol.* 13, 97–110.

Brunet, E., Sarfate, Y., Hardy-Bayle, M. C. and Decety, J. (2000). A PET investigation of the attribution of intentions with a nonverbal task. *Neuroimage* 11, 157–66.

Burkhalter, A. (1993). Development of forward and feedback connections between areas V1 and V2 of human visual cortex. *Cerebral Cortex* 3, 476–87.

Castelli, F., Happé, F., Frith, U. and Frith, C. D. (2000). Movement and mind: a functional imaging study of perception and interpretation of complex intentional movement patterns. *Neuroimage* 12, 314–25.

Castelli, F., Frith, C., Happé, F. and Frith, U. (2002). Autism, Asperger syndrome and brain mechanisms for the attribution of mental states to animated shapes. *Brain* 125, 1839–49.

Chakrabarti, S. and Fombonne, E. (2001). Pervasive developmental disorders in preschool children. *J. Am. Medical Association* 285, 3093–99.

Cody, H., Pelphrey, K. and Piven, J. (2002). Structural and functional magnetic resonance imaging of autism. *Int. Devl Neurosci.* 766, 1–18.

Courchesne, E., Yeung-Courchesne, R., Press, G. A., Hesselink, J. R. and Jernigan, T. L. (1988). Hypoplasia of cerebellar vermal lobule-Vi and lobule-Vii in autism. *New England J. Med.* 318, 1349–54.

Courchesne, E., Karns, C. M., Davis, H. R., Ziccardi, R., Carper, R. A., Tigue, Z. D., *et al.* (2001). Unusual brain growth patterns in early life in patients with autistic disorder: a MRI study. *Neurology* 57, 245–54.

Critchley, H. D., Daly, E. M., Bullmore, E. T., Williams, S. C., Van Amelsvoort, T., Robertson, D. M., *et al.* (2000). The functional neuroanatomy of social behaviour: changes in cerebral blood flow when people with autistic disorder process facial expressions. *Brain* 123, 2203–12.

Dawson, G., Munson, J., Estes, A., Osterling, J., McPartland, J., Toth, K., *et al.* (2002). Neurocognitive function and joint attention ability in young children with autism spectrum disorder versus developmental delay. *Child Devl* 73, 345–58.

Dewey, M. (1991). Living with Asperger's syndrome. In *Autism and Asperger syndrome* (ed. U. Frith), pp. 184–206. Cambridge University Press.

Farrington, C. P., Miller, E. and Taylor, B. (2001). MMR and autism: further evidence against a causal association. *Vaccine* 19, 3632–35.

Fink, G. R., Halligan, P. W., Marshall, J. C., Frith, C. D., Frackowiak, R. S. J. and Dolan, R. J. (1997). Neural mechanisms involved in the processing of global and local aspects of hierarchically organized visual stimuli. *Brain* 120, 1779–91.

Fletcher, P. C., Happé, F., Frith, U., Baker, S. C., Dolan, R. J., Frackowiak, R. S. J., *et al.* (1995). Other minds in the brain: a functional imaging study of 'theory of mind' in story comprehension. *Cognition* 57, 109–28.

Frith, C. D. (2003). What do imaging studies tell us about the neural basis of autism? In *Autism: neural basis and treatment possibilities* (ed. M. Rutter), Novartis Foundation. Chichester, UK: Wiley.

Frith, U. (2003). *Autism. Explaining the enigma,* 2nd ed. Oxford: Blackwell.

Frith, U. (2001). Mindblindness and the brain in autism. *Neuron* **32**, 969–79.

Frith, U. and Snowling, M. (1983). Reading for meaning and reading for sound in autistic and dyslexic children. *J. Devl Psychol.* **1**, 329–42.

Gallagher, H., Happé, F., Brunswick, N., Fletcher, P. C., Frith, U. and Frith, C. D. (2000). Reading the mind in cartoons and stories: a fMRI study of 'theory of mind' in verbal and non-verbal tasks. *Neuropsychologia* **38**, 11–21.

Gerland, G. (1997). *A real person: life on the outside.* (trans. J. Tate). London: Souvenir.

Gilchrist, A., Green, J., Cox, A., Burton, D., Rutter, M. and Le Couteur, A. (2001). Development and current functioning in adolescents with Asperger syndrome: a comparative study. *J. Child Psychol. Psychiatry* **42**, 227–40.

Gillberg, C. and Coleman, M. (2000). *The biology of the autistic syndromes,* 3rd edn. London: MacKeith Press.

Griffith, E. M., Pennington, B. F., Wehner, E. A. and Rogers, S. J. (1999). Executive functions in young children with autism. *Child Dev.* **70**, 817–32.

Halsey, N. A. and Hyman, S. L. (2001). Measles–mumps–rubella vaccine and autistic spectrum disorder: report from the New Challenges in childhood immunizations conference convened in Oak Brook, Illinois, June 12–13. *Pediatrics* **107**, E84.

Happé, F. G. E. (1994). An advanced test of theory of mind: understanding of story characters' thoughts, and feelings by able autistic, mentally handicapped, and normal children and adults. *J. Autism Devl Disorder* **24**, 129–54.

Happé, F. G. E. (1997). Central coherence and theory of mind in autism: reading homographs in context. *Br. J. Devl Psychol.* **15**, 1–12.

Happé, F. (1999). Autism: cognitive deficit or cognitive style? *Trends Cogn. Sci.* **3**, 216–222.

Happé, F., Briskman, J. and Frith, U. (2001). Exploring the cognitive phenotype of autism: weak 'central coherence' in parents and siblings of children with autism: I. experimental tests. *J. Child Psychol. Psychiatry* **42**, 299–307.

Happé, F., Ehlers, S., Fletcher, S., Frith, U., Johannsson, M., Gillberg, C., *et al.* (1996). 'Theory of mind' in the brain. Evidence from a PET scan study of Asperger syndrome. *Neuroreport* **8**, 197–201.

Haznedar, M. M., Buchsbaum, M. S., Wei, T. C., Hof, P. R., Cartwright, C., Bienstock, C. A., *et al.* (2001). Limbic circuitry in patients with autism spectrum disorders, studies with positron emission tomography and magnetic resonance imaging. *Am. J. Psychiatry* **157**, 1994–2001.

Heaton, R. K., Chelune, G. J., Talley, J. L., Kay, G. G. and Curtiss, G. (1993). *Wisconsin card sorting test manual: revised and expanded.* Odessa, FL: Psychological Assessment Resources.

Heinze, H. J., Hinrichs, H., Scholz, M., Burchert, W. and Mangun, R. (1998). Neural mechanisms of global and local processing: a combined PET and ERP study. *J. Cogn. Neurosci.* **10**, 485–98.

Hermelin, B. (2002). *Bright splinters of the mind. A personal story of research with autistic savants.* London: Jessica Kingsley.

Hobson, R. P. (1993). *Autism and the development of mind.* Hove, Sussex: Lawrence Erlbaum Associates.

Hughes, C. and Russell, J. (1993). Autistic children's difficulty with mental disengagement from an object: its implications for theories of autism. *Devl Psychol.* **29**, 498–510.

Hughes, C., Russell, J. and Robbins, T. W. (1994). Evidence for executive dysfunction in autism. *Neuropsychologia* **32**, 477–492.

Hughes, C., Leboyer, M. and Bouvard, M. (1997). Executive function in parents of children with autism. *Psychol. Med.* **27**, 209–20.

Hughes, C., Plumet, M.-H. and Leboyer, M. (1999). Towards a cognitive phenotype for autism: increased prevalence of executive dysfunction and superior spatial span amongst siblings of children with autism. *J. Child Psychol. Psychiatry* **40**, 705–18.

Huttenlocher, P. R. and Dabholkar, A. S. (1997). Regional differences in synaptogenesis in human cerebral cortex. *J. Comp. Neurol.* **387**, 167–78.

International Molecular Genetic Study of Autism Consortium (1998). A full genome screen for autism with evidence for linkage to a region on chromosome 7q. *Hum. Mol. Genet.* **7**, 571–78.

Jolliffe, T. and Baron-Cohen, S. (1997). Are people with autism or Asperger syndrome faster than normal on the embedded figures test? *J. Child Psychol. Psychiatry* **38**, 527–34.

Jolliffe, T. and Baron-Cohen, S. (1999). A test of central coherence theory: linguistic processing in high-functioning adults with autism or Asperger syndrome: is local coherence impaired? *Cognition* **71**, 149–85.

Kanner, L. (1943). Autistic disturbances of affective contact. *Nervous Child* **2**, 217–50.

Kemper, K. L. and Bauman, M. L. (1998). Neuropathology of infantile autism. *J. Neuropathol. Exp. Neurol.* **57**, 645–52.

Klin, A., Jones, W., Schultz, R., Volkmar, F. and Cohen, D. (2002). Defining and quantifying the social phenotype in autism. *Am. J. Psychiatry* **159**, 895–908.

Lainhart, J. E., Piven, J., Wzorek, M., Landa, R., Santangelo, S. L., Coon, H., *et al.* (1997). Macrocephaly in children and adults with autism. *J. Am. Acad. Child Adolescent Psychiatry* **36**, 282–90.

Maestrini, E., Paul, A., Monaco, A. P. and Bailey, A. (2000). Identifying autism susceptibility genes. *Neuron* **28**, 19–24.

Mottron, L. and Belleville, S. (1993). A study of perceptual analysis in a high-level autistic subject with exceptional graphic abilities. *Brain Cogn* **23**, 279–309.

Mottron, L., Peretz, I. and Ménard, E. (2000). Local and global processing of music in high-functioning persons with autism: beyond central coherence? *J. Child Psychol. Psychiatry* **41**, 1057–65.

Ohnishi, T., Matsuda, H., Hashimoto, T., Kunihiro, T., Nishikawa, M., Uema, T., *et al.* (2000). Abnormal regional cerebral blood flow in childhood autism. *Brain* **123**, 1838–44.

Ozonoff, S. (1995). Reliability and validity of the Wisconsin card sorting test in studies of autism. *Neuropsychology* **9**, 491–500.

Ozonoff, S. and Jensen, J. (1999). Brief report: specific executive function profiles in three neurodevelopmental disorders. *J. Autism Devl Disorders* **29**, 171–77.

Ozonoff, S. and McEvoy, R. E. (1994). A longitudinal study of executive function and theory of mind development in autism. *Devl Psychopathol.* **6**, 415–31.

Ozonoff, S., Pennington, B. F. and Rogers, S. J. (1991). Executive function deficits in high-functioning autistic individuals: relationship to theory of mind. *J. Child Psychol. Psychiatry* **32**, 1081–105.

Pierce, K., Muller, R. A., Ambrose, J., Allen, G. and Courchesne, E. (2001). Face processing occurs outside the fusiform 'face area' in autism: evidence from functional MRI. *Brain* **124**, 2059–73.

Plaisted, K. (2001). Reduced generalization in autism: an alternative to weak central coherence. In *The development of autism: perspectives from theory and research* (ed. J. A. Burack, T. Charman, N. Yirmiya and P. Zelazo), pp. 149–69. Mahwah, NJ: Lawrence Erlbaum Associates.

Prior, M. R. and Hoffmann, W. (1990). Brief report: neuropsychological testing of autistic children through an exploration with frontal lobe tests. *J. Autism Devl Disorders* **20**, 581–90.

Prior, M., Eisenmajer, R., Leekam, S., Wing, L., Gould, J., Ong, B., *et al.* (1998). Are there subgroups within the autistic spectrum? A cluster analysis of a group of children with autistic spectrum disorder. *J. Child Psychol. Psychiatry* **39**, 893–902.

Rimland, B. and Fein, D. (1988). Special talents of autistic savants. In *The exceptional brain* (ed. L. K. Obler and D. Fein), pp. 474–92. New York: Guildford.

Ring, H. A., Baron-Cohen, S., Wheelwright, S., Williams, S. C. R., Brammer, M., Andrew, C., *et al.* (1999). Cerebral correlates of preserved cognitive skills in autism: a functional MRI study of embedded figures task performance. *Brain* **122**, 1305–15.

Robbins, T. W. (1997). Integrating the neurobiological and neuropsychological dimensions of autism. In *Autism as an executive disorder* (ed. J. Russell), pp. 21–53. Oxford: Oxford University Press.

Rumsey, J. M. and Hamburger, S. D. (1988). Neuropsychological findings in high-functioning men with infantile autism. *J. Autism Devl Disorders* **20**, 155–68.

Russell, J. (1997). *Autism as an executive disorder*. Oxford: Oxford University Press.

Russell, J. (2002). Cognitive theories of autism. In *Cognitive deficits in brain disorders* (ed. J. E. Harrison and A. M. Owen), pp. 295–323. London: Martin Dunitz.

Russell, J. and Hill, E. L. (2001). Action-monitoring and intention reporting in children with autism. *J. Child Psychol. Psychiatry* **42**, 317–28.

Schultz, R. T., Gauthier, I., Klin, A., Fulbright, R. K., Anderson, A. W., Volkmar, F., *et al.* (2000). Abnormal ventral temporal cortical activity during face discrimination among individuals with autism and Asperger syndrome. *Arch. Gen. Psychiatry* **57**, 331–40.

Shah, A. and Frith, U. (1983). An islet of ability in autistic children: a research note. *J. Child Psychol. Psychiatry* **24**, 613–20.

Shah, A. and Frith, U. (1993). Why do autistic individuals show superior performance on the block design task? *J. Child Psychol. Psychiatry* **34**, 1351–64.

Shallice, T. (1988). *From neuropsychology to mental structure*. Cambridge University Press.

Szatmari, P., Bartolucci, G., Bremner, R., Bond, S. and Rich, S. (1989). A follow-up study of high-functioning autistic children. *J. Autism Devl Disorders* **19**, 213–25.

Tager-Flusberg, H. (2001). A re-examination of the theory of mind hypothesis of autism. In *The development of autism: perspectives from theory and research* (ed. J. A. Burack, T. Charman, N. Yirmiya and P. Zelazo), pp. 173–93. Mahwah, NJ: Lawrence Erlbaum Associates.

Taylor, B., Miller, E., Farrington, C. P., Petropoulos, M.-C., Favot-Mayaud, I., Li, J., *et al.* (1999). Autism and measles, mumps, and rubella vaccine: no epidemiological evidence for a causal association. *Lancet* **353**, 2026–29.

Vogeley, K., Bussfeld, P., Newen, A., Herrmann, S., Happé, F., Falkai, P., *et al.* (2001). Mind reading: neural mechanisms of theory of mind and self-perspective. *Neuroimage* **14**, 170–81.

Williams, J. H. G., Whiten, A., Suddendorf, T. and Perrett, D. I. (2001). Imitation, mirror neurons and autism. *Neurosci. Biobehav. Rev.* **25**, 287–95.

Witkin, H. A., Oltman, P. K., Raskin, E. and Karp, S. (1971). *A manual for the embedded figures test*. Palo Alto, CA: Consulting Psychologists Press.

World Health Organization (1992). *The ICD-10 classification for mental and behavioural disorders: clinical descriptions and diagnostic guidelines*. Geneva, Switzerland: WHO.

Zilbovicius, M., Boddaert, N., Belin, P., Poline, J. B., Remy, P., Mangin, J. F., *et al.* (2000). Temporal lobe dysfunction in childhood autism: a PET study. *Am. J. Psychiatry* **157**, 1988–93.

Glossary

DZ: dizygotic
fMRI: functional magnetic resonance imaging
IQ: intelligence quotient
MZ: monozygotic
PET: positron emission tomography

2

A retrospective analysis of the clinical case records of 'autistic psychopaths' diagnosed by Hans Asperger and his team at the University Children's Hospital, Vienna

Kathrin Hippler and Christian Klicpera

To date, it is questionable whether the diagnostic criteria for Asperger syndrome (AS) as stated by ICD-10 or DSM-IV still reflect Asperger's original account of 'autistic psychopathy' (AP) from the 1940s. The present study examined 74 clinical case records of children with AP diagnosed by Hans Asperger and his team at the Viennese Children's Clinic and Asperger's private practice between 1950 and 1986. The characteristic features of the children are outlined, including reasons for referral, parental background, behavioural problems, cognitive functioning, communication and interests. Results show that the patients of Asperger described in our study represent a subgroup of children with very high intellectual functioning, specific circumscribed interests and talents but impaired social, communication and motor skills. Sixty-eight percent of the sample met ICD-10 criteria for AS, while 25% fulfilled the diagnostic criteria for autism. Implications for the diagnosis of AS are discussed.

Keywords: Asperger syndrome; 'autistic psychopathy'; high-functioning autism; diagnostic criteria

2.1 Introduction

AS or 'autistic psychopathy'—as the syndrome was originally termed by Hans Asperger—still constitutes a much discussed and controversial diagnostic category. Asperger, a Viennese paediatrician, described a series of children, mainly boys, with a typical pattern of deficits and assets, which he referred to as AP. In his summary of the typical features of this disorder, he delineates the children's appearance, their distinct intellectual functioning including their learning difficulties and attention problems, their problematic behaviour in social situations and their impairment of emotions and instincts. Asperger (1944, 1952) believed that AP was a constitutionally based personality disorder merging into the 'normal' continuum, that is, a group of eccentric, withdrawn, but often highly gifted, individuals who manage social integration despite their somewhat odd social interaction or communication. He stated that AP corresponded with autism as described by Kanner (1943) in wide terms but emphasized his belief that these disorders had a genetic background and were not caused 'exogenously'. In his view, the two main diagnoses to be differentiated from AP included cerebral organic conditions and schizophrenic psychoses (Asperger 1952). While several symptoms supposedly overlapped with both disorders (e.g. the social impairment or 'contact disorder', the bizarre stereotypes or pedantic rituals) he saw AP as a life-long, stable type of personality without the quality of a progressing fragmentation of personality typically seen in schizophrenia. Also, he stated that it was possible for 'autistic psychopaths' to form certain close interpersonal relationships in the course of their life while schizophrenic psychotic individuals were more likely to lose their ability to form close relationships over time.

From the 1920s onwards, several concepts had appeared in the literature all referring to similar or overlapping patterns of personality traits and problematic behaviours in children (mostly boys) as described by Asperger (for a historic literature review see Gillberg 1998, Wing 1998, or Wolff 1991a). Different terms were in use, for example, schizoid character, schizothymia, schizoid personality disorder, children with circumscribed interests or, later, Asperger's AP.

In 1981, Lorna Wing described the clinical picture of Asperger's AP for the first time in more detail in an English-language journal, making the condition known to a wider scientific community (Wing 1981). She coined the term 'Asperger's syndrome' and slightly altered and extended Asperger's account. Wing observed some additional items in the developmental history of children with AS (e.g. a lack of interest or pleasure in human company in the first year of life) and pointed out that AP may also occur in individuals with learning disabilities. This was, in fact, mentioned by Asperger in his 1944 paper but seems to have been overlooked by researchers and even Asperger himself in his later papers (Frith 1991 in Wing 2000). Wing proposed a spectrum of autistic disorders with a triad of impairments, namely impairment of social interaction, communication and imagination.

Confusion over the definition of AS further increased with the introduction of several diagnostic criteria, including Gillberg and Gillberg's criteria of 1989 (outlined in Gillberg 1991), the criteria of Szatmari et al. (1989), ICD-10 (World Health Organization 1992, 1993) and DSM-IV (American Psychiatric Association 1994) criteria. For a diagnosis of Asperger's disorder to be made, both ICD-10 and DSM-IV require at least two manifestations of social impairment and one area of restricted interest or behaviour from a list of symptoms originally defining autistic disorder (Kanner syndrome). In contrast to autistic disorder, language development in AS is not supposed to be delayed and normal cognitive and self help skills need to present during the first three years of life—a requirement many researchers find problematic (Gillberg and Gillberg 1989; Miller and Ozonoff 1997; Leekam et al. 2000; Szatmari 2000; Wing 2000). In both diagnostic systems, 'dual diagnoses' of AS and autistic disorder are not possible. Therefore, autistic disorder takes precedence over AS if the child is delayed in aspects of his/her early development and meets at least six criteria from the 'autism list', even if s/he demonstrates problems that are quite characteristic for AS.

In contrast to DSM-IV and ICD-10, the criteria of Gillberg and Gillberg (1989) and those of Szatmari *et al.* (1989) do not require 'normal' early development for a diagnosis of AS to be made, and view language and communication peculiarities as a defining feature. Additionally, Gillberg and Gillberg proposed that motor control problems (poor performance on neuro-developmental examination) have to be present.

The introduction of diagnostic criteria brought with it discussion of whether AS constitutes a valid diagnostic entity and can be differentiated from autism. Volkmar and Klin (2000) name several features that have been discussed in the literature to be of relevance in this debate. A later onset, the presence of special interests combined with amassing large amounts of factual information, poor motor functioning, interest in others but failure to establish friendships, a certain communication style (verbosity, tangentiality, certain prosodic deviancies), and associated problems, such as conduct disorders, have all been proposed as being specific markers for AS. Also, higher intellectual functioning (Miller and Ozonoff 1997) accompanied by better verbal than performance IQ (Klin *et al.* 1995) may differentiate AS from autism. Szatmari (2000) holds an alternative view in this debate by regarding AS as one possible pathway of different disorders of the autistic spectrum or pervasive developmental disorders. This implies that a person's diagnosis may, for instance, change from autism to AS over time. Similarly, Wing (2000) argues that a mixture of symptoms that are typical for autism and AS can often be found in the same individual and changes in symptoms may occur over time.

To date, it is highly questionable whether Asperger's original description of AP fits today's diagnostic criteria of AS in DSM-IV and ICD-10. Miller and Ozonoff (1997) examined the four cases of AP described by Asperger in his seminal paper and found that according to current DSM-IV and ICD-10 criteria all of them would be diagnosed with autistic disorder, rather than Asperger disorder due to the precedence rule in both diagnostic systems. The authors conclude that current criteria may not identify the syndrome that Asperger originally described and suggest areas of potential difference between Asperger disorder and autism (e.g. the presence of motor problems, higher intellectual functioning, better theory of mind). Leekam *et al.* (2000) found that of 200 individuals with autistic spectrum disorders, all met ICD-10 criteria for autism, whereas only 1% met criteria for Asperger disorder. However, 45% fulfilled Gillberg's criteria for AS. Again, the difference was due to the ICD-10 requirement for normal development of language, cognitive skills, curiosity and self-help skills.

In order to investigate this issue, our study tried to identify and analyse the clinical case records of children who were seen by Asperger and his team at the paediatric clinic in Vienna. The questions motivating the present study were as follows: (i) What were the characteristic features of AP? (ii) Which features were important for making the diagnosis? (iii) Do these features correspond with ICD-10 criteria? Other areas of interest include:

(i) family background, genetic factors,
(ii) developmental milestones,
(iii) social integration, social behaviour,
(iv) communication and language,
(v) apraxia, motor coordination problems and clumsiness,
(vi) special interests and skills,
(vii) intellectual ability, and
(viii) additional or reactive disorders.

In an attempt to keep the translation of the words and labels from German as clear as possible, in this article, the original label AP is used. In the German language, 'psychopathy' did not quite have the negative connotation it now has in English. It was merely a term for describing personality disorders and did not seek to stress the patients' proneness to criminality.

2.2 Sampling methods

The search for Asperger's original files turned out to be rather difficult, which probably results from the separate storage of the various records and the loss of data due to the war years. Eventually, two major sources were used: the archives of the remedial pedagogical ward at the Vienna University Children's Hospital and the card files of Asperger's private practice stored at the Institute of Medical History in Vienna.

(a) Data from the Pedagogical Department,
University Children's Clinic, Vienna

All stored files of the remedial pedagogical unit were checked for diagnosis of AP. To compare the percentage of admissions, the cases with Kanner's autism and autistic features were also counted. Thirty-seven files of children with a clear diagnosis of AP could be identified and were selected for further analysis. As the original hospital building was destroyed during World War II, unfortunately no files dating from Asperger's famous publication on 'autistic psychopaths' in 1944 up to the 1960s could be found. The files originate from 1964 to 1986. Asperger became head of the Viennese University Children's Clinic in 1962 and remained in this post until 1977. Twenty-seven of the 37 children with AP (73%) were diagnosed or seen by Asperger himself during his weekly rounds on the remedial ward. Most of the remaining 10 children ($n = 7$) were diagnosed and treated by his direct follower and student (Dr Kuszen) who had worked with Asperger for a long time. It can therefore be assumed that the majority of children were either seen by Asperger himself or diagnoses made were in accordance with his account of the disorder. The diagnosis of AP seemed most frequent during the 1970s, obviously the time when Asperger had the greatest influence in his career as head of the clinic. It seems that later the more general term 'autism' was used in favour of the term AP, which made it harder to select children with AS. The files are quite detailed, containing biographic histories, medical and psychological reports, and notes on the child's behaviour and progress on the ward. Often, various other materials were included, such as letters the children wrote to their parents, short notes by the medical staff, or the children's school work and drawings. Four additional patient records of 'autistic psychopaths' were obtained from the private card file of one of Asperger's former colleagues at the Viennese clinic (Dr Wurst). These records are from 1950 and 1951 and consist of less detailed descriptions. The children outlined had been admitted to the remedial pedagogical ward in Vienna and had been seen by Asperger and Wurst together.

(b) Data from Asperger's private practice

The legacy of Asperger's private practice in Vienna's Burggasse was given to the Institute of Medical History by his daughter. It consists of several boxes with thousands of file cards sorted by years. Again, all boxes were checked for the diagnoses of AP, AK and AFs. One hundred and thirty patients with autistic spectrum disorders could be found, 33 of which had received a definite diagnosis of AP. The patient records originate from 1951 to 1980 and include children and adolescents who were seen by Asperger in his private practice and were sometimes, in the course of the treatment, also admitted to the remedial pedagogical ward as inpatients. Many of the records are handwritten or in a hard-to-decipher shorthand and contain brief descriptions of each child, medical letters, letters of referral, etc. Only those children who were also admitted to the ward have more detailed files ($n = 9$).

2.3 Results

(a) Admissions to the remedial pedagogical ward

The admission books from 1950 to 1986 were checked for: (i) total number of admissions per year; (ii) number of 'autistic psychopaths' admitted; (iii) number of children with AK admitted; (iv) and number of children with AFs admitted. The AP group includes all children with a clear diagnosis of AP or 'Asperger autism'. The AK group consists of all children with the diagnoses 'autism and low intelligence' or 'Kanner's autism'. The AF group constitutes a more heterogeneous group without a final diagnostic formulation. We included children with normal to high intelligence who either had an explicit statement saying that they showed distinct or mild AFs or who were described with a combination of social impairment (difficulty of integration into peer group) together with restricted interests/activities, language and communication peculiarities or motor apraxia.

A total of 6459 children were admitted to the ward between 1950 and 1986, with a mean rate of 175 referrals per year. Of the 6459 children, 228 (3.5%) had autistic spectrum disorders. The distribution among the three subgroups (AP, AK, AF) was relatively even: 'autistic psychopaths' comprised 1.15% ($n = 74$) of all referrals, children with early infantile autism 1.23% ($n = 83$) and children with AFs 1.1% ($n = 71$). However, if the number of 'autistic psychopaths' is added to the number of children with AFs, this group comprises 2.25% of all admissions.

For the whole group of autism spectrum disorders, a male : female ratio of 9 : 1 could be found. For the children with AK this ratio decreased to 4 : 1, whereas for the children with AP it was as high as 24 : 1.

(b) Referrals to Asperger's practice

All file cards in the 23 boxes stored at the Institute of Medical History were counted and checked for diagnoses of autism spectrum disorders. According to the card file, Asperger saw approximately 9800 children between 1951 and 1980. Two hundred and thirteen children (2.17%) had disorders on the autistic spectrum. Similarly to the remedial pedagogical ward, 1.15% ($n = 113$) were recorded as having a clear diagnosis of AP. Fewer children had AK (0.68%; $n = 67$), and 0.35% ($n = 34$) were described as having AFs.

(c) Analysis of the clinical case records and files

(i) Cases included for detailed analysis
Only cases with explicitly stated diagnoses of AP ($n = 74$) were selected for further analysis. Detailed files from the time the children were inpatients at the ward were available for 46 of these cases (37 from the remedial pedagogical ward, 9 from Asperger's private card file). For categories that have several rating possibilities (e.g. several initial reasons for referral or types of language peculiarities) only the 46 detailed files were included as it is not certain whether missing values would indicate normalcy or not. For more factual information (e.g. IQ, father's profession) the whole AP sample ($n = 74$) was included, and lacking data were coded as missing values.

(ii) Rating methods
The information from the files was entered into a database containing variables covering the following aspects:

   (i) general data (age at first referral, gender, school attended, etc.),
   (ii) reasons for referral or admission,
   (iii) diagnosis and additional diagnostic labels,
   (iv) intelligence,

  (v) family background,
 (vi) pregnancy, birth and early developmental milestones,
(vii) behaviour at home/on the ward/at school,
(viii) language and communication,
 (ix) non-verbal communication,
  (x) special interests and skills, and
 (xi) additional information (e.g. suspected prognosis, physical problems).

Most variables had a simple coding of $0 = $ not true/no, $1 = $ true/yes. There were only a few variables with alternative ratings (e.g. type of school).

The charts were reviewed and rated by a clinical psychologist as part of her PhD (first author). Parts of the data were re-rated by four psychology students who worked on this project (in an extended form) for their Master's theses. All raters had experience with autistic patients and patients with AS, either in clinical practice or care settings. The raters' training was carried out with the project's supervisor (second author) and consisted of group practice on the ratings of several cases, as well as an independent rating of one case each followed by discussion.

(iii) Inter-rater reliability
Twenty-six cases (35% of the whole AP sample) were re-rated. To determine inter-rater reliability, we used kappa coefficients. The average agreement on the initial reasons for referral was 84%, kappa values ranged from 0.519 to 1.00. Ratings on diagnoses were more consistent and an inter-rater agreement of 87% was reached (kappa values between 0.709 and 0.881). Average agreement on behavioural difficulties was 85% (kappa between 0.505 and 1.00) and 83% on language and communication deviancies (kappa from 0.489 to 1.00). No systematic difference across raters was found.

(d) Description of the sample

The children included in the analysis were seen between 1950 and 1986. They were born between 1938 and 1979 (and are now 23–64 years of age). Seventy-four percent of the admitted children (the majority) were inpatients on the ward between 1969 and 1979. Ninety-five percent of the children with this type of diagnosis were boys ($n = 70$), whereas only four girls showed full AP.

The age range of the children was between 4 and 17 years. The mean age at which the child was first seen at the clinic or at Asperger's practice was 8.2 years (s.d. $= 2.5$). Most children (66%) attended primary school at the time of the first admission or consultation; 11% were in kindergarten, 10% were at high school/college (Gymnasium) while 6% attended grammar school (Hauptschule). Another 6% were at special schools (Sonderschule).

Fifty children (68%) had been inpatients at the remedial pedagogical ward at some point; 24 (32%) were seen only by Asperger at his private practice. Forty-six of the 50 children admitted to the ward had detailed files. For those

Table 2.1   Most frequent reasons for referral to the pedagogical ward in the AP group
with detailed files ($n = 46$).

reasons for referral	n	percentage
learning difficulties, attention deficits, academic problems	27	69
social and interactive difficulties with peers	26	57
disciplinary problems at school	16	35
behavioural difficulties, aggression and opposition	12	26
educational difficulties, parental problems in child-rearing	12	26
isolation, withdrawal, solitariness	11	24
lack of independence and life skills	9	20
temper tantrums	6	13
anxiety attacks, phobia (e.g. fear of other children, physical education, darkness)	5	11

children who were inpatients, the duration of their stay on the ward ranged
from 1 to 10 weeks (for children who had more than one stay, the weeks of
admission were added up). The average duration of admission was four and a
half weeks (s.d. = 1.71). Most of the admitted children were inpatients on the
ward once (88%); 10% of the children were admitted twice; one child had
three stays.

(i) Initial reasons for admission
All children with detailed files from the ward ($n = 46$) were included in the
analysis. Combinations of more than one reason for referral were common.
The most frequent reasons for referral consisted of learning difficulties at
school, followed by difficulties in mixing with the peer group and disciplinary
problems (for an overview see Table 2.1).

Seven children (15%) had to be admitted to the ward because their behaviour was no longer acceptable at school and exclusion was imminent. A smaller
number of children were referred because of developmental delay, enuresis/
encopresis, sleeping or eating disorders. Difficulties occasionally reported as
being the reason for referral included depressive episode, lack of drive, obsessive imitation of animal voices, elective mutism or whispering, maliciousness,
nervous symptoms, obscene language, speech and language difficulties,
unusual obsessions or compulsions, and hallucinations.

(ii) Additional diagnostic labels
The diagnostic formulation usually consisted of several labels to amplify and
add to the main diagnosis. The diagnoses given most often in addition to AP
were 'contact disorder' and 'instinct disorder'. According to clinicians who
worked with Asperger, the term 'instinct disorder' was used to refer to the children's lack of common sense, their impaired 'practical intelligence' in everyday situations including deficient social understanding. In contrast to knowing
'instinctively' how to behave in a social situation or how to master day-to-day

Table 2.2   Diagnostic labels in the AP group with detailed files ($n = 46$).

additional diagnostic labels	n	percentage
contact disorder	40	87
'instinct disorder'	35	76
learning difficulties, academic failure	31	68
apraxia, motor coordination problems, clumsiness	27	59
disciplinary problems	22	48
reduced sense of reality	17	37
obsessive and compulsive behaviours, rituals	17	37
familial and socio-economic difficulties	14	30

problems, it was believed that children with AP had to learn these skills through their intellect. 'Contact disorder' referred to the patient's difficulty in forming real interpersonal relationships. Despite good intellectual skills, approximately two-thirds of the children were also diagnosed with severe learning and/or attention deficits often leading to academic failure (for an overview of diagnostic labels see Table 2.2).

(iii) Additional information
In four of the 46 children admitted to the ward (9%), schizophrenia was either suspected or put forward as a future prognosis. What Asperger called 'autistic malice' was observed in seven patients (15%); these children were described as seemingly good observers, showing intentional acts of malice, with malicious pleasure and apparent pride in what they had done. Some of the children were said to 'experiment' on others, that is, they seemed to do things on purpose to see how others reacted or to provoke a certain reaction. Eight children (17%) were reported as being hypersensitive towards criticism and jokes by others. For nine patients (20%) sensory deviancies were so striking that they were mentioned in the files (e.g. hypersensitivity to certain noises, obsession with smells).

(iv) Intellectual functioning
For 62 children, a brief general judgement of intellectual functioning (low intelligence–good intelligence–above average intelligence) was available. Twelve children (27%) were described as being of average intelligence while only one child (2%) was reported as being below average. Twenty-five (57%) children's intelligence was claimed to be above average. Six children (14%) were described as having low to average intelligence at present or being too young for testing but were given the prognosis that intellectual functioning would increase with age.

Results for 42 children from the HAWIK (which is equivalent to the WISC) were available. No children were below average (i.e. IQ lower than 85): 45% were of average intelligence while, in fact, 55% of the children functioned in

Table 2.3 FSIQ, VIQ and PIQ in children with AP and controls as measured by the HAWIK (German version of the WISC).

	AP group ($n = 38$) mean (s.d.) range	controls ($n = 2318$)[a] mean
FSIQ	116.21 (16.95) 85–153	105.91
VIQ	117.68 (15.40) 92–152	102.96
PIQ	110.34 (17.56) 75–150	107.65
sex (m : f)	35 : 3	1746 : 525

[a] From Schubert & Berlach (1982); no information on s.d. and range was available, only confidence intervals (likelihood: 99%) were reported (FSIQ, 105–107; VIQ, 102.1–103.8; PIQ, 106.7–108.6).

the high to superior range. Comparison data were taken from the study of Schubert and Berlach (1982) of 2318 children tested with the HAWIK at the remedial pedagogical ward between 1962 and 1979. They found a mean FSIQ of 106, VIQ of 103 and PIQ of 108. These figures, although slightly upwardly skewed (Schubert and Berlach argued for a revision of the HAWIK due to their findings), are still clearly lower than the measures in our sample. Schubert and Berlach also found a slightly higher PIQ than VIQ, whereas in the AP sample the opposite pattern was observed (see Table 2.3).

(v) Comparing VIQ and PIQ

In many files (54%), it was mentioned that the children showed excellent verbal abilities with good formal and abstract thinking as well as general knowledge, whereas 'practical' intelligence (i.e. visual–spatial skills, social intelligence or visual–motor coordination) seemed impaired. For 38 cases, measured VIQ and PIQ could be compared. VIQ and PIQ were rated as discrepant if a 9-point difference or higher could be observed between the two measures. Applying this rule, 48% showed a higher VIQ than PIQ, whereas 18% demonstrated the opposite pattern. For 38%, VIQ and PIQ measures showed no significant differences.

Special gifts and abilities

Nineteen percent of the 46 children with detailed files were reported as being capable of original, sometimes even philosophical, thinking processes. Fourteen percent were said to have a special gift for abstract thinking and logical reasoning. A special insight into themselves (self-reflection and consciousness) was reported for another 17%. These children were described as being capable of looking at themselves from an outside or dispassionate view, but Asperger often mentioned that they did not draw conclusions from these insights and could not use them in the social context (i.e. see themselves through the eyes of *others* and behave accordingly). An outstanding mathematical talent was reported in 23%. Some children were said to invent their own calculation methods that were highly complicated but did not always lead to correct results. Other abilities mentioned included eidetic memory (14%) and musical or artistic talent (12%).

Specific learning disabilities
Eight children (17%) had problems in reading and writing (i.e. either isolated spelling or reading disorder or both combined), while only one child was reported as having problems in mathematics (dyscalculia). Four children (9%) showed difficulty in handwriting ('grapho-motor skills').

(vi) Family background
For 35 fathers and 31 mothers of the sample, details about their educational qualifications were mentioned. More than half of the fathers ($n = 20$; 57%) and 42% of mothers ($n = 13$) had finished high school with A-levels ('Matura'). Almost one-third of the fathers ($n = 10$) and 23% of the mothers ($n = 7$) had a university degree, which seems to point to an upwardly skewed educational level compared with the normal population. To determine whether these figures are merely a selection bias due to the type of clients coming to the clinic, a control group was identified consisting of 82 files from the archives of the remedial pedagogical ward taken from 1958–1982. The children included were mainly diagnosed with behavioural problems (48%), learning/concentration/ attention difficulties (27%), cerebral disorders (26%) and family problems (21%). In the control group, only a quarter of the fathers ($n = 19$) had completed A-levels, which is significantly less often than in the AP group ($\chi^2 = 11.489$, d.f. $= 1, p = 0.001$). Similarly, only 17% of the mothers ($n = 12$) in the control group had A-levels, compared with 42% in the AP sample ($\chi^2 = 7.090$, d.f. $= 1, p = 0.008$). Furthermore, university degrees were significantly less common in the control group than in the AP group. Thirty-one percent of fathers of children with AP as opposed to 12% of control fathers had a university degree ($\chi^2 = 6.561$, d.f. $= 1, p = 0.010$).

In 37 cases, the father's profession was mentioned. The most common profession among the fathers of children with AP was technical professions, which is significantly different from the control group ($\chi^2 = 9.588$, d.f. $= 1, p = 0.002$). In the control group, most fathers were in manual work, followed by commercial jobs (see also Table 2.4).

The most frequently seen profession for fathers in our sample was engineer or electrical engineer (22%; $n = 8$). Compared with the control group, only 6% ($n = 5$) were engineers, which constitutes a significant difference ($\chi^2 = 5.922$, d.f. $= 1, p = 0.015$).

(vii) Similarity with family members
In 32 files, a short description of the impression the staff had of the parent's personality was available. Some resemblance between the child with AP and one or more family members was observed in 53% of the sample. Fourteen fathers (52%) were reported as being similar to their child in personality (e.g. aloof, odd, 'nervous') showing deviant behaviours or low social competence.

Table 2.4 Area of fathers' professions in the AP sample compared with controls (figures do not add up to 100% as 11% of the jobs did not fit into the categories given).

area of fathers' professions	AP group (%) ($n = 37$)	controls (%) ($n = 80$)
technical (e.g. engineer, electrical engineer, technician)[a]	27	8
commercial	16	15
skilled manual (e.g. carpenter, builder)[b]	14	31
professionals (e.g. lawyer, doctor, journalist)	11	8
civil services	8	6
public services (e.g. post, transport)	5	14
clergy	5	0
teaching	3	1
unskilled worker (e.g. shelf stacker)	0	9

[a] Significant difference between the groups ($\chi^2 = 9.588$, d.f. = 1, $p = 0.002$).
[b] Marginally significant difference ($\chi^2 = 3.823$, d.f. = 1, $p = 0.051$).

Additionally, for four mothers (15%) and two siblings (7%) similarities with the presented child were mentioned.

(viii) Pregnancy, birth and early developmental milestones
Information about the mother's pregnancy, the child's birth, and his/her early development was available for the 46 cases with detailed files from the ward. Twenty-eight percent of the mothers had had difficulties during pregnancy, including bleeding, infection or extreme nausea. In 33% of the cases, difficulties during birth were reported.

Twenty-six percent of the children were late in being potty trained, or had phases of enuresis or soiling during their early childhood. Only 11% were reported as having been delayed in their motor development. By contrast, 20% of the children showed language delay (first words after 2 years). It was mentioned that seven children (15%) started to talk quite unexpectedly, that is, they did not talk at all until a certain age and were then suddenly capable of saying a number of words or even whole sentences. Four of these cases had been significantly delayed in saying their first words (2 years or more) but then rapidly developed a good use of phrases before the age of three.

(ix) Behaviour on the ward/at home/at school
The greatest behavioural difficulty of the 46 children admitted to the ward consisted of lack of integration into the peer group. Over 90% were reported as having severe deficits in this area. For the great majority, these problems consisted of a combination of being 'out of the group', having no friends, being ignored, disliked or bullied by the others. It was not so much that they were not interested in their peers but rather that they approached them in an

inappropriate way or that their unpredictable behaviour (i.e. aggressive out-bursts) made them unpopular with the others. Three-quarters of the children were described as being clumsy during their stay on the ward (i.e. it was mentioned in their files that they showed impaired fine and gross motor skills, poor motor coordination or difficulty in participating in sports and games) although not all of them received a diagnosis of apraxia (see Table 2.2). The motor problems were sometimes also reflected in the children's poor drawing skills and particularly poor results in the 'man-drawing-test', pointing to a deficient 'body schema' which was described as a lack of knowledge about their own body in space and the body's proportions. Other frequently seen problems concerned the children's difficulty in finishing school work. They were reported as being too slow, too pedantic or too careless because they were preoccupied with other things (e.g. their special interests) or had major attention deficits. Asperger often regarded the children as being 'distracted from within/or by themselves'. Furthermore, half of the children displayed disciplinary problems, negativism or conduct difficulties, particularly at school; they did not listen to what the teacher said or only followed their own 'spontaneous', idiosyncratic ideas. They were described as disrespectful towards authority, and could come across as impudent and blunt because they would speak out freely without thinking while being quite unaware of the situation or the status of the person to whom they were talking. Sometimes disciplinary problems went so far that s/he had to be expelled from school or excluded from PE lessons (20%). For a detailed overview see Table 2.5.

(x) Special interests and hobbies
For 44 cases with detailed files, information on special interests was available. Eighty-two percent were reported as having special, original and narrow interests and hobbies. Asperger and his team often described these interests as highly scientific and distinctive, while other interests were rather obscure or atypical for children that age (e.g. eye muscles, rubbish bins, earthworms, religious hymns, gangsters). For 33 children, the nature of the interests was mentioned and a categorization was attempted (see Table 2.6).

(xi) Language and communication
Ninety-five percent of the admitted patients displayed some kind of language and communication deviancies that can be regarded as typical for AS (excluding common speech problems, like stuttering, or problems not specific for AS, such as talking too fast or too quietly).

Asperger considered the 'autistic psychopath's' language peculiarities as one of the most dominant characteristics of the disorder. When describing the more able children's language, Asperger (and his team) most often referred to their unusually sophisticated and distinguished language, their good verbal ability. The children supposedly spoke like scholars or professors about their chosen field often using original expressions or unusual words. Asperger drew a connection between their language and their thought processes, which he

Table 2.5 Behavioural difficulties in children with AP who were admitted to the remedial pedagogical ward.

behavioural difficulties	n	percentage
no integration into peer group (lack of friends, victim of bullying, etc.)	42	91
marked clumsiness during stay on the ward	34	74
difficulty with completing school work (only follows his/ her own interests, is too slow, too careless, etc.)	28	61
attention problems, poor concentration	27	59
problems with accepting authority, disciplinary problems, conduct disorder	23	50
absent-mindedness, 'in a world of his/her own'	23	50
verbal and physical aggression	20	44
inappropriate social behaviour (lack of personal distance to others)	19	41
stereotyped behaviour, tics	16	35
hyperactivity	16	35
anxiety, phobia	13	28
affective lability	9	20
'playing the fool' (in class)	7	15
temper tantrums	6	13

Table 2.6 Special interests and hobbies in children with AP ($n = 33$). (Thirty per cent of the children with special interests had hobbies which could not be categorized, such as a fascination with puns, letters, comics, Mickey Mouse, gangsters, national socialism, clocks, inventing own methods for calculation.)

special interests	n	percentage
animals and nature	10	30
technical and/ or scientific interests	9	27
obsessive reading, collecting facts	8	24
public transport systems, trains, cars	6	18
religion	4	12
drawing	4	12
music	3	9
space, astronauts	2	6

thought of as often being creative, spontaneous and original. For many children, deviant prosody and quality of voice was reported (e.g. monotonous speech, singing quality of voice, high pitched tone, over-precise articulation). The children were frequently regarded as ignorant of the social situation when speaking, and sometimes seemed to talk to themselves, commenting on their

Table 2.7   Speech and language characters in children with AP ($n = 43$).

language and communication	n	percentage
ignorant of social situation when talking	29	68
talking in monologues, commenting on own actions, talking to him/herself	24	56
distinguished language, good verbal ability	23	54
deviant modulation (e.g. monotonous) and articulation (e.g. over-exact)	23	54
associative language, 'derailment of thoughts', getting off-topic	14	33
pedantic, long-winded, complicated speech	13	30
verbosity, 'endless talking'	12	28
'obsessional' questioning, 'getting into endless debates'	11	26
precocious, 'know-it-all'	9	21
neologisms, original or unusual words and phrases	9	21
common speech problems (e.g. stutter, lisp)	9	21
echolalia and verbal perseverations	8	19

own actions or giving monologues without needing a listener. One-third of the children showed associative, tangential language and were unable to stay with one topic for a longer period of time (unless they talked about their interests). One-quarter were reported as showing 'obsessional' questioning or were said to have some kind of need to debate things endlessly. Common speech problems, like stuttering or lisping, were present in a smaller number of children. For an overview of language and communication deviancies see Table 2.7.

(xii) Non-verbal communication
Facial expression was regarded as limited or different in 80% of the admitted children. More than one-third of these children lacked emotional expression; 13% seemed tense; 17% had facial twitches/tics or an unnatural expression (e.g. permanent smile or grin); 17% appeared unusually serious and not child-like in their facial expression.

Thirty-five percent of the children showed deviant eye contact (no or reduced eye contact 29%, unusual gaze, for example, staring 7%). Limited use of gestures (11%) or stereotyped movements (9%) were reported less frequently than rather bizarre, gauche or clumsy body language and gait which was seen in a third of the admitted children (33%).

(e) Application of ICD-10 criteria

In order to determine whether Asperger's patients would fit the diagnostic criteria for Asperger's disorder today, 44 children with AP were analysed according to ICD-10 research criteria (World Health Organization 1993). Twelve cases (29%) were double-rated by four students. For points A, B and D of the diagnostic criteria, 100% agreement could be reached. For point C (circumscribed interest or restricted, repetitive and stereotyped behaviour patterns) there was disagreement on one case. For the sub-scores, reliability coefficients (kappa) ranged between 0.66 and 1.00.

The results show that 68% of the children would be diagnosed with AS according to current ICD-10 criteria. Twenty-five percent of the children ($n = 11$) did not meet the requirement of normal development before the age of three. Six of these cases showed delayed language development (first words after 2 years), one child had delayed cognitive development, one displayed deficient self-help skills and three showed a combination of delayed language and impaired self-help skills. Nearly all of the children fulfilled the criteria for points B (abnormal reciprocal social interaction) and C (circumscribed interest or restricted, repetitive and stereotyped patterns of behaviour). In 11 cases (all cases with some kind of developmental delay), autism took precedence over Asperger's disorder. One child was also diagnosed with OCD and therefore could not be diagnosed with Asperger's disorder at the same time. Five percent of the children ($n = 2$) clearly diagnosed with AP by Asperger and his team would not be captured by ICD-10 criteria at all. Table 2.8 provides a symptom count on ICD-10 criteria for AS.

Table 2.8   ICD-10 symptom count for 44 cases with AP.

point	ICD-10 criteria applied to Asperger's clients with AP	n
A	lack of delay in spoken and receptive language or cognitive development	33 (75%)
B	qualitative abnormalities in reciprocal social interaction	43 (98%)
	(i) failure adequately to use eye-to-eye gaze, facial expression, body posture, . . .	26 (61%)
	(ii) failure to develop peer relationships . . .	40 (91%)
	(iii) lack of social–emotional reciprocity . . .	41 (93%)
	(iv) lack of spontaneous seeking to share enjoyment, interests, . . .	12 (29%)
C	unusually intense, circumscribed interest or restricted, repetitive and stereotyped patterns of behaviour, interests and activities	42 (96%)
	(i) encompassing preoccupation with one or more stereotyped and restricted patterns of interest . . .	33 (77%)
	(ii) apparently compulsive adherence to specific, non-functional routines or rituals	15 (35%)
	(iii) stereotyped and repetitive motor mannerisms . . .	14 (32%)
	(iv) preoccupations with part-objects or non-functional elements of play . . .	4 (9%)
D	the disorder is not attributable to other varieties of pervasive developmental disorder; simple schizophrenia; schizotypal disorder; OCD; anankastic personality disorder; reactive and disinhibited attachment disorders of childhood	32 (73%)
Does the diagnosis of AS apply?		30 (68%)
Autism taking precedence over AS		11 (25%)
No diagnosis or other diagnosis (OCD)		3 (7%)

Apart from the requirement for delayed development, 45% of the children also met the ICD-10 criteria for autism, i.e. they fulfilled points B1 (social impairment), B2 (communication impairment) and B3 (restricted behaviour), and met six or more criteria for the symptoms listed under point B, as well as criteria C. A high number of children showed language deviancies (table 7) and, to an extent, these were captured by ICD-10 criteria for autism: 25% had delayed language, 33% showed marked impairment in the ability to initiate or sustain a conversation with others, 39% demonstrated stereotyped and repetitive use of language or idiosyncratic language, and 8% displayed a lack of varied, spontaneous make-believe play or social imitative play.

2.4 Discussion

In the present study we wanted to outline how Asperger and his team characterized their clients with AP, which features led to a diagnosis, and how this conforms with today's diagnostic criteria of AS. After systematically analysing 74 descriptions of 'autistic psychopaths' delineated by Asperger and his team from 1950 to 1986, we hope that a somewhat clearer picture of 'what Asperger meant' may arise.

Limitations to the study lie in the fact that different types of files with varying amounts of information were included in the analysis. In particular, the file cards from Asperger's private practice lacked information. In these files, Asperger apparently only recorded what he found most striking about the individual child and what would have been most useful for further intervention. Owing to this problem, we had to confine the sample to a much smaller number of 46 cases with detailed files from the ward for many of the categories described. Another limitation is that raters who re-examined the cases for interrater reliability were not blind to diagnosis as they had all been involved in the process of identifying and collecting data and were therefore familiar with the case files analysed.

Results show that 'autistic psychopaths' comprised over 1% of all referrals to the remedial pedagogical unit of the children's clinic or to Asperger's practice. Added to the number of children with affiliated disorders without an explicit diagnosis of AP the percentage lies between 1.5% and 2.3%. Only 5% of the analysed cases were females. Typically, the children were first referred in middle childhood (mean age 8 years), the initial reasons for their referral being mostly learning difficulties, academic failure and attention deficits. The children were described with several diagnostic labels, most commonly 'contact and instinct disorder', i.e. a combination of low social competence and a lack of *instinctive* knowledge about how to solve everyday problems or how to behave appropriately in a variety of situations. The most dominant behavioural difficulty of the children consisted of lack of integration into the peer group. The children seemed to others to be isolated and were often ignored, bullied or disliked by their classmates. Although they did not lack interest in others, their social approaches were often awkward and inappropriate—a feature which has been discussed as characteristic for AS compared with HFA (Volkmar and Klin 2000) and may correspond to the 'active but odd' group of Wing and Gould (1979). The ability to concentrate on schoolwork was usually poor, and disciplinary problems and conduct disorder were seen in half of the children of the sample. These children were not capable of following the rules and joining in with the normal school routine. Usually, typical pedagogical measures proved to have no effect on the child's behaviour, but rather made it worse. More extreme forms of aggression ('autistic malice') were reported less often. Over 80% of the children had special interests, most of which consisted of a fascination for certain animals and aspects of nature or were of a technical kind.

Intellectual functioning was clearly higher in the AP sample than in other children referred to the clinic at about the same time. No child was below average, whereas over half of the children showed high to superior intellectual skills—a finding that seems quite surprising considering the fact that Asperger (1944) did mention that AP could occur in less able individuals as well. Clinicians who worked with Asperger in the 1970s report that it was an 'unspoken rule' (set by Asperger) that a diagnosis of AP was usually only considered in children with good to high intelligence, which would explain why Asperger in his later papers 'overlooked' the coexistence of AP and learning disabilities he had suggested before (Wing 2000). Whether it was Asperger's intention to exclude less able individuals from the diagnosis is unclear.

Looking at VIQ and PIQ in the admitted children of our sample, we found that a significantly higher VIQ than PIQ was more than twice as common as the converse (44% versus 18%). The former pattern has been proposed as being typical for AS (Klin et al. 1995; Miller and Ozonoff 1997). A meta-analysis on studies measuring IQ profiles in subjects with HFA and AS by Lincoln et al. (1998) confirmed the assumption that individuals with AS typically demonstrate higher VIQ than PIQ, whereas subjects with HFA display the opposite pattern.

Examining the cases in our sample according to ICD-10 research criteria (World Health Organization 1993) it could be found that, unlike the results of Leekam et al. (2000), 68% of the present sample did fulfil the criteria for AS. However, a closer analysis led to somewhat contrasting results.

In one way, ICD-10 criteria seem over-inclusive, as they capture neither impaired verbal/non-verbal communication nor motor problems. In our sample, we found that 95% of the children had some form of language deviancies most often connected with the pragmatic aspects of language use followed by prosodic differences. Although, in the present sample, early motor development was not found to be delayed very often, 59% had an additional diagnosis of motor apraxia, almost three-quarters showed motor clumsiness during their stay on the ward and another third displayed awkward or gauche body language and gait. It has been suggested that developmental motor delay and the presence of motor clumsiness (Gillberg 1991) may be a defining feature of AS but so far no evidence has been found of clumsiness as a specific marker for AS in comparison with HFA (Ghaziuddin *et al.* 1994). Both language deviancies and motor clumsiness, however, seemed crucial for a diagnosis of AP in the present sample.

However, ICD-10 criteria appeared too narrow, as 25% of the children examined (some of which were described as 'classic autistic psychopaths') did not fit the diagnosis due to early developmental delays, mostly regarding language. Forty-five percent fulfilled point B of the diagnostic criteria for autism. For the rest, the impairments in communication required for autism did not conform to the communication difficulties in the children with AP. It could be assumed that the rather high intellectual functioning and excellent verbal ability found in our sample may lead to a different appearance of language and communication impairments.

Ghaziuddin and Gerstein (1996) suggested that 'pedantic speech' may be specific to AS, defining it as 'that type of speech in which the speaker conveys more information than the topic and goals of the conversation demand, violating expectations of relevancy and quantity; sentence structure may have the formality and vocabulary display the erudition expected of written language. Conversational turns resemble rehearsed monologues rather than contributions to a jointly managed dialogue. Articulation may be precise and intonation formal' (p. 589). Although the word 'pedantic' was rarely used in our sample (and if so it mainly referred to somewhat lengthy, complicated speech), many single features listed above were mentioned in the files when describing the children's language, particularly the distinguished, 'scholarly' language, the precise articulation, the ignorance of the social context when talking and the tendency to speak in monologues. The inclusion of specific language issues into current diagnostic criteria for AS are therefore considered as highly important.

Other more selected results of the present study also coincide with other authors' findings. The parents of the children in our sample, for instance, had significantly higher educational qualifications than the parents of other patients visiting the clinic (which might derive directly from the clinicians' habit of only diagnosing AP in children with higher intellectual functioning). However, fathers of children with AP also more often worked in technical professions (particularly engineering) compared with controls, which confirms the suggestion of Baron-Cohen *et al.* (1997) that there may be a link between autism and engineering or, generally spoken, superior functioning in the domain of 'folk physics'. The authors presume that the very same genes leading to high ability in 'folk physics' may, in some cases, lead parents to have a child with autism. A number of children with AP whose files we examined also showed high mathematical and/or technical ability, often even working on 'new inventions'. However, these were often described as not being very usable. Half of the fathers were reported as resembling their child in personal characteristics supporting Asperger's own observation of a genetic background to the disorder.

Furthermore, a certain overlap of our cases with Sula Wolff's sample of 'schizoid' children exists (Wolff 1991a,b). The author pointed out that maybe 'schizoid' children come closer to Asperger's account of AP than the commonly used diagnosis of AS today. She stated that 'schizoid' children were usually of higher intelligence than children diagnosed with AS today and their social handicaps did sometimes not manifest until school age—findings that can be confirmed by the results of this study. The majority of 'schizoid' children were described as being less disabled and superficially resembling children with reactive conduct disorder or emotional disorder, having more specific but not pervasive developmental delays (Wolff 1991b). This also applies to our sample, especially regarding the additional presence of conduct disorders. Furthermore, Wolff (1991a) mentions a better outcome for 'schizoid children' than that described for children with AS by other authors. Asperger also often emphasized the good outcome in his clinical records, provided the child would find a niche in which his/her special abilities could be of use.

In sum, the patients of Asperger described in our study represent a subgroup of children with high intellectual functioning, specific circumscribed interests and talents but impaired social, communication and motor skills who partly resemble Sula Wolff's description of 'schizoid' individuals. However, a quarter of these children also fulfil diagnostic criteria for autism, which points to the possibility of a mixture of symptoms regarded as typical for AS and autism. The authors would therefore agree with the point of view of Wing (2000) that AS cannot be clearly distinguished from autism but may still be clinically useful as a diagnostic category (also Szatmari 2000). As can be seen in this analysis, the phenotypic appearance of children with AS can be very distinct from that normally associated with Kanner's autism. Specific areas of difference might perhaps be a function of the higher (verbal) intelligence.

In any case, current ICD-10 and DSM-IV criteria for AS do not quite capture the individuals originally described by Asperger and his team. They appear to differentiate AS from autism solely based on the onset criteria, regardless of the patient's social impairment later in life (Volkmar and Klin 2000, p. 44). In particular, motor and social clumsiness as well as speech and communication deviancies should be taken into consideration in further discussion of diagnostic criteria for AS.

We thank Professor Elisabeth Wurst and Professor Maria Asperger-Felder for their support and their help in gaining access to the relevant data. The authors are indebted to Thomas Harmer, Ilian Ivanov, Andreas Mühlberger, Carolin Steidl, and Theresia Viehhauser for collecting and re-rating parts of the data. They are also grateful to Dr Francesca Happé for her valuable comments on this manuscript. K.H. was supported by the Austrian Academy of Science (Österreichische Akademie der Wissenschaften) during her work.

References

American Psychiatric Association (1994). *Diagnostic and statistical manual of mental disorders*, 4th edn. Washington, DC: American Psychiatric Association.

Asperger, H. (1944). Die autistischen Psychopathen im Kindesalter. *Arch. Psychiat. Nervenkrank.* **177**, 76–137.

Asperger, H. (1952). *Heilpädagogik. Einführung in die Psychopathologie des Kindes für Ärzte, Lehrer, Psychologen und Fürsorgerinnen.* Wien: Springer.

Baron-Cohen, S., Wheelwright, S., Stott, C., Bolton, P. and Goodyer, I. (1997). Is there a link between engineering and autism? *Autism* **1**, 101–109.

Ghaziuddin, M. and Gerstein, L. (1996). Pedantic speaking style differentiates Asperger syndrome from high-functioning autism. *J. Autism Devl Disorders* **26**, 585–95.

Ghaziuddin, M., Butler, E., Tsai, L. and Ghaziuddin, N. (1994). Is clumsiness a marker for Asperger syndrome? *J. Intellect. Disab. Res.* **38**, 519–27.

Gillberg, C. (1991). Clinical and neurobiological aspects of Asperger syndrome in six family studies. In *Autism and Asperger syndrome* (ed. U. Frith), pp. 122–46. Cambridge University Press.

Gillberg, C. (1998). Asperger syndrome and high-functioning autism. *Br. J. Psychiat.* **172**, 200–09.

Gillberg, I. C. and Gillberg, C. (1989). Asperger syndrome—some epidemiological considerations: a research note. *J. Child Psychol. Psychiat.* **30**, 631–38.

Kanner, L. (1943). Autistic disturbances of affective contact. *Nervous Child* **2**, 217–50.

Klin, A., Volkmar, F. R., Sparrow, S. S., Cicchetti, D. V. and Rourke, B. P. (1995). Validity and neuropsychological characterisation of Asperger syndrome. *J. Child Psychol. Psychiat.* **36**, 1127–40.

Leekam, S., Libby, S., Wing, L., Gould, J. and Gillberg, C. (2000). Comparison of ICD-10 and Gillberg's criteria for Asperger syndrome. *Autism* **4**, 11–28.

Lincoln, A. J., Courchesne, E., Allen, M., Hanson, E. and Ene, M. (1998). Neurobiology of Asperger Syndrome: seven case studies and quantitative magnetic resonance imaging findings. In *Asperger syndrome or high functioning autism?* (ed. E. Schopler, G. B. Mesibov and L. J. Kunce), pp. 145–66. New York: Plenum.

Miller, J. N. and Ozonoff, S. (1997). Did Asperger's cases have Asperger disorder? A research note. *J. Child Psychol. Psychiat. Allied Disciplines* **38**, 247–51.

Schubert, M. T. and Berlach, G. (1982). Neue Richtlinien zur Interpretation des Hamburg-Wechsler-Intelligenztests. *Zeit. Klin. Psychol.* **4**, 253–79.

Szatmari, P. (2000). Perspectives on the classification of Asperger syndrome. In *Asperger syndrome* (ed. A. Klin, F. R. Volkmar and S. S. Sparrow), pp. 403–17. New York: Guilford Press.

Szatmari, P., Bartolucci, G. and Bremner, R. (1989). Asperger's syndrome and autism: comparisons on early history and outcome. *Devl Med. Child Neurol.* **31**, 287–99.

Volkmar, F. R. and Klin, A. (2000). Diagnostic issues in Asperger syndrome. In *Asperger syndrome* (ed. A. Klin, F. R. Volkmar and S. S. Sparrow), pp. 25–71. New York: Guilford Press.

Wing, L. (1981). Asperger's syndrome: a clinical account. *Psychol. Med.* **11**, 115–29.

Wing, L. (1998). The history of Asperger syndrome. In *Asperger syndrome or high functioning autism?* (ed. E. Schopler, G. B. Mesibov and L. J. Kunce), pp. 61–76. New York: Plenum.

Wing, L. (2000). Past and future of research on Asperger syndrome. In *Asperger syndrome* (ed. A. Klin, F. R. Volkmar and S. S. Sparrow), pp. 418–32. New York: Guilford Press.

Wing, L. and Gould, J. (1979). Severe impairments of social interaction and associated abnormalities in children: epidemiology and classification. *J. Autism Devl Disorders* **9**, 11–29.

Wolff, S. (1991*a*). Schizoid personality in childhood and adult life. I: the vagaries of diagnostic labelling. *Br. J. Psychiat.* **159**, 615–20.

Wolff, S. (1991*b*). Schizoid personality in childhood and adult life. III: the childhood picture. *Br. J. Psychiat.* **159**, 629–35.

World Health Organization (1992). *The ICD-10 classification of mental and behavioural disorders. Clinical descriptions and diagnostic guidelines*. Geneva: World Health Organization.

World Health Organization (1993). *The ICD-10 classification of mental and behavioural disorders. Diagnostic criteria for research*. Geneva: World Health Organization.

Glossary

AF: autistic feature
AK: autism (Kanner type)
AP: autistic psychopathy
AS: Asperger syndrome
FSIQ: full-scale intelligence quotient
HAWIK: Hamburg–Wechsler-Intelligenztest für Kinder
HFA: high-functioning autism
OCD: obsessive–compulsive disorder
PIQ: performance intelligence quotient
VIQ: verbal intelligence quotient
WISC: Wechsler Intelligence Scale for Children

3

Identifying neurocognitive phenotypes in autism

Helen Tager-Flusberg and Robert M. Joseph

Autism is a complex disorder that is heterogeneous both in its phenotypic expression and its etiology. The search for genes associated with autism and the neurobiological mechanisms that underlie its behavioural symptoms has been hampered by this heterogeneity. Recent studies indicate that within autism, there may be distinct subgroups that can be defined based on differences in neurocognitive profiles. This paper presents evidence for two kinds of subtypes in autism that are defined on the basis of language profiles and on the basis of cognitive profiles. The implications for genetic and neurobiological studies of these subgroups are discussed, with special reference to evidence relating these cognitive phenotypes to volumetric studies of brain size and organization in autism.

Keywords: autism; phenotype; cognitive profile; specific language impairment; language; macrocephaly

3.1 Introduction

Autism is a neurodevelopmental disorder that is defined on the basis of behavioural symptoms. Among the major goals of research in this field are to find the underlying causes and to develop novel treatments that will alleviate the severe and debilitating effects of autism on children and their families. These goals can only be achieved when the disorder can be objectively and reliably diagnosed, and has a clearly defined phenotype. Over the past decade international consensus has been reached on the clinical diagnostic criteria for autism and other ASDs within ICD-10 and DSM-IV (World Health Organization 1993; American Psychiatric Association 1994). These criteria have been implemented in the ADI-R (Lord *et al*. 1994) and the ADOS (Lord *et al*. 1999), which are now widely used to obtain reliable and valid classification of individuals with ASD for research purposes.

The introduction of these diagnostic criteria and gold-standard instruments has led to a significant increase in studies investigating the etiology of autism. Genetic studies have shown the greatest promise in this area, and twin and family studies indicate that the heritability estimates for autism are over 90%, far exceeding other psychiatric disorders (Bailey *et al*. 1995). Evidence indicates that anywhere from 2 to 10 interacting genes are involved (Pickles *et al*. 1995; Santangelo and Folstein 1999) and numerous studies using different methodological strategies have been launched to find these genes by using advances in human genome research and molecular biology (see Lamb *et al*. (2000), Rutter (2000) and Folstein and Rosen-Sheidley (2001) for recent reviews). Some cases of autism are associated with other medical conditions, including known genetic disorders (e.g. fragile X syndrome). However, recent estimates indicate that these cases account for only 10–15% of all cases of autism (Rutter *et al*. 1994; Barton and Volkmar 1998) and they are generally excluded from genetic studies of 'idiopathic' autism. Despite the advances that have been made, and reports of some positive findings from both linkage and association genetic studies, thus far not a single susceptibility gene for autism has been identified. The current view is that each locus identified in these studies contains genes with only small or moderate effects on the etiology of autism. These small effect sizes make the identification of specific genes significantly more difficult, especially given the relative rarity of the disorder and the fact that it involves both phenotypic and genetic heterogeneity.

Numerous researchers have argued that new approaches, which go beyond the standard methods, will be needed for real advances to be made in finding genes for autism over the next few years (Szatmari 1999; Risch *et al*. 1999; Rutter 2000). One way to enhance the possibility of finding a larger genetic effect size is to reduce the phenotypic variability in the sample in ways that go beyond simply excluding non-idiopathic cases (cf. Miles and Hillman 2000). By constraining the phenotype, one might expect a more homogeneous genetic etiology (Leboyer *et al*. 1998; but cf. Le Couteur *et al*. 1996). There are several methods available for narrowing down the phenotype of autism. One involves identifying *subtypes* within autism (Szatmari 1999). Several studies have used this approach by looking for meaningful groupings within the diagnostic classifications for ASD (e.g. Asperger syndrome, pervasive developmental disorder). With the exception of Rett syndome, now known to be caused by mutations in a single gene (Amir *et al*. 1999), these studies have yielded mixed results and have not had a significant impact on genetic research (e.g. Mahoney *et al*. 1998; Prior *et al*. 1998).

In this paper, we report on a different approach for finding subtypes within autism that may be useful for genetic studies, one focusing on aspects of the phenotype that are not part of the core defining features of the disorder. The particular strategy we have taken is to investigate cognitive characteristics that are found in some, but not all, children with autism, thus providing more homogeneous subtypes that are defined along dimensions that could potentially be linked to specific patterns of neuropathology. We describe our research on the two most promising subtypes in autism that we have investigated thus far:

(i) distinguishing between children with normal language abilities from those who are language impaired, and

(ii) distinguishing between children with discrepantly high NV intelligence scores from those who do not show this cognitive profile on standardized psychometric tests.

3.2 Language abilities in autism

Deficits in language and communication are among the defining symptoms of autism (American Psychiatric Association 1994), although Kanner (1943) did not consider these features to be central to what distinguished autism as a unique syndrome. Most studies have focused on identifying deficits in the language domain that are universally and uniquely found in autism, and there is general agreement that pragmatic and discourse skills represent core areas of dysfunction in this disorder (for reviews, see Lord and Paul 1997, Wilkinson 1998 and Tager-Flusberg 1999). Relatively little research in recent years has investigated other aspects of language in autism, yet it is clear that most children with autism have language deficits that go beyond impaired pragmatic ability. For example, most children with autism show significant delays in acquiring language, and about half remain essentially NV (Bailey *et al.* 1996). Many of those children who acquire some spontaneous use of language show deficits in vocabulary and the acquisition of complex syntax and morphology (e.g. Bartak *et al.* 1975). Thus, in autism there are often problems in both structural and pragmatic aspects of language (Ballaban-Gil *et al.* 1997; Rapin and Dunn 1997). However, the former are more variable, are not unique to autism and are not necessarily correlated with the degree of severity of core autism features or level of cognitive functioning.

We conducted two studies designed to investigate language impairments in autism with particular interest in exploring the variability in structural aspects of language. We followed up these behavioural studies with an investigation of structural brain patterns in children with autism, using MRI to detect regional brain volume differences that might be related to the language impairments that were found in the behavioural studies.

(a) Study Ia: language profiles in autism

A large sample of 89 children with autism (9 girls and 80 boys), between the ages of 4 and 14, participated in this study (Kjelgaard and Tager-Flusberg 2001). They were selected on the basis of having at least some language, defined as the ability to use some two-word utterances, and were diagnosed using the DSM-IV criteria on the basis of algorithm scores on the ADI-R and ADOS, and confirmed by an expert clinician. The research form of the ADI-R (Lord *et al.* 1994) and the ADOS (Lord *et al.* 2000) were administered by specially trained personnel who demonstrated reliability in scoring with the authors of the instruments and on-site trainers. The IQ of each child was assessed with the DAS (Elliott 1990). For this sample, the mean IQ was 68 and scores ranged from 25 (floor) to 141.

A battery of standardized tests was individually administered to the children to measure their phonological, lexical and higher-order semantic and grammatical language abilities. Phonological skills were assessed using the Goldman–Fristoe Test of Articulation (Goldman and Fristoe 1986) that measures the accuracy of productive phonology for the consonant sounds of English, and the RNW test taken from the Developmental Neurophysiological Assessment Battery (Korkman *et al.* 1998). This latter test measures the ability to analyse and reproduce phonological knowledge by asking the child to repeat nonsense words that are presented on an audiotape. Lexical knowledge was assessed using the PPVT (Dunn and Dunn 1997), a widely used measure of lexical comprehension, and the EVT (Williams 1997), a measure of productive vocabulary. Higher-order semantic and grammatical skills were assessed using the CELF (Wiig *et al.* 1992; Semel *et al.* 1995). This is an omnibus test comprised of six subtests designed to measure receptive and expressive grammatical morphology, syntax, semantics and working memory for language. For each test, the child's standard score was computed, based on a mean of 100 and a standard deviation of 15 points.

Owing to the wide variability in the language skills of the children, in many cases not all the tests were completed. We were able to obtain standard scores on the Goldman–Fristoe test, the PPVT and EVT for almost all the children in the sample, but only about half could be scored on the CELF and the RNW test. In general, regardless of age, those children with higher IQ scores were more likely to complete these more complex tests, which have considerable attentional, working memory and other test-related factors associated with them.

Our primary interest was in exploring differences in language profiles across the standardized tests in children with relatively good language skills compared with those with clear impairments. We present here the data based on those children who were able to complete all the language tests. Most of the 44 children in this group had NV IQ scores in the normal range. This group was divided into three subtypes based on their total CELF standard scores. The participants in the *normal language subtype* group had CELF scores 85 or higher (within 1 s.d. of the mean), and included 10 children, or 23% of the children. The participants in the *borderline language subtype* group had CELF scores between 70 and 84; more than 1 s.d. below the mean but less than 2. There were 13 children in the borderline subtype, representing 30% of the sample. The participants in the *impaired-language subtype* group had CELF scores below 70, more than 2 s.d. below the mean. There were 21 children in this subtype; 47% of the group who were able to complete all the standardized language tests.

Figure 3.1 presents the profile of scores across the language tests for the participants within each of the subtypes. The PPVT and EVT scores were combined since they were highly correlated with one another and the tests were

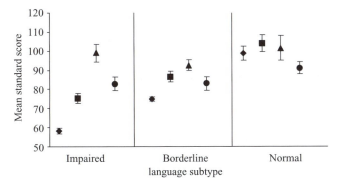

Fig. 3.1 The profile of performance across the standardized test by the impairment, borderline and normal language subtype groups. Diamonds, CELF total; squares, PPVT + EVT; triangles, Goldman–Fristoe test; circles, RNW.

normed on the same sample. At a group level, the children in the normal language subtype had scores on all the language measures that were well within the normal range, representing a relatively flat profile. These children had normal phonological, lexical, morphological and syntactic skills, as measured by the standardized tests used in this study. By contrast, the children in the borderline and impaired subtypes had deficits in higher-order syntax and semantics, vocabulary and the ability to represent and reproduce novel phonological sequences, as measured by the RNW test. Differences between the subtypes were statistically significant for vocabulary scores ($F_{2,41} = 19.45$, $p < 0.0001$), but did not reach significance on the RNW test ($F_{2,28} = 1.77$, n.s.). The impaired children did not have deficits in basic articulation skills, as can be seen by their scores on the Goldman–Fristoe test, which fell within the normal range; this was confirmed in a one-way ANOVA showing no differences among the subtypes on this test ($F_{2,39} = 0.82$, n.s.).

At the individual level, there was good consistency in meeting the subtype profiles for the children in the normal and impaired groups. Within the normal subtype eight of the ten children fitted the profile of scores within the normal range across all the language tests; the remaining two children fell one point below the normal range on RNW. Of the 21 children in the impaired subtype, 14 (two-thirds) met the profile with scores more than 1 or 2 s.ds below the mean across all the tests (not including the Goldman–Fristoe). The other seven children in this group had scores in the normal range on either the vocabulary measure (one child) or on RNW (six children). Only three of the 13 children met the profile of performance (defined as more than 1 s.d. below the mean but less than 2) in the borderline subtype, indicating that this group is more heterogeneous, and less clearly defined as language impaired. The remaining children had scores in the normal range on vocabulary (four children) or RNW (five children) or both (one child).

The language test profiles for most of the children in the language-impaired subtype are particularly revealing about the nature of language impairments in autism. The pattern of their performance is strikingly similar to what has been reported for children with a SLI, a developmental language disorder that is diagnosed on the basis of performance on language tests that fall significantly below age expectations, but in the absence of other conditions such as hearing loss, mental retardation, autism or frank neurological pathology. The patterns of performance shown in figure 1 match the profile found across these same kinds of tests in children with SLI (Tomblin and Zhang 1999). For example, scores on the vocabulary measures were somewhat higher than the CELF scores, indicating that lexical knowledge is generally less impaired than higher-order language abilities.

The most interesting finding was the poor performance by the children in the language-impaired subtype on RNW. Given that children with autism are known for their excellent echolalic skills, one might have predicted that, across the board, the children in this study would have done well on this test, as they did on the Goldman–Fristoe test. Figure 3.1 shows that this was clearly not the case: performance on RNW distinguished well between children with normal language ($M = 91$) and children with borderline ($M = 83$) or impaired ($M = 83$) language. This test was included in our language battery because it is one on which children with SLI demonstrate significant deficits (e.g. Gathercole and Baddeley 1990; Bishop *et al.* 1996; Dollaghan and Campbell 1998; Weismer *et al.* 2000). Indeed, poor performance on nonword repetition tests is now considered one of the primary clinical markers of SLI (Tager-Flusberg and Cooper 1999). Taken together, we argue that children with autism with language impairments, probably including many children in both the borderline and impaired subtypes identified in this study, have a language disorder that is overlapping with the disorder of SLI (see also Rapin 1998; Bishop and Norbury 2002).

(b) Study Ib: grammatical deficits in autism

Current research on SLI has identified another important clinical marker of this disorder. This second marker involves measures of children's knowledge and processing of finite-verb morphology. Several studies have found that children with SLI tend to omit several finite verb-related morphemes in obligatory contexts, including the third-person present tense-s (e.g. *Susan skip-s*) or the past-tense regular (e.g. *Susan walk-ed*) or irregular (e.g. *Susan left*) forms (Rice *et al.* 1995; Rice and Wexler 1996; Bedore and Leonard 1998). We followed up our findings of potential overlap between autism and SLI by exploring whether the children with autism in our initial study who fell into the language-impaired subtype would also show problems in marking tense (Roberts *et al.* 2000).

For this study, data were collected from 62 (54 boys and eight girls) of the children in the original sample of 89, 41 of whom had also participated in study Ia. They were given two experimental tasks, drawn from Rice and Wexler's groundbreaking work on tense in SLI (Rice *et al.* 1995). One task used linguistic probes to elicit the past tense, the other used probes to elicit the third-person singular present-tense marker. On the past-tense task, children were shown pictures of people engaged in activities and asked questions such as, 'What happened?' or 'What did he do with the rake?'. There were 11 trials designed to elicit regular past-tense forms on lexical verbs (e.g. wash, colour) and eight intermixed trials to elicit irregular forms (e.g. catch, fall). On each trial the experimenter first modelled the verb and then asked the probe questions. For the third-person task, 12 pictures depicting people in various occupations (e.g. doctor, painter) were presented to the children. They were asked questions such as: 'Tell me what a doctor does' and 'What does a painter do?'. Children were probed until they produced a verb in the third person (e.g. *He help(-s) people*).

The 62 children were divided into normal, borderline and impaired subtypes, based on standardized language test scores. Figure 3.2 shows the performance of the children on the tense-marking tasks for the normal (25 children; 40%) and impaired subtypes (20 children; 32%). The children in the normal language subtype gave almost twice as many correct responses as

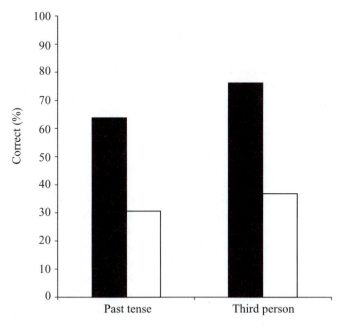

Fig. 3.2 Performance on the past tense and third person present tense tasks by the normal and impaired language subtype groups. White bars, normal subtype; black bars, impaired subtype.

those in the impaired subtype, whose performance was between 30% and 40% correct on both tasks. Differences between the children in the impaired subtype and the other subtypes were highly significant on both the third-person singular ($F_{2,59} = 10.7$, $p < 0.0001$; impaired < normal, $t(44) = 4.91$, $p < 0.0001$) and on the past tense ($F_{2,59} = 8.13$, $p < 0.001$; impaired < normal, $t(44) = 3.93$, $p < 0.0001$). The most common error pattern was to omit any morphological marking on the verb stem, the error that is also most frequently reported for children with SLI. The children in the impaired subtype produced significantly more of these errors than the other children on the past-tense task ($F_{2,59} = 3.16$, $p < 0.05$; impaired > normal, $t(44) = 2.25$, $p < 0.03$), but the differences between the groups did not reach significance on third-person singular ($F_{2,59} = 0.63$, n.s.). On the past-tense task the children were equally likely to produce these bare-stem errors on the regular and irregular verbs, and made few over-regularization errors (e.g. *falled*). Again, studies on children with SLI report similar findings (Marchman *et al.* 1999; Rice 1999). The findings from this study provide further support for the view that autism and SLI are overlapping disorders in some, but not all, children with autism. Thus, this group of children with SLI represents a subtype within autism because there are clearly children with autism but without any linguistic deficits, as in our normal language subtype (cf. Bishop 2000).

(c) Study Ic: morphometric analysis of brain asymmetry in autism

If there were a subtype in autism that is overlapping with SLI, defined on the basis of similar language phenotypes, then one would hypothesize that they would show similar atypical patterns of brain structure. Thus far there have been several studies of brain structure in SLI. The most consistent finding in studies of children and adults with SLI is that they show different patterns of brain asymmetry, as compared with non-SLI controls. In normal individuals, left (L) cortical regions, especially in key language areas (perisylvian region, planum temporale and Heschel's gyrus), are enlarged relative to the size of those regions in the right (R) hemisphere. By contrast, individuals with SLI or with language-based learning disorders show reduced or reversed asymmetries in these areas (Galaburda 1989; Jernigan *et al.* 1991; Plante *et al.* 1991; Leonard *et al.* 1996; Gauger *et al.* 1997; Clark and Plante 1998).

Our group has recently completed a MRI study comparing 16 boys with autism (all with normal NV IQ scores) to 15 age, sex and handedness matched normal controls who were part of a different cohort of children from those participating in the language studies described here (Herbert *et al.* 2002). MR scans were obtained on a 1.5 T scanner and included a T1-weighted sagittal scout series, a coronal T2-weighted sequence, and a coronal volumetric T1-weighted spoiled gradient echo-imaging sequence for morphometric analysis. The images were processed with custom software, and head position was normalized by re-slicing each volume with 3 mm thickness along the coronal plane, perpendicular to the anterior commissure–posterior commissure plane, without scaling the image size.

Neuroanatomic segmentation of grey and white matter and ventricles was performed using semi-automated procedures based on intensity contour mapping and differential intensity contour algorithms (for more details of the methods used see Filipek *et al.* 1994 and Caviness *et al.* 1996). The neo-cortical ribbon was then parcellated into 48 primarily gyral-based parcellation units per hemisphere (Kennedy *et al.* 1998). We compared the volumes in parcellation regions in the L and R hemispheres, expressed as a symmetry index. For each structure in the brain this index was calculated as: $[2 \times (L - R)/(L + R)] \times 100$.

We focused our group comparisons on the language regions of the cortex. In inferior lateral frontal language cortex (pars opercularis, associated with Broca's area) the boys with autism were significantly different from controls ($F_{1,30} = 5.58, p < 0.02$). This region was 27% larger in the R hemisphere in the boys with autism by contrast with the control boys, who had 17% larger volume in the L hemisphere. Other differences between the groups did not reach statistical significance. The reversed asymmetry found in the boys with autism is strikingly similar to what has been reported in studies of boys with SLI (e.g. Jernigan *et al.* 1991; Gauger *et al.* 1997). Unfortunately, language phenotypic data were not available for the boys with autism in this study, and so individual difference patterns and relationships between brain and behavioural data could not be examined. Nevertheless, based on other reports from which this autistic sample was drawn, we know that it included primarily children with language impairments (Rapin 1996).

These three studies indicate that there is a subtype among children with autism who have a neurocognitive phenotype that is the same as has been reported in the literature for SLI. Children with autism in the language-impaired subtype performed poorly on standardized and experimental language tests that are sensitive to deficits that characterize SLI, and they showed the same reversal of asymmetry in frontal language regions of the brain. To what extent does the identification of this putative SLI subtype in autism have implications for genetic studies of autism? Studies have found among family members of children with autism, there are significantly elevated rates of documented histories of language delay and language-based learning deficits that go well beyond pragmatic difficulties (Bolton *et al.* 1994; Fombonne *et al.* 1997; Piven *et al.* 1997; Bailey *et al.* 1998). Twin studies have also reported that co-twins discordant for autism had high rates of language deficits that resemble the pattern described as SLI (Folstein and Rutter 1977; Le Couteur *et al.* 1996). There is also evidence that in families identified on the basis of having a child with SLI, there is a significantly elevated risk of autism among the siblings. Hafeman and Tomblin (1999) recently reported that in a population-based sample of children diagnosed with SLI, 4% of the siblings met criteria for autism. This rate is much higher than would be expected based on the current prevalence estimates of around 1 in 500 (Fombonne 1999), and is similar to the 6% risk recurrence rates in autism families (Santangelo and Folstein 1999).

In addition to this behavioural evidence, recent genetic linkage and association studies may offer further clues to some shared genetic basis for these disorders. The KE family in England has been intensively investigated because they represent a large multi-generational pedigree in which a severe speech and language disorder has been transmitted in a manner indicating a single dominant gene. The locus of the gene was found on chromosome 7q31 (Fisher *et al.* 1998) and it has recently been identified as the FOXP2 gene (Lai *et al.* 2001). Tomblin and his colleagues took their population-based sample of children with SLI (Tomblin *et al.* 1998), and found a significant association between SLI and an allele of the CFTR gene. This gene is in the 7q31 region where FOXP2 is located, although more recent studies have not found an association between SLI and FOXP2 (Meaburn *et al.* 2002; Newbury *et al.* 2002). Nevertheless, there is some evidence from Tomblin *et al.* that there is a gene (or genes) located on the long arm of chromosome 7 that contributes to SLI. Another locus for a gene associated with SLI has been recently been found on chromosome 13 (13q21), based on the analysis of five large pedigrees (Bartlett *et al.* 2002).

Genetics studies have consistently identified 7q31 as a region that is likely to include a susceptibility gene for autism (International Molecular Genetic Study of Autism Consortium 1998). However, it does not appear that FOXP2 is a candidate autism gene (Newbury *et al.* 2002; Wassink *et al.* 2002). Another locus for a susceptibility gene for autism has been found on 13q (CLSA 1999). However, as noted earlier, all the genome scans conducted thus far have found only modest signals in all studies using linkage analysis. The parallels between the loci that have been linked to autism and SLI are striking, and recently the CLSA explored the possibility of incorporating a phenotypically defined subgroup in their genetic analysis (CLSA 2001). Using only the subgroup of probands with autism who had no language or clearly impaired language and whose parents had a history of language difficulties, the linkage signals on both 7q and 13q were significantly increased, indicating that these signals were mainly attributable to the language-impaired subtype within autism. These genetic findings hold out some promise that defining language phenotypic subtypes within the autism population may provide important benefits to genetic studies (cf. Dawson *et al.* 2002).

3.3 Cognitive profiles in autism

Autism is often characterized by unevenly developed cognitive skills. Unevenness in the cognitive abilities of individuals with autism has been most frequently documented in terms of IQ profiles. Although an IQ profile in which NV, visuospatial abilities are significantly superior to V abilities has been most strongly associated with autism (see Lincoln *et al.* 1988), this profile is not universal among individuals with autism, and is not even necessarily the modal cognitive profile in autism (Siegel *et al.* 1996). Further, higher-functioning individuals with autism often evidence V abilities that are superior to their visuospatial skills in IQ testing (Manjiova and Prior 1999; Ozonoff *et al.* 2000).

We conducted three additional studies that examined cognitive profiles in school-age children with autism, focusing particularly on discrepancies between V and NV skills. In the first study, we investigated whether any specific neurocognitive profile might be associated with increased susceptibility to autistic symptomatology and might thereby index important aspects of the underlying brain pathology. In the second and third study, we examined the relationship between cognitive profiles and two putative indices of autistic brain pathology: abnormally increased head circumference and brain volume.

(a) Study IIa: cognitive profiles and symptom severity in autism

Our first study (Joseph *et al.* 2002) investigated whether different cognitive profiles were associated with differences in the severity of the core communication and reciprocal social interaction symptoms in autism. The participants were 47 children (five girls and 42 boys) with DSM-IV clinical diagnoses of autism or PDDNOS, who ranged from 6 to 13 years in age (mean of 8 years 11 months). They were administered the ADI-R and ADOS by specially trained personnel who demonstrated reliability in scoring with the authors of the instruments and on-site trainers. All participants met criteria for autism on the ADI-R diagnostic algorithm. On the ADOS, 41 children met diagnostic criteria for autism, 5 children met criteria for a less severe diagnosis of ASD, and 1 child met criteria for ASD in the reciprocal social interaction domain, but not in the communication domain. Given that children met clinical diagnostic criteria for autism or PDDNOS, and ADI-R criteria for autism, we chose to include children who did not necessarily meet criteria for autism on the ADOS to allow for a wider range of variance in scores, which we were using as quantitative measures of current symptom severity. The communication and reciprocal social interaction scores from the ADOS diagnostic algorithms served as the dependent variables, with higher scores reflecting a greater degree of impairment.

To assess cognitive functioning, we used the DAS (Elliott 1990). The DAS consists of six core subtests that yield a V and a NV IQ score, which we have argued are conceptually more homogeneous and can provide a more valid estimate of differential cognitive abilities than the Wechsler (1991, 1997) Verbal and Performance subscales (Joseph *et al.* 2002). DAS V–NV difference scores were calculated by subtracting the NV IQ score from the V IQ score, and V–NV discrepancies were identified on the basis of the minimum difference between V and NV IQ scores required for significance at the 0.05 level of probability (Elliott 1990).

Table 3.1   Study IIa: age, IQ and ADOS scores as a function of V–NV discrepancy group.

	V–NV discrepancy group		
	V < NV (n = 16) M (s.d.)	V = NV (n = 18) M (s.d.)	V > NV (n = 13) M (s.d.)
age	8;6 (2;0)	8;9 (1;10)	9;7 (1;10)
full-scale IQ	91 (25)	77 (17)	87 (19)
V IQ	73 (22)	77 (17)	103 (19)
NV IQ	102 (24)	80 (15)	80 (16)
ADOS symptom severity			
communication	5.9 (1.6)	4.7 (2.1)	4.6 (1.6)
social interaction	11.0 (2.1)	8.6 (2.4)	8.2 (2.0)

Analysis of children's cognitive profiles revealed a high rate of V–NV discrepancies (62%), which occurred at a much higher frequency than in the DAS normative sample (around 30%), and which occurred nearly equally in both directions. Of the 47 participants, 16 exhibited a V < NV profile, 13 exhibited a V > NV profile, and 18 exhibited no discrepancy. Table 3.1 displays mean age, IQ scores and ADOS scores for each of the V–NV discrepancy groups. The V–NV groups did not differ significantly in age, $F_{2,44} = 0.1$, n.s. A one-way ANOVA comparing the groups on full-scale IQ was not significant, $F_{2,44} = 2.0$, but pair-wise comparisons showed a marginally significant difference ($p < 0.06$) between the V < NV group, which had the highest full-scale IQ, and the V = NV group, which had the lowest. As can be seen in Table 3.1, the V and NV IQ scores for the two discrepancy groups were nearly the converse of each other, and the low score for each discrepancy group was similar to that found in the nondiscrepancy group. This pattern of scores indicated that the V–NV discrepancies reflected a genuine strength in one domain or the other, rather than differing levels of V ability across groups who shared the same level of NV ability.

Correlational analyses showed that V IQ was inversely related to ADOS communication score, $r(45) = -0.48$, $p < 0.01$, and social interaction score, $r(45) = -0.32$, $p < 0.05$.

Although NV IQ was unrelated to ADOS scores, the V–NV difference score was specifically correlated with the ADOS social interaction score, $r(45) = -0.45$, $p < 0.01$, such that the higher a child's NV IQ was relative to V IQ, the more impaired he or she was in reciprocal social functioning. This relationship remained significant even when absolute level of V ability was partialled from the correlation, $r(44) = -0.35$, $p < 0.05$.

A one-way MANCOVA was conducted to examine differences in ADOS symptom severity among the V–NV groups. As V IQ was correlated with

ADOS scores, it was included as covariate in order to control for the effect of group differences in the absolute level of V ability. For communication symptoms, there was a significant effect of the covariate V IQ, $F_{1,45} = 8.74$, $p < 0.01$, but no effect of the V–NV group. By contrast, for social interaction symptoms, there was no effect of the covariate, but a significant effect of V–NV group, $F_{2,44} = 5.09$, $p < 0.02$. Pairwise comparisons showed that the ADOS social interaction score was significantly higher in the V < NV group than in the V = NV and V > NV groups, which did not differ from each other on this score.

In summary, we found a high rate of V–NV discrepancies in this group of children with autism, and these discrepancies were in favour of V ability nearly as often as NV ability. In addition, we found an interesting pattern of relationships between measures of cognitive ability and symptom severity. First, V ability was inversely related to symptoms in the reciprocal social interaction and, particularly, the communication domain. This finding is consistent with evidence that level of language functioning is an important mediating factor in the expression of autistic symptoms (Bailey *et al.* 1996). Our second and novel finding was that children with discrepantly superior NV skills exhibited increased impairments in reciprocal social skills that were independent of absolute level of V ability and overall ability. By contrast, children with cognitive discrepancies of a comparable magnitude, but in favour of V abilities, did not exhibit increased symptoms. One possibility could be that the children in the V > NV group were able to use their relatively superior V skills to help compensate for their deficits in the social interaction domain. However, although children in the nondiscrepancy group had V IQ scores that were much lower than in the V > NV group, and similar to those in the V < NV group, they were no more impaired in social-communicative functioning than children with relatively superior V skills. This has led us to argue (Joseph *et al.* 2002) that the imbalance in cognitive abilities represented by the V < NV profile may reflect a particularly severe disturbance in brain development and organization and, as such, may provide a marker for an etiologically significant subtype of autism.

Although superior NV abilities in individuals with autism have traditionally been conceived in terms of a 'sparing' of visual–perceptual skills relative to V skills (Lincoln *et al.* 1988), a more recent, alternative view is that these apparently preserved skills are not achieved by virtue of a selective sparing of normal cognitive capacities and their neurobiological substrates, but are the outcome of fundamental differences in neurocognitive development and organization (Karmiloff-Smith 1997, 1998; Happé 1999). For example, enhanced visuoperceptual capacities in autism have been attributed to local processing biases resulting from a failure of the normal propensity for 'central coherence' (Frith and Happé 1994; Happé 1999) or, alternatively, from the abnormal development of lower-level perceptual processes (Plaisted *et al.* 1998; Plaisted 2000; Elgar and Campbell 2001). Efforts to link these functional abnormalities or differences to their neuroanatomical underpinnings has recently given rise to the hypothesis that isolated visuoperceptual skills in autism may be related to increased neuronal growth or reduced cortical pruning and connectivity (Cohen 1994; Happé 1999). One way of testing this hypothesis, at least indirectly, would be to examine whether discrepantly strong NV skills in autism are associated with increased head and brain size.

(b) Study IIb: cognitive correlates of large head circumference in autism

Enlarged head circumference, or macrocephaly, occurs at an unusually high frequency among children with autism and their nonautistic relatives (Davidovitch *et al.* 1996; Woodhouse *et al.* 1996; Lainhart *et al.* 1997; Stevenson *et al.* 1997; Fombonne *et al.* 1999; Fidler *et al.* 2000). However, efforts to link macrocephaly to other clinical and cognitive features of autism have proven largely unsuccessful, raising doubts as to whether macrocephaly indexes a homogeneous and etiologically meaningful autism subtype. In this study (Deutsch and Joseph 2003), we examined the relationship between head circumference in autism and a wide range of potential clinical and cognitive correlates, including V–NV difference scores.

Participants were 63 children (54 males) with DSM-IV clinical diagnoses of autism or PDDNOS, who ranged from 4 to 14 years in age (mean of 7 years 4 months). All children met criteria for autism on the ADI-R, and for either autism ($n = 58$) or ASD ($n = 5$) on the ADOS. Of the 63 participants, 25 had also participated in study IIa, described in Section 3a. Head measurements included circumference, length and width, all of which were converted to standardized (z) scores, adjusted for age and sex using the Farkas (1994) database. Other measures included DAS V IQ, NV IQ and V–NV difference score; expressive and receptive language; executive functions; and ADOS symptom severity.

Using the conventional clinical criterion of $z > 1.88$ (i.e. >97th percentile), we found that macrocephaly occurred at a rate of 14% in our sample, which was significantly higher than the expected rate of 3%, $\chi^2(1, N = 63) = 27.57$, $p < 0.001$ and similar to rates reported in several previous studies (Lainhart *et al.* 1997; Fombonne *et al.* 1999). Large head size ($z > 1.28$, >90th percentile) that did not necessarily meet the criterion for macrocephaly was also common, occurring at a rate of 33%, which was much higher than the expected rate of 10%, $\chi^2(1, N = 63) = 38.11$, $p < 0.001$. By contrast, microcephaly did not occur at a rate higher than expected.

Correlational analyses revealed a significant inverse relationship between head circumference and V–NV difference scores, $r(57) = -0.38$, $p < 0.01$, indicating that children with larger head circumference tended to have discrepantly higher NV scores on the DAS. This relationship remained significant when absolute level of V ability (V IQ score) was partialled from the correlation, $r(56) = -0.35$, $p < 0.02$. (Only 59 of the original 63 participants

Table 3.2 Study IIb: age, IQ scores and head size as a function of V–NV discrepancy group.

	V–NV discrepancy group		
	V < NV ($n = 27$) M (s.d.)	V = NV ($n = 21$) M (s.d.)	V > NV ($n = 11$) M (s.d.)
age	6;8 (2;0)	7;8 (2;4)	8;3 (2;10)
full-scale IQ	84 (19.3)	73 (17.2)	73 (18.3)
V IQ	72 (16.8)	74 (17.3)	89 (18.8)
NV IQ	97 (18.5)	75 (16.0)	66 (17.8)
head circumference[a]	1.3 (1.2)	0.3 (1.4)	0.1 (1.3)
head width	1.0 (1.1)	0.6 (0.8)	0.01 (1.0)
head length	0.3 (1.1)	−0.1 (0.9)	−0.2 (0.9)

[a] All head measurement figures are based on standardized z-scores.

were included in these analyses because four children were not of sufficient cognitive ability to generate separate V and NV IQ scores.) Head circumference was not correlated with age, V or NV IQ, language, executive functions or ADOS symptom severity.

Table 3.2 displays mean age, IQ and standardized head circumference scores for each V–NV profile group, defined using the same criteria as in study IIa. The groups did not differ significantly in age, $F_{2,56} = 2.32$, n.s. An ANCOVA covarying V IQ revealed no effect of the covariate, $F_{1,56} = 1.19$, n.s., but did show a main effect of V–NV group on head circumference, $F_{2,56} = 3.69, p < 0.05$. Pairwise comparisons showed that head circumference was significantly larger in the V < NV group than in the V = NV and V > NV groups, which did not differ from each other in head circumference.

We conducted *post-hoc* analyses to examine whether the V–NV profile groups differed in head width, length or both. A one-way MANOVA showed a significant effect of V–NV group on head width, $F_{2,56} = 3.52, p < 0.05$, but not on head length, $F_{2,56} = 1.75$, n.s. Table 3.2 displays mean standardized head width and length for each V–NV group.

In summary, we identified a subgroup of children with autism who have discrepantly high NV skills accompanied by large head circumference, thus providing further evidence that the V < NV profile may index an etiologically significant subtype of autism. This finding indicates that macrocephaly and unevenly developed NV skills reflect the same underlying disturbance in neuro-cognitive development and organization. Although preliminary and in need of replication, these results are consistent with suggestions that isolated visual–perceptual skills in autism may be related to neuronal overgrowth or reduced neuronal pruning and connectivity (Cohen 1994; Happé 1999). Recent evidence supporting this possibility includes the finding that there is disproportionate growth of the posterior cerebral cortex in autism (Piven *et al.* 1996), and the finding that enlarged head circumference in autism is primarily due to an increase in head width (Deutsch *et al.* 2003). Increased head width in autism would be consistent with enlargement of parieto-temporal cortex and is conceivably related to abnormal development of the visuoperceptual skills mediated by these brain regions. In keeping with this possibility, the $V < NV$ group in this study was differentiated from the other groups by head width rather than length. However, more detailed, regional measurements of brain volume in macrocephalic children with autism would be necessary to determine if these phenomena are truly related.

(c) Study IIc: V–NV discrepancies and brain volume in autism

Given prior evidence that increased head size is associated with increased brain volume in autism (Deutsch *et al.* 2001), the purpose of this final study was to determine:

(i) if the $V < NV$ profile is associated with increased brain volume in autism; and

(ii) if there is any pattern of regional brain enlargement specifically associated with the $V < NV$ profile in autism.

Participants were 16 male children with DSM-IV clinical diagnoses of autism or PDDNOS. All children met the criteria for autism on the ADI-R, and had been participants in study IIb. The sample was evenly divided between children who manifested a $V < NV$ discrepancy on the DAS and those who did not. As can be seen in Table 3.3, the two groups were well-matched on age and fullscale IQ ($p > 0.8$). Brain scans were acquired and analysed in a similar way to those described in study Ic.

We conducted a series of exploratory t-tests to assess potential differences in brain volumes between the two groups. As can be seen in Table 3.3, total brain volume was significantly higher in the $V < NV$ group than in the $V = NV$ group, $t(14) = 2.5$, $p < 0.05$. In order to assess whether the increase in total brain volume was generalized across brain structures, we compared group differences in cerebral volume to those in cerebellar volume. Cerebral volume was significantly higher in the $V < NV$ group, $t(14) = 2.5$, $p < 0.05$, but there was no difference between the groups in cerebellar volume, $t(14) = 1.2$, n.s. Subsequent analyses showed that the group differences in cerebral volume were due to differences in cortical grey matter, $t(14) = 3.0$, $p < 0.01$, rather than in cerebral white matter, $t(14) = 1.3$, n.s. In a final set of analyses, we examined whether increased cortical volume in the $V < NV$ group was specific to any region(s) of the cortex. As shown in Table 3.3, the increases in cortical volume found in the $V < NV$ group were generally consistent across the frontal, parietal, temporal and occipital lobes, and the paralimbic cortex.

In summary, this final study provides evidence linking the $V < NV$ profile to enlarged brain volume in addition to enlarged head circumference. Although

Table 3.3 Study IIc: age, IQ and brain volumes (cm^3) as a function of V–NV discrepancy group.

	V < NV (n = 8) M (s.d.)	V = NV (n = 8) M (s.d.)	t(14)	p
age	9;10 (2;3)	10;0 (1;8)	0.2	n.s.
full-scale IQ	89 (25)	87 (15)	0.2	n.s.
V IQ	75 (18)	89 (17)	1.6	n.s.
NV IQ	101 (25)	88 (14)	1.3	n.s.
total brain	1530 (87)	1385 (139)	2.5	<0.05
cerebrum	1347 (78)	1212 (132)	2.5	<0.05
cerebral cortex	814 (61)	719 (66)	3.0	<0.01
cerebral white matter	454 (28)	419 (70)	1.3	n.s.
cerebellum	156 (11)	149 (11)	1.2	n.s.
cortical regions				
frontal cortex	272 (18)	244 (27)	2.4	<0.05
parietal cortex	133 (14)	119 (10)	2.3	<0.05
temporal cortex	174 (15)	147 (17)	3.4	<0.01
occipital cortex	160 (18)	142 (12)	2.3	<0.05
paralimbic cortex	68 (5)	61 (6)	2.4	<0.05

our preliminary evidence indicates that the increases in brain volume associated with discrepantly strong visual–spatial skills primarily affect cortical grey matter, we were not able to identify any pattern of regional differences in cortical size.

3.4 Summary and conclusions

We have presented evidence for two different subtypes in autism—one based on language abilities and the other based on IQ discrepancy scores. Our behavioural studies indicate that there is a subtype in autism that overlaps with SLI. In a separate study of brain structure, we found reversed asymmetry in a group of boys with autism in the frontal language area, a pattern similar to that found in SLI. Our data thus far do not permit a direct link between the SLI subtype and the reversed asymmetry, but this is clearly an important direction for future studies on this language subtype within autism. Discrepantly high NV IQ scores were shown to be related to autism severity, and to larger head size and brain volume. Genetic studies of autism have found that dividing samples on the basis of language impairment (although the phenotypes used in the CLSA (2001) study were more crudely defined than those presented here) may be useful for identifying genes associated with this component of autistic disorder. As yet, no genetic studies have attempted to use IQ discrepancy scores, so we do not know whether the subtype with high NV IQ represents one that is meaningful for genetic studies of autism.

As research advances on the etiology of autism, more detailed information about the phenotypes of probands promises to speed the search for specific autism genes. Thus far, we have focused on cognitive and behavioural data for defining phenotypes in autism. Adding structural and functional brain data will help to bridge the connection between genes and behaviour and will advance our understanding of how mutations in genes associated with autism lead to abnormalities in brain development that are expressed in different patterns of behaviour.

There are many questions that remain regarding the putative subtypes presented here. For example, are they qualitatively distinct subtypes, as we have argued, or do they represent quantitative variation along dimensions that we have measured using psychometric tests? Do these phenotypic subtypes extend to family members, and can they thus be considered 'endophenotypes' for autism (cf. Leboyer *et al.* 1998)? As more studies are conducted on these and other components of the autism phenotype, genuine progress will be made in uncovering its underlying causes, which in turn will lead to important advances in developing novel and effective treatments for this devastating disorder.

The authors thank the following individuals for their assistance in preparing the data reported in this paper, and the manuscript: S. Hodge, L. McGrath, L. Stetser, and A. Verbalis. They are especially grateful to the children and families who participated in this research. This research was supported by grants from the National Institutes of Health (NIDCD: PO1 DC 03610; NINDS: RO1 NS 38668), and was conducted as part of the NICHD–NIDCD-funded Collaborative Programs of Excellence in Autism.

References

American Psychiatric Association (1994). *Diagnostic and statistical manual of mental disorders (DSM-IV)*, 4th edn. Washington, DC: American Psychiatric Association.

Amir, R., Van den Veyver, I., Wan, M., Tran, C., Francke, U. and Zoghbi, H. (1999). Rett syndrome is caused by mutations in X-linked MECP2, encoding methyl-CpG-binding protein 2. *Nature Genet.* **23**, 185–88.

Bailey, A., Le Couteur, A., Gottesman, I., Bolton, P., Simonoff, E., Yuzda, F., *et al.* (1995). Autism as a strongly genetic disorder: evidence from a British twin study. *Psychol. Med.* **25**, 63–77.

Bailey, A., Phillips, W. and Rutter, M. (1996). Autism: towards an integration of clinical, genetic, neuropsychological, and neurobiological perspectives. *J. Child Psychol. Psychiat.* **37**, 89–126.

Bailey, A., Palferman, S., Heavey, L. and LeCouteur, A. (1998). Autism: the phenotype in relatives. *J. Autism Dev. Disord.* **28**, 369–92.

Ballaban-Gil, K., Rapin, I., Tuchman, R. and Shinnar, S. (1997). Longitudinal examination of the behavioral, language, and social changes in a population of adolescents and young adults with autistic disorder. *Pediatric Neurol.* **16**, 353.

Bartak, L., Rutter, M. and Cox, A. (1975). A comparative study of infantile autism and specific developmental receptive language disorder: I. The children. *Br. J. Psychiat.* **126**, 127–45.

Bartlett, C., Flax, J., Logue, M., Vieland, V., Bassett, A., Tallal, P., *et al.* (2002). A major susceptibility locus for specific language impairment is located on 13q21. *Am. J. Hum. Genet.* **71**, 45–55.

Barton, M. and Volkmar, F. (1998). How commonly are known medical conditions associated with autism? *J. Autism Dev. Disord.* **28**, 273–78.

Bedore, L. M. and Leonard, L. B. (1998). Specific language impairment and grammatical morphology: a discriminant function analysis. *J. Speech Lang. Hearing Res.* **41**, 1185–92.

Bishop, D. V. M. (2000). Pragmatic language impairment. In *Speech and language impairments in children: causes, characteristics, intervention and outcome* (ed. D. V. M. Bishop and L. B. Leonard), pp. 99–113. Hove, UK: Psychology Press.

Bishop, D. V. M. and Norbury, C. F. (2002). Exploring the borderlands of autistic disorder and specific language impairment: a study using standardized diagnostic instruments. *J. Child Psychol. Psychiat.* **43**, 917–29.

Bishop, D., North, T. and Donlan, C. (1996). Nonword repetition as a behavioural marker for inherited language impairment: evidence from a twin study. *J. Child Psychol. Psychiat.* **36**, 1–13.

Bolton, P., Macdonald, H., Pickles, A., Rios, P., Goode, S., Crowson, M., *et al.* (1994). A case-control family history study of autism. *J. Child Psychol. Psychiat.* **35**, 877–900.

Caviness, V., Meyer, J., Makris, N. and Kennedy, D. (1996). MRI-based topographic parcellation of human neocortex: an anatomically specified method with estimate of reliability. *J. Cogn. Neurosci.* **8**, 566–87.

CLSA (1999). An autosomal genomic screen for autism. Collaborative linkage study of autism. *Am. J. Med. Genet.* **88**, 609–15.

CLSA (2001). Incorporating language phenotypes strengthens evidence of linkage to autism. *Am. J. Med. Genet.* **105**, 539–47.

Clark, M. M. and Plante, E. (1998). Morphology of the inferior frontal gyrus in developmentally language-disordered adults. *Brain Lang.* **61**, 288–303.

Cohen, I. L. (1994). An artificial neural network analogue of learning in autism. *Biol. Psychiat.* **36**, 5–20.

Davidovitch, M., Patterson, B. and Gartside, P. (1996). Head circumference measurements in children with autism. *J. Child Neurol.* **11**, 389–93.

Dawson, G., Webb, S., Schellenberg, G., Dager, S., Friedman, S., Aylward, E., *et al.* (2002). Defining the broader phenotype of autism: genetic, brain, and behavioral perspectives. *Dev. Psychopathol.* **14**, 581–611.

Deutsch, C. and Joseph, R. M. (2003). Cognitive correlates of enlarged head circumference in children with autism. *J. Autism Dev. Disord.* (In the press.)

Deutsch, C., Hodge, S., Tager-Flusberg, H., Folstein, S., Steele, S., Laurer, E., *et al.* (2001). Macrocephaly and brachycephaly in autism: correspondence of brain and cranial size/shape. Paper presented at the First International Meeting for Autism Research, San Diego, CA.

Deutsch, C. K., Folstein, S. E., Gordon-Vaughn, K., Tager-Flusberg, H., Schmid, C., Martino, B., *et al.* (2003). Macrocephaly and cephalic disproportion in autistic probands and their first-degree relatives. *Am. J. Med. Genet.* (In the p⁓ ⁓s.)

Dollaghan, C. and Campbell, T. (1998). Nonword repetition and child language impairment. *J. Speech Lang. Hearing Res.* **41**, 1136–46.

Dunn, L. M. and Dunn, L. M. (1997). *Peabody picture vocabulary test*, 3rd edn. Circle Pines, MN: American Guidance Service.

Elgar, K. and Campbell, R. (2001). Annotation: the cognitive neuroscience of face recognition: implications for developmental disorders. *J. Child Psychol. Psychiat.* **42**, 705–17.

Elliott, C. D. (1990). *Differential ability scales: introductory and technical handbook.* New York: Psychological Corporation.

Farkas, L. G. (1994). *Anthropometry of the head and face*, 2nd edn. New York: Raven.

Fidler, D., Bailey, J. and Smalley, S. (2000). Macrocephaly in autism and other pervasive developmental disorders. *Dev. Med. Child Neurol.* **42**, 737–40.

Filipek, P., Richelme, C. and Caviness, V. (1994). The young adult human brain: an MRI-based morphometric analysis. *Cerebr. Cortex* **4**, 344–60.

Fisher, S. E., Vargha-Khadem, F., Watkins, K. E., Monaco, A. P. and Pembrey, M. E. (1998). Localisation of a gene implicated in a severe speech and language. *Nature Genet.* **18**, 168–70.

Folstein, S. and Rutter, M. (1977). Infantile autism: a genetic study of 21 twin pairs. *J. Child Psychol. Psychiat.* **18**, 297–321.

Folstein, S. and Rosen-Sheidley, B. (2001). Genetics of autism: complex aetiology for a heterogeneous disorder. *Nature Rev. Genet.* **2**, 943–55.

Fombonne, E. (1999). The epidemiology of autism: a review. *Psychol. Med.* **29**, 769–86.

Fombonne, E., Bolton, P., Prior, J., Jordan, H. and Rutter, M. (1997). A family study of autism: cognitive patterns and levels in parents and siblings. *J. Child Psychol. Psychiat.* **38**, 667–84.

Fombonne, E., Rogé, B., Claverie, J., Courty, S. and Frémolle, J. (1999). Microcephaly and macrocephaly in autism. *J. Autism Dev. Disord.* **29**, 113–19.

Frith, U. and Happé, F. (1994). Autism: beyond 'theory of mind'. *Cognition* **50**, 115–32.

Galaburda, A. (1989). Ordinary and extraordinary brain development: anatomical variation in developmental dyslexia. *Ann. Dyslexia* **39**, 67–79.

Gathercole, S. and Baddeley, A. (1990). Phonological memory deficits in language disordered children: is there a causal connection? *J. Memory Lang.* **29**, 336–60.

Gauger, L., Lombardino, L. and Leonard, C. (1997). Brain morphology in children with specific language impairment. *J. Speech Lang. Hearing Res.* **40**, 1272–84.

Goldman, R. and Fristoe, M. (1986). *Goldman–Fristoe test of articulation.* Circle Pines, MN: American Guidance Service.

Hafeman, L. and Tomblin, J. B. (1999). Autism behaviors in the siblings of children with specific language impairment. *Mol. Psychiat.* **4**(Suppl. 1), S14.

Happé, F. (1999). Autism: cognitive deficit or cognitive style? *Trends Cogn. Sci.* **3**, 216–22.

Herbert, M., Harris, G. J., Adnen, K. T., Ziegler, D. A., Makris, N., Kennedy, D. N., *et al.* (2002). Abnormal asymmetry in language association cortex in autism. *Ann. Neurol.* **52**, 588–96.

International Molecular Genetic Study of Autism Consortium (1998). A full genome screen for autism with evidence for linkage to a region on chromosome 7q. *Hum. Mol. Genet.* **7**, 571–78.

Jernigan, T., Hesselink, J., Sowell, E. and Tallal, P. A. (1991). Cerebral structure on magnetic resonance imaging in language- and learning-impaired children. *Arch. Neurol.* **48**, 539–45.

Joseph, R. M., Tager-Flusberg, H. and Lord, C. (2002). Cognitive profiles and social-communicative functioning in children with autism. *J. Child Psychol. Psychiat.* **6**, 807–21.

Kanner, L. (1943). Autistic disturbances of affective contact. *Nervous Child* **2**, 217–50.

Karmiloff-Smith, A. (1997). Crucial differences between developmental cognitive neuroscience and adult neuropsychology. *Dev. Neuropsychol.* **13**, 513–24.

Karmiloff-Smith, A. (1998). Development itself is the key to understanding developmental disorders. *Trends Cogn. Sci.* **2**, 389–398.

Kennedy, D., Lange, N., Makris, N., Bates, J., Meyer, J. and Caviness, V. (1998). Gyri of the human neocortex: an MRI-based analysis of volume and variance. *Cerebr. Cortex* **8**, 372–84.

Kjelgaard, M. and Tager-Flusberg, H. (2001). An investigation of language impairment in autism: implications for genetic subgroups. *Language Cogn. Processes* **16**, 287–308.

Korkman, M., Kirk, U. and Kemp, S. (1998). *NEPSY: a developmental neuropsychological assessment.* San Antonio, TX: Psychological Corporation/Harcourt Brace.

Lai, C., Fisher, S., Hurst, J., Vargha-Khadem, F. and Monaco, A. (2001). A forkhead-domain gene is mutated in a severe speech and language disorder. *Nature* **413**, 465–66.

Lainhart, J. E., Piven, J., Wzorek, M., Landa, R., Santangelo, S. L., Coon, H., *et al.* (1997). Macrocephaly in children and adults with autism. *J. Am. Acad. Child Adolescent Psychiat.* **36**, 282–90.

Lamb, J. A., Moore, J., Bailey, A. and Monaco, A. P. (2000). Autism: recent molecular genetic advances. *Hum. Mol. Genet.* **9**, 861–68.

Leboyer, M., Bellivier, F., Nosten-Bertrand, M., Jouvent, R., Pauls, D. and Mallet, J. (1998). Psychiatric genetics: search for phenotypes. *Trends Neurosci.* **21**, 102–05.

Le Couteur, A., Bailey, A., Goode, S., Pickles, A., Robertson, S., Gottesman, I., *et al.* (1996). A broader phenotype of autism: the clinical spectrum in twins. *J. Child Psychol. Psychiat.* **37**, 785–801.

Leonard, C., Lombardino, L. J., Mercado, L. R., Browd, S., Breier, J. and Agee, O. (1996). Cerebral asymmetry and cognitive development in children: a magnetic resonance imaging study. *Psychol. Sci.* **7**, 79–85.

Lincoln, A. J., Courchesne, E., Kilman, B. A., Elmasian, R. and Allen, M. (1988). A study of intellectual abilities in high-functioning people with autism. *J. Autism Dev. Disord.* **18**, 505–23.

Lord, C. and Paul, R. (1997). Language and communication in autism. In *Handbook of autism and pervasive development disorders*, 2nd edn (ed. D. J. Cohen and F. R. Volkmar). New York: Wiley.

Lord, C., Rutter, M. and LeCouteur, A. (1994). Autism Diagnostic Interview—Revised: a revised version of a diagnostic interview for caregivers of individuals with possible pervasive developmental disorders. *J. Autism Dev. Disord.* **24**, 659–68.

Lord, C., Rutter, M., DiLavore, P. C. and Risi, S. (1999). *Autism Diagnostic Observation Schedule–WPS (ADOS–WPS).* Los Angeles, CA: Western Psychological Services.

Lord, C., Risi, S., Lambrecht, L., Cook, E. H., Lenventhal, B. L., DiLavore, P. S., *et al.* (2000). The Autism Diagnostic Observation Schedule–Generic: a standard measure of social and communication deficits associated with the spectrum of autism. *J. Autism Dev. Disord.* **30**, 205–23.

Mahoney, W., Szatmari, P., MacLean, J., Bryson, S., Bartolucci, G., Walter, S., *et al.* (1998). Reliability and accuracy of differentiating pervasive developmental disorder subtypes. *J. Am. Acad. Child Adolescent Psychiat.* **37**, 278–85.

Manjiviona, J. and Prior, M. (1999). Neuropsychological profiles of children with Asperger syndrome and autism. *Autism* **3**, 327–56.

Marchman, V. A., Wulfeck, B. and Weismer, S. E. (1999). Morphological productivity in children with normal language and SLI: a study of the English past tense. *J. Speech Lang. Hearing Res.* **42**, 206–19.

Meaburn, E., Dale, P., Craig, I. and Plomin, R. (2002). Language-impaired children: no sign of the FOXP2 mutation. *Neuroreport* **13**, 1075–77.

Miles, J. and Hillman, R. E. (2000). Value of a clinical morphology examination in autism. *Am. J. Med. Genet.* **91**, 245–53.

Newbury, D., Bonora, E., Lamb, J. A., Fisher, S. E., Lai, C. S., Baird, G., *et al.* (2002). FOXP2 is not a major susceptibility gene for autism or specific language impairment. *Am. J. Hum. Genet.* **70**, 1318–27.

Ozonoff, S., South, M. and Miller, J. (2000). DSM-IV-defined Asperger disorder: cognitive, behavioral, and early history differentiation from high-functioning autism. *Autism* **4**, 29–46.

Pickles, A., Bolton, P., Macdonald, H., Bailey, A., Le Couteur, A., Sim, L., *et al.* (1995). Latent class analysis of recurrent risk for complex phenotypes with selection and measurement error: a twin and family history study of autism. *Am. J. Hum. Genet.* **57**, 717–26.

Piven, J., Arndt, S., Bailey, J. and Andreasen, N. (1996). Regional brain enlargement in autism: a magnetic resonance imaging study. *J. Am. Acad. Child Adolescent Psychiat.* **35**, 530–36.

Piven, J., Palmer, P., Landa, R., Santangelo, S., Jacobi, D. and Childress, D. (1997). Personality and language characteristics in parents from multiple-incidence autism families. *Am. J. Med. Genet.* **74**, 398–411.

Plaisted, K. C. (2000). Aspects of autism that theory of mind cannot explain. In *Understanding other minds: perspectives from autism and developmental cognitive neuroscience*, 2nd edn (ed. S. Baron-Cohen, H. Tager-Flusberg and D. Cohen), pp. 222–50. Oxford University Press.

Plaisted, K., O'Riordan, M. and Baron-Cohen, S. (1998). Enhanced discrimination of novel, highly similar stimuli by adults with autism during a perceptual learning task. *J. Child Psychol. Psychiat.* **39**, 765–75.

Plante, E., Swisher, L., Vance, R. and Rapcsak, S. (1991). MRI findings in boys with specific language impairment. *Brain Lang.* **41**, 52–66.

Prior, M., Eisenmajer, R., Leekam, S., Wing, L., Gould, J., Ong, B., *et al.* (1998). Are there subgroups within the autistic spectrum? A cluster analysis of a group of children with autistic spectrum disorders. *J. Child Psychol. Psychiat.* **39**, 893–902.

Rapin, I. (ed.) (1996). *Preschool children with inadequate communication.* London: Mac Keith Press.

Rapin, I. (1998). Understanding childhood language disorders. *Curr. Opin. Pediatrics* **10**, 561–66.

Rapin, I. and Dunn, M. (1997). Language disorders in children with autism. *Semin. Pediatric Neurol.* **4**, 86–92.

Rice, M. L. (1999). Specific grammatical limitations in children with specific language impairment. In *Neurodevelopmental disorders* (ed. H. Tager-Flusberg), pp. 331–59. Cambridge, MA: MIT Press.

Rice, M. L. and Wexler, K. (1996). Toward tense as a clinical marker of specific language impairment in English-speaking children. *J. Speech Hearing Res.* **39**, 1239–57.

Rice, M. L., Wexler, K. and Cleave, P. L. (1995). Specific language impairment as a period of extended optional infinitive. *J. Speech Hearing Res.* **38**, 850–63.

Risch, N., Spiker, D., Lotspeich, L., Nouri, N., Hinds, D., Hallmayer, J., *et al.* (1999). A genomic screen of autism: evidence for a multilocus etiology. *Am. J. Hum. Genet.* **65**, 493–507.

Roberts, J., Rice, M. and Tager-Flusberg, H. (2000). Tense marking in children with autism: further evidence for overlap between autism and SLI. Paper presented at the Symposium on Research in Child Language Disorders, Madison, WI (June).

Rutter, M. (2000). Genetic studies of autism: from the 1970s into the millennium. *J. Abnormal Child Psychol.* **28**, 3–14.

Rutter, M., Bailey, A., Bolton, P. and Le Couteur, A. (1994). Autism and known medical conditions: myth and substance. *J. Child Psychol. Psychiat.* **35**, 311–22.

Santangelo, S. L. and Folstein, S. E. (1999). Autism: a genetic perspective. In *Neurodevelopmental disorders* (ed. H. Tager-Flusberg), pp. 431–447. Cambridge, MA: MIT Press.

Semel, E., Wiig, E. H. and Secord, W. A. (1995). *Clinical evaluation of language fundamentals*, 3rd edn. San Antonio, TX: Psychological Corporation/Harcourt Brace.

Siegel, D. J., Minshew, N. J. and Goldstein, G. (1996). Wechsler IQ profiles in diagnosis of high-functioning autism. *J. Autism Dev. Disorders* **26**, 389–406.

Stevenson, R. E., Schroer, R. J., Skinner, C., Fender, D. and Simensen, R. J. (1997). Autism and macrocephaly. *Lancet* **349**, 1744–45.

Szatmari, P. (1999). Heterogeneity and the genetics of autism. *J. Psychiat. Neurosci.* **24**, 159–65.

Tager-Flusberg, H. (1999). A psychological approach to understanding the social and language impairments in autism. *Int. Rev. Psychiat.* **11**, 325–34.

Tager-Flusberg, H. and Cooper, J. (1999). Present and future possibilities for defining a phenotype for specific language impairment. *J. Speech Lang. Hearing Res.* **42**, 1001–04.

Tomblin, J. B. and Zhang, X. (1999). Language patterns and etiology in children with specific language impairment. In *Neurodevelopmental disorders* (ed. H. Tager-Flusberg), pp. 361–82. Cambridge, MA: MIT Press/Bradford Books.

Tomblin, J. B., Nishimura, C., Zhang, X. and Murray, J. (1998). Association of developmental language impairment with loci at 7q31. *Am. J. Hum. Genet.* **63**(Suppl. 2), A312.

Wassink, T., Piven, J., Vieland, V., Pietila, J., Goedken, R., Folstein, S., *et al.* (2002). Evaluation of FOXP2 as an autism susceptibility gene. *Am. J. Med. Genet.* **114**, 566–69.

Wechsler, D. (1991). *Wechsler Intelligence Scale for Children*, 3rd edn. San Antonio, TX: Psychological Corporation.

Wechsler, D. (1997). *Wechsler Adult Intelligence Scale*, 3rd edn. San Antonio, TX: Psychological Corporation.

Weismer, S. E., Tomblin, J. B., Zhang, X., Buckwalter, P., Chynoweth, J. G. and Jones, M. (2000). Nonword repetition performance in school-age children with and without language impairment. *J. Speech Lang. Hearing Res.* **43**, 865–878.

Wilkinson, K. (1998). Profiles of language and communication skills in autism. *Mental Retardation Dev. Disabilities Res. Rev.* **4**, 73–79.

Wiig, E. H., Secord, W. and Semel, E. (1992). *Clinical evaluation of language fundamentals— preschool*. San Antonio, TX: Psychological Corporation/Harcourt Brace.

Williams, K. T. (1997). *Expressive vocabulary test*. Circle Pines, MN: American Guidance Service.

Woodhouse, W., Bailey, A., Rutter, M., Bolton, P., Baird, G. and Le Couteur, A. (1996). Head circumference in autism and other pervasive developmental disorders. *J. Child Psychol. Psychiat.* **37**, 665–71.

World Health Organization (1993). *The international classification of diseases*, 10th edn. Geneva: World Health Organization.

Glossary

ADI-R: autism diagnostic interview—revised
ADOS: autism diagnostic observation schedule
ASD: autism spectrum disorder
CELF: clinical evaluation of language fundamentals—preschool or III
CLSA: collaborative linkage study of autism
DAS: differential abilities scale
EVT: expressive vocabulary test
IQ: intelligence quotient
MRI: magnetic resonance imaging
NV: non-verbal
PDDNOS: pervasive developmental disorder not otherwise specified
PPVT: Peabody picture vocabulary test—III
RNW: repetition of nonsense words
SLI: specific language impairment
V: verbal

4

Why is joint attention a pivotal skill in autism?

Tony Charman

Joint attention abilities play a crucial role in the development of autism. Impairments in joint attention are among the earliest signs of the disorder and joint attention skills relate to outcome, both in the 'natural course' of autism and through being targeted in early intervention programmes. In the current study, concurrent and longitudinal associations between joint attention and other social communication abilities measured in a sample of infants with autism and related pervasive developmental disorders at age 20 months, and language and symptom severity at age 42 months, were examined. Extending the findings from previous studies, joint attention ability was positively associated with language gains and (lower) social and communication symptoms, and imitation ability was also positively associated with later language. Some specificity in the association between different aspects of joint attention behaviours and outcome was found: declarative, triadic gaze switching predicted language and symptom severity but imperative, dyadic eye contact behaviours did not. Further, although joint attention was associated with later social and language symptoms it was unrelated to repetitive and stereotyped symptoms, suggesting the latter may have a separate developmental trajectory. Possible deficits in psychological and neurological processes that might underlie the impaired development of joint attention in autism are discussed.

Keywords: autism; joint attention; play; imitation; language; symptom severity

4.1 Introduction

(a) The role of psychological theory in understanding autism

Psychological theory helps us understand autism at two levels.[1] First, it describes and delineates, in psychological terms, the behaviours that characterize individuals with autism. Second, and more powerfully, it attempts to explain, at a psychological level, the underlying processes that contribute to the abnormal development seen in individuals with autism. Abnormal psychological processing is not the primary pathogenesis that 'causes' autism. It is well established that autism is a neuro-developmental condition whose ultimate aetiology is due to the influence of genetic and other organic disruptions to brain development and organization (Lord and Bailey 2002). It is also likely that the behavioural phenotype encompassed by the label 'autism' and the broader autism spectrum disorders includes individuals with different and complex aetiologies. However, a 'dynamic systems approach' to neurodevelopmental disorders (Bishop 1997; Karmiloff-Smith 1997) highlights ways in which abnormal psychological development, consequent on abnormal brain development, can have secondary effects on later brain and psychological development and organization. Primary neurobiological deficits may impact on optimal behavioural responses and lead to secondary neurological and psychological disturbance, via the interaction of the developing brain system with the organization of input available to children from their processing of, and interaction with, the environment ('experience expectant neural development'; Greenough et al. 1987).

This paper summarizes the evidence base and presents new data that highlight the pivotal role that joint attention plays in the development of autism. Two outstanding questions are discussed:

(i) In what way might impairments in the development of joint attention have secondary effects on later development in autism?

(ii) What primary pathogenic processes at the psychological and neurological level might lead to impaired development of joint attention in autism?

'Pivotal' can refer both to 'acting as a fulcrum' and to 'being of crucial importance' or 'the thing on which progress depends' (Anonymous 1994). Both meanings are relevant to discussion of the pivotal role that joint attention plays in the psychopathology of autism. Evidence comes from several sources, including parental reports of the earliest recognized signs of abnormality, early videotapes of infants who later go on to receive a diagnosis of autism, attempts to prospectively screen for autism, longitudinal studies of early predictors of language and social outcome and intervention studies.

In typical development, joint attention behaviours emerge between 6 and 12 months and involve the triadic coordination or sharing ('jointness'; Leekam and Moore 2001) of attention between the infant, another person, and an object or event (Bakeman and Adamson 1984). The term encompasses a complex of behavioural forms including gaze and point following, showing and pointing. A distinction has been made between two different functions that joint attention behaviours serve. Imperative triadic exchanges serve an instrumental or requesting function, whereas declarative triadic exchanges serve to share awareness, or the experience, of an object or event (Gómez et al. 1993; Mundy et al. 1993). Individuals with autism are impaired in the development of both imperative and declarative acts, although impairments in the latter are more severe (Ricks and Wing 1975; Mundy et al. 1986, 1993; Sigman et al. 1986; Baron-Cohen 1989, 1993;). More recently, it has been shown that the critical distinction may not be the imperative versus declarative level. Rather, the degree to which a child is monitoring and regulating the attention (or attitude) of the other person in relation to objects and events determines the severity of the deficit seen in autism (Mundy *et al*. 1994; Phillips *et al*. 1995; Charman 1998).

(b) Evidence for the pivotal role of joint attention in the early development of autism

The first line of evidence for the central role that joint attention plays in the development of autism comes from studies that have systematically elicited retrospective parental reports of early symptoms between 12 and 18 months (Ohta *et al*. 1987; Gillberg *et al*. 1990; Stone *et al*. 1994). There is some evidence of early abnormalities in sensory, motor and RSBs, and when such behaviours are present they are highly characteristic of autism (Rogers 2001; Charman and Baird 2002). However, most studies concur that the best discriminators at this age are likely to be the social and communicative impairments, in particular, joint attention behaviours such as eye contact, gaze monitoring and response to name (Stone *et al*. 1997; Charman 2000).

The second source of evidence is the retrospective analysis of home videos taken before children are diagnosed with autism. Adrien *et al*. (1993) found that within the first year children with autism showed impairments in social interaction, lack of social smile and facial expression, hypotonia and poor attention. In the second year of life, additional impairments included ignoring people, preference for aloneness, lack of eye contact and lack of appropriate gestures. In a study examining home videos taken at first birthday parties, Osterling and Dawson (1994) found that children with autism were less likely to look at others, to show an object or point to objects, and to orient to their name, compared with typically developing controls. In an extension of this study, Werner *et al*. (2000) found that in videotapes taken between eight and 10 months of age children with autism were differentiated from typically developing children on the basis of less frequent orienting to name. Baranek (1999) found that abnormalities in orientation to visual stimuli, aversion to touch and delayed response to name, all characterized autism (but not developmental delay or typical development) as early as at nine months of life. In summary, these studies suggest that alongside a lack of effect, and in a few cases sensory abnormalities, pre-verbal social communication and social orientating behaviours, including joint attention acts, are the most reliably identified early abnormalities (retrospectively) seen towards the end of the first year of life in children with autism.

Another demonstration of the importance of joint attention behaviours in the early development of autism comes from studies that have attempted to prospectively identify cases of autism using screening instruments (Baird *et al*. 2001). These have been applied both to general populations (Baron-Cohen *et al*. 1996; Baird *et al*. 2000; Dietz *et al*. 2001; Robins *et al*. 2001) and to referred and highrisk populations (Baron-Cohen *et al.* 1992; Scambler *et al.* 2001). Different aspects of giving, showing, following eye gaze, and producing and following points, form a key part of all the screens for autism developed thus far. In the CHAT screening study (Baird *et al.* 2000), two aspects of joint attention behaviour—a lack of gaze monitoring and a lack of pointing for interest—in combination with an absence of simple pretend play at 18 months of age, was highly predictive of autism. A proportion of the children prospectively identified had only failed (by parental report and health practitioner observation) the items asking about pointing for interest. An important caution is that although the CHAT screen had a high positive predictive value its sensitivity was moderate at best, identifying only 38% of cases. It may be that the majority of infants with autism did not show impairments in joint attention and play behaviours at this age (but might have shown other developmental impairments and abnormal behaviours not measured in the study). Alternatively, the threshold of impairment in these skills may have been set too high (the CHAT asked if children had *ever* produced such behaviours).

Several studies have examined the longitudinal associations between joint attention in the pre-school years and later language and social development. Mundy *et al.* (1990) found that joint attention behaviours (alternating gaze, pointing, showing and gaze following) measured at 45 months were associated with language ability 12 months later. Social interaction, requesting behaviour, and initial age, IQ and language ability were not associated with language at follow-up. Sigman and Ruskin (1999) found that responding to joint attention bids measured at the initial time-point was associated with gain in EL at age 12 years. Further, joint attention behaviours measured at 4 years of age were also associated with social and peer group behaviour 8 years later (Sigman and Ruskin 1999). Stone and Yoder (2001) reported a similar association between early joint attention ability and later EL ability from 2 to 4 years of age.

Another aspect of the pivotal role played by joint attention in the development of autism is demonstrated by evidence that intervention approaches that have placed an emphasis on the development of non-verbal social–communicative skills promote enhanced language and social development (Rogers and Lewis 1989; Koegel 2000; Lord 2000). Although few, if any, well-controlled randomized control trials exist, numerous small series case studies have suggested that promoting the NVC competence of children with autism enhances the communicative use of the language (Rollins *et al.* 1998; Kasari *et al.* 2001).

The convergence of these sources of evidence suggests that joint attention plays a critical role in the early development of autism. Impairments in joint attention behaviours are among the earliest abnormalities noticed in autism, becoming apparent around the end of the first year of life. Screening instruments that assess (among other things) joint attention behaviours can prospectively identify some cases of autism. Individual differences in joint attention ability relate to later language and social outcomes over time-periods as long as 8 years, and joint attention behaviours are emerging as a key target for psycho-educational approaches to early intervention. This does not mean that joint attention impairments 'cause' autism. However, it does suggest that joint attention is a critical 'downstream' effect of earlier brain psychopathology. Understanding why the development of joint attention skills is impaired in individuals with autism, and the mechanisms by which joint attention behaviours are related to later outcomes, are important future enterprises for psychological research.

(c) The present study

The present study took advantage of a small group of infants ($n = 18$) with autism and related pervasive developmental disorders prospectively identified in the CHAT screening study (Baron-Cohen et al. 1996, 2000; Baird et al. 2000). We have previously reported findings from a series of experimental tasks of joint attention, attention switching, imitation, play and empathy conducted at 20 months of age (Charman et al. 1997, 1998; Swettenham et al. 1998). In brief, the group of infants with autism and pervasive developmental disorder showed very low production of some behaviours, including empathic responding, pretend play, gaze switching and imitation, in contrast to infants with language delay. The present study reports on the longitudinal associations between performance on these experimental measures conducted in infancy, and language and behavioural outcomes (symptom severity) from a follow-up conducted when the children were aged 42 months.

Although the sample was relatively small, the study provides a unique contribution because the cohort is significantly younger than those previously studied. Previous studies with older samples of children have found positive longitudinal associations between early joint attention behaviour and later language. Consistent with the thesis that joint attention is a pivotal skill in the development of autism, we expected to replicate this finding with our younger sample but, in addition, made the prediction that joint attention ability would associate more strongly with language than imitation and play ability. Few studies have examined the association between early joint attention behaviours and later symptom severity but again consistent with our 'pivotal skill' thesis we predicted that early joint attention ability would be (negatively) associated with later symptom severity.

4.2 Methods

(a) Participants

The participant characteristics are shown in Table 4.1. Non-verbal ability was measured using the D and E scales of the Griffiths Scale of Infant Development (Griffiths 1986) at age 20 months, and either the Griffiths or the Leiter International Performance Scale (Leiter 1952) at age 42 months.

Table 4.1   Age, non-verbal mental age, language scores
and ADI-R scores of participants at both time points.

	time 1	time 2
	$n = 18$ mean (s.d.)	$n = 18$ mean (s.d.)
age in months	20.6 (1.3)	42.5 (3.6)
non-verbal IQ	80.6 (10.1)	83.6 (25.8)
EL[a] raw score	7.3 (3.5)	24.3 (10.5)
RL[b] raw score	4.8 (2.5)	24.9 (9.5)
RSI[c]	12.4 (6.3)	12.2 (7.0)
NVC[d]	9.4 (4.0)	8.8 (4.3)
RSB[e]	1.8 (1.4)	2.6 (1.8)

[a] Reynell EL score.
[b] Reynell RL score.
[c] Reciprocal social behaviour domain of the ADI-R.
[d] NVC domain of the ADI-R.
[e] RSB domain of the ADI-R.

A non-verbal IQ was calculated by dividing the age equivalent score by the child's chronological age (MA/CA). RL and EL abilities were assessed at both time-points using the Reynell Developmental Language Scales (Reynell 1985). At age 42 months, nine subjects met ICD-10 (World Health Organization 1993) criteria for autism and nine subjects met criteria for atypical autism or pervasive developmental disorder—unspecified (see Cox *et al.* (1999) for details of diagnostic assessments). Given the restricted sample size, we adopted an autism spectrum approach (Lord and Risi 1998) and results were analysed for the group as a whole.

(b) Experimental measures conducted at age 20 months

Full details of the experimental measures taken at age 20 months are given in Charman *et al.* (1997, 1998). For the present analyses, only the key variables entered into the crosssectional and longitudinal analyses are described.

(i) Spontaneous play task

When the child entered the room the following sets of toys were available (all at once), spread out on the floor: a toy tea-set; a toy kitchen stove with miniature pots and pans, spoon, pieces of green sponge; and junk accessories (e.g. brick, straw, rawlplug, cotton-wool, cube, box) and conventional toy accessories (toy animals, cars, etc.). This combination of objects was based on studies by Baron-Cohen (1987) and Lewis and Boucher (1988). The child's parents and the experimenters remained seated and offered only minimal and non-specific responses to child-initiated approaches. Each child was filmed for 5 min. The presence of any functional and pretend play acts on a two-point scale (0 = no functional or pretend play; 1 = functional play; 2 = pretend play) was entered into the current analysis.

(ii) Joint attention tasks
Activated toy task

A series of three active toy tasks based on those described by Butterworth and Adamson-Macedo (1987) was conducted. The child stood or sat between their mother and the experimenter. A series of mechanical toys, designed to provoke an ambiguous response, that is, to provoke a mixture of attraction and uncertainty in the child, were placed one at a time onto the floor of the room 1–2 m from the child. The toys were a robot, which flashed, beeped and moved around in circular sweeps; a car that followed a circular path around the room; and a pig that made 'oinking' noises and shunted backwards and forwards. The toys were controlled by the experimenter. They were active for a period of 1 min, during which time they stopped and restarted twice. The proportion of trials on which the infant produced the key joint attention behaviour—a gaze switch between the toy and adult (experimenter or parent)—was entered into the current analysis.

Goal-detection tasks

A series of tasks described by Phillips *et al.* (1992) were conducted at different times throughout the testing session: (i) *The blocking task*: when the child was manually and visually engaged with a toy, the experimenter covered the child's hands with his own, preventing the child from further activity, and held the block for 5 s. This was repeated four times during the session. (ii) *The teasing task*: the experimenter offered the child a toy. When the child looked at the toy and began to reach out for it, the experimenter withdrew the toy and held it out of reach for 5 s. The experimenter then gave the toy to the child. This was repeated four times during the session. The key behaviour recorded on each trial was whether the child looked up towards the experimenter's eyes during the 5 s period immediately after the block or the tease. The teasing and blocking scores were highly intercorrelated ($r = 0.83$, $p < 0.001$). To reduce the number of variables entered into the analysis, a composite goaldetection task score of the proportion of trials in which the infant looked up towards the experimenter on the teasing and blocking trials combined, was entered into the analysis.

(iii) Imitation

The materials and method for the procedural imitation task followed those employed by Meltzoff (1988). The child sat opposite the experimenter. Four actions were modelled, all on objects designed to be unfamiliar to the child. Each act was performed three times. At the end of the modelling period (around 2 min in total), the objects were placed, in turn, in front of the child. One non-specific prompt ('What can you do with this?') was given if the child failed to pick up or manipulate the object at once. The response period was

20 s for each object. The proportion of trials on which the infant imitated the modelled action on the objects was entered into the current analysis.

(c) Symptom severity measured at 20 months and 42 months

The ADI (ADI-R; Lord *et al.* 1994) is a semi-structured, standardized diagnostic interview that asks parents about the current (and past) functioning. The ADI-R algorithm has three domains or clusters of items that map onto the three symptom areas by which autism is defined in ICD-10 (World Health Organization 1993): *Qualitative impairments in reciprocal social interaction* (*RSI* or Dimension B), *Impairments in verbal and NVC* (*VNVC* or Dimension C), and *Repetitive behaviours and stereotyped patterns* (*RSB* or Dimension D) (see Lord *et al.* (1994) for details). ADI-R interviews were conducted with parents of all children at both the initial (age 20 months) and follow-up (age 42 months) assessments. For the purposes of the present study the summary algorithm scores (that is, the items that correspond most closely to characteristic autism symptoms) for each of the three domains of behaviour will be entered into the analysis. None of the children had sufficient language (phrase speech) for the higher-level verbal items (e.g. stereotyped and idiosyncratic language) to be scored at 20 months, and only half had sufficient language at 42 months. Therefore, the NVC algorithm score was entered into the analysis for all participants. The ADI-R algorithm domain scores are shown in Table 4.1.

4.3 Results

The raw scores of the experimental variables are presented in Table 4.2. The strategy for analysis was to present zero-order correlations, followed by partial correlations with IQ at 20 months which were partialled out. Given the sample size, regression analysis was not conducted.

Table 4.2   Scores for all experimental variables.

	n	%
(*a*) number of children showing		
no function or pretend play	4	22.2
functional play	12	66.7
pretend play	2	11.1
	mean (%)	s.d. (%)
(*b*) percentage of trials key behaviours observed		
gaze switch task	45.4	44.2
goal-detection task	37.7	42.2
imitation task	43.1	35.2

Table 4.3 Full and IQ-partialled correlations between the experimental measures and language at 20 and 42 months.

	20 months		42 months	
	EL	RL	EL	RL
(a) full correlations				
play	0.16	0.30	0.43	0.34
gaze switch	0.28	0.54*	0.55*	0.74***
goal-detection composite	−0.07	0.06	0.41	0.34
imitation	0.04	0.25	0.46	0.63**
(b) IQ-partialled correlations[a]				
play	0.16	0.29	0.42	0.33
gaze switch	0.28	0.52*	0.54*	0.74***
goal-detection composite	−0.09	0.00	0.40	0.32
imitation	0.02	0.18	0.47	0.65**

[a] IQ at 20 months partialled out.
* $p < 0.05$, **$p < 0.01$, ***$p < 0.001$.

Concurrent associations between the experimental measures and the EL and RL ability at 20 months, and longitudinal associations with EL and RL at 42 months, are shown in Table 4.3. Concurrently, only the correlation between gaze switching and RL was significant ($r = 0.54$, $p < 0.05$) and remained so when the effects of IQ were partialled out ($r = 0.52$, $p < 0.05$). Longitudinally, the presence of functional and pretend play at the initial assessment was not associated with language ability at 42 months. The proportion of trials in which a child's gaze switched in the joint attention task was significantly correlated with both EL ($r = 0.55$, $p < 0.05$) and RL ($r = 0.74$, $p < 0.001$). In contrast, the proportion of trials in which a child made eye contact in the goal-detection tasks was not associated with later language ability. Imitation scores were significantly correlated with RL ($r = 0.63$, $p < 0.01$). When initial IQ was partialled out, the correlations between gaze switches in the joint attention task and EL ($r = 0.54$, $p < 0.05$) and RL ($r = 0.74$, $p < 0.001$) remained significant. The partial correlation between imitation and RL was also significant ($r = 0.65$, $p < 0.01$).

Concurrent associations between the experimental measures and ADI-R symptom domain scores at 20 months and longitudinal associations with ADI-R scores at 42 months are shown in Table 4.4. Concurrent performance on the play, gaze switch and imitation tasks was significantly (negatively) associated with 20-month symptom severity measured by the ADI-R algorithm domain scores. Several of these associations remained significant for play (NVC: $r = -0.61$, $p < 0.01$; RSB: $r = -0.53$, $p < 0.05$) and for gaze switch (RSI: $r = -0.80$, $p < 0.001$; NVC: $r = -0.59$, $p < 0.05$; RSB: $r = -0.69$, $p < 0.01$) when the effect of IQ was partialled out. Fewer associations were found

Table 4.4 Full and IQ-partialled correlations between the experimental measures and symptom severity at 20 and 42 months.

	20 months			42 months		
	RSI[b]	NVC[c]	RSB[d]	RSI[b]	NVC[c]	RSB[d]
(a) full correlations						
play	−0.45	−0.59*	−0.52*	−0.08	−0.27	−0.15
gaze switch	−0.81	−0.62**	−0.65**	−0.51*	−0.66**	−0.30
goal-detection composite	−0.14	−0.42	−0.38	−0.32	−0.12	−0.27
imitation	−0.23	−0.48*	−0.29	−0.37	−0.52*	−0.14
(b) IQ-partialled correlations[a]						
play	0.44	−0.61**	−0.53*	−0.03	−0.25	−0.14
gaze switch	−0.80***	−0.59*	−0.69**	−0.46	−0.65**	−0.27
goal-detection composite	−0.10	−0.35	−0.41	−0.22	0.02	−0.23
imitation	−0.16	−0.31	−0.38	−0.14	−0.34	−0.05

[a] IQ at 20 months partialled out.
[b] Reciprocal social behaviour domain of the ADI-R.
[c] NVC domain of the ADI-R.
[d] RSB domain of the ADI-R.
*$p < 0.05$, **$p < 0.01$, ***$p < 0.001$.

between performance on the experimental measures at 20 months and symptom severity at 42 months. In the full correlations, performance on the gaze switch task was associated with scores on the RSI ($r = -0.51$, $p < 0.05$) and NVC ($r = -0.66$, $p < 0.01$) domains of the ADI-R and imitation was associated with NVC ($r = -0.52$, $p < 0.05$). When the effect of IQ was partialled out, only one correlation remained significant: performance on the gaze switch task was associated with NVC score at 42 months ($r = -0.65$, $p < 0.01$), although the correlation between gaze switch and RSI fell only just short of significance ($r = -0.46$, $p = 0.06$). Performance on the goal-detection tasks was not associated with symptom severity scores cross-sectionally or longitudinally.

4.4 Discussion

A clear pattern of findings emerged in terms of the concurrent and longitudinal associations between the experimental measures at 20 months and language ability and symptom severity at 20 and 42 months. One measure of joint attention (frequency of gaze switches in the active toy task) and the measure of imitation were associated with language ability, both concurrently and longitudinally for the former, but only longitudinally for the latter. By contrast, the other joint attention measure (proportion of trials in which a child looked to the adult in the goaldetection tasks) and the measure of functional and pretend play were not associated with language ability either concurrently or longitudinally. The play, gaze switch and imitation measures were all associated with measures of symptom severity, across all three domains of symptoms, concurrently at 20 months. However, only gaze switches on the active toy task and imitation were associated with symptom severity at 42 months. The gaze switch measure was more robustly associated with later symptom severity than imitation, in that it was associated with both the RSI and the NVC ADI-R domains, and these associations held up when the effect of initial IQ was controlled. By contrast, none of the experimental measures taken at 20 months was associated with severity of RSB measured by the ADI-R at 42 months.

These results extend downwards in age the findings of previous studies that have shown longitudinal associations between early social communication behaviours and later language ability in samples seen first in the third and fourth years of life (Mundy *et al*. 1990; Stone *et al*. 1997; Sigman and Ruskin 1999; Stone and Yoder 2001). This demonstrates that within the present sample of infants with autism individual differences in early social communication skills relate to one critical outcome measure: language ability. They also extend previous findings by examining longitudinal associations with symptom severity as well as language ability. That is, the greater the facility a child demonstrated in gaze switching during the active toy task at 20 months of age, the less severe were that child's social and communication symptoms at 42 months. This is consistent with a recent finding that an early joint attention behaviour (looking at an object held out by other), rated retrospectively from home videos of first birthday parties, was associated with symptom severity (rated on the Childhood Autism Rating Scale; Schopler *et al*. (1980)) at age 5 years (Osterling *et al*. 2002). The findings are also consistent with many studies that have demonstrated longitudinal associations between joint attention abilities, including proto-declarative pointing, following eye gaze and pointing, and language learning and later language ability in typically developing infants (Bates *et al*. 1979; Tomasello and Farrar 1986; Mundy and Gomes 1996; Carpenter *et al*. 1998).

Taken together, this pattern of findings provides further support for the thesis that joint attention is a pivotal skill in autism. Only joint attention abilities were significantly related to both later language ability *and* symptom levels. Further, the present study demonstrates that the pivotal role of joint attention can be demonstrated in infants with autism, representing the youngest cohort of children with autism studied to date. However, although one measure of joint attention (gaze switches in the active toy task) was associated with later language and symptom severity, another measure of joint attention (looks to the experimenter in the blocking and teasing tasks) was not. This suggests that the underlying competencies tapped by the two tasks may differ, despite the fact that both have been described under the umbrella term 'joint attention tasks'. Previously, it has been suggested that looking to the experimenter in the blocking and teasing tasks might be a questioning ('What are you doing?';

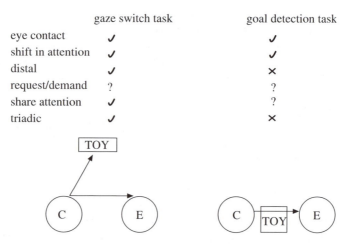

	gaze switch task	goal detection task
eye contact	✓	✓
shift in attention	✓	✓
distal	✓	✗
request/demand	?	?
share attention	✓	?
triadic	✓	✗

Fig. 4.1 Differences in the form and function of joint attention behaviours in the gaze-switching and goal-detection tasks.

Phillips *et al.* (1992)) or an imperative communicative act ('Give me that back!'; Charman 1998). This differs in both nature and form from the more clear declarative act involved in switching gaze between the active toy and an adult in the active toy task. One suggestion is that the triangulation and shifting of attention in this task may have a more direct social goal ('Look at that!') and this may involve sharing one's mental state of perception with others.

An analysis of the differences in both the form and the function of the two joint attention tasks is shown in Fig. 4.1. Both forms of joint attention behaviour involve eye contact (or at least looking to an adult's face) and a shift in attention, and both might have an imperative function ('Start up that toy!' in the gaze-switch task; 'Give me that back!' in the goal-detection task). The aspects of *communicative form* that characterize the gaze switch but not the goal-detection response include the distal position of the object and the triadic nature of attention focus (child–toy–adult). The aspects of *communicative function* that characterize the gaze switch, but not the goal-detection task, are that the former but not the latter involves shared attention and a directly referential goal ('Look at that!'). It has been suggested that these aspects—shared attention and communicative reference—of joint attention behaviour are early evidence for the infant's emerging understanding of others as intentional agents, and that understanding the mental state of attention in episodes of shared attention may be a precursor to understanding mental states or 'theory of mind' ability (Baron-Cohen 1993; Tomasello 1995). Some empirical evidence from typically developing children supports this claim (see Charman *et al.* 2000). The present study demonstrates that individual differences in these specific aspects of joint attention in infants with autism are related to later language ability and social and communication symptoms more than other joint attention skills and imitation and play.

One other notable finding emerged. Although early joint attention and imitation abilities were related to both later language and symptom severity (above and beyond initial IQ), this only held for social and communication symptoms and not for repetitive behaviours and stereotyped patterns. This suggests that the developmental trajectories, and perhaps at a psychological level the underlying psychopathology, of these symptom domains may be separable. There is other evidence to suggest that this might be the case (see Charman and Swettenham 2001, for a review). Tanguay *et al.* (1998), for example, found that three factors derived from factor analysis of the social and communication items on the ADI-R ('affective reciprocity', 'joint attention' and 'theory of mind') did not correlate with scores on the repetitive behaviours and stereotyped interests ADI-R domain score. At least two studies have found that RSBs were identified less consistently in the second and third years of life compared with older samples of 4- and 5-year-old children with autism (see Cox *et al.* 1999; Stone *et al.* 1999). Consistent with this, two recent studies have found social communication impairments (including in joint attention) but not executive function deficits in 3-year-olds with autism relative to controls, in contrast to studies with school-age children with autism (see Griffith *et al.* 1999; Dawson *et al.* 2002). It is possible that in at least a subgroup of children with autism, repetitive, restricted and stereotyped abnormalities only begin to emerge in children with autism after infancy, later than the social and communication deficits are apparent.

Thus, although joint attention may be a pivotal skill in the development of individuals with autism, it may not be related to RSBs and restricted interests, which may be due to different underlying pathology at both the psychological and neurological level. It is not well understood how the social and communication symptoms in autism 'hang together' with the repetitive and stereotyped symptoms. This has implications both for our understanding of autism and for interventions. Whereas there is evidence that intervention approaches that place an emphasis on the development of non-verbal social–communicative skills promote enhanced language and social development (Rogers and Lewis 1989; Koegel 2000; Lord 2000; Kasari *et al.* 2001), we do not know if such approaches have a direct effect on RSBs. Although some of the latter may be secondary to communication difficulties they might also be expected to ameliorate as communication improves. However, direct interventions that target RSBs may be required (National Research Council 2001).

(a) What are the origins of the joint attention deficit in autism?

Much theoretical interest has focused on the role of joint attention behaviours as 'precursors' to later language (Tomasello 1995) and theory of mind development (Charman *et al.* 2000) in both typically developing children and children with

autism. Acting as a 'precursor' involves either joint attention growing or trans-
forming into language or theory of mind ability (i.e. it is an earlier form of these
behaviours) or via experiences gained through the precursor behaviour (e.g.
jointly attending to events in the world) the child acquires the later abilities.
However, recognition that joint attention is not a starting point but merely a stag-
ing post in early social communicative development, and hence a 'postcursor' of
earlier psychological and developmental processes (Tomasello 1995), focuses
attention on what earlier impairments underlie the impaired development of joint
attention skills in autism. Several candidate precursors have been suggested.

Using a paradigm measuring spontaneous attention switching during free
play, Swettenham *et al.* (1998) found that, compared with controls, infants
with autism looked less and for shorter duration at people, and more and for
longer duration at objects. They also switched attention less frequently
between social and non-social stimuli. This mirrors recent findings using a
sophisticated eye-tracking methodology to examine where adults with autism
look when watching film of social interactions (Klin *et al.* 2002*b*). Thus, individuals with autism (from a very early age) may have less exposure to people
and the facial, gestural and eye gaze information that, in the typical case, draw
them into social interaction and an understanding of the social world. In one
sense, this reduced exposure to social information means that they are less
'expert' in social interactions than typically developing children. What might
underlie this preference for directing attention to objects rather than to people?

Mundy and colleagues have proposed a 'social orienting' model of autistic
pathology, whereby disturbances to frontally mediated neuroaffective motiva-
tion systems, that serve to prioritize social information processing, are apparent in development in advance of cognition as the primary regulator of
behaviour (Mundy 1995; Mundy and Neal 2001). Dawson and colleagues
have developed a similar account and provided experimental evidence of a
deficit in social orienting in pre-school children with autism (Dawson and
Lewy 1989; Dawson *et al.* 1998; see also Hobson 1993). Consistent with
this account, Leekam *et al.* (2000) found that children with autism were
unimpaired in low-level exogenous orienting to objects but they were
impaired in exogenous orienting to a social cue (a head turn), and the latter
was strongly related to joint attention behaviour (gaze following). This
suggests that impairments in dyadic social engagement may be present in
autism and may relate to the triadic social engagement impairments, most
notably in joint attention behaviours (Leekam and Moore 2001). Under such
accounts, primary neurobiological deficits that underlie impaired social
orienting impact on optimal behavioural responses from as early as the first
few months of life. This may lead to secondary neurological (and later
psychological) disturbance via the interaction of the developing brain system
with the organization of social input available to the children from their
processing of, and interaction with, the environment ('experience expectant
neural development'; Greenough *et al.* 1987) (see Mundy and Crowson 1997;
Mundy and Neal 2001).

Another clue as to what impairments might underlie disturbances in joint attention behaviours in autism is provided by a secondary finding from the study of Dawson *et al.* (1998). Although the impairment in orienting found in children with autism was greatest for social stimuli (e.g. name called), they also showed impairments in orienting to non-social stimuli (e.g. jack-in-the-box). Results from studies examining attention orienting to non-social stimuli are mixed, with some studies finding slow spatial orienting to cues implicating cerebella dysfunction (Townsend *et al.* 1996) and others finding no deficit in automatic shifts of attention, but impairments in suppression of context-inappropriate responses implicating executive brain systems in the prefrontal and parietal cortex (Minshew *et al.* 1999). Other, more recent, lines of research suggest that the fundamental cognitive impairments that underlie these abnormalities might be at a more basic, low-level perceptual processing level (Happé 1999; Plaisted *et al.* 1999; Milne *et al.* 2002) or at the level of processing and understanding emotions (Baron-Cohen *et al.* 2000; Klin *et al.* 2002*a*).

The association between executive deficits and joint attention impairments has been directly explored in several recent studies of 3- and 4-year-old children with autism. As noted above, two recent studies have found no executive function deficits in 3-year-olds with autism relative to controls, in contrast to studies with school-age children (see Griffith *et al.* 1999; Dawson *et al.* 2002). Both studies also examined the longitudinal associations between executive measures and joint attention. Griffith *et al.* (1999) found that performance on a spatial reversal task at age 3 years was associated with joint attention ability at age 4 years (but not vice versa) for children with autism but not for controls. Dawson *et al.* (2002) found that tasks tapping ventromedial but not dorsolateral prefrontal function were correlated with joint attention ability. They suggested that impairments in rule learning regarding the relations between stimuli and reward that is mediated by the ventromedial system may underlie the deficits in the development of joint attention (and later theory of mind) abilities in autism.

Even when these developmental processes are better understood, the need to study and understand joint attention and other early social communication impairments in autism will not disappear. The pivotal role that joint attention appears to play in the course and outcome of development for individuals with autism, and its potential as a target for intervention, will remain, whatever its neurological and psychological antecedents. One example is a recent study by Siller and Sigman (2002) who found that individual differences in the degree to which mothers synchronized their focus of attention with that of their child were associated with child language gains up to 16 years later. The authors suggest several mechanisms that may underlie this association. These include providing attentional, social and language experiences that partly compensate for the child's attentional impairments, providing a more consistent model of being an agent directing attention (and having intentions) in relation to objects and events in the world, or simply being a more fun and motivational partner in social exchanges (Siller and Sigman 2002). Understanding how early psychopathological processes affect joint attention ability, and what the mechanism of transmission is of the associations identified between joint attention and later social and language development, remain important goals for psychological research into autism.

The author is grateful to his research collaborators on the CHAT project for many discussions over the years that have helped develop and inform his views on this topic: Simon Baron-Cohen, Gillian Baird, Antony Cox, John Swettenham, Auriol Drew, and Sally Wheelwright.

Endnote

1. For reasons of parsimony the term 'autism' will be used throughout to describe individuals with autism and the related 'pervasive developmental disorders' described in DSM-IV (American Psychiatric Association 1994) and ICD-10 (World Health Organization 1993), commonly referred to as 'autism spectrum disorders'.

References

Adrien, J. L., Lenoir, P., Martineau, J., Perrot, A., Hameury, L., Larmande, C., *et al.* (1993). Blind ratings of early symptoms of autism based upon family home movies. *J. Am. Acad. Child Adol. Psychiat.* **32**, 617–26.

American Psychiatric Association (1994). *Diagnostic and statistical manual of mental disorders (DSM-IV)*, 4th edn. Washington, DC: American Psychiatric Association.

Anonymous (1994). *Collins English dictionary*, 3rd edn. Glasgow: Harper Collins.

Baird, G., Charman, T., Baron-Cohen, S., Cox, A., Swettenham, J., Wheelwright, S., *et al.* (2000). A screening instrument for autism at 18 month of age: a six-year follow-up study. *J. Am. Acad. Child Adol. Psychiat.* **39**, 694–702.

Baird, G., Charman, T., Cox, A., Baron-Cohen, S., Swettenham, J., Wheelwright, S., *et al.* (2001). Screening and surveillance for autism and pervasive developmental disorders. *Arch. Dis. Child* **84**, 468–75.

Bakeman, R. and Adamson, L. B. (1984). Coordinating attention to people and objects in mother–infant and peer–infant interaction. *Child Dev.* **55**, 1278–89.

Baranek, G. T. (1999). Autism during infancy: a retrospective video analysis of sensory-motor and social behaviours at 9–12 months of age. *J. Autism Devl Disord.* **29**, 213–24.

Baron-Cohen, S. (1987). Autism and symbolic play. *Br. J. Devl Psychol.* **5**, 139–48.

Baron-Cohen, S. (1989). Perceptual role-taking and protodeclarative pointing in autism. *Br. J. Devl Psychol.* **7**, 113–27.

Baron-Cohen, S. (1993). From attention–goal psychology to belief–desire psychology: the development of a theory of mind and its dysfunction. In *Understanding other minds: perspectives from autism* (ed. S. Baron-Cohen, H. Tager-Flusberg and D. Cohen), pp. 59–82. Oxford: Oxford University Press.

Baron-Cohen, S., Allen, J. and Gillberg, C. (1992). Can autism be detected at 18 months? The needle, the haystack, and the CHAT. *Br. J. Psychiat.* **161**, 839–43.

Baron-Cohen, S., Cox, A., Baird, G., Swettenham, J., Nightingale, N., Morgan, K., *et al.* (1996). Psychological markers of autism at 18 months of age in a large population. *Br. J. Psychiat.* **168**, 158–63.

Baron-Cohen, S., Ring, H. A., Bullmore, E. T., Wheelwright, S., Ashwin, C. and Williams, S. C. (2000). The amygdala theory of autism. *Neurosci. Biobehav. Rev.* **24**, 355–64.

Bates, E., Benigni, L., Bretherton, I., Camaioni, L. and Volterra, V. (1979). *The emergence of symbols: cognition and communication in infancy.* New York: Academic Press.

Bishop, D. V. M. (1997). Cognitive neuropsychology and developmental disorders: uncomfortable bedfellow. *Q. J. Exp. Psychol.* A **50**, 899–923.

Butterworth, G. E. and Adamson-Macedo, E. (1987). The origins of pointing: a pilot study. In *Annual Conference of the Developmental Psychology Section of the British Psychological Society York, September, UK.* [Abstract.]

Carpenter, M., Nagell, K. and Tomasello, M. (1998). Social cognition, joint attention and communicative competence from 9 to 15 months of age. *Monog. Soc. Res. Child Dev.* **63**, 1–143.

Charman, T. (1998). Specifying the nature and course of the joint attention impairment in autism in the preschool years: implications for diagnosis and intervention. *Autism* **2**, 61–79.

Charman, T. (2000). Theory of mind and the early diagnosis of autism. In *Understanding other minds: perspectives from autism and developmental cognitive neuroscience,* 2nd edn (ed. S. Baron-Cohen, H. Tager-Flusberg and D. Cohen), pp. 422–41. Oxford: Oxford University Press.

Charman, T. and Baird, G. (2002). Practitioner review: diagnosis of autism spectrum disorder in 2- and 3-year-old children. *J. Child Psychol. Psychiat.* **43**, 289–305.

Charman, T. and Swettenham, J. (2001). Repetitive behaviors and social-communicative impairments in autism: implications for developmental theory and diagnosis. In *The development of autism: perspectives from theory and research* (ed. J. A. Burack, T. Charman, N. Yirmiya and P. R. Zelazo), pp. 325–45. Hillsdale, NJ: Lawrence Erlbaum Associates.

Charman, T., Swettenham, J., Baron-Cohen, S., Cox, A., Baird, G. and Drew, A. (1997). Infants with autism: an investigation of empathy, pretend play, joint attention and imitation. *Devl Psychol.* **33**, 781–89.

Charman, T., Baron-Cohen, S., Swettenham, J., Cox, A., Baird, G. and Drew, A. (1998). An experimental investigation of social-cognitive abilities in infants with autism: clinical implications. *Infant Mental Hlth J.* **19**, 260–75.

Charman, T., Baron-Cohen, S., Swettenham, J., Baird, G., Cox, A. and Drew, A. (2000). Testing joint attention, imitation and play as infancy precursors to language and theory of mind. *Cogn. Dev.* **15**, 481–98.

Cox, A., Klein, K., Charman, T., Baird, G., Baron-Cohen, S., Swettenham, J., *et al.* (1999). Autism spectrum disorders at 20 and 42 months of age: stability of clinical and ADI-R diagnosis. *J. Child Psychol. Psychiat.* **40**, 719–32.

Dawson, G. and Lewy, A. (1989). Arousal, attention and the social impairments of individuals with autism. In *Autism: nature, diagnosis and treatment* (ed. G. Dawson), pp. 49–74. New York: Guilford Press.

Dawson, G., Meltzoff, A. N., Osterling, J., Rinaldi, J. and Brown, E. (1998). Children with autism fail to orient to naturally occurring social stimuli. *J. Autism Devl Disord.* **28**, 479–85.

Dawson, G., Munson, J., Estes, A., Osterling, J., McPartland, J., Toth, K., *et al.* (2002). Neurocognitive function and joint attention ability in young children with autism spectrum disorder versus developmental delay. *Child Dev.* **73**, 345–58.

Dietz, C., Willemsen-Swinkels, S. H. N., Buitelaar, J. K., van Daalen, E. and van Engeland, H. (2001). Early detection of autism: population screening. Presentation at the *Bienn. Meeting Soc. Res. Child Development, Minneapolis, April.*

Gillberg, C., Ehlers, S., Schaumann, H., Jakobsson, G., Dahlgren, S. O., Lindblom, R., *et al.* (1990). Autism under age 3 years: a clinical study of 28 cases referred for autistic symptoms in infancy. *J. Child Psychol. Psychiat.* **31**, 921–34.

Gómez, J. C., Sarria, E. and Tamarit, J. (1993). The comparative study of early communication and theories of mind: ontogeny, phylogeny and pathology. In *Understanding other minds: perspectives from autism* (ed. S. Baron-Cohen, H. Tager-Flusberg and D. Cohen), pp. 397–426. Oxford: Oxford University Press.

Greenough, W. T., Black, J. E. and Wallace, C. S. (1987). Experience and brain development. *Child Dev.* **58**, 539–59.

Griffith, E. M., Pennington, B. F., Wehner, E. A. and Rogers, S. J. (1999). Executive functions in young children with autism. *Child Dev.* **70**, 817–32.

Griffiths, R. (1986). *The abilities of babies.* London: University of London Press.

Happé, F. (1999). Autism: cognitive deficit or cognitive style? *Trends Cogn. Sci.* **3**, 216–22.

Hobson, R. P. (1993). *Autism and the development of mind.* London: Lawrence Erlbaum.

Karmiloff-Smith, A. (1997). Crucial differences between developmental cognitive neuroscience and adult neuropsychology. *Devl Neuropsychol.* **13**, 513–24.

Kasari, C., Freeman, S. F. N. and Paparella, T. (2001). Early intervention in autism: joint attention and symbolic play. *Int. Rev. Res. Mental Retard.* **23**, 207–37.

Klin, A., Jones, W., Schultz, R., Volkmar, F. and Cohen, D. (2002*a*). Defining and quantifying the social phenotype in autism. *Am. J. Psychiat.* **159**, 895–908.

Klin, A., Jones, W., Schultz, R., Volkmar, F. and Cohen, D. (2002*b*). Visual fixation patterns during viewing of naturalistic social situations as predictive of social competence in individuals with autism. *Arch. Gen. Psychiat.* **59**, 809–16.

Koegel, L. K. (2000). Interventions to facilitate communication in autism. *J. Autism Devl Disord.* **30**, 383–91.

Leekam, S. and Moore, C. (2001). The development of attention and joint attention in children with autism. In *The development of autism: perspectives from theory and research* (ed. J. A. Burack, T. Charman, N. Yirmiya and P. R. Zelazo), pp. 105–29. Hillsdale, NJ: Lawrence Erlbaum Associates.

Leekam, S. R., López, B. and Moore, C. (2000). Attention and joint attention in preschool children with autism. *Devl Psychol.* **36**, 261–73.

Leiter, R. G. (1952). *Leiter international performance scale.* Wood Dale, IL: Stoetling.

Lewis, V. and Boucher, J. (1988). Spontaneous, instructed and elicited play in relatively able autistic children. *Br. J. Devl Psychol.* **6**, 325–39.

Lord, C. (2000). Commentary: achievements and future directions for intervention in communication and autism spectrum disorders. *J. Autism Devl Disord.* **30**, 393–398.

Lord, C. and Bailey, A. (2002). Autism spectrum disorders. In *Child and adolescent psychiatry: modern approaches*, 4th edn (ed. M. Rutter and E. Taylor), pp. 636–63. Oxford: Blackwell Scientific.

Lord, C. and Risi, S. (1998). Frameworks and methods in diagnosing autism spectrum disorders. *Mental Retard. Devl Disab. Res. Rev.* **4**, 90–96.

Lord, C., Rutter, M. and Le Couteur, A. (1994). Autism diagnostic interview-revised. *J. Autism Devl Disord.* **24**, 659–686.

Meltzoff, A. N. (1988). Infant imitation and memory: ninemonth-olds in immediate and deferred tests. *Child Dev.* **59**, 217–25.

Milne, E., Swettenham, J., Hansen, P., Campbell, R., Jeffries, H. and Plaisted, K. (2002). High motion coherence thresholds in children with autism. *J. Child Psychol. Psychiat.* **43**, 255–63.

Minshew, N. J., Luna, B. and Sweeney, J. A. (1999). Oculomotor evidence for neocortical systems but not cerebellar dysfunction in autism. *Neurology* **52**, 917–22.

Mundy, P. (1995). Joint attention and social-emotional approach behavior in children with autism. *Dev. Psychopathol.* **7**, 63–82.

Mundy, P. and Crowson, M. (1997). Joint attention and early social communication: implications for research on intervention with autism. *J. Autism Devl Disord.* **27**, 653–76.

Mundy, P. and Gomes, A. (1996). Individual differences in joint attention skill development in the second year. *Infant Behav. Dev.* **21**, 469–82.

Mundy, P. and Neal, R. (2001). Neural plasticity; joint attention and autistic developmental pathology. *Int. Rev. Res. Mental Retard.* **23**, 139–68.

Mundy, P., Sigman, M., Ungerer, J. and Sherman, T. (1986). Defining the social deficits of autism: the contribution of non-verbal communication measures. *J. Child Psychol. Psychiat.* **27**, 657–69.

Mundy, P., Sigman, M. and Kasari, C. (1990). A longitudinal study of joint attention and language development in autistic children. *J. Autism Devl Disord.* **20**, 115–28.

Mundy, P., Sigman, M. and Kasari, C. (1993). The theory of mind and joint attention in autism. In *Understanding other minds: perspectives from autism* (ed. S. Baron-Cohen, H. Tager-Flusberg and D. Cohen), pp. 181–203. Oxford: Oxford University Press.

Mundy, P., Sigman, M. and Kasari, C. (1994). Joint attention, developmental level, and symptom presentation in young children with autism. *Devl Psychopathol.* **6**, 389–401.

National Research Council (2001). *Educating children with autism. Committee on educational interventions for children with autism*. Division of Behavioral and Social Sciences and Education. Washington, DC: National Academy Press.

Ohta, M., Nagai, Y., Hara, H. and Sasaki, M. (1987). Parental perception of behavioral symptoms in Japanese autistic children. *J. Autism Devl Disord.* **17**, 549–63.

Osterling, J. and Dawson, G. (1994). Early recognition of children with autism: a study of first birthday home videotapes. *J. Autism Devl Disord.* **24**, 247–57.

Osterling, J. A., Dawson, G. and Munson, J. A. (2002). Early recognition of 1-year-old infants with autism spectrum disorder versus mental retardation. *Devl Psychopathol.* **14**, 239–51.

Phillips, W., Baron-Cohen, S. and Rutter, M. (1992). The role of eye-contact in goal-detection: evidence from normal toddlers and children with autism or mental handicap. *Devl Psychopathol.* **4**, 375–84.

Phillips, W., Gómez, J. C., Baron-Cohen, S., Laá, V. and Riviére, A. (1995). Treating people as objects, agents, or 'subjects': how children with autism make requests. *J. Child Psychol. Psychiat.* **36**, 1383–98.

Plaisted, K. C., Swettenham, J. and Rees, L. (1999). Children with autism show local precedence in a divided attention task and global preference in a selective attention task. *J. Child Psychol. Psychiat.* **40**, 733–42.

Reynell, J. K. (1985). *Reynell developmental language scales*, 2nd edn. Windsor, UK: NFER Nelson.

Ricks, D. N. and Wing, L. (1975). Language, communication, and symbols in normal and autistic children. *J. Autism Child Schizophrenia* **5**, 191–22.

Robins, D. L., Fein, D., Barton, M. L. and Green, J. A. (2001). The modified checklist for autism in toddlers: an initial study investigating the early detection of autism and pervasive developmental disorders. *J. Autism Devl Disord.* **31**, 131–44.

Rogers, S. (2001). Diagnosis of autism before the age of 3. *Int. Rev. Mental Retard.* **23**, 1–31.

Rogers, S. and Lewis, H. (1989). An effective day treatment model for young children with pervasive developmental disorders. *J. Am. Acad. Child Adol. Psychiat.* **28**, 207–14.

Rollins, P. R., Wambacq, I., Dowell, D., Mathews, L. and Reese, P. B. (1998). An intervention technique for children with autistic spectrum disorders: joint attentional routines. *J. Commun. Disord.* **31**, 181–93.

Scambler, D., Rogers, S. J. and Wehner, E. A. (2001). Can the checklist for autism in toddlers differentiate young children with autism from those with developmental delays? *J. Am. Acad. Child Adol. Psychiat.* **40**, 1457–63.

Schopler, E., Reichler, R. J., DeVellis, R. and Daly, K. (1980). Towards objective classification of childhood autism: childhood autism rating scale (CARS). *J. Autism Devl Disord.* **10**, 91–103.

Sigman, M., Mundy, P., Sherman, T. and Ungerer, J. (1986). Social interactions of autistic, mentally retarded and normal children and their caregivers. *J. Child Psychol. Psychiat.* **27**, 647–56.

Sigman, M. and Ruskin, E. (1999). Continuity and change in the social competence of children with autism, Down syndrome and developmental delays. *Monogr. Soc. Res. Child Dev.* **64**, 1–114.

Siller, M. and Sigman, M. (2002). The behaviors of parents of children with autism predict the subsequent development of their children's communication. *J. Autism Devl Disord.* **32**, 77–89.

Stone, W. L. and Yoder, P. J. (2001). Predicting spoken language in children with autistic spectrum disorders. *Autism* **5**, 341–61.

Stone, W. L., Hoffman, E. L., Lewis, S. E. and Ousley, O. Y. (1994). Early recognition of autism: parental reports vs. clinical observation. *Arch. Ped. Adol. Med.* **148**, 174–79.

Stone, W. L., Ously, O. Y. and Littleford, C. D. (1997). Motor imitation in young children with autism: what's the object? *J. Abn. Child Psychol.* **25**, 475–85.

Stone, W. L., Lee, E. B., Ashford, L., Brissie, J., Hepburn, S. L., Coonrod, E. E., *et al.* (1999). Can autism be diagnosed accurately in children under three years? *J. Child Psychol. Psychiat.* **40**, 219–26.

Swettenham, J., Baron-Cohen, S., Charman, T., Cox, A., Baird, G., Drew, A., *et al.* (1998). The frequency and distribution of spontaneous attention shifts between social and non-social stimuli in autistic, typicallydeveloping and non-autistic developmentally delayed infants. *J. Child Psychol. Psychiat.* **39**, 747–54.

Tanguay, P. E., Robertson, J. and Derrick, A. (1998). A dimensional classification of autism spectrum disorder by social communication domains. *J. Am. Acad. Child Adol. Psychiat.* **37**, 271–77.

Tomasello, M. (1995). Joint attention as social cognition. In *Joint attention: its origins and role in development* (ed. C. Moore and P. Dunham), pp. 85–101. Hillsdale, NJ: Lawrence Erlbaum Associates.

Tomasello, M. and Farrar, M. J. (1986). Joint attention and early language. *Child Dev.* **57**, 1454–63.

Townsend, J., Harris, N. S. and Courchesne, E. (1996). Visual attention abnormalities in autism: delayed orienting to location. *J. Int. Neuropsychol. Soc.* **2**, 541–50.

Werner, E., Dawson, G., Osterling, J. and Dinno, N. (2000). Brief report: recognition of autism spectrum disorder before one year of age: a retrospective study based on home videotapes. *J. Autism Devl Disord.* **30**, 157–62.

World Health Organization (1993). *Mental disorders: a glossary and guide to their classification in accordance with the 10th revision of the international classification of diseases: research diagnostic criteria (ICD-10).* Geneva: World Health Organization.

Glossary

ADI: autism diagnostic interview
ADI-R: autism diagnostic interview—revised
CHAT: CHecklist for Autism in Toddlers
EL: expressive language
IQ: intelligence quotient
NVC: non-verbal communication
RL: receptive language
RSB: repetitive and stereotyped behaviour
RSI: reciprocal social interaction

5

Does the perception of moving eyes trigger reflexive visual orienting in autism?

John Swettenham, Samantha Condie, Ruth Campbell,
Elizabeth Milne, and Mike Coleman

Does movement of the eyes in one or another direction function as an automatic attentional cue to a location of interest? Two experiments explored the directional movement of the eyes in a full face for speed of detection of an aftercoming location target in young people with autism and in control participants. Our aim was to investigate whether a low-level perceptual impairment underlies the delay in gaze following characteristic of autism. The participants' task was to detect a target appearing on the left or right of the screen either 100 ms or 800 ms after a face cue appeared with eyes averting to the left or right. Despite instructions to ignore eye-movement in the face cue, people with autism and control adolescents were quicker to detect targets that had been preceded by an eye movement cue *congruent* with target location compared with targets preceded by an *incongruent* eye movement cue. The attention shifts are thought to be reflexive because the cue was to be ignored, and because the effect was found even when cue–target duration was short (100 ms). Because (experiment two) the effect persisted even when the face was inverted, it would seem that the direction of movement of eyes can provide a powerful (involuntary) cue to a location.

Keywords: autism; visual orienting; joint attention; perception; face processing

5.1 Introduction

The ability to follow another person's direction of gaze arises in infancy and marks an important breakthrough in the development of social communication (Butterworth and Jarrett 1991; Corkum and Moore 1995; Emery 2000). Although infants are sensitive to whether others are making direct eye contact with them (mutual gaze) from birth (Bakti *et al.* 2000; Farroni *et al.* 2002), and respond to eye contact with smiles and teasing facial expressions during the first few months (Aitken and Trevarthen 1997), it is not until at least four months of age that they can perceive the movement in another's gaze shift as a directional cue, facilitating saccadic reaction time to targets appearing in the visual field (Hood *et al.* 1998; Farroni *et al.* 2000). By nine months, infants can use another's head turn to search for an object at a particular location even when that object is not present (Corkum and Moore 1998), and by 18 months they can use eye movements alone as cues to follow direction of gaze (Butterworth and Jarrett 1991). The gaze direction of another person can be important not only because it may reveal an interesting location or object in the environment, but also because it reveals what another person is attending to. Gaze following can therefore allow the infant to establish triadic joint attention with others, whereby the child becomes aware that both itself and the other person are attending to the same object (Butterworth and Jarrett 1991). The developing child's gaze-following behaviour and engagement in triadic joint attention is commonly thought to be important for language and social development (Baron-Cohen 1995).

There is now considerable evidence that children with autism are impaired in the processing of gaze. Lack of gaze following is apparent in autism at 18 months of age, one of the earliest detectable symptoms (Baron-Cohen *et al.* 1996; Baird *et al.* 2000), and an insensitivity to direction of gaze is reflected in impairments in joint attention: the ability to coordinate attention between people and objects (Curcio 1978; Loveland and Landry 1986; Baron-Cohen 1989; Mundy *et al.* 1994; Lord 1995; Leekam *et al.* 1997). Although some children with autism eventually develop the ability to follow gaze (particularly if they have an IQ of 70 or above), the onset of this ability is still severely delayed relative to children of equivalent mental age (Leekam *et al.* 1998, 2000).

Two main views have emerged regarding the origins of the joint attention impairment in autism. One is that the origin of the impairment is *affective*. According to this view children with autism have difficulty engaging in joint attention either as a result of a deficit in intersubjective relatedness (see Hobson 1993), or because of a deficit in social-emotional approach (see Mundy 1995). The other view is that the impairment is *cognitive*. The origin of the impairment, according to this view, is in understanding and representing the psychological relationship between oneself, another person and an object: that oneself and another person are 'attending' to the same object (Baron-Cohen 1995).

More recently, a third view has emerged, that children with autism may have a low-level *attentional* or *perceptual* impairment affecting their ability to make a response to another's head or eye movements. It is this theory that has informed the studies reported here. Leekam and Moore (2001) point out that even if children with autism have difficulty understanding another person's focus of attention or experience, it is still surprising that they do not at least use gaze as an instrumental cue to the location of an object or event in the environment. For example, Povinelli and Eddy (1997) have shown that chimpanzees can use gaze direction as a cue to the location of an object, even though they do not initiate joint attention acts like pointing and showing (Tomasello *et al.* 1993) and are unlikely to be representing another's attention or sharing affective experience when following gaze. Leekam and colleagues therefore tested the ability to execute shifts of overt attention in young children with autism by measuring head turn responses to mechanical objects or the viewed head turn of the experimenter. They found that low-functioning children with autism were able to overtly disengage attention and turn to look from a centrally viewed object towards an object appearing in peripheral vision (Leekam *et al.* 2000). In such a task, attention can be automatically captured by the target appearing in the periphery. It was therefore argued that exogenous orienting and the ability to disengage from a central stimulus may be intact. Exogenous orienting refers to a reflexive system driven by the physical characteristics of the information in the visual field (Posner 1980) and is characteristic of attention in the early months of normal development (Atkinson *et al.* 1992). However, the same children with autism had difficulty overtly shifting attention from a face to search for an object not present in the visual field (Leekam *et al.* 1998). This task, they argued, involved interpreting the meaning of the cue as a predictor of location (particularly as the target was absent). The results therefore indicated an impairment in endogenous orienting. Endogenous orienting is considered to be goal directed and under voluntary control, involving cognitive interpretation of stimuli and the formation of expectation from predictive cues (Jonides 1981; Lauwereyns 1998), and it seems to develop later in the first year of life (Gilmore and Johnson 1995).

Evidence from the attentional literature on autism, using non-social stimuli and testing adolescents or adults has also indicated an attentional impairment in autism, but the pattern of intact exogenous orienting and impaired endogenous orienting is less clear. In these non-social tasks measures are typically of covert orienting (rather than overt head turns) and involve verbal instruction and key presses in response to the detection of targets on a computer display. Although the disadvantage of these studies is that they can only be used with older adolescents or adults who understand the instructions, the advantage is that they do not rely on overt head turns or looking behaviour as measures. This may be important because it is possible to orient attention even without making a head turn or eye movement. In addition they can identify subtle differences in the efficiency of attentional orienting by measuring reaction time and accuracy under highly controlled conditions. With respect to exogenous orienting the results are mixed, some studies suggesting an impairment and others suggesting intact orienting response to visual or auditory stimuli (Courchesne *et al.* 1985, 1994; Rincover and Ducharme 1987; Burack and Iarocci 1995; Townsend *et al.* 1996; Wainwright and Bryson 1996). Studies of endogenous orienting, for example where a central arrow cue indicates the location of an oncoming target, have also suggested that individuals with autism have difficulty shifting attention efficiently to a peripheral target (Casey *et al.* 1993; Wainwright-Sharp and Bryson 1993). However, it remains unclear whether this is because of a difficulty in disengaging attention from a central cue, or in forming an expectation from the 'symbolic' central arrow cue (Burack *et al.* 1997).

The attentional literature using non-social stimuli indicates impairments in attentional orienting in autism, but how might this relate to attentional orienting in response to faces? Recent work using adaptations of traditional cueing tasks indicate that head and face cues may elicit a reflexive orienting response in an adult viewer: a result not traditionally found in response to non-social cues (Friesen and Kingstone 1998; Driver *et al.* 1999; Hietanen 1999; Langton and Bruce 1999; Vuilleumier 2002). In other words a directional face cue is a special sort of stimulus which is hard to ignore, rapidly and reflexively effecting a shift of attention in a viewer in the direction of seen gaze. Whether this is because of an innate mechanism or whether the automatic cueing effects are acquired through experience (overlearning) remains controversial (Vecera and Johnson 1995). In either case it is important to know whether gaze direction cues reflexive orienting in children with autism. If gaze direction has a special reflexive orienting effect in typically developing children, but not children with autism, then this would indicate a failure to develop a specialized reflexive response in children with autism.

The experiments reported here therefore examine whether perceived gaze direction can elicit reflexive shifts of spatial attention in children with autism. Our questions were as follows: is the special mechanism present in normal adults, eliciting reflexive shifts of attention in response to perceived gaze direction, present in normally developing children? Is this mechanism working to the same extent in children with autism?

The cueing tasks that have demonstrated these reflexive orienting effects in normal adults (Friesen and Kingstone 1998; Driver *et al.* 1999; Hietanen 1999; Langton and Bruce 1999; Vuilleumier 2002) typically involve detecting a target stimulus that appears either to the left or right of the screen shortly after the appearance of a centrally placed directional face cue. In some cases the cue used has been a directional head profile and in others it has been averted eyes within a full face. On each trial the gaze direction of the cue is either congruent with target location (validly predicting location) or incongruent (invalid). The consistent finding has been that even when the gaze cue is *not predictive* overall (i.e. only valid on 50% of trials), and participants are told to ignore it, attention is still recruited to the location congruent with gaze direction, indicating that the allocation of attention is *reflexive*. The viewer is unable to ignore the gaze direction cue. Therefore targets appearing at locations congruent with gaze direction are responded to more quickly than incongruently cued targets.

5.2 Experiment one

In the first experiment, we examined the influence of the to-be-ignored eye movement cue on the speeded detection of an aftercoming target. The full face cue appeared in the centre of the screen and the eyes moved to the left or right. After a delay of either 100 ms or 800 ms a target stimulus appeared to the left or right of the screen. The use of variable delay meant that it was not possible to predict when the target would appear. If the viewer cannot resist shifting attention in direction of gaze this would be reflected in faster detection of validly cued target compared with an invalidly cued target. This would indicate a reflexive attention shift. If spatial cueing effects were found even after a short duration delay of 100 ms, allowing little time to prepare a voluntary attention shift, this would be even stronger evidence that the cue triggers reflexive shifts of attention. The dependent variable was speed of response to detect the target.

We predicted that the perceived direction of eye movement would reflexively trigger attention shifts in the typically developing children but our predictions were open with respect to children with autism.

(a) Methods

(i) Participants

Fifteen high-functioning children with autism and 15 typically developing children took part in the study. The children with autism had all been diagnosed using the ADI-R (Lord *et al.* 1994) and all met established criteria for autism, as specified in DSM-IV (American Psychiatric Association 1994). Each child with autism was individually matched to a typically developing child according to chronological age and raw score on the Raven's progressive matrices (a non-verbal IQ test). Participants were aged between 8 years, eight months and 11 years, two months. Table 5.1 shows the mean chronological age and Raven's matrices raw score for the two groups of children. Independent sample *t*-tests revealed that there were no significant group differences in either chronological age ($t = -0.57, p = 0.96$), or Raven's matrices ($t = -0.18$, $p = 0.99$).

(ii) Materials

Digital grey-scale photographs of a male face were used as the cues. The face was 70 mm in height presented on a lap-top computer monitor. Five images of a face were used. In all the images the head was facing forwards. In the first

Table 5.1 Mean (and s.d.) chronological age and Raven's progessive matrices scores for the group of children with autism and typically developing children

group	age (years:months)	Raven's matrices scores
autism ($n = 15$)		
mean	10:2	37.6
(s.d.)	(0:9)	(10.3)
control ($n = 15$)		
mean	10:2	37.7
(s.d.)	(0:9)	(10.4)

image the eyes were central (looking forward); and in the four remaining images the eyes were averted increasingly to the left. Mirror images of these five photographs were also used, with eyes therefore averted to the right. The 'eyes forward' image followed by rapid presentation of the four images with eyes increasingly averted laterally created the impression of eyes moving (looking) to one side. There was also a fixation cross (0.5 cm $\times$ 0.5 cm) and a target asterisk (0.5 cm $\times$ 0.5 cm). The display was viewed 60 cm away from a 15 inch monitor.

(iii) Procedure
Participants were asked to press the space bar on the keyboard, as quickly as they could, when they detected a target asterisk on the screen. The asterisk would appear on each trial to the right or left of a centrally placed face cue. Participants were told that on each trial the face would appear and the eyes would look either to the left or to the right. It was emphasized that the face would provide no information about where the asterisk would appear, but that they should keep looking at the face throughout each trial. Participants then received 10 practice trials, and the experimenter checked carefully that the child had understood the task.

The sequence of events for each trial was as follows: a central cross appeared as a fixation point for either 1000 ms or 2000 ms. The random duration of the fixation point was intended to stop participants from anticipating the cue onset. The face then appeared on the screen, with eyes forward, for 500 ms. The eyes 'looked' to the left or right (56 ms total, each brief display lasting 14 ms), and then following a delay between cue and target of either 100 ms or 800 ms an asterisk appeared on either the left or right of the screen. Both cue and target remained on the screen until the participant made a response. Each response was followed by an inter-trial interval of 1000 ms, and then the fixation point appeared again marking the onset of a new trial. Figure 5.1a,b illustrates the sequence of events for an example trial.

The experiment consisted of four blocks of 64 trials. The direction of eye gaze provided a valid cue to the location of the target on 50% of the trials. The direction of gaze (left or right), location of target asterisk (left or right), and the length of SOA (100 ms or 800 ms) were randomly generated but equiprobable in appearance. Anticipatory responses (less than 100 ms before target appearance) and responses that were too long (more than 1500 ms) were followed by a warning method and excluded from the analysis. These error trials were replaced with repeat trials.

(b) Results

We aimed to examine whether the gaze cue produced a *validity effect*: i.e. when the target appeared in a position indicated by the gaze cue (valid) its processing should be relatively more efficient (e.g. faster detection) than when it was not. The median reaction times were derived for each participant for each condition (valid/invalid; 100 ms/800 ms SOA). Figure 5.2 shows the mean median reaction times for each group. The validity effect at each SOA can be seen by the difference in reaction time to valid versus invalidly cued targets.

The data were analysed using ANOVA with one between-subjects factor of group (autism, typically developing) and two within-subjects factors of cue validity (valid, invalid) and SOA (100 ms, 800 ms).

ANOVA revealed a main effect of validity ($F_{(1,28)} = 13.41, p < 0.01$) indicating that participants in both groups were faster to respond to valid versus invalidly cued targets. Both groups were affected by the eye gaze cue. There was also a main effect of SOA ($F_{(1,28)} = 26.26, p < 0.01$) indicating that participants were faster overall to respond to targets appearing 800 ms after the cue onset compared with targets appearing at 100 ms SOA. In addition, there was a group by SOA interaction ($F_{(1,28)} = 4.98, p < 0.05$); *post hoc* analysis using Tukey's HSD revealed that typically developing children made faster

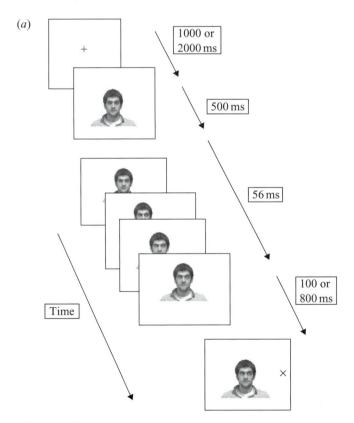

Fig. 5.1   (*Continued.*)

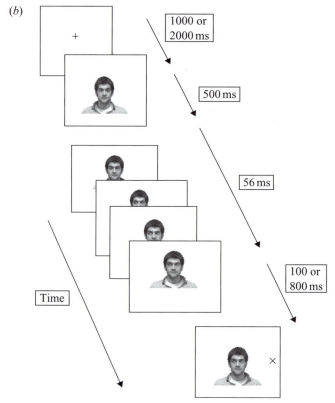

Fig. 5.1   Frame by frame sequence of events presented on the computer: (*a*) upright face, valid trials; and (*b*) upright face, invalid trials.

responses at 800 ms SOA than children with autism ($p < 0.05$). There was no group difference at 100 ms SOA.

(c) Discussion

In this experiment perceived direction of gaze triggered reflexive orienting in both the typically developing children and the children with autism. It is likely that the orienting effects were reflexive for two reasons. First, the effects were found even though the perceived direction of eye gaze was random with the respect to the location of the target and the participants were aware that the direction of eye gaze should be ignored. Second, the effects were found even when the delay between the eyes moving and the onset of the target was short (100 ms SOA) allowing little time for a voluntary cognitive strategy to be

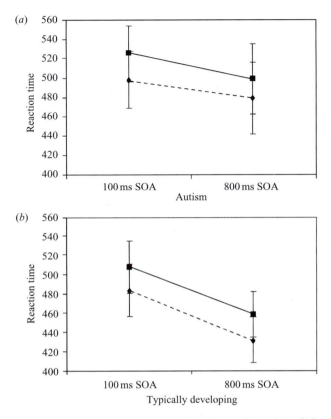

Fig. 5.2 Mean median reaction times for validly (diamonds) and invalidly (squares) cued targets in (*a*) children with autism and (*b*) typically developing children. Upright face (error bar, 1 s.e.m.).

recruited. Typically, reflexive orienting effects are found with a short duration between cue and target (Posner 1980). These data provide powerful evidence for the existence of a specialized mechanism, present in both typically developing and autistic children, which results in a reflexive orienting response to perceived direction of gaze. No evidence was found here supporting the hypothesis that the delay in the development of gaze is due to a perceptual or attentional impairment.

We also found a small but significant interaction between group and SOA, so that when the cue–target delay is 800 ms, the children with autism tended to respond more slowly, regardless of whether the cue was valid or invalid. Despite the instruction to ignore the cue, and the randomness of validity, participants may still follow gaze direction voluntarily at 800 ms SOA because the longer delay allows for the recruitment of voluntary attention. One possibility is that for longer duration cue–target intervals, voluntary orienting mechanisms could be recruited on at least some trials. If this were the case then the generally slower responses of the autistic children at 800 ms SOA might reflect impairments in voluntarily orienting attention (Wainwright-Sharp and Bryson 1993; Wainwright and Bryson 1996). However, a simpler explanation for the slower responses to longer SOAs might be that children with autism are slower to prepare and initiate any response to an imperative cue, independent of the context of attentional shifts or social gaze processing.

5.3 Experiment two

The reflexive orienting effect found in experiment one indicates that perception and attentional orienting are intact in high-functioning adolescents with autism at least for responses to eye direction in a face. However, despite the similarity in orienting responses of the two groups, it is still possible that they were perceiving the face stimuli differently (see Grelotti *et al.* (2002) for a review of face perception in autism). Research on general perceptual processing in autism has revealed a preference for processing individual features rather than global properties (Frith 1989). One possibility is that the children with autism are perceiving two moving features, while the typically developing children are perceiving eyes moving in the context of the configuration of the whole face. If this were the case then we might expect the two groups to respond differently when the face is inverted. For example, when the face cue is inverted, accuracy judgements of gaze direction are disrupted (Campbell *et al.* 1990) and the reflexive orienting effect is reduced in normal adults (Langton and Bruce 1999).

Our second experiment used an inverted face stimulus with moving eyes. Our prediction was that the children with autism would continue to be cued by the direction of eye movement even within an inverted face, as people with autism are relatively insensitive to face configuration (Langdell 1978; Volkmar *et al.* 1989; Davies *et al.* 1994). However, in normally developing children, the upright face may be an important determinant of sensitivity to gaze, so that inverting the face abolishes the validity effect.

(a) Methods

The participants who took part in experiment one also took part in experiment two (see Table 5.1 for details). The second experiment differed from the first only in that an inverted version of the face cue with moving eyes was used as a cue (see Fig. 5.3*a,b*). In all other respects the procedures were the same.

(b) Results

The median reaction times for each participant were derived for each condition (valid/invalid; 100 ms/800 ms SOA) for the inverted face stimuli. Figure 5.4

shows the mean median reaction times for each group. The validity effect at each SOA can be seen by the difference in reaction time to valid versus invalidly cued targets.

The data were analysed using ANOVA with one between-subjects factor of group (autism, typically developing) and two within-subjects factors of cue validity (valid, invalid) and SOA (100 ms, 800 ms).

ANOVA revealed a main effect of validity ($F_{(1,28)} = 27.67$, $p < 0.01$) indicating that participants in both groups were faster to respond to valid versus invalidly cued targets. Both groups were affected by the inverted eye gaze cue. There was also a main effect of SOA ($F_{(1,28)} = 30.07$, $p < 0.01$) indicating that participants were faster overall to respond to targets appearing 800 ms after the cue onset compared with targets appearing at 100 ms SOA. There were no significant interactions and no main effect of group.

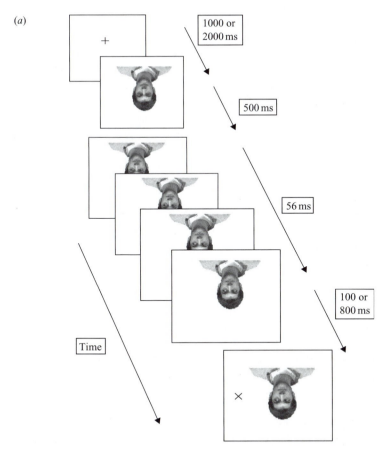

Fig. 5.3 (*Continued.*)

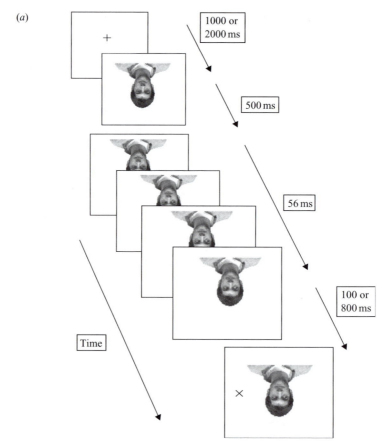

Fig. 5.3   Frame by frame sequence of events presented on the computer: (*a*) inverted
face, valid trials; and (*b*) inverted face, invalid trials.

(c) Discussion

The results of experiment two revealed that both the typically developing children and the children with autism were unable to resist the eye movement cue,
even in an inverted face. Both groups were faster to detect targets appearing
on the side of the screen towards which the eyes moved, compared with the
opposite side. This was despite the fact that the direction of movement was
random with respect to the location of the target, and participants had been
told to ignore the cue. Moreover, this validity effect was found in both groups
when there was a short cue–target delay of 100 ms as well as a longer cue–
target delay of 800 ms. The result indicates that the moving eyes trigger rapid
reflexive shifts of visual attention.

   We had hypothesized that inverting the face might eliminate the reflexive
cueing effect of the moving eyes in typically developing children but not the

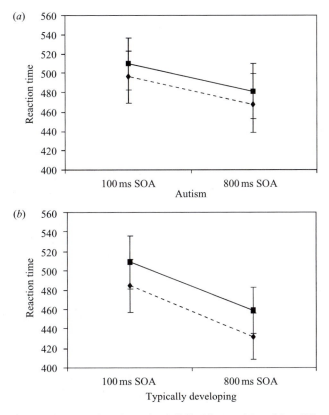

Fig. 5.4 Mean median reaction times for validly (diamonds) and invalidly (squares) cued targets in (*a*) children with autism and (*b*) typically developing children. Inverted face (error bar, 1 s.e.m.).

children with autism. This prediction was made because the face appears to lose configural information when inverted, disrupting face processing in typically developing children but not autistic children (Langdell 1978; Volkmar *et al.* 1989; Davies *et al.* 1994). In addition, Langton and Bruce (1999) have reported that inverting the face cue significantly reduces the strength of the reflexive cueing effect in adult viewers. Looking at experiment two compared with experiment one, both groups maintained reflexive cueing effects with the inverted cue, and showed an equally strong validity effect (faster responses to valid rather than invalid trials). Although it was somewhat surprising that the face inversion did not suppress reflexive gaze effects (particularly in the control group), this may have been because the stimuli were repeatedly displayed. Face inversion experiments do not normally involve such a large number of presentations. Alternatively, the perception of eye movements independent of face configuration may be producing the reflexive orienting effects in both groups. It would be interesting, for example, to test whether eyes alone (i.e. not in a face) trigger reflexive orienting.

5.4 General discussion

In two experiments this study showed that children with autism, when matched to a group of typically developing children, show an equal sensitivity to the disruptive effect of a gaze cue. Neither group were able to ignore an incongruent cue, reflexively orienting in the direction of seen gaze. The reflexive response would seem to be insensitive to facial configuration because the effects are similar in both experiments one and two. We were surprised that there were so few group differences in our findings. One interpretation of this could be that our tasks and analyses were relatively insensitive to any possible group differences. However, the mean reaction times with similar standard deviations in the two groups seemed to us to indicate that our tasks were sensitive to any group differences should these be present. The one small group difference that we did find was in experiment one: children with autism were slower than typically developing children to respond in general to cues presented at 800 ms SOA. The simplest explanation for this result would be that children with autism are slower to prepare and initiate any response to an imperative cue, independent of the context of gaze processing or attention shifting.

Children with autism are impaired in a range of joint attention behaviours (Curcio 1978; Loveland and Landry 1986; Landry and Loveland 1988; Baron-Cohen 1989; Mundy *et al.* 1994; Lord 1995; Charman *et al.* 1997; Leekam *et al.* 1997, 2000). One of the earliest recognizable symptoms is an absence of gaze following (Baron-Cohen *et al.* 1996; Baird *et al.* 2000). Direction of gaze is an important social signal (Argyle and Cook 1976; Kleinke 1986), indicating the location of objects or events that others are attending to. A delay in the development of gaze following could be expected to impair the development of subsequent social communication skills, including theory of mind (Baron-Cohen 1995). Recent work with autistic individuals has suggested an attentional impairment which may underlie the joint attention impairment (Courchesne *et al.* 1985; Rincover and Ducharme 1987; Casey *et al.* 1993; Wainwright-Sharp and Bryson 1993; Burack and Iarocci 1995; Wainwright and Bryson 1996; Leekam *et al.* 1998, 2000). The study reported here looked specifically at attentional orienting in response to gaze direction cues to establish whether an attentional impairment might be the origin of the gaze-following impairment. Recent work in the literature about adult attention has shown that gaze direction cues may differ from non-social directional cues, such as arrows, in that they trigger reflexive orienting responses in the viewer (Friesen and Kingstone 1998; Driver *et al.* 1999; Hietanen 1999; Langton and Bruce 1999; Vuilleumier 2002). We therefore decided to test whether moving eyes in a full face would trigger reflexive shifts of attention in the children with autism and typically developing children.

Our initial hypotheses were open with respect to autism, although given autistic children's behavioural delay in gaze following (Leekam *et al*. 1998), we suspected they may have shown reduced sensitivity to gaze direction in a face. However, we found strong evidence that moving eyes did trigger reflexive shifts of attention not only in typically developing children, but also in a group of children with autism.

If eye direction reflexively orients attention in children with autism, why have previous observational studies shown a lack of gaze following (Leekam *et al*. 1997, 2000)? First, previous studies have tested autistic children who are at an earlier stage of development (either in terms of chronological age or mental age). In other words, a developmental delay evident in early behaviour has been overcome in these older, high-functioning participants. Second, Leekam *et al*. measured overt attentional orienting (the child's own head turns) which may function independently of covert orienting measured in our tasks here. One interpretation is that the origin of the gaze-following deficit in general, is not related to a low-level perceptual or attentional deficit. Instead, the origin is either cognitive (e.g. Baron-Cohen 1995) or affective (Hobson 1993; Mundy 1995). However, our results do not rule out the possiblity that children with autism are *delayed* in the onset of a reflexive orienting response. It would be possible to test this by doing the same experiments with younger children.

The notion that the reflexive response may take longer to develop in people with autism would be consistent with the idea that it is acquired through over-learning. Lambert and Sumich (1996) have demonstrated using arbitrary pairings between word categories and side of a subsequent target, that learned associations between cue events and the subsequent position of targets can produce a reliable orienting response in normal adults, even when participants are unaware of contingency between cue and target. In the case of gaze direction, the repeated pairing of another person's direction of gaze and the location of interesting objects or events through extensive social experience may have resulted in association being so over-learned that it becomes reflexive. Given the evidence that early in development young children with autism look less at people (Swettenham *et al*. 1998) then we might expect them to only have enough exposure to acquire a reflexive response later in development. According to this view the reflexive response to gaze direction develops as a consequence of exposure to the association of seen gaze direction and objects. Children must first be following gaze before the reflexive response develops. The relationship between the development of overt gaze following and reflexive orienting could be tested in future experiments. A plausible *developmental* scenario could be that in all children an 'innate' or at least early sensitivity to direction of gaze (proto-reflexive orienting) operates to allow young infants to shift attention in response to gaze cues without further inferential work.

Indeed, this function may well be specific only to humans and some primate species (Emery 2000). However, the further development of this skill to sustain joint attention abilities involving the reading of intention in others (Baron-Cohen 1995) will depend on further developmental factors, some of which may be anomalous in people with autism. Thus, it may be possible for the young child with autism to follow the gaze of another to some extent and be 'captured' by the direction of gaze of another, although s/he may not be able to make further use of this skill.

Although the results suggest that moving eyes reflexively orient attention in the direction of seen gaze we cannot be sure from these experiments whether such effects are only found for moving *social* stimuli. The inclusion of a non-social but moving cue, matched for stimulus complexity, would be useful as a control condition in future experiments. It is also possible that other social cues including whole face orientation may produce different effects to eyes. For example, recent experiments indicate that a face profile may fail to produce a reflexive orienting response in children with autism (Swettenham *et al.* 2003).

Do our results mean that perception and attention in general are intact in autism? This still seems unlikely given the number of studies demonstrating perceptual and attentional impairments in autism (e.g. Courchesne *et al.* 1985; Rincover and Ducharme 1987; Casey *et al.* 1993; Wainwright-Sharp and Bryson 1993; Burack and Iarocci 1995; Wainwright and Bryson 1996). Our findings only apply to responses to eye direction, and given that gaze direction seems to elicit powerful effects not traditionally found in laboratory cueing tasks it would be unwise to generalize to other attentional studies. Our findings of no difference between the groups in the magnitude of the validity effect indicates that some exogenous orienting mechanisms, at least, may be intact in autism.

This research was conducted by S.C. as part of her final year BSc dissertation in the Department of Human Communication Science, UCL. The work reported here has developed from ESRC project no. R000222988 awarded to J.S., R.C. and Kate Plaisted. We are grateful to the teachers and children at The Marlborough Unit, Kent, and Roseacre Junior School.

References

Aitken, K. J. and Trevarthen, C. (1997). Self/other organization in human psychological development. *Devl Psychol.* **9**, 653–77.

American Psychiatric Association (1994). *Diagnostic and statistical manual of mental disorders*, 4th Edition (DSM-IV). Washington, DC: American Psychiatric Association.

Argyle, M. and Cook, M. (1976). *Gaze and mutual gaze*. Cambridge University Press.

Atkinson, J., Hood, B., Wattam-Bell, J. and Braddick, O. (1992). Changes in infants' ability to switch visual attention in the first three months of life. *Perception* **21**, 643–53.

Baird, G., Charman, T., Baron-Cohen, S., Cox, A., Swettenham, J., Wheelwright, S., *et al.* (2000). A screening instrument for autism at 18 months of age: a six year follow-up. *J. Am. Acad. Child Adolescent Psychiatry* **39**, 694–702.

Bakti, A., Baron-Cohen, S., Wheelwright, S., Connellan, J. and Ahluwalia, J. (2000). Is there an innate gaze module? Evidence from human neonates. *Infant Behav. Dev.* **23**, 223–29.

Baron-Cohen, S. (1989). Perceptual role taking and protodeclarative pointing in autism. *Br. J. Devl Psychol.* **7**, 113–27.

Baron-Cohen, S. (1995). *Mindblindness: an essay on autism and theory of mind.* Cambridge, MA: MIT Press.

Baron-Cohen, S., Cox, A., Baird, G., Swettenham, J., Nightingale, N., Morgan, K., *et al.* (1996). Psychological markers in the detection of autism in infancy in a large population. *Br. J. Psychiatry* **168**, 158–63.

Burack, J. A. and Iarocci, G. (1995). Visual filtering and covert orienting in devlopmentally disordered persons with and without autism. Paper presented at the meeting of the Society for Research in Child Development, Indianapolis, IN, March 1995.

Burack, J. A., Enns, J. T., Stauder, J. E. A., Mottron, L. and Randolph, B. (1997). Attention and autism: behavioural and electrophysiological evidence. In *Handbook of autism and developmental disorders*, 2nd edn (ed. D. J. Cohen and F. R. Volkmar), pp. 226–47. New York: Wiley.

Butterworth, G. and Jarrett, N. (1991). What minds have in common in space: spatial mechanisms serving joint visual attention in infancy. *Br. J. Devl Psychol.* **9**, 55–72.

Campbell, R., Heywood, C. A., Cowey, A., Regard, M. and Landis, T. (1990). Sensitivity to eye gaze in prosopagnosic patients and monkeys with superior temporal sulcus ablation. *Neuropsychologia* **28**, 1123–42.

Casey, B. J., Gordon, C. T., Mannheim, G. T. and Rumsey, J. M. (1993). Dysfunctional attention in autistic savants. *J. Clin. Exp. Neuropsychol.* **15**, 933–46.

Charman, T., Swettenham, J., Baron-Cohen, S., Cox, A., Baird, G. and Drew, A. (1997). Infants with autism: an investigation of empathy, pretend play, joint attention and imitation. *Devl Psychol.* **33**, 781–89.

Corkum, V. and Moore, C. (1995). Development of joint visual attention in infancy. In *Joint attention: its origins and role in development* (ed. C. Moore and P. J. Durham), pp. 61–83. Hillsdale, NJ: Lawrence Erlbaum Associates.

Corkum, V. and Moore, C. (1998). The origin of joint visual attention in infants. *Devl Psychol.* **34**, 28–38.

Courchesne, E., Lincoln, A. J., Kilman, B. A. and Galambos, R. (1985). Event-related brain potential correlates of the processing of novel visual and auditory information in autism. *J. Autism Devl Disorders* **15**, 55–76.

Courchesne, E., Townsend, J., Ashoomoff, N. A., Saitoh, O., Yeung-Courchesne, R., Lincoln, A., *et al.* (1994). Impairments in shifting attention in autistic and cerebellar patients. *Behav. Neurosci.* **108**, 848–65.

Curcio, F. (1978). Sensorimotor functioning and communication in mute autistic children. *J. Autism Childhood Schizophrenia* **8**, 282–92.

Davies, S., Bishop, D., Manstead, A. S. R. and Tantam, D. (1994). Face perception in children with autism and Asperger's syndrome. *J. Child Psychol. Psychiatry* **35**, 1033–57.

Driver, J., Davis, G., Ricciardelli, P., Kidd, P., Maxwell, E. and Baron-Cohen, S. (1999). Gaze perception triggers reflexive visual orienting. *Visual Cogn* **6**, 509–40.

Emery, N. J. (2000). The eyes have it: the neuroethology, function and evolution of social gaze. *Neurosci. Biobehav. Rev.* **24**, 581–604.

Farroni, T., Johnson, M. H., Brockbank, M. and Simion, F. (2000). Infants use of gaze direction to cue attention: the importance of perceived motion. *Visual Cogn.* **7**, 705–18.

Farroni, T., Csibra, G., Simion, F. and Johnson, M. H. (2002). Eye contact detection in humans from birth. *Proc. Natl Acad. Sci. USA* **99**, 9602–05.

Friesen, C. and Kingstone, A. (1998). Reflexive orienting is triggered by a nonpredictive gaze cue. *Psychol. Bull. Rev.* **5**, 490–95.

Frith, U. (1989). *Autism: explaining the enigma*. Oxford: Blackwell Science.

Gilmore, R. O. and Johnson, M. H. (1995). Working memory in six month old infants revealed by versions of oculomotor delayed response task. *J. Exp. Child Psychol. Psychiatry* **59**, 397–418.

Grelotti, D. J., Gauthier, I. and Schultz, R. T. (2002). Social interest and the development of cortical specialisation: what autism teaches us about face processing. *Devl Psychobiol.* **40**, 213–25.

Hietanen, J. (1999). Does your gaze direction and head orientation shift my visual attention? *Neuroreport* **10**, 3443–47.

Hobson, P. (1993). *Autism and the development of mind*. Hove, UK: Lawrence Erlbaum Associates.

Hood, B. M., Willen, J. D. and Driver, J. (1998). Adult's eyes trigger shifts of visual attention in human infants. *Psychol. Sci.* **9**, 276–336.

Jonides, J. (1981). Voluntary versus automatic control over mind's eye movement. In *Attention and performance*, vol. 9 (ed. J. Long and A. Baddely), pp. 187–203. Hillsdale, NJ: Lawrence Erlbaum Associates.

Kleinke, C. (1986). Gaze and eye contact: a research review. *Psychol. Bull.* **100**, 78–100.

Lambert, A. and Sumich, A. L. (1996). Spatial orienting controlled without awareness: a semantically based implicit learning effect. *Q. J. Exp. Psychol.* **49A**, 490–518.

Landry, S. and Loveland, K. A. (1988). Communication behaviours in autism and developmental language delay. *J. Child Psychol. Psychiatry* **29**, 621–34.

Langdell, T. (1978). Recognition of faces: an approach for the study of autism. *J. Child Psychol. Psychiatry* **19**, 255–68.

Langton, S. R. H. and Bruce, V. (1999). Reflexive visual orienting in response to the social attention of others. *Visual Cogn* **6**, 541–68.

Lauwereyns, J. (1998). Exogenous/endogenous control of space based/object-based attention: four types of visual selection? *Eur. J. Cogn. Psychol.* **10**, 41–74.

Leekam, S. R. and Moore, C. (2001). The development of attention and joint attention in children with autism. In *The development of autism: perspectives from theory and practice* (ed. J. A. Burack, T. Charman, N. Yirmiya and P. R. Zelazo), pp. 105–29. New Jersey: Lawrence Erlbaum.

Leekam, S. R., Baron-Cohen, S., Perrett, D., Milders, M. and Brown, S. (1997). Eye-direction detection: a dissociation between geometric and joint attention skills in autism. *Br. J. Devl Psychol.* **15**, 77–95.

Leekam, S. R., Hunnisett, E. and Moore, C. (1998). Targets and cues: gaze following in children with autism. *J. Child Psychol. Psychiatry* **39**, 951–62.

Leekam, S. R., Lopez, B. and Moore, C. (2000). Attention and joint attention in pre-school children with autism. *Devl Psychol.* **36**, 261–73.

Lord, C. (1995). Follow-up of two year olds referred for autism. *J. Child Psychol. Psychiatry* **36**, 1365–82.

Lord, C., Rutter, M. and LeCouteur, A. (1994). Autism diagnostic interview revised: a revised version of a diagnostic interview for caregivers of individuals with possible pervasive developmental disorders. *J. Autism Devl Disorders* **24**, 659–85.

Loveland, K. and Landry, S. (1986). Joint attention and language in autism and developmental language delay. *J. Autism Devl Disorders* **16**, 335–49.

Mundy, P. (1995). Joint attention and social emotional approach behaviour in children with autism. *Devl Psychopathol.* **7**, 63–82.

Mundy, P., Sigman, M. and Kasari, C. (1994). Joint attention, developmental level and symptom presentation in autism. *Devl Psychopathol.* **6**, 389–401.

Posner, M. I. (1980). Orienting attention. *Q. J. Exp. Psychol.* **32**, 3–25.

Povinelli, D. J. and Eddy, T. J. (1997). Specificity of gaze following in young chimpanzees. *Br. J. Devl Psychol.* **15**, 213–222.

Rincover, A. and Ducharme, J. M. (1987). Variables influencing stimulus over-selectivity and 'tunnel-vision' in developmentally delayed children. *Am. J. Mental Deficiency* **91**, 422–430.

Swettenham, J., Baron-Cohen, S., Charman, T., Cox, A., Baird, G. and Rees, L. (1998). The frequency and distribution of spontaneous attention shifts between social and non-social stimuli in autistic, typically developing and non-autistic developmentally delayed infants. *J. Child Psychol. Psychiatry* **39**, 747–753.

Swettenham, J., Plaisted, K., Milne, E., Campbell, R. and Coleman, M. (2003). Visual orienting in response to social and non-social stimuli in typically developing children and children with autism. (Submitted.)

Tomasello, M., Kruger, A. C. and Ratner, H. H. (1993). Cultural learning. *Behav. Brain Sci.* **16**, 495–511.

Townsend, J., Courchesne, E. and Egaas, B. (1996). Slowed orienting of covert visual-spatial attention in autism: specific deficits associated with cerebellar and parietal abnormalities. *Devl Psychopathol.* **8**, 563–84.

Vecera, S. P. and Johnson, M. H. (1995). Gaze detection and the cortical processing of faces: evidence from infants and adults. *Visual Cogn* **2**, 59–87.

Volkmar, F. R., Sparrow, S. S., Rende, R. D. and Cohen, D. J. (1989). Facial perception in autism. *J. Child Psychol. Psychiatry Allied Disciplines* **30**, 591–98.

Vuilleumier, P. (2002). Perceived gaze direction in faces and spatial attention: a study in patients with parietal damage and unilateral neglect. *Neuropsychologia* **40**, 1013–26.

Wainwright, J. A. and Bryson, S. E. (1996). Visual orienting in autism. *J. Autism Devl Disorders* **26**, 423–38.

Wainwright-Sharp, J. A. and Bryson, S. E. (1993). Visual orienting deficits in high functioning people with autism. *J. Autism Devl Disorders* **23**, 1–13.

Glossary

IQ: intelligence quotient
HSD: Tukey's Honestly Significant Difference test
SOA: stimulus onset asynchrony

6

The pathogenesis of autism: insights from congenital blindness

R. Peter Hobson and Martin Bishop

There is substantial heterogeneity in the aetiology and clinical presentation of autism. So how do we account for homogeneity in the syndrome? The answer to this question will be critical for any attempt to trace the links between brain pathology and the psychological disabilities that characterize autism. One possibility is that the source of homogeneity in autism is not to be found 'in the child', but rather in dysfunction of the system constituted by child-in-relation-to-other. We have been exploring this hypothesis through the study of congenitally blind children, among whom features of autism, and the syndrome of autism itself, are strikingly common. To justify such an approach, one needs to establish that the clinical features in blind children have qualities that are indeed 'autistic-like'. We conducted systematic observations of the social interactions of two matched groups of congenitally blind children who do *not* have autism, rating their social engagement, emotional tone, play and language during three sessions of free play in the school playground. The qualities of social impairment in the more disabled children were similar to those in sighted children with autism. Additional evidence came from independent ratings of the children in a different play setting: on the childhood autism rating scale (CARS), the socially impaired children had 'autistic-like' abnormalities in both social and non-social domains. If we can determine the way in which congenital blindness predisposes to features of autism, we shall be in a better position to trace the developmental pathways that lead to the syndrome in sighted children.

Keywords: autism; blindness; intersubjectivity; social relations

6.1 Introduction

In this paper, we attempt to do three things. Our first aim is theoretical: we shall propose that to determine what makes autism a syndrome, it may be necessary to consider it as an interpersonal disorder. Second, we shall consider how research with congenitally blind children bears upon this thesis. Finally, we shall describe a formal exploratory study with non-autistic congenitally blind children that provides evidence for this account.

It is one of the striking things about autism, that it is both a relatively homogeneous and clinically valid constellation of clinical features, and a syndrome that has diverse aetiology and marked individual differences in clinical presentation. On a clinical-descriptive level, for example, Kanner's view was that each of his 11 cases were characterized by an 'inability to form the usual, biologically provided affective contact with people' (Kanner 1943, p. 250), and among a range of other characteristic abnormalities, those in the pragmatic aspects of language are almost universal (Tager-Flusberg 2000). On an epidemiological level, classic studies by Wing and Gould (1979) demonstrated that 'autism' really does exist as a triad of social impairments. However, despite evidence that genetic or other identifiable physical factors are important in a substantial number of children with autism, the goal of defining a common underlying physical substrate has proved elusive. On a psychological level, too, attempts to capture a dysfunction or set of dysfunctions that is universal to individual children, of early onset, and responsible for the characteristic pattern of clinical features, have met with only partial success. Even in those respects that have been most productive—and here, theory of mind approaches top the list (Frith 1989; Hobson 1993; Happé 1995; Baron-Cohen *et al*. 2000)—it remains unclear how far the children's limitations in understanding people's minds are the cause or the result of their abnormalities in non-verbal communication, or the cause or the result (or neither) of their ritualistic behaviour and relatively inflexible thinking.

There are two main alternatives to the idea that we should seek a single and specific underlying 'cause' for autism, whether on a physical or psychological level. The first is to reject the notion that there is a final common pathway to autism, and to suppose instead that the syndrome is the manifestation of several distinct areas of disability (e.g. Wing and Wing 1971; Goodman 1989). The second, equally radical alternative is to hold that there may be a final common pathway of psychological disorder to the syndrome, but to locate this essential factor in what happens or fails to happen *between* people. According to this hypothesis—which is emphatically not a return to the damaging psychogenic theories of earlier decades—there may be several different psychological abnormalities (as well as different neurological abnormalities and different underlying aetiological factors) in individual children with autism, but that whatever those abnormalities are, they interact with what the environment provides to result in a special kind of breakdown in social engagement between the affected child and others. It is this breakdown and its development sequelae that become manifest in the special 'autistic' quality of social and communicative impairment.

The claim here is that without taking into account the interpersonal quality and level of disorder, one will never arrive at a satisfactory theory of why the particular clinical features of autism co-occur in the way that they do. The claim is not that the interpersonal level underpins all the phenomena of autism. On the contrary, there will be 'lower-level' psychological abnormalities in most if not all cases, because there must be reasons why the disruption in social engagement is happening, and these abnormalities will have additional manifestations that may or may not be universal to autism. Perhaps the most obvious case in point is that brain pathology is often manifest in a degree of 'general' mental retardation, and one does not need to claim either that the general mental retardation is totally irrelevant in causing the autism (which it may or may not be, in any given case), nor that it results from social impairment (although this may exacerbate the cognitive impairment). What *is* being claimed is that the social impairment itself is a necessary and probably sufficient condition for the characteristic constellation of clinical features to develop over the early period of a child's life. There are central features of autism that are explicable in terms of 'lower-level' impairments only insofar as these operate through disrupting interpersonal engagement and interaction.

This kind of interpersonal account faces two immediate challenges. First, we need a more detailed specification of which aspects of interpersonal engagement are deficient in children with autism, and how these then give rise to at least some of the essential features of the syndrome. Here, the suggestion is that a young child needs emotional engagement and identification with the attitudes of other people not only to derive concepts of mind and to employ language with flexibility and context-sensitivity, but also to disembed from a one-track perspective *on the world* and to acquire the ability to symbolize in characteristically human ways; and that such emotional engagement and identification is seriously impaired in children with autism (see, for example, Hobson 1989, 2002; Hobson and Lee 1998, 1999). Second, we need to know just how much this account is meant to explain: how many of the characteristic abnormalities are supposed to be the developmental outcome of disorder that occurs in interpersonal transactions, and how many are spin-off deficits that arise from lower-order impairments that do not implicate this social level of explanation.

If one adopts the approach of developmental psychopathology, one is prompted not only to compare typical and atypical development (in the present case, 'normal' development and autism), but also to compare developmental processes and outcomes that are 'typically atypical' (in this case, classically autistic) with those that are 'atypically atypical'. If there are atypical forms of autism, their very unusualness may draw one's attention to otherwise neglected causal processes and psychological mechanisms in the pathogenesis of the syndrome. For example, autism may be observed in circumstances that (arguably) implicate relevant kinds of disruption in the system of child-inrelation-to-other, and restrict the critical kinds of childhood social experience. Two potential cases in point are children who early in life suffered terrible deprivation and privation in the orphanages of Romania (Rutter *et al.* 1999), and children who are congenitally blind.

There are special hazards in following this line of explanation. If one is drawing comparisons between features of typical and atypical autism, how similar is similar enough to justify such a comparison? Is it even permissible to think in terms of autism in this context, or should we confine ourselves to noting 'autistic-like' clinical features in atypical cases? The danger of the latter approach is that it seems to presuppose that there is a clear boundary in phenomenology and pathogenesis between 'typical' and 'less typical' instances of autism. If a child meets formal diagnostic criteria for the syndrome, then we should accept that child has the syndrome of autism *in certain important respects*. It is a subsidiary matter to tease out the ways in which the syndrome is atypical, for example with respect to particular clinical features or to natural history. Only in this way shall we recognize previously unrecognized diversity in more typical cases, and appreciate how there may be different routes to the syndrome and potentially at least, different routes by which the syndrome may evolve (and even partly remit) subsequently.

6.2 The case of congenital blindness

First, to state the obvious: even total congenital blindness is not sufficient to cause autism. The fact is that there are congenitally blind individuals who do not manifest features of autism (as illustrated later in this paper). However, there have been many clinical reports of autism or autistic-like conditions in children with congenital blindness (see, for example, Keeler 1958; Wing 1969; Chess 1971; Fraiberg and Adelson 1977; Rogers and Newhart-Larson 1989), and recent systematic investigations of relatively large groups of congenitally blind children reveal that a surprisingly high number—almost half the sample of 24 children between the ages of 3 and 9 years studied in special schools by Brown *et al.* (1997)—meet the formal diagnostic criteria for autism. Moreover, when Hobson *et al.* (1999) made close comparisons between a subgroup of the congenitally blind children with autism, and an age- and IQ-matched group of sighted children with autism, there were marked similarities and only suggestive evidence of group differences (especially in the less markedly 'autistic' quality of the blind children's social impairment). When it came to focus on the congenitally blind children without autism, systematic observations by Brown *et al.* (1997) revealed that they displayed a significantly greater number of 'autistic features' than matched sighted children; and in a separate study on different groups of nonautistic congenitally blind and matched sighted children, the blind children were significantly impaired on 'theory of mind' tasks (Minter *et al.* 1998; and see Hobson *et al.* 1997 for an overview of these studies).

  The possibility arises that the 'effective environment' of congenitally blind children—that is, the environment as experienced by the children—may have conjoined with other factors in causing features of autism to develop in a substantial number of cases. However, we need to be critical in exploring this possibility. As Baron-Cohen (2002, p. 792) has recently remarked, '. . . might this be no more than a surface similarity? We should be careful not to assume that just because two church bells are ringing simultaneously they are causally connected by the same rope'. In addressing this challenge, one avenue of research is to explore the nature and neurofunctional basis of blind children's autistic-like psychological difficulties (e.g. O'Connor and Hermelin 1978). Another is to examine in more detail whether in congenitally blind children, there is coherence between an 'autistic-like' quality of social impairment—something beyond the kinds of difficulty in social relatedness one might expect in all blind children—and other clinical features of autism. Such study may enable us to discern whether there is an intrinsic link between the children's abnormal social relations and experience, and their other deficits.

6.3 The present study

There has been surprisingly little study of social interactions among children with congenital blindness. Apart from in-depth studies of the interactions between blind infants and their mothers (see, for example, Urwin 1983; Rowland 1983; Rogers and Puchalski 1984; Preisler 1991; Troster and Brambring 1992), most accounts of the social relations of young blind children have been contained in clinical-descriptive studies. In a report of young blind children in nursery school, Preisler (1993) (also Curson 1979; Sandler and Hobson 2001) described how the blind children seldom participated in sighted children's play or initiated contact with the other children, and there was little exchange of ideas or meanings. The play of blind children has also been described as impoverished and 'primitive', more often directed at adults than other children (Burlingham 1961; Wills 1968; Tait 1972*a,b*; Schneekloth 1989; Troster and Brambring 1994; Ferguson and Buultjens 1995; Skellenger *et al.* 1997). Not only do blind children rarely imitate others, except in the special case of vocalizations (Sandler and Wills 1965; Fraiberg 1977), but also they often appear muted in their affective expression (Burlingham 1961; Fraiberg 1968; Wills 1970, 1981) or reciprocal positive feelings to others (e.g. Kekelis 1992). Kekelis (1992) describes how the children may be preoccupied with their own thoughts and actions, abruptly shift topics of conversation, and pay little attention to other people's points of view, interests, language or other behaviour (see also Chernus-Mansfield *et al.* 1985; Andersen and Kekelis 1986; Skellenger *et al.* 1992).

In the extreme case, as we have seen, congenitally blind children may present with 'autistic-like' clinical features or with a more or less full picture of autism. But it may be argued that in those blind children with the syndrome of autism, the social impairment is simply a reflection of coincidental autism: there need be no intrinsic connection with the lack of visual input. This argument is less persuasive because one finds a spectrum of severity of 'autistic features' in blind children. Therefore special interest is attached to the clinical presentation of socially impaired blind children who are *not* classically autistic. Is there evidence that in these children, the social impairment is (i) like that of sighted children with autism and (ii) associated with other features of autism? If so, then perhaps there is some intrinsic connection between blind children's social impairment and their 'autistic-like' clinical features: in this case, the connection may also have a bearing on the pathogenesis of the full syndrome when it occurs in blind children; and if this is so, there may be lessons to be learnt for what leads to autism in sighted children.

In our study of these issues, we needed to establish that the qualities of the social and other impairments under review were not simply a reflection of behavioural strategies common to all children who are congenitally blind, nor a reflection of low IQ in the context of blindness. Therefore we constituted two IQ- and age-matched groups of congenitally blind children according to teachers' reports of their abilities to engage with others. The MS blind children served as a control group for those who were socially impaired (LS children). This allowed us to explore a matter that has not been addressed previously: within the population of congenitally blind children who do not have autism, is there a specific association between autistic-like social impairments and autistic-like non-social abnormalities when the children's age and IQ are taken into account?

We adopted two approaches to evaluating the children's social impairments. The first approach was to observe the children in free play in the school playground. Our observational technique and rating procedures drew on the approaches of several earlier workers such as Rubin *et al.* (1976), Connolly and Doyle (1984) and Guralnick and Groom (1987). Our interest focused on the quality and emotional tone of the children's social engagement, the types and sociability of their play, and the social and pragmatic aspects of their language use. Our predictions were that the LS children would contrast with the MS children in having more periods in which they were isolated and relatively unexpressive ('placid') emotionally, and in which they would fail to show play and more specifically, fail to engage in reciprocal play. On ratings of language use, we predicted that the LS group would show fewer periods of language directed towards other children, and make fewer utterances to others involving comments on things or events.

Our second approach was to invite an independent judge who was unaware of group constitution to rate videotapes of the children engaged in play with someone. This rater employed the CARS of Schopler *et al.* (1988) to assess the degree to which children displayed both social *and* non-social abnormalities that were 'autistic-like' in quality.

(a) Participants

Participants were 18 congenitally blind children selected on the basis that they were between 4 and 8 years of age (inclusive), they did *not* satisfy DSM-IV criteria for autism, they were not exhibiting high degrees of repetitive mannerisms which might have prevented interactions in the free-play settings, they had an IQ above that of severe learning disability (an IQ of 55), and finally, they fell into the appropriate subgroups according to teacher ratings of social ability. Nearly all of the children had been totally blind from birth; the exceptions were two of the MS children and two of the LS children, each of whom had light perception only. None of the children had been in their present nursery school for less than a year, so it was unlikely that their behaviour reflected adjustment to a new school.

For teacher ratings, two qualified class teachers who knew each of 25 children were asked to fill in a questionnaire which included the question: 'on a scale of 1–5, how would you rate this child's behaviour in the ability to relate to adults and peers (rated separately), establishing normal mutual interpersonal contact with them?' The threshold at which children qualified for the socially impaired (LS) group was set at a mean score across adult and peer ratings of equal to or less than 3, with neither of the teachers' ratings higher than 3 for the child's relations with either adults or peers. Nine children met these criteria. We selected a corresponding group of nine MS children on the basis that they were similar in age and achieved the highest scores (4 or more) on the scale.

Children were tested on the verbal subtests of the Wechsler Preschool and Primary Scale of Intelligence (Wechsler 1967), or for the older children, the Wechsler Intelligence Scale for Children: Revised (Wechsler 1976). It should be noted from Table 6.1 that although the two groups were closely similar in CA and MA, there was a modest discrepancy in the mean IQ scores. Across the whole sample of children, there was not a significant correlation between the scores for interpersonal relations on the teacher questionnaire, and CA, MA, nor IQ.

(b) Procedure

(i) Playground observations
Children were observed for three sessions in their school playground during regular free play periods, in nearly all cases on three different days. There was at least one class of pupils in the playground at any one time, supervised by an adult. One of us (M.B.) acted as the observer. He followed a given child for around 5 min in any given session, and made judgements on a total of five 20 s observation periods. Each observation session was begun when a child was within 1.8 m of at least one other child, without an adult in the immediate vicinity. This established a common starting point for all children. After a period of 20 s of undistracted observation, the observer would spend around 40 s recording what he had observed by ticking off items on a prepared scoring schedule (described below). Once the scoring had been completed (minimum 40 s), the next 20 s observation period would commence. Overall, therefore, each child was observed for fifteen 20 s observation periods (see Appendix A for examples).

(ii) Rating schedule for social interactions
The rating schedule followed the format of Tables 6.2 and 6.3, except that there were blank boxes to check off instead of the results presented. In addition, for each observation a rating was made of the child's proximity to another child

Table 6.1 Participant characteristics.

child	CA (months)	IQ	MA (months)	diagnosis	teachers' 'social' ratings (max. = 5)
more social group					
1	107	57	61.0	optic atrophy hydrocephalus	5
2	76	96	73.0	retinopathy of prematurity	5
3	72	104	74.9	retinopathy of prematurity	5
4	93	87	80.9	retinopathy of prematurity	4.5
5	75	109	81.7	microphthalmiaa (prostheses)	5
6	98	85	83.3	retinopathy of prematurity	4
7	96	101	97.0	uncertain: optic pathway disorder	4
8	90	115	103.5	retinopathy of prematurity	4.5
9	101	117	118.2	retinal aplasia	5
mean	89.8	96.8	85.9		4.7
s.d.	12.6	18.6	17.4		0.4
less social group					
1	76	65	49.4	retinopathy of prematurity	2
2	63	89	56.1	retinopathy of prematurity	2
3	102	62	63.2	congenital optic nerve hypoplasia	1.5
4	96	72	69.1	retinopathy of prematurity	3
5	76	106	80.6	Leber's amaurosis	2.5
6	85	96	81.6	Leber's amaurosis	2.5
7	109	85	92.6	Leber's amaurosis	3
8	104	100	104	Leber's amaurosis	3
9	113	112	126.6	Norries disease	3
mean	91.6	87.4	80.4		2.5
s.d.	17.3	17.9	24.5		0.6

[a] Isolated condition: not part of a wider syndrome or association.

(distant, within 1.8 m; within 0.9 m; or touching). With one exception the items within each category were constructed so that they were mandatory to complete and mutually exclusive, and the observer simply ticked the item that best characterized the child's behaviour for each category during the 20 s observation period. Thus, for example, after an observation period the observer would begin by judging the typical degree of proximity, and would then move to rate social engagement (choosing one of cooperative, conflictual or isolated), and so on. If he was in doubt about which of two items captured the most frequent behaviour in a particular 20 s, he would select the most social/affective. Because a child was scored for 15 observation periods, the maximum score for any given item was 15; and the total score across the potential items for any category (for example, the total of cooperative, conflictual and isolated ratings in the category of social engagement) was 15.

Table 6.2 Mean number of observation periods for which each item of behaviour was most characteristic.

	MS group ($n = 9$)		LS group ($n = 9$)	
	mean	range	mean	range
social engagement				
cooperative	12.28	5–15	4.83	0–11
conflictual	0.89	0–2	1.94	0–7
isolated	1.83	0–8	8.22	3–15
emotional tone				
placid	6.22	0–12	8.67	5–12
pleasure	7.89	2–12	3.39	0–7
distress	0.89	0–3	2.94	0–6
type of play				
absence of play	3.33	0–9	9.83	3–15
rough and tumble	7.17	0–15	1.39	0–7
functional/exploratory	1.22	0–6	1.33	0–7
symbolic with props	1.78	0–5	1.33	0–12
symbolic verbal	1.50	0–6	0.78	0–4
other	0	0	0.33	0–2
sociability of play				
(absence of play)	3.33	0–9	9.83	3–15
alone	1.22	0–7	1.78	0–6
parallel	1.44	0–5	1.06	0–3
reciprocal (equivocal)	2.22	0–4	1.89	0–6
reciprocal (definite)	6.78	2–10	0.44	0–2

Table 6.3 (a) Mean number of observation periods for which each item of social language was characteristic. (b) Number of observation periods featuring each pragmatic use of language (not mutually exclusive).

	MS group ($n = 9$)		LS group ($n = 9$)	
	mean	range	mean	range
(a)				
none	2.50	0–8	5.39	1–9
self-directed	0.22	0–2	0.56	0–3
non-specifically outward	0.94	0–2	2.39	0–4
directed to other	0.72	0–2	2.78	0–9
reciprocal (equivocal)	3.44	0–6	2.50	0–5
reciprocal (definite)	7.17	2–11	1.39	0–4
(b)				
request	2.44	0–6	1.61	0–4.5
instruction	5.06	1.5–9	3.78	0–7
comment	9.39	5–13.5	4.78	1–9

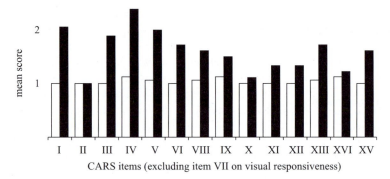

CARS items (excluding item VII on visual responsiveness)

Fig. 6.1 CARS group profiles: MS (open bars) versus LS (black bars) groups. (I, relating to people; II, imitation; III, emotional response; IV, body use; V, object use; VI, adaptation to change; VIII, listening response; IX, taste, smell and touch response and use; X, fear or nervousness; XI, verbal communication; XII, non-verbal communication; XIII, activity level; XIV, level and consistency of intellectual response; XV, general impressions.) Note that scores above unity indicate abnormality.

The one set of items that were not mutually exclusive, and that were not always rated because they required that a child spoke (which did not always happen), concerned pragmatic language use. Here, a given child could score positively for any or all items if he/she made *any* instruction, request or comment during a given rating period.

(iii) Ratings on the CARS
The children were assessed on the CARS of Schopler *et al.* (1988), within around 12 months of the playground observations. This was possible because for a separate investigation, we made half-hour videotapes of the children engaging with an adult in play, and an independent clinician (blind to the MS and LS group membership) was able to complete the CARS by reviewing these videotapes. The setting was that the child was invited to play with several toys, and then an investigator would model a theme and invite the child to continue. The CARS involves ratings on 15 items (see Fig. 6.1), each of which is scored from one (for age-appropriate behaviour) to four (for severely abnormal autistic-like behaviour). Children with scores lower than 30 are considered non-autistic, although it should be noted that the omission of item VII on visual responsiveness reduces by four the maximum achievable score.

6.4 Results

(a) Playground ratings

(i) Reliability of ratings
The ratings were made by one of the investigators (M.B.) who was aware of the group of each child. To locate children with profound visual impairment

but no other diagnosed neurological or other handicap, he visited several English regional schools for children with visual impairment. Therefore it was not possible to employ multiple raters for most observations. To check the reliability of his ratings, a second person who was unaware of the hypotheses underlying the study accompanied him to one school and conducted independent ratings of one observation session each with four randomly selected children. On the ratings for each category, the weighted kappa coefficients of agreement (with the percentages of exact agreement in brackets) for each category of behaviour were as follows: for emotional tone, kappa = 0.60 (85%); for social engagement, kappa = 0.88 (85%); for type of play, kappa = 1.0 (100%); for sociability of play, kappa = 0.98 (90%); and for social language, kappa = 0.87 (75%). According to the criteria of Landis and Koch (1977), kappa values of 0.61 and above represent 'substantial' agreement, and 0.81 and above 'almost perfect' agreement.

(ii) Observations
For most observation periods, the children of both groups remained within 0.6 m of a peer (in 82% of the observations of MS children, and 66% of those of LS children), but in 8% of periods for MS children and 24% of periods for LS children, the children were more distant than 1.8 m from others. Across all observations, only one child in the MS group and two children in the LS group spent more than half their time at a distance greater than 0.6 m from a peer. These results indicate that group differences in the remaining ratings were not simply a reflection of the LS children moving away from their peers.

Ratings of social engagement, emotional tone, and type and sociability of play
The results from these ratings are presented in Table 6.2. We have presented mean rather than median scores out of 15 on each item for clarity of exposition. Within each category, the mean item scores add up to a total of 15.

In relation to the within-category items that exemplified our predictions most closely, one-tailed Mann–Whitney p-values for group differences (with the LS children showing the LS forms of behaviour) were as follows: for social engagement, the item of isolation ($U = 4$, $p < 0.001$); for emotional tone, the item of placidity turned out to yield a non-significant group difference, but on a two-tailed test the LS children showed significantly less pleasure ($U = 8$, $p < 0.005$); for type of play, the absence of play ($U = 8$, $p < 0.005$); and for the presence of equivocal or definite reciprocal play ($U = 4.5$, $p < 0.001$). Only two LS children showed more than three observation periods that included either definite or equivocal reciprocal play, and three showed no reciprocal play at all; by contrast, all but one MS child showed six or more periods involving reciprocal play, and four of the children showed 10 or more.

Ratings on use of language
The results from the ratings of social language and pragmatic language use are presented in Table 6.3. We repeat that the ratings of pragmatic language use

differ from the other ratings because the items of instruction, request and comment were not mutually exclusive. A child might be scored positively for each of these types of utterance, if he or she made at least one such utterance during a given observation period.

In keeping with our prediction, the LS children showed fewer periods in which they directed language towards other children (summing the items of 'direct to other', equivocally reciprocal and definitely reciprocal in Table 6.3, Mann–Whitney $U = 11, p < 0.005$, one-tailed). Only one out of nine MS children but seven of the nine LS children had more ratings of non-reciprocal speech than speech that was equivocally or definitely reciprocal (Fisher's exact test, $p < 0.01$, one-tailed).

With regard to our second prediction, it was the case that the LS children showed fewer periods in which they offered comments to their peers (Mann–Whitney $U = 6.5, p < 0.001$, one-tailed). Six of the nine MS children made comments in at least 10 of the 15 observation periods, whereas none of the LS children did so. However, the dearth of comments was not absolute: four of the LS children were observed to make comments in more than five of the 15 periods, and although comments were rare among the remaining five children, all but one of them made comments on at least three occasions.

(b) Ratings on the CARS

The results on the CARS are presented in Fig. 6.1. Among those children who were socially engaged (MS), there was one child unavailable for testing on the CARS; otherwise in this group, for only one child and only on one item (level and consistency of intellectual response) was an item scored elevated by more than 0.5, and the highest overall score for a child was 15.5 (where 14 is the minimum score). Three children showed no abnormalities at all, three showed minor elevation of scores on a single item (body use, activity level, and level and consistency of intellectual response), and two showed abnormalities in smell and touch responses along with those in body and/or object use and/or listening response. These results indicate that in cases with little social impairment, congenital blindness *per se* is not necessarily associated with 'autistic-like' features.

These results may be compared with those from the socially impaired group (LS), in whom the range of individual scores was 17.5–27.5 (mean = 22.3, s.d. = 3.6). In Fig. 6.1 it can be seen that minor but significant abnormalities were present across most of the items of the CARS. This pattern is representative of individual children. For example, if one takes the criterion of an item score of at least two for 'autistic-like' abnormality, the numbers of children (out of nine) rated abnormal were as follows: six for relating to people, five for emotional response, seven for body use, six for object use, three for adaptation to change, five for activity level and four for 'general impressions' of autism (an item on which only two children showed no abnormality). There were three individuals who scored *above* two for four items, two who did so for two items, and one for one item. Thus, there was evidence both that the social impairment had some 'autistic-like' quality, and that the range of abnormalities spread across the range of clinical features characteristic of autism.

6.5 Discussion

The aim of this exploratory study was to examine the 'autistic-like' quality and breadth of abnormalities in socially impaired but not autistic congenitally blind children. The study was unusual in that it involved congenitally blind children *both* in index *and* control groups. The rationale was to control for the effects of blindness in shaping children's social relations, so that one could discern what is special about the social *and* non-social abnormalities that occur in those children with severe impairments in personal relatedness. The results indicated that in comparison with their MS blind peers, those whom teachers judged to be socially impaired were observed in the playground to be more socially isolated, less likely to express pleasure, and less likely to play or be involved in reciprocal play. The results highlight the nature and severity of the relative lack of reciprocal interpersonal engagement seen in some socially impaired blind children. Further observations pointed to additional parallels with deficits that are typical of sighted children with autism, for example in the children's relative dearth of comments on things and events.

In independent CARS ratings for 'autistic-like' abnormalities in a different play setting, a substantial majority of the socially impaired group were given elevated scores both for the autistic-like quality of their relating to people, and for 'general impressions' of autism. Moreover, the socially impaired but not the highly social children were also given moderately elevated scores for additional, relatively non-social clinical features characteristic of sighted children with autism, such as body and object use. The group differences occurred despite the fact that the two groups were closely similar in chronological and mental age (albeit not exactly matched for IQ, with the mean IQ of the LS group approximately nine points lower than that of the MS group).

A limitation of the study was that inter-rater reliabilities of the playground observations were established on a relatively small sample of the ratings. It might also be objected that there is a circularity in the methodology we have adopted, as we constituted the two groups of blind children according to teachers' ratings of sociability, and then proceeded to demonstrate that indeed one group was more social than the other. However, one aim of our study was to demonstrate something about the *qualities* of the social impairments of the more disabled group of children. For example, it is not simply that they tend to avoid other people, because even when they are close by their peers there are limitations to how they interact; it is not simply that they are clumsy in their social interactions, because they are less engaged with others in reciprocal interactions, whether emotionally or in language or in play. These observations highlight how there are wide-ranging individual differences in blind children's capacity for reciprocal engagement with others, and that such differences are not simply a reflection of intellectual ability. Both playground observations and separate CARS ratings indicated that the social impairments were of a kind reminiscent of autism. The second major finding was that additional, relatively non-social 'autistic-like' abnormalities were present almost exclusively in the socially impaired group.

The present study was not designed to address whether severe social impairments among blind children are associated with particular disorders. Although there have been suggestions that children with conditions such as Leber's amaurosis might have a special predisposition to autistic-like clinical features (Rogers and Newhart-Larson 1989), there is also evidence from our own previous research that such features may be associated with a range of medical conditions (Brown *et al.* 1997). In the present study, it was the case that all four children with the diagnosis of Leber's amaurosis were in our LS group, whereas the eight children with the diagnosis of retinopathy of prematurity were spread across the two groups.

To explain the association between the different kinds of 'autistic-like' abnormality in socially impaired blind children, there are several theoretical options. One might argue that there is something special about the physical constitution of some blind children: perhaps some form of minimal brain damage associated with the conditions that led to blindness (Cass *et al.* 1994) that predisposes both to the social disabilities of these children and to their 'autistic-like' clinical features. Or one might consider that there are several sources of social impairment in blind children, including both physical and environmental factors, and that when potentiated by the children's lack of vision, these result in specific forms of impoverishment in interpersonal experiences that have developmental consequences which include several autistic-like features. We would stress that the socially impaired blind children of our study demonstrated a limited *reciprocal engagement with others*. Such engagement is pivotal for drawing a typically developing child into a flexible and creative engagement with other people's relatedness to the world, and prompting the child to grasp alternative meanings in reality and play.

Central to this thesis is that the syndrome of autism, whether in blind *or* sighted children, is the developmental outcome of profound disruption in the usual patterns of intersubjective coordination between the affected individual and others. The present results reveal how there are blind children who do *not* satisfy the diagnostic criteria for autism, but who nevertheless have marked impairments in interpersonal engagement. These are the very same children who also manifest several additional 'autistic features'. Our own preferred explanation is that vision has a special role in linking children with other people and with others' attitudes towards a shared world. Whether or not this proves to be correct, the findings indicate that there might be a variety of functional abnormalities—and correspondingly, a variety of conditions in the brains and/or perceptual systems and/or the environments of children—that can predispose to autism. And, however we explain the pathogenesis of autism, our explanation needs to encompass the phenomena of autism and autistic-like features in congenitally blind children.

The empirical study reported in this paper was supported by a studentship from the Mary Kitzinger Trust to M.B. The Hayward Foundation also contributed financial support. We are very grateful to Tony Lee for all his help. We thank the pupils and staff of the following schools, who were so generous in making the study possible: Dorton House School, Sevenoaks; West of England School, Exeter; Joseph Clarke School, London; Linden Lodge School, Wimbledon; Temple Bank School, Bradford; St Vincent's School for the Blind, Liverpool; RNIB Sunshine House School, Northwood; and Priestley Smith School, Birmingham.

Appendix A

The following observation sessions concern two of the LS children. Each observation consists of five successive 20 s periods (labelled (i) to (v)), separated by periods of *around* 40 s while ratings were recorded.

A 6-year-old girl in the playground at lunchtime:

 (i) she moved from an initially close position to become distant from the other children, involved with noone, seemingly distressed and isolated; in using direct language, called out loud for a particular teacher; not involved in any play;

 (ii) still distant, and distressed and isolated; showing no language or play;

(iii) moved within 0.6 m of both an adult and another child; still distressed and isolated; gave an undirected outward scream; no play;

(iv) still within 0.6 m of both an adult and child; distressed and in conflict; she suddenly called out, with a non-specific instruction—'don't do that!'; showing no play;

 (v) within 0.6 m of an adult and now two other children; placid yet cooperative; engaged in an equivocally reciprocal exchange, making a verbal request, 'When we go in, can I hear your beautiful voice this afternoon?'; no play.

A 9-year-old boy during lunchtime outside: he was sitting on some steps while others were playing a game, calling out letters to each other.

 (i) He was within touching distance of three other children who were playing the letter game; showing a placid emotional tone yet cooperative in social engagement; though no language or play.

 (ii) He was led away by the hand by a girl classmate, reacting placidly yet cooperatively to this, though without showing any speech or play.

(iii) Being pulled around; distressed and conflicted, calling out to the other child to stop leading him around; no play.

(iv) Still being led by the other child, though now placid and cooperative again; no language or play.

(v) Still being led; distressed and isolated; giving an instruction to her, but not talking reciprocally; no play.

References

Andersen, E. S. and Kekelis, L. S. (1986). The role of sibling input in the language socialisation of younger blind children. *S. California Occasional Pap. Linguistics, Social Cogn. Perspectives Lang.* **11**, 141–56.

Baron-Cohen, S. (2002). I am loved, therefore I think. Book review of *The Cradle of Thought* by R. P. Hobson. *Nature* **416**, 791–92.

Baron-Cohen, S. Tager-Flusberg, H. and Cohen, D. J. (eds) (2000). *Understanding other minds: perspectives from developmental cognitive neuroscience*, 2nd edn. Oxford: Oxford University Press.

Brown, R., Hobson, R. P., Lee, A. and Stevenson, J. (1997). Are there 'autistic-like' features in congenitally blind children? *J. Child Psychol. Psychiatry Allied Disciplines* **38**, 693–703.

Burlingham, D. (1961). Some notes on the development of the blind. *Psychoanalytic Stud. Child* **16**, 121–45.

Cass, H. D., Sonksen, P. M. and McConachie, H. R. (1994). Developmental setback in severe visual impairment. *Arch. Dis. Childhood* **70**, 192–96.

Chernus-Mansfield, N., Hayashi, D. and Kekelis, L. S. (1985). *Talk to me II: common concerns*. Los Angeles, CA: Blind Children's Centre.

Chess, S. (1971). Autism in children with congenital rubella. *J. Autism Childhood Schizophrenia* **1**, 33–47.

Connolly, J. A. and Doyle, A.-B. (1984). Relation of social fantasy play to social competence in preschoolers. *Devl Psychol.* **20**, 797–806.

Curson, A. (1979). The blind nursery school child. *Psychoanalytic Stud. Child* **34**, 51–83.

Ferguson, R. and Buultjens, M. (1995). The play behaviour of young blind children and its relationship to developmental stages. *Br. J. Vis. Impairment* **13**, 100–107.

Fraiberg, S. (1968). Parallel and divergent patterns in blind and sighted infants. *Psychoanalytic Stud. Child* **26**, 264–300.

Fraiberg, S. (1977). *Insights from the blind*. London: Souvenir.

Fraiberg, S. and Adelson, E. (1977). Self-representation in language and play. In *Insights from the blind* (ed. S. Fraiberg), pp. 248–70. London: Souvenir.

Frith, U. (1989). *Autism: explaining the enigma*. Oxford: Blackwell.

Goodman, R. (1989). Infantile autism: a syndrome of multiple primary deficits? *J. Autism Devl Disorders* **19**, 409–24.

Guralnick, M. J. and Groom, J. M. (1987). The peer relations of mildly delayed and nonhandicapped preschool children in mainstreamed playgroups. *Child Dev.* **58**, 1556–72.

Happé, F. (1995). *Autism: an introduction to psychological theory*. Harvard University Press.

Hobson, R. P. (1989). Beyond cognition: a theory of autism. In *Autism: nature, diagnosis, and treatment* (ed. G. Dawson), pp. 22–48. New York: Guildford.

Hobson, R. P. (1993). *Autism and the development of mind*. Hillsdale, NJ: Lawrence Erlbaum Associates.

Hobson, R. P. (2002). *The cradle of thought*. London: Macmillan.

Hobson, R. P. and Lee, A. (1998). Hello and goodbye: a study of social engagement in autism. *J. Autism Devl Disorders* **28**, 117–26.

Hobson, R. P. and Lee, A. (1999). Imitation and identification in autism. *J. Child Psychol. Psychiatry* **40**, 649–59.

Hobson, R. P., Brown, R., Minter, M. E. and Lee, A. (1997). 'Autism' revisited: the case of congenital blindness. In *Blindness and psychological development in young children* (ed. V. Lewis and G. M. Collis), pp. 99–115. Leicester, UK: The British Psychological Society.

Hobson, R. P., Lee, A. and Brown, R. (1999). Autism and congenital blindness. *J. Autism Devl Disorders* **29**, 45–56.

Kanner, L. (1943). Autistic disturbances of affective contact. *Nervous Child* **2**, 217–50.

Keeler, W. R. (1958). Autistic patterns and defective communication in blind children with retrolental fibroplasia. In *Psychopathology of communication* (ed. P. H. Hoch and J. Zubin), pp. 64–83. New York: Grune and Stratton.

Kekelis, L. S. (1992). Peer interactions in childhood: the impact of visual impairment. In *The development of social skills by blind and visually impaired students* (ed. S. Z. Sacks, L. S. Kekelis and R. J. Gaylord-Ross), pp. 13–35. New York: American Foundation for the Blind.

Landis, J. R. and Koch, G. G. (1977). The measurement of observer agreement for categorical data. *Biometrics* **33**, 159–74.

Minter, M. E., Hobson, R. P. and Bishop, M. (1998). Congenital visual impairment and 'theory of mind'. *Br. J. Devl Psychol.* **16**, 183–96.

O'Connor, N. and Hermelin, B. (1978). *Seeing and hearing and space and time.* London: Academic.

Preisler, G. M. (1991). Early patterns of interaction between blind infants and their sighted mothers. *Child: Care Hlth Dev.* **17**, 65–90.

Preisler, G. M. (1993). A descriptive study of blind children in nurseries with sighted children. *Child: Care Hlth Dev.* **19**, 295–315.

Rogers, S. J. and Newhart-Larson, S. (1989). Characteristics of infantile autism in five children with Leber's congenital amaurosis. *Devl Med. Child Neurol.* **31**, 598–608.

Rogers, S. J. and Puchalski, C. B. (1984). Development of symbolic play in visually impaired young children. *Topics in Early Childhood Special Education* **3**, 57–63.

Rowland, C. (1983). Patterns of interaction between three blind infants and their mothers. In *Language acquisition in the blind child: normal and deficient* (ed. A. E. Mills), pp. 114–32. London: Croom Helm.

Rubin, K. H., Maioni, T. L. and Hornung, M. (1976). Free play behaviors in middle- and lower-class preschoolers: Parten and Piaget revisited. *Child Dev.* **47**, 414–19.

Rutter, M., Andersen-Wood, L., Bechett, C., Bredenham, D., Castle, J., Groothues, C., *et al.* (1999). Quasi-autistic patterns following severe early global privation. *J. Child Psychol. Psychiatry* **40**, 537–49.

Sandler, A.-M. and Hobson, R. P. (2001). On engaging with people in early childhood: the case of congenital blindness. *Clin. Child Psychol. Psychiatry* **6**, 205–22.

Sandler, A.-M. and Wills, D. M. (1965). Preliminary notes on play and mastery in the blind child. *J. Child Psychotherapy* **1**, 7–19.

Schneekloth, L. H. (1989). Play environments for visually impaired children. *J. Vis. Impairment Blindness* **83**, 196–210.

Schopler, E., Reichler, R. J. and Renner, B. R. (1988). *The childhood autism rating scale (CARS).* Los Angeles, CA: Western Psychological.

Skellenger, A.C., Hill, M.M. and Hill, E. (1992). Social functioning of young children with visual impairments. In *Social competence of young children with disabilities: issues and strategies for intervention* (ed. S. Odom, S. McConnell and M. A. Covey), pp. 165–88. Baltimore, MD: Brooks Publishing.

Skellenger, A. C., Rosenblum, L. P. and Jager, B. K. (1997). Behaviors of preschoolers with visual impairments in indoor play settings. *J. Vis. Impairment Blindness* **91**, 519–30.

Tager-Flusberg, H. (2000). Language and understanding minds: connections in autism. In *Understanding other minds: perspectives from developmental cognitive neuroscience*, 2nd edn (ed. S. Baron-Cohen, H. Tager-Flusberg and D. J. Cohen), pp. 124–49. Oxford: Oxford University Press.

Tait, P. E. (1972*a*). Behavior of young blind children in a controlled play situation. *Perceptual and Motor Skills* **34**, 963–69.

Tait, P. E. (1972*b*). A descriptive analysis of the play of young blind children. *Educ. Vis. Handicapped* **4**, 12–15.

Troster, H. and Brambring, M. (1992). Early social–emotional development in blind infants. *Child: Care Hlth Dev.* **18**, 207–27.

Troster, H. and Brambring, M. (1994). The play behavior and play materials of blind and sighted infants and preschoolers. *J. Vis. Impairment Blindness* **88**, 421–32.

Urwin, C. (1983). Dialogue and cognitive functioning in the early language development of three blind children. In *Language acquisition in the blind child: normal and deficient* (ed. A. E. Mills), pp. 142–61. London: Croom Helm.

Wechsler, D. (1967). *Wechsler preschool and primary scale of intelligence*. Cleveland, OH: Psychological Corporation.

Wechsler, D. (1976). *The Wechsler intelligence scale for children: revised*. Sidcup, Kent, UK: Psychological Corporation.

Wills, D. M. (1968). Problems of play and mastery in the blind child. *Br. J. Med. Psychol.* **41**, 213–22.

Wills, D. M. (1970). Vulnerable periods in the early development of blind children. *Psychoanalytic Study of the Child* **34**, 85–117.

Wills, D. M. (1981). Some notes on the application of the diagnostic profile to young blind children. *Psychoanalytic Study of the Child* **36**, 217–37.

Wing, L. (1969). The handicaps of autistic children: a comparative study. *J. Child Psychol. Psychiatry* **10**, 1–40.

Wing, L. and Gould, J. (1979). Severe impairments of social interaction and associated abnormalities in children: epidemiology and classification. *J. Autism Devl Disorders* **9**, 11–20.

Wing, L. and Wing, J. K. (1971). Multiple impairments in early childhood autism. *J. Autism Childhood Schizophrenia* **1**, 256–66.

Glossary

CA: chronological age
CARS: childhood autism rating scale
IQ: intelligence quotient
LS: less social
MA: mental age
MS: more social

7

The enactive mind, or from actions to cognition: lessons from autism

Ami Klin, Warren Jones, Robert Schultz, and Fred Volkmar

Normative-IQ individuals with autism are capable of solving explicit social cognitive problems at a level that is not matched by their ability to meet the demands of everyday social situations. The magnitude of this discrepancy is now being documented through newer techniques such as eye tracking, which allows us to see and measure how individuals with autism search for meaning when presented with naturalistic social scenes. This paper offers an approach to social cognitive development intended to address the above discrepancy, which is considered a key element for any understanding of the pathophysiology of autism. This approach, called the enactive mind (EM), originates from the emerging work on 'embodied cognitive science', a neuroscience framework that views cognition as bodily experiences accrued as a result of an organism's adaptive actions upon salient aspects of the surrounding environment. The EM approach offers a developmental hypothesis of autism in which the process of acquisition of embodied social cognition is derailed early on, as a result of reduced salience of social stimuli and concomitant enactment of socially irrelevant aspects of the environment.

Keywords: autism; enactive mind; embodied cognition; theory of mind

7.1 Social functioning in explicit versus naturalistic situations

One of the most intriguing puzzles posed by individuals with autism is the great discrepancy between what they can do on explicit tasks of social reasoning (when all of the elements of a problem are verbally given to them), and what they fail to do in more naturalistic situations (when they need to spontaneously apply their social reasoning abilities to meet the moment-by-moment demands of their daily social life) (Klin *et al.* 2000). While even the most intellectually gifted individuals display deficits in some complex social reasoning problems (Happé 1994; Baron-Cohen *et al.* 1997), some, particularly those without cognitive deficits, can solve such problems at relatively high levels (Bowler 1992; Dahlgren and Trillingsgaard 1996) without showing commensurate levels of social adaptation. This discrepancy is troublesome because, while it is possible to teach them better social reasoning skills, such new abilities may have little impact on their real-life social or communicative competence (Ozonoff and Miller 1995; Hadwin *et al.* 1997).

There has been little systematic research to investigate the magnitude of this discrepancy. Nevertheless, an indicator of its size can be derived from a sample of 40 older adolescents and adults with autism followed in our centre. Their full-scale IQs are within the normative range, whereas their mean age equivalent score on the interpersonal relationships sub-domain of the *Vineland Adaptive Behaviour Scales* (Sparrow *et al.* 1984) is 4 years. These individuals have many cognitive, linguistic, knowledge-based and potentially useful vocational assets, and yet this social adaptive score would suggest that if left to their own devices in a challenging social situation, their 'social sur-vival' skills or 'street smarts' might be equivalent to those of young children. However, many of these individuals are capable of a degree of self-sufficiency that is much higher than 4 years. It is possible that they are able to achieve this level of independence despite significant social disabilities by choosing highly structured and regimented life routines that avoid novelty and the inherent unpredictability of typical social life. In other words, they may be able to constrain the inevitable complexity of social life by setting themselves a routine of rigid rules and habits, adhering very closely to this lifestyle in what is, typically, a very solitary life.

Some recent studies focusing on responses to naturalistic social situations suggest that the discrepancy between performance on structured as against naturalistic tasks may be even greater than hitherto thought possible. Consider the following two examples from eye-tracking studies of normative-IQ adolescents and adults with autism. In these experiments (Klin *et al.* 2002*a,b*), eye-tracking technology allows researchers to see and measure what a person is visually focusing on when viewing complex social situations. This paradigm allows for an appreciation of a person's spontaneous reactions to naturalistic demands inherent in seeking meaning in what is viewed. In real-life social sit-uations, many crucial social cues occur very rapidly. Failure to notice them may lead to a general failure in assessing the meaning of entire situations, thus precluding adaptive reactions to them. Figure 7.1 shows a still image of two characters from a film: a young man on the left and a young woman on the right. Overlaid on the image are crosses that mark, in black, the focus of a normative-IQ adult with autism and, in white, the focus of a typical adult viewer matched for gender and IQ. The boldest crosshairs mark each viewer's point-of-regard at the moment of this still, while the gradated crosses reveal the path of each viewer's focus over the preceding five frames. The image in this figure is a still from a shot immediately following an abrupt camera cut. In the pre-ceding shot, a character smashes a bottle in the right half of the frame (where both viewers were focused). The camera cuts to show the reaction of the young man and woman, and both viewers respond immediately. While the typical

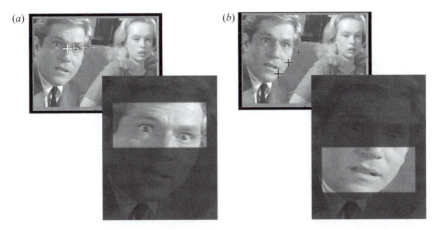

Fig. 7.1   Focus on eyes versus mouth: cut to shocked young man. (*a*) Focus of typically developing viewer. (*b*) Focus of viewer with autism.

Fig. 7.2   Group data (*n* = 16) illustrating focus on eyes versus mouth. Viewers with autism: black crosses; typically developing viewers: white crosses.

viewer responds directly to the look of surprise and horror in the young man's wide eyes, the viewer with autism is seen trying to gather information from the young man's mouth. The young man's mouth is slightly open but quite expressionless, and it provides few clues about what is happening in the scene.

This discrepancy in viewing patterns is also seen in group data. Figure 7.2 plots the focus of eight normative-IQ adults with autism (in black) and eight age-, IQ- and gender-matched typical controls (in white) (this is a sub-sample from the data in Klin *et al.* 2002*b*) for one frame of this video sequence. This sub-sample is used here to visually illustrate the findings obtained for the entire sample summarized below. While typical viewers converge on the eye region, some individuals with autism converge on the mouth region, whereas others' focus is peripheral to the face. When the visual fixation patterns were summarized for the entire sample in this study ($n = 30$, 15 participants in each group), individuals with autism, relative to controls, focused twice as much time on the mouth region of faces and 2.5 times less on the eye region of faces when viewing dynamic social scenes. There was virtually no overlap in the distributions of visual fixation patterns across the two groups of participants. Figure 7.3 presents these data as per cent of overall viewing time focused on eyes and on mouths.

These results contrast markedly with another recent study of face scanning in autism (van der Geest *et al.* 2002), in which participants showed normative visual fixation patterns when viewing photographs of human faces relative to controls. The difference between the two studies was that while in the latter investigation participants were presented with static pictures of faces, in the former study participants were presented with dynamic (i.e., video) depictions of social interactions, coming perhaps closer to replicating a more naturalistic social situation (i.e., we almost never encounter static depictions of faces in our daily social interactions). In such more 'spontaneous situations', the deviation from normative face-scanning patterns in autism seems to be magnified. And the magnitude of this deviation is put in context if one appreciates the fact that preferential looking at the eyes rather than at the mouths of an approaching person has been shown in infants as young as three months of age (Haith *et al.* 1979).

A second example from the same eye-tracking studies (Klin *et al.* 2002*a*) focuses on a developmental skill that emerges and is fully operational by the time a child is approximately 12–14 months of age. It involves the joint-attention skill of following a pointing gesture to the target indicated by the direction of pointing (Mundy and Neal 2000). Pointing, like many other non-verbal social cues, can both modify and further specify what is said. For effective communication exchange, verbal and non-verbal cues need to be quickly integrated. Figure 7.4 shows a scene from a film in which the young man enquires about a painting hanging on a distant wall. In doing so, he first points to a specific painting on the wall and then asks the older man (who lives in the house) 'Who did the painting?' While the verbal request is more general (as there are several pictures on the wall), the act of pointing has already specified the painting in which the young man is interested. The figure shows the visual scanning paths of the adult viewer with autism (in black) and the typical viewer (in white). As can be seen in Fig. 7.4*a*, and more clearly in the schematic renditions in Fig. 7.4*b,c*, the viewer with autism does not follow the pointing gesture but instead waits until he hears the question and then appears to move from picture to picture without knowing which one the conversation

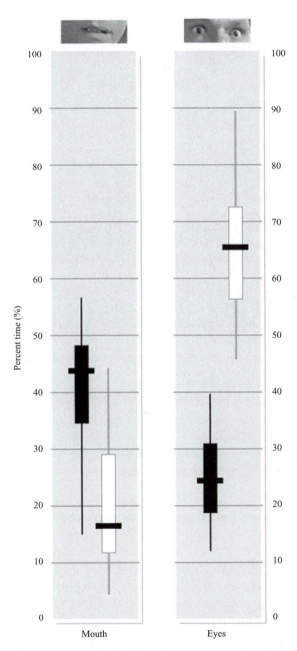

Fig. 7.3 Box plot comparison of visual fixation time on mouth and eye regions for 15 viewers with autism and 15 typically developing viewers (controls). The upper and lower boundaries of the standard box plots are the 25th and 75th percentiles. The horizontal line across the box marks the median of the distribution and the vertical lines below and above the box extend to the minimum and maximum, respectively. Viewers with autism: areas shaded in black; typically developing viewers: white areas.

Fig. 7.4 Scanning patterns in response to social visual versus verbal cues. Viewer with autism: black trace in (*a*) and (*b*); typically developing viewer: white trace in (*a*) and (*c*).

is about. The typical viewer (white track) follows the young man's pointing immediately, ending up, very deliberately, on the correct (large) picture. Hearing the question, he then looks to the older man for a reply and back to the young man for his reaction. The visual path he follows clearly illustrates his ability to use the non-verbal gesture to immediately inspect the painting referenced by the young man. By contrast, the viewer with autism uses primarily the verbal cue, neglecting the non-verbal gesture, and in doing so, resorts to a much more inefficient pursuit of the referenced painting. When the viewer with autism was later questioned, in an explicit fashion, about whether he knew what the pointing gesture meant, he had no difficulty defining the meaning of the gesture. And yet, he failed to apply this knowledge spontaneously when viewing the scene from the film.

That normative-IQ adolescents and adults with autism fail to display normative reactions exhibited by typical young children does not mean, of course, that their ability to function in the world is at this very early stage of development. Rather, it raises the possibility that these individuals learn about the social world in a different manner. What form this developmental path takes is of both clinical and research importance. Collectively, the various examples presented here suggest a need to explain the discrepancy between performance on structured and explicit, as against naturalistic and spontaneous, tasks, and in so doing, to explore what might be a unique social developmental path evidenced in autism. This paper contends that theories of the social dysfunction in autism need to address both of these phenomena. Traditionally, theories of social cognitive development have relied on a framework delineated by computational models of the mind and of the brain (Gardner 1985), which focus on abstracting problem-solving capacities necessary to function in the social environment. The methodologies used typically employ explicit and often verbally mediated tasks to probe whether or not a person has these capacities. In real life, however, social situations rarely present themselves in this fashion. Rather, the individual needs to go about defining a social task as such by paying attention to, and identifying, the relevant aspects of a social situation prior to having an opportunity to use their available social cognitive problem-solving skills. Thus, in order to study more naturalistic social adaptation, there may be some justification in using an alternative theoretical framework that centres around a different set of social cognitive phenomena, for example, people's predispositions to orient to salient social stimuli, to naturally seek to impose social meaning on what they see and hear, to differentiate what is relevant from what is not, and to be intrinsically motivated to solve a social problem once such a problem is identified. The framework presented in this paper is called enactive mind (EM) in order to highlight the central role of motivational predispositions to respond to social stimuli and a developmental process in which social cognition results from social action.

The emphases of the EM framework differ from those in computational models in a number of ways:

(i) instead of assuming a social environment that consists of a pre-given set of definitions and regularities, and a perceiving social agent (e.g. a child) whose mind consists of a pre-given set of cognitive capacities that can solve problems as they are explicitly presented to it, this framework proposes an active mind that sets out to make sense of the social environment and that changes itself as a result of this interaction (Mead 1924);

(ii) moving from a focus on abstracted competencies (what an organism can do), this framework focuses on the adaptive functions which are subserved by these competencies (i.e. how an agent engages in the process of acquiring such competencies in the first place) (Klin *et al.* 2000);

(iii) moving away from a focus on cognition, this framework rekindles a once more prominent role given to affect and predispositional responses in the process of socialization (Damasio 1999); and

(iv) it shifts the focus of investigation from what can be called 'disembodied cognition', or insular abstractions captured by computational cognition (e.g. algorithms in a digital computer) to 'embodied cognition', or cognitive traces left by the action of an organism upon an environment defined by species-specific regularities and by a species-specific topology of differential salience (i.e. some things in the environment are more important than others).

Of particular importance in this framework is the premise that agents may vary in what they are seeking in the environment, resulting in highly disparate 'mental representations' of the world that they are interacting with (Varela *et al.* 1991; Clark 1999). This process, in turn, leads to individual variation in neurofunctional specialization given that more prominence is given in this framework to the notion of the brain as a repository of experiences (LeDoux 2002); that is, our 'brain becomes who we are' or experience repeatedly.

Specifically, the EM approach is offered as an avenue to conceptualize phenomena deemed essential for understanding social adaptation, and which are typically not emphasized in research based on computational models of the social mind. These include the need to consider the complexity of the social world, the very early emerging nature of a multitude of social adaptive mechanisms and how these mechanisms contextualize the emergence of social cognition, as well as important temporal constraints on social adaptation. Our formulation of the EM framework is primarily based on Mead's Darwinian account of the emergence of mind (Mead 1924), the work of Searle *et al.* (1980) and Bates (1976, 1979) in respect to the underlying functions of communication, the philosophy of perception of Merleau-Ponty (1962), and, particularly, on a framework for cognitive neuroscience outlined by Varela *et al.* (1991), from which the term 'enactive mind' is borrowed. Excellent summaries of psychological and neurofunctional aspects of this framework have been provided by Clark (1999) and Iacoboni (2000*a*). Some of the views proposed here have long been part of discussions contrasting information processing and ecological approaches to every aspect of the mind, including attention and sensorimotor integration, memory and language, among other psychological faculties (Gibson 1963; Neisser 1997).

7.2 The social world as an 'open domain task'

In the EM approach, a fundamental difference between explicit and naturalistic social tasks is captured in the distinction between 'closed domains' and 'open domains' of operation (Winograd and Flores 1986). Research paradigms based on computational models of the social mind often reduce the social word to a set of pre-given rules and regularities that can be symbolically represented in the mind of a young child. In other words, the social world is simplified into a 'closed domain task', in which all essential elements to be studied can be fully represented and defined. This is justified in terms of the need to reduce the complexity of the social environment into a number of easily tested problem-solving tasks. By contrast, the EM approach embraces the open-ended nature of social adaptation. The social world as an 'open domain task' implies the need to consider a multitude of elements that are more or less important depending on the context of the situation and the person's perceptions, desires, goals and ongoing adjustment. Successful adaptation requires from a person a sense of relative salience of each element in a situation, preferential choices based on priorities learned through experience, and further moment-by-moment adjustments. For example, if one were to represent the skills of driving a car successfully, one could define the 'driving domain' as involving wheels, roads, traffic lights and other cars. However, this domain is hardly complete without encompassing a host of other factors including attention to pedestrians (sometimes but not always), driving regulations (but these can be overridden by safety factors), local customs (in some cities or countries more than others), variable weather conditions, signals from other drivers, and so on. This rich texture of elements defines the 'background' of knowledge necessary to solve problems in the driving domain. Similarly, the social domain consists of people with age, gender, ethnic and individual differences, facial and bodily gestures, language and voice/prosodic cues in all of their complexity and context-dependent nature, posture, physical settings and social props, and situation-specific conventions, among a host of other factors. Successful driving, or social adaptation, would require more than knowing a set of rules—at times referred to as 'Knowing That'. Rather, it would require 'Knowing How', or a learning process that is based on the accumulation of experiences in a vast number of cases that result in being able to navigate the background environment according to the relative salience of each of the multitude of elements of a situation, and the moment-by-moment emerging patterns that result from the interaction of the various elements. In autism, one of the major limitations of available teaching strategies, including forms of social skills training (Howlin *et al.* 1999), is the difficulty in achieving generalization of skills; in other words, how to translate a problem-solving capacity learned in a closed-domain environment (e.g. therapeutic methods relying on explicit rules and drilling) into a skill that the person avails himself, or herself, of in an open-domain environment (e.g. a naturalistic social situation). This may also be the reason why individuals with autism have difficulty in spontaneously using whatever social cognitive skills they may have learned through explicit teaching. Incidentally, driving is an equally challenging task to individuals with autism.

In the EM approach, the child 'enacts the social world', perceiving it selectively in terms of what is immediately essential for social action, whereas mental representations of that individualized social world arise from repeated experiences resulting from such perceptually guided actions (Varela *et al.* 1991). In this way, the surrounding environment is reduced to perceptions that are relevant to social action; a great simplification if one is to consider the richness of what is constantly available for an agent to hear, see and otherwise experience. Similarly, the mental representations (i.e. social cognition) available for the child to reason about the social environment are deeply embedded in the child's history of social actions, thereby constituting a tool for social adaptation. Thus, there are two principles underlying the EM approach to naturalistic social situations as 'open-domain tasks'. First, the vast complexity of the surrounding environment is greatly simplified in terms of a differential 'topology of salience' that separates aspects of the environment that are irrelevant (e.g. light fixtures, a person turned away) from those that are crucially important (e.g. someone staring at you). Second, this topology of salience is established in terms of perceptually or cognitively guided actions subserving social adaptation.

These principles imply, however, that the surrounding environment will be 'enacted' or recreated differently based on differences in predispositions to respond in a certain way (Maturana and Varela 1973). In autism, our eye-tracking illustrations are beginning to show what this social landscape may look like from the perspective of individuals with this condition. Consider, for example, the illustration in Fig. 7.5, showing the point of regard (signalled by the white cross in the centre of the black circle) of a normative-IQ adult with autism who is viewing a romantic scene. Rather than focusing on the actors in the foreground, he is foveating on the room's light-switch on the left. In Fig. 7.6, a 2-year-old boy with autism is viewing a popular American

Fig. 7.5 Adult viewer with autism (white cross circled in black): focus on non-essential inanimate details.

Fig. 7.6   Toddler viewer with autism: focus on non-essential inanimate details.

children's show. His point of regard on the video frame presented as well as his scan-path immediately before and after that frame (seen in black at the right-hand corner of the picture) indicate that rather than focusing on the pro- tagonists of the show and their actions, this child is visually inspecting inanim- ate details on the shelves. By 'enacting' these scenes in this manner it is likely that, from the perspective of the two viewers with autism, the scenes are no longer social scenes, however clear their social nature might be to a typical viewer. It is also quite probable that if these viewers were explicitly asked or prompted to observe the social scenes and perform a task about them, they might be able to fare much better. The fact that they did not orient to the essen- tial elements in the scene, however, suggests that were they to be part of such a situation, their adjustment to the environmental demands (e.g. to fit in the ongoing play taking place between the two child protagonists) would be greatly compromised.

7.3 Developmental elements in the emergence of mental representations

Computational models of the social mind make use of cognitive constructs that could help a child successfully navigate the social environment (Baron- Cohen 1995). There is less emphasis on how these constructs emerge within a broader context of early social development, which is a justifiable way of modelling the more specific, targeted social cognitive skills. By contrast, the EM approach depends on this broader discussion of early social predis- positions to justify the need to consider complex social situations in terms of a differential 'topology of salience'. In other words, why should some aspects of the environment be more salient than others? In order to address this question, there is a need to outline a set of early social reactions that may precede and accompany the emergence of social cognitive skills.

In the EM approach, the perceptual make-up of typical human infants is seen as consisting of a specific set of somatosensory organs that are constantly seeking salient aspects of the world to focus on, particularly those that have survival value. To invoke the notion of survival value implies the notion of adjustment to, or action upon, the environment. In this context, the gravitation towards and engagement of conspecifics is seen as one of the important survival functions. Thus, social stimuli are seen as having a higher degree of salience than competing inanimate stimuli (Bates 1979; Klin *et al.* 2000). The possibility that, in autism, the relative salience of social stimuli might be diminished (Klin 1989; Dawson *et al.* 1998) could be the basis for a cascade of developmental events in which a child with this condition fails to enact a relevant social world, thus failing to accrue the social experiences suggested in the EM approach to be the basis for social cognitive development.

A large number of social predispositions have been documented in the child development literature, some of which appear to be greatly reduced in children with autism. To limit the discussion to early social orientation skills, we consider only infants' reactions to human sounds and faces. The human voice appears to be one of the earliest and most effective stimuli conducive of social engagement (Eimas *et al.* 1971; Mills and Melhuish 1974; Alegria and Noirot 1978; Eisenberg and Marmarou 1981), a reaction that is not observed in autism (Adrien *et al.* 1991; Klin 1991, 1992; Osterling and Dawson 1994; Werner *et al.* 2000). In fact, the lack of orientation to human sounds (e.g. when the infant hears the voice of a nearby adult) has been found to be one of the most robust predictors of a later diagnosis of autism in children first seen at the age of 2 years (Lord 1995). In the visual modality, human faces have been emphasized as one of the most potent facilitators of social engagement (Bryant 1991). For example, 2-day-olds look at their mother rather than at another unknown woman (Bushnell *et al.* 1989). Three-month-olds focus on the more emotionally revealing eye regions of the face (Haith *et al.* 1979), and 5-month-olds are sensitive to very small deviations in eye gaze during social interactions (Symons *et al.* 1998) and can match facial and vocal expressions based on congruity (Walker 1982). In autism, a large number of face perception studies have shown deficits and abnormalities in such basic visual social processing situations (Langdell 1978; Hobson *et al.* 1988; Klin *et al.* 1999) which, incidentally, are not accompanied by failure in developmentally equivalent tasks in the physical (non-social) domain. For example, one study demonstrated adequate visual processing of buildings as against faces (Boucher and Lewis 1992). Another study asked children with autism to sort people who varied in terms of age, sex, facial expressions of emotion and the type of hat that they were wearing (Weeks and Hobson 1987). In contrast to typical children who grouped pictures by emotional expressions, the partici-pants with autism grouped the pictures by the type of hat the people were wearing. Such studies indicate not only abnormalities in face processing but also preferential ori-entation to inanimate objects, a finding corroborated in other studies (Dawson *et al*. 1998). In a more recent study (Dawson *et al*. 2002), children with autism failed to exhibit differential brain event-related potentials to familiar versus unfamiliar faces, but they did show differences relative to familiar versus unfamiliar objects.

While computational models of the social mind are often modular in nature (Leslie 1987), that is, certain aspects of social functioning could be preserved while others are disrupted, the EM approach ascribes importance to early disruptions in sociability because of its central premise that normative social cognition is embedded in social perception and experience. This principle states that social perception is perceptually guided social action, and social cognitive processes emerge only from recurrent sensorimotor patterns that allow action to be perceptually guided (hence the notion of 'embodied cogni-tion'; Varela *et al*. 1991). The radical assumption of this framework, therefore, is that it is not possible to disentangle cognition from actions, and that if this happened (e.g. a child was taught to perform a social cognitive task following an explicit drill rather than acquiring the skill as a result of repeated social engagement and actions), the given skill would represent a 'disembodied cog-nition', or a reasoning skill that would not retain its normative functional value in social adaptation (Markman and Dietrich 2000). For example, an infant may be attracted to the face of his mother, seeking to act upon it, and in the context of acting upon it the infant learns a great deal about faces and moth-ers, although this knowledge is a function of the child's active experiences with that face. These experiences may include learning of contingencies (e.g. vocal sounds and lip movements go together; certain voice inflections go with certain face configurations such as smiles and frowns), and that these contin-gencies have pleasurable value (thus leading to approach or an attempt at re-enactment of the situation) or unpleasurable value (thus leading to with-drawal). Studies of infants' early social development have shown not only that they are sensitive to affective salience, but that they also act upon that salience through reactions that are appropriate to emotional signals (Haviland and Lelwica 1987). They react negatively to their mothers' depressed affect (Tronick *et al*. 1986), and appropriately to the emotional content of praise or prohibition (Fernald 1993). From an early age, they expect contingency between their actions and those of their partners (Tarabulsy *et al*. 1996). Fewer developmental phenomena have demonstrated this effect more clearly than studies using the 'still-face paradigm' (Tronick *et al*. 1978). When mothers, who have previously been stimulating their babies in a playful fashion, with-draw the smiles and vocalization and assume a still-face, infants as young as 2–3 months old first make attempts to continue the interaction but then stop smiling, avert their gaze, and may protest vigorously (Field *et al*. 1986;

Gusella *et al.* 1988). One study of the still-face effect involving children with autism has failed to document this normative pattern of response (Nadel *et al.* 2000).

In summary, in the EM approach early social predispositions are thought to create the basis and the impetus for the subsequent emergence of mental representations that, because of their inseparability from social action (i.e. they are 'embodied'), retain their adaptive value. Infants do not build veridical models of the social world based on 'universals' or context-invariant representations. Rather, their models or expectations of the world follow their salience-guided actions upon an ever-changing environment that needs to be coped with in an adaptive, moment-by-moment and context-dependent manner (Engel *et al.* 2001).

7.4 Contextual elements in the emergence of mental representations

The classical computational model in cognitive science assumes that cognitive processes are rule-based manipulations of symbols representing the external environment (Newell 1991). Similarly, computational models of the social mind build on the notion that to operate socially is to execute algorithms involving mental representations (Baron-Cohen 1994). By contrast, the EM approach raises the non-trivial question of how a representation acquires meaning to a given child, the so-called 'mind–mind problem' (Jackendoff 1987). The question is, what is the relationship between computational states (e.g. manipulation of mental representations) and a person's experience of the real-life referent of the computational state? How do we progress from having a representation of a person's intention, to experiencing that intention by reacting to it in a certain way? In the computer world, we do know where the meaning of the computational algorithms comes from, namely the programmer. But how do mental representations acquire meaning to a developing child? In autism, individuals often acquire a large number of symbols and symbolic computations that are devoid of shared meaning with others, i.e. the symbols do not have the meaning to them that they have to typical children. Examples are: (i) hyperlexia (reading decoding skills go unaccompanied by reading comprehension; Grigorenko *et al.* 2002); (ii) echolalia and echopraxia (echoing of sounds or mimicry of movements; Prizant and Duchan 1981; Rogers 1999); (iii) 'metaphoric language' (e.g. neologisms, words used in idiosyncratic ways; Lord and Paul 1997); and (iv) prompt-dependent social gestures, routines or scripts (e.g. waving bye-bye without eye contact, staring when requested to make eye contact), among others. While it is difficult for one to conceive of a dissociation between knowing a symbol and acting upon it (e.g. knowing what is the meaning of the pointing gesture and spontaneously turning one's head when somebody is pointing somewhere), this actually happens

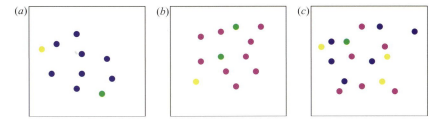

Plate 1. Illustrations of the stimuli presented in feature trials (*a,b*) and in configural trials (*c*) in experiment 2. The absolute numbers of dots and their positions on the computer screen were varied across trials. A random number of green and yellow dots were added to each stimulus to increase the overall difficulty of the discrimination. (See Chapter 9, p. 195.)

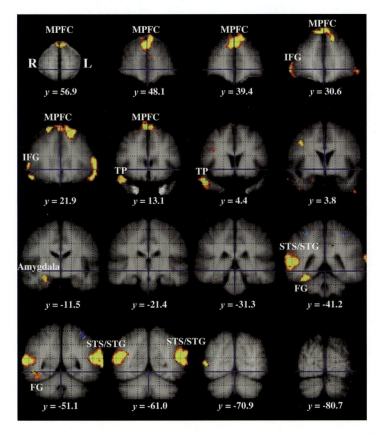

Plate 2. Composite *t*-map for 12 healthy controls, contrasting the social attribution (yellow/red) and the bumper car (blue/purple) tasks ($p < 0.0005$). Right and left are reversed by convention. Abbreviations: BA, Brodman area; FG, fusiform gyrus; IFG, inferior frontal gyrus; MPFC, medial prefrontal cortex; STG, superior temporal gyrus; *Y*-coordinates are from the system of Talairach and Tournoux (1988). (See Chapter 13, p. 275.)

(a) SAT versus bumber car: FFA activation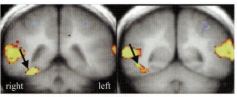

(b) Enlargement and alignment of FFA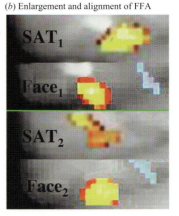

(c) Face versus object discrimination: FFA activation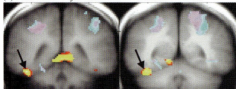

Plate 3. (a) Composite ($n = 12$) t-map at two slices showing significant ($p < 0.0005$) activation for the SAT contrast (yellow/red) with the bumper car control task (blue/purple). (b) Composite ($n = 9$) t-map at two slices showing significant ($p < 0.05$) activation for the face (yellow/red) versus object discrimination (blue/purple). This contrast defines the FFA. (c) Subregions of composite t-maps shown in (a) and (b) are enlarged and aligned to demonstrate the overlap of activation in the FG for the SAT and face discrimination activations. Subscripts 1 and 2 refer to the first (more anterior) and second coronal slices with significant activation. (See Chaper 13, p. 279.)

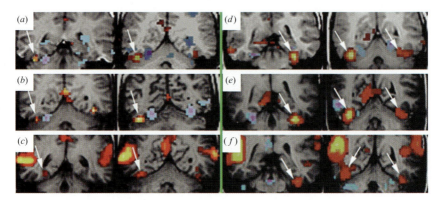

Plate 4. Scans of two individuals across three different occasions showing the reproducibility of FFA activations at two timepoints, and relationship to SAT activations. (a–c) are from a 23-year-old male; (d–f) are from a 24-year-old female. Panels are arranged chronologically. (a,d) The first face versus object experiment. (b,e) The second face versus object scan. (c,f) SAT versus bumper car contrast. Both coronal slices are shown where there was FFA ($t \geqslant 1.5$ in yellow/red) or SAT activation ($t \geqslant 3.0$ in yellow/red). Arrows point to FG activity (right and left are reversed by convention). As in the group results (figure 13.2), the SAT activation is centred slightly more medially along the MFS. Left FG activation shown in these two subjects does not survive thresholding in the group composite (figure 13.2). Control tasks (object discrimination, bumper car) are shown in purple/blue. (See Chapter 13, p. 280.)

in autism, as shown in Fig. 7.3 and in the other examples given above. We know that children with autism can learn associatively (e.g. a symbol becomes paired with a referent). This happens, for example, in vocabulary instruction using simple behavioural techniques. However, one of the big challenges for these children is often to pair a symbol with the adaptive action subsumed by the symbol (Wetherby *et al.* 2000).

In the EM approach, symbols or cognition in general have meaning to the child using them because they are 'embodied actions' (Johnson 1987; Clark 1999), meaning that 'cognition depends upon the experiences that come from having a body with various sensorimotor capacities', and that 'perception and action are fundamentally inseparable in lived cognition' (Varela *et al.* 1991, p. 173). An artificial separation of cognition from the other elements would render the given cognitive construct a 'mental ghost' once again. One can exemplify the inseparability of cognition and action through the classic studies of Held and Hein (1963) and Held (1965) of perceptual guidance of action. They raised kittens in the dark and exposed them to light only under controlled conditions. One group of kittens was allowed to move around normally, but each of them was harnessed to a carriage that contained a second group of kittens. While the groups shared the same visual experience, the second group was entirely passive. When the kittens were released after a few weeks of this treatment, members of the first group (the one that moved around) behaved normally, whereas members of the second group (the one that was passively carried by the others) behaved as blind, bumping into objects and falling off edges. These experiments illustrate the point that meaningful cognition of objects (i.e. the way we see them and adjust to them) cannot be formed by means of visual extraction alone; rather, there is a need for perceptual processes to be actively linked with action in order to guide further action upon these objects. Studies of adaptation of disarranged hand–eye coordination in humans (Held and Hein 1958), tactile vision substitution in blind humans (Bach-y-Rita 1983) and neural coding of body schema in primates (Iriki *et al.* 1996) among others (see Iacoboni 2000*b*) support this point. A striking example is provided in a study (Aglioti *et al.* 1996) of a patient with right-brain damage who denied the ownership of her left hand and of objects that were worn by her left hand (such as rings). When the same objects were worn by the right hand, the patient recognized them as her own. In infancy research, a wide range of phenomena, from haptic and depth perception (Bushnell and Boudreau 1993) to Piagetian milestones (Thelen *et al.* 2001) have began to characterize developmental skills as 'perception-for-action' systems, while neuroimaging studies have shown overlapping brain circuitry subserving action observation and action generation (Blakemore and Decety 2001).

Perception-for-action systems are particularly relevant to a discussion of social adaptation. Consider the skill of imitation, one of the major deficits in autism (Rogers 1999). It is interesting that while children with autism have great difficulty in learning through imitation, they do exhibit a great deal of 'mirroring' or 'copying' behaviours, both vocally (e.g. echoing what other people say) and motorically (e.g. making the same gesture as another person). However, these are typically devoid of the function that these behaviours serve to typical people displaying them. One theory derived from the EM approach would predict that this curious discrepancy originates from the aspect of the typical person's action that is most salient in the child's perception. Whereas typical children may see a waving gesture as a motion embedded in the act of communication or emotional exchange, children with autism may dissociate the motion from the social context, focusing on the salient physical facts and thus repeating the gesture in a mechanical fashion. This is not unlike what a typical child might do in a game of imitating meaningless gestures, or what a neonate might do when protruding his or her tongue in response to seeing an adult doing so (Meltzoff and Moore 1977). This theory originates from the notion that while perception-for-action may occur in the absence of social engagement (e.g. in neonates), in typical infants, around the middle of their second year of life, imitation is much more likely to serve social engagement and social learning than to occur outside the realm of social interaction, as in autism. Supporting this theory is a series of studies in which, for example, 18-month-old infants were exposed to a human or to a mechanical device attempting to perform various actions. The children imitated the action when it was performed by the human model, but not when it was performed by the mechanical device (Meltzoff 1995).

Perception-for-action systems are of particular interest in the context of survival abilities (e.g. responding to a threatening person or a lethal predator). A central example of such systems is the ability to perceive certain patterns of movement as biological motion. This system allows humans, as well as other species, to discern the motion of biological forms from motion occurring in the inanimate environment. In the wild, an animal's survival would depend on its ability to detect approaching predators and predict their future actions. In humans, this system has been linked to the emergence of the capacity to attribute intentions to others (Frith and Frith 1999). The study of biological motion has traditionally used the paradigm of human motion display created by Johansson (1973). In his work, the motion of the living body is represented by a few bright spots describing the motions of the main joints. In this fashion, the motion pattern is dissociated from the form of people's bodies. The moving presentation of this set of bright spots evokes a compelling impression of basic human movements (e.g. walking, running, dancing) as well as of social movements (e.g. approaching, fighting, embracing). Figure 7.7 illustrates a series of static images of the human form rendered as point-light animations. The phenomenon studied by Johansson, however, can only be fully appreciated when the display is set in motion.

Using this paradigm, several studies have documented adult's abilities to attribute gender, emotions and even personality features to these moving dots (Koslowski and Cutting 1978; Dittrich *et al.* 1996). Even 3-month-old infants

Fig. 7.7   Series of static images of the human form rendered as point-light displays.

are able to discriminate between the moving dots depicting a walking person and the same dot displays moving randomly (Fox and McDaniel 1982). The presence of this ability at such a young age, as well as its presence in other species including monkeys (Oram and Perrett 1994) and birds (Regolin *et al*. 2000), and the demonstrated singularity of biological motion relative to other forms of motion from the perspective of the visual system (Neri *et al*. 1998) suggest that this is a highly conserved and unique system that makes possible the recognition of movements of others in order to move towards or away from them. Several neuroimaging studies have singled out the superior temporal sulcus as an important structure involved in the perception of biological motion (Grossman and Blake 2000; Grossman *et al*. 2000; Grezes *et al*. 2001), a region also associated with basic 'survival' reactions such as evaluating facial expressions and/or direction of eye gaze (Puce *et al*. 1998). A positron emission tomography study attempting to separate decontextualized human motions (point-light displays depicting a hand bringing a cup to one's mouth) from what can be seen as a more naturalistic human motion (a person dancing) showed that the perception of the latter also implicated limbic structures such as the amygdala (Bonda *et al*. 1996). This finding is consistent with a perception-for-action system that not only perceives to act, but one that is embedded in an approach/withdrawal, affective-based context (Gaffan *et al*. 1988).

Given the fundamental and adaptive nature of perception of biological motion, one would expect this system to be intact in even very disabled children. One study so far has shown the system to be intact in children with profound spatial deficits and a degree of mental retardation (Jordan *et al*. 2002). By contrast, our own preliminary data suggest, to date, that this system may be compromised in young children with autism. We used Johansson point-light displays to depict a series of social approaches that are part of the typical experiences of young children (e.g. an animated adult trying to attract the attention of a young toddler, 'pat-a-cake', 'peek-a-boo'). Scenes were presented in two formats simultaneously, one on each of the two horizontal halves of a computer screen. The scenes were identical except that one was oriented correctly and the other was upside-down. The child heard the corresponding sound effects of that social scene (e.g. the verbal approach of an adult). The experiment followed a visual preference paradigm in which the child looked at one of the two scenes presented. By requiring the child to choose between an upside-down and a correctly oriented animation matching the sound effects of the social interaction, we were able to test the child's ability to impose mental representations of human movement interactions on the ambiguous visual stimuli. This paradigm is illustrated in Fig. 7.8. Our preliminary data for 11 2-year-old toddlers, 5 with a diagnosis of autism and 6 typical children are given in Fig. 7.9. Overall, the typically developing toddlers demonstrated a marked preference for the correctly oriented figure (83% of total viewing time versus 17% for upside-down display), while the toddlers with autism showed a pattern closer to a random choice (56% versus 44%). We also analysed initial fixations and final fixations (defined by the figure the child was focusing on at the end of the animation) as a rudimentary view of how understanding of the animation's content might progress during viewing. We recorded the number of times the toddlers with autism shifted their focus from the upright to the inverted figure, relative to typically developing controls. These results are depicted graphically in Fig. 7.10. While typically developing toddlers and toddlers with autism both exhibited initial fixations at chance or near-chance levels, the typically developing infants were focused on the upright figure at the end of more than 75% of all trials, while the toddlers with autism remained at chance level. Of similar interest are group differences in the pattern of shifting between the upright and inverted figures. Toddlers with autism shifted more frequently than typically developing toddlers, a trend suggestive of increased difficulty in adequately understanding either of the two displays. If corroborated in larger studies, this finding would point to a major disruption in a highly conserved skill that is thought to be a core ability underlying social engagement and, subsequently, the capacity to attribute intentionality to others.

7.5 Temporal constraints on models of social adaptation

Computational models of the mind place less emphasis on the temporal unfolding of the cognitive processes involved in a task (Newell 1991). This stance is justified when a given task is explicit and fully defined. However, in naturalistic situations there are important temporal constraints in social adaptation, as failure to detect an important but fleeting social cue, or a failure to detect temporal relationships between two social cues, may lead to partial or even misleading comprehension of the situation, which may in turn lead to ineffective adjustment to the situation. For example, if the viewer of a scene fails to monitor a non-speaker in a social scene who is clearly embarrassed by what another person is saying, the viewer is unlikely to correctly identify the meaning of that situation (Klin *et al.* 2002*a*). In this way, the EM approach sees social adaptation along the same principles currently being considered in research into 'embodied vision' (Churchland *et al.* 1994). This view holds that the task of the visual system is not to generate exhaustive mental models of a veridical surrounding environment but to use visual information to perform real-time, real-life adaptive reactions. Rather than creating an inner mirror of the outside world to formulate problems and then to solve them ahead of

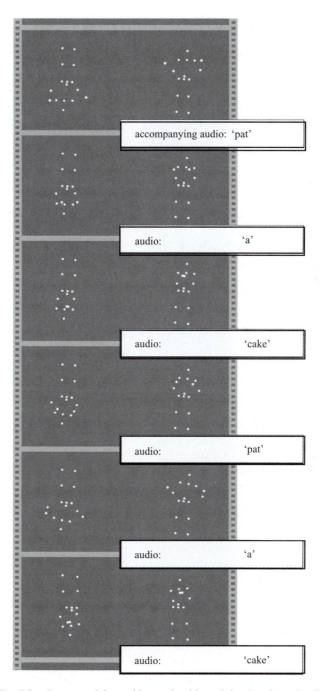

Fig. 7.8 Cross-modal matching task with social animation stimuli.

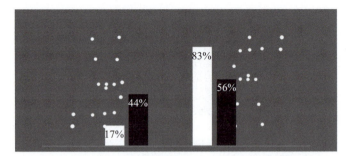

Fig. 7.9 Percentage of total viewing time spent on upright versus inverted figures. Black bars: toddlers with autism; white bars: typically developing toddlers.

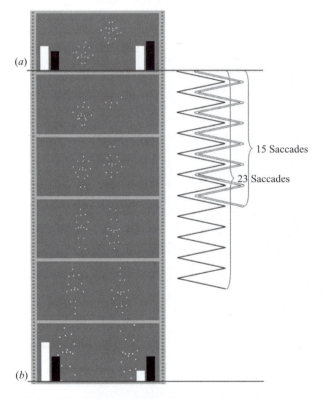

Fig. 7.10 Initial and final fixation data, and number of saccades between upright and inverted figures. Toddlers with autism, filled bars; typically developing toddlers, open bars. (*a*) Initial fixation: toddlers with autism 40% upright, 60% inverted; typically developing toddlers 50% upright, 50% inverted. (*b*) Final fixation: toddlers with autism 50% upright, 50% inverted; typically developing toddlers 79% upright, 21% inverted. Number of saccades between upright and inverted figures: toddlers with autism 23 saccades min^{-1}, typically developing toddlers 15 saccades min^{-1}.

acting upon them, vision is seen as the active retrieval of useful information as it is needed from the constantly present and complex visual environment. From the organism's adaptive perspective, the topology of salience of this visual tapestry, from light reflections to carpet patterning, to furniture and clothing, to mouths and eyes, is far from flat. We would be overwhelmed and paralysed by its richness if we were to start from a position of equal salience to every aspect of what is available to be visually inspected. Rather, we actively retrieve aspects of the visual environment that are essential for quick, adaptive actions by foveating on sequential locations where we expect to find them. These 'expectations' are generated by a brain system dedicated to salience (a lion entering the room is more important than the light-switch next to the door), and an ever more complex (going from infancy to adulthood) understanding of the context of the situation, the so-called 'top-down' approach to vision (Engel *et al.* 2001).

A pertinent example of this view of vision is the analysis of a baseball game by Clark (1999, p. 346) in which an outfielder positions himself or herself to catch a fly ball: 'It used to be thought that this problem required complex calculations of the arc, acceleration and distance of the ball. However, more recent work suggests a computationally simpler strategy (McBeath *et al.* 1995). Put simply, the fielder continually adjusts his or her run so that the ball never seems to curve towards the ground, but instead appears to move in a straight line in his or her visual field. By maintaining this strategy, the fielder should be guaranteed to arrive in the right place at the right time to catch the ball' (p. 346). Piaget (1973) provided similar examples from children's play, and Zajonc (1980) provided similar examples from intersubjective adaptation. Consistent with these examples, the EM approach considers the 'social game' to be not unlike the outfielder's effort. A typical toddler entering a playroom pursues a sequence of social adaptive reactions to split-second environmental demands with moment-by-moment disregard of the vast majority of the available visual stimulation. Such a child is ready to play the social game. For individuals with autism, however, the topology of salience, defined as the 'foveal elicitation' of socially relevant stimuli (as exemplified in our eye-tracking illustrations and in studies of preferential attention to social versus non-social entities; see above), is much flatter. The social worlds enacted by individuals with autism and by their typical peers, if viewed in this light, may be strikingly different.

7.6 Social cognition as social action

The radical assumption made in the EM approach is that mental representations as described in computational models of the mind are proxies for the actions that generated them and for which they stand (Varela *et al.* 1991; Thelen and Smith 1994; Lakoff and Johnson 1999). This counter-intuitive view can be traced back to the account of Mead (1924) of the social origins of mind. Mead saw the emergence of mind as the capacity of an individual to make a 'gesture' (e.g. bodily sign, vocal sound) that means to the other person seeing or hearing it the same as for the person making it. The meaning of the gesture, however, is in the reaction of the other. A gesture used in this way becomes a symbol, i.e. something that stands for the predicted reaction of the other person. Once a child has such a symbolic gesture, she can then uphold it as a representation for the reaction of the social partner, thus being able to take a step back from the immediate experience and then to contemplate alternatives of action using such symbols as proxies for real actions. In the EM approach, the fact that the emergence and evolution of a symbol are tied to actions of adaptation, which in turn are immersed in a context of somatosensory experiences, salience and perceptually guided actions, makes the symbol a proxy for these elements of the action. When we uphold and manipulate symbols in our mind, therefore, we are also evoking a network of experiences resulting from a life history of actions associated with that symbol.

This view, connecting social cognition with social action, is useful in our attempt to explore possible reasons why accomplishments in social reasoning in individuals with autism are not accompanied by commensurate success in social action. Consider an example from research on face perception. While face recognition deficits are very pronounced in young children with autism (Klin *et al.* 1999), the size of this deficit is much smaller in older and more cognitively able adolescents (Celani *et al.* 1999). The possibility that older individuals might perform such tasks using atypical strategies relative to their peers was investigated in our recent fMRI study of face recognition in autism (Schultz *et al.* 2000) in which normative-IQ individuals with autism and controls were presented with face versus object recognition tasks. In contrast to controls for whom face processing was associated with fusiform gyrus (FG) activation, in individuals with autism face processing was associated with activation in inferior temporal gyrus structures, an activation pattern that was obtained for controls when they were processing objects. These results indicated that individuals with autism did not rely on the normal neural substrate during face perception (Kanwisher *et al.* 1997) but rather engaged brain areas that were more important to non-face, object processing (Haxby *et al.* 1999). In other words, they failed to treat faces as a special form of visual stimulus, treating them instead as ordinary objects.

It would be tempting from these results to suggest that a circumscribed area of the brain, namely the FG, and the mechanism it represents, namely perception of face identity, were causally related to autism. Given the centrality of face perception in interpersonal interactions, this would be a plausible theory of autism. However, other recent studies (Gauthier and Tarr 1997; Gauthier *et al.* 1999) have suggested that the FG is not necessarily the brain site for face recognition, appearing instead to be a site associated with visual expertise, so that when a person becomes an expert on a given object category (say Persian carpets), selective activation of the FG occurs when the person is looking at an instance of that object. This notion suggests a reinterpretation of our face recognition results in autism. The FG was not selectively activated when individuals with autism were looking at faces because they were not experts on faces. By contrast, typically developing individuals have a lifetime to develop this expertise, a result of a very large number of recurrent experiences of focusing on and acting upon other people's faces beginning in very early infancy. As previously described, faces have little salience to young children with autism and would thus represent a much less frequent target of recurrent actions necessary to produce expertise.

Considering this interpretation, if individuals with autism were to be asked to perform a visual recognition task using stimuli on which they had expertise, one might observe FG activation. Preliminary results supportive of this suggestion were obtained in an fMRI study of an individual with autism whose expertise area is *Digimon* characters (a large series of cartoon figures) (Grelotti *et al.* 2003). Interestingly, fMRI activations for *Digimon* characters in this individual with autism also included the amygdala, suggesting salience-driven rewards associated with the characters. Results such as these are beginning to delineate a developmental profile of functional brain maturation in autism in which hardwired social salience systems are derailed from very early on, following a path marked by seeking physical entities (not people) and repeatedly enacting them and thus neglecting social experiences (Klin *et al.* 2002*a*). This proposal is consistent with the notion of functional brain development as 'an activity-dependent process' that emphasizes the infancy period as a window of maximal plasticity (Johnson 2001). An interesting line of research supporting this theory is the case of people with a period of visual deprivation early in postnatal life due to bilateral congenital cataracts. Although early surgical correction was associated with rapid improvement of visual acuity, deficits in configural processing of faces remained even after many years post-surgery (Maurer *et al.* 1999; Le Grand *et al.* 2001). Configural processing of a class of visual stimuli (say, faces) represents a developmental shift from processing an object from its parts to processing objects in a Gestalt manner (Tanaka *et al.* 1998), which, in turn, is a mark of the acquisition of perceptual expertise (Diamond and Carey 1986; Gauthier and Nelson 2001). Thus, studies of early visual deprivation seem to highlight the effects of reduced early 'visual enactment' of a class of visual stimuli on later, automatic, and more efficient ways of processing that class of stimuli.

Returning to the fMRI example in which individuals with autism treated faces as objects (Schultz *et al.* 2000), it is of considerable interest that all participants could perform relatively well on the behavioural task of face recognition. They could correctly match faces, albeit using a strategy that differed markedly from controls. Thus, an analysis of results on the behavioural task by itself would have unveiled no significant differences between the two groups. One may, however, consider what would be the behavioural impact of failing to process faces as a special class of objects. Most people are able to recognize possibly thousands of faces very quickly, whereas their ability to recognize, say, pieces of luggage is much more limited. Thus, some of us are quite likely to mistake our bags when coming to pick them up from a luggage carousel at the airport, but we are very unlikely to mistake our mother-in-law rushing to greet us from the surrounding crowd.

The point illustrated in this example is the importance of developmental and contextual aspects of social development in making social cognitive accomplishments into tools of social action. Temporal constraints on social adaptation require skills to be displayed spontaneously and quickly, without the need for an explicit translation of what requirements are to be met in a given social task. There is a need to seek socially relevant information, and to maintain on-line, as it were, a continuous process of imposing social meaning to what is seen. This comes easily and effortlessly to typical individuals. By contrast, the most challenging task in the daily lives of individuals with autism involves the need to adjust to commonplace, naturalistic social situations. Consider, for example, an adolescent with autism entering a high school cafeteria. There is usually an array of interrelated social events taking place, each one consisting of a vast amount of social cues including language exchange, voice/prosody cues, facial and bodily gestures, posture and body movements, among many others. These cues are embedded in a complex visual and auditory setting, with some physical stimuli being relevant to the social events (i.e. representing specific social contexts—a cafeteria—or specific 'props'— a costume worn by one of the students), and other physical stimuli being entirely irrelevant (e.g. light switches or fixtures, number of doors, detailing in the walls). Such situations are so challenging because there is hardly any aspect of the social event that is explicitly defined. Faced with a highly complex and ambiguous social display that demands a reaction (e.g. where to sit down, how to insert oneself in an unfolding social event), they need to make sense of what they see and hear by imposing social meaning onto essential social aspects of the situation (e.g. facial expressions) while ignoring irrelevant stimuli (e.g. light fixtures).

In order to study how difficult it might be for individuals to make sense of such a situation, one can use an experimental metaphor that measures a person's spontaneous tendency to impose social meaning on ambiguous visual stimuli. More specifically, it measures how salient the social meaning of an array of ambiguous visual stimuli is to a viewer, and how socially relevant the viewer's thinking is when making an effort to make sense of the presented visual stimuli. The paradigm involves the presentation of a classic animation in which geometric shapes move and act like humans (Heider and Simmel 1944; Fig. 7.11). Typical viewers immediately recognize the social nature of the cartoon, and provide narratives that include a number of social attributions involving relationships portrayed there (e.g. being a bully, being a friend), the meaning of specific actions (e.g. trapping, protecting), and attributions of

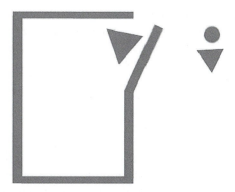

Fig. 7.11   Screen shot showing cast of characters from a cartoon from Heider & Simmel (1944).

mental states (e.g. being shy, thinking, being surprised) to the characters. By contrast, cognitively able adolescents and adults with autism have great difficulty in doing so. In one study (Klin 2000), they were, on average, able to recognize only a quarter of the social elements deemed essential to understanding the plot of the story. A large proportion of them limited their narratives to faithful descriptions of the geometric events depicted in the cartoon, but without any social attributions. This was quite surprising considering that an inclusionary condition in this study required participants to 'pass' a relatively advanced social reasoning task (a second-order theory of mind task; Tager-Flusberg and Sullivan 1994). Thus, these individuals' ability to solve explicit social cognitive problems was no assurance that they would use these skills spontaneously. Some of them were unable to make any social attributions at all. Yet, such spontaneous attributions of intentionality to these geometric cartoons have been documented in infants (Gergely *et al.* 1995), and even primates (Uller and Nichols 2000). Some of the individuals with autism did, however, make a meaningful effort to make sense of the cartoon, but in doing so provided entirely irrelevant attributions, explaining the movements of the geometric shapes in terms of physical meaning (e.g. magnetic forces), not social meaning. Translated into a task of social adjustment to a naturalistic setting such as the high school cafeteria, the results of this study would suggest that some of these individuals might have no access to the social cues (not even noticing them), whereas others might search for causation relationships in the wrong domain, namely physical rather than social.

   To impose social meaning on an array of visual stimuli is an adaptive reaction displayed by typical children, from infancy onwards, at an ever-increasing level of complexity. This spontaneous skill is cultivated in countless hours of recurrent social engagement. From discerning the meaning of facial expressions and detecting human motion and forms of human action, to attributing intentionality and elaborate mental states to others, the act of adjusting to social demands imbues social cognitive accomplishments with their functional value. It is in this light that the above examples suggest that in autism there is a breakdown in the process through which social cognitive skills and social action become inseparable.

7.7 Conclusions

This paper began with an intriguing puzzle posed by normative-IQ individuals with autism: how can they learn so much about the world and yet still be unable to translate this knowledge into real-life social adaptive actions? A framework different from the prevailing computational models of social cognitive development was offered—enactive mind (EM)—as a way of exploring this puzzle. This framework is based on the emerging embodied cognitive neuroscience. EM views cognition as embedded in experiences resulting from a body's actions upon salient aspects of its surrounding environment. Social cognition is seen as the experiences associated with a special form of action, namely social interaction. These are tools of social adaptation that can be abstracted in the form of symbols and used to reason about social phenomena, although they retain their direct connection to the composite of enactive experiences that originated and shaped them over the lifetime of the child.

In autism, the EM approach proposes the theory that the above process is derailed from its incipience, because the typical overriding salience of social stimuli is not present. In its place is a range of physical stimuli, which attracts the child's selective attention, leading into a path of ever greater specialization in things rather than people. Clearly, individuals with autism are capable of acquiring language and concepts, and even a vast body of information on people. But these tools of thought are acquired outside the realm of active social engagement and the embodied experiences predicated by them. In a way, they possess what is, typically, the rooftop of social development. However, this rooftop is freestanding. The constructs and definitions are there, but their foundational experiences are not. The EM approach contends that without the set of embodied social cognitive tools required to produce moment-by-moment social adaptive reactions in naturalistic social situations, social behaviour becomes truncated, slow and inefficient.

A corollary of this theory is that individuals with autism learn about people in a way that departs from the normative processes of social development. The fact that cognitively able individuals with autism are able to demonstrate so much social cognitive understanding in some situations is as interesting as the fact that they fail to make use of these skills in other situations. The study of possible compensatory paths and the degrees to which they help these individuals to achieve more independence is as important a research endeavour as to document their social cognitive failures, but to do so there will be a need to go beyond results on explicit tasks. There will be a need both to explore more deeply the atypical processes used by these individuals to perform explicit tasks, and to increase our arsenal of methodologies capable of studying social adaptation in more naturalistic settings (Klin *et al.* 2002*a*).

References

Adrien, J., Faure, M., Perrot, A., Hameury, L., Garreau, B., Barthelemy, C., *et al.* (1991). Autism and family home movies: preliminary findings. *J. Autism Devl Disorders* **21**, 43–49.

Aglioti, S., Smania, N., Manfredi, M. and Berlucchi, G. (1996). Disownership of left hand and objects related to it in a patient with right brain damage. *NeuroReport* **8**, 293–96.

Alegria, J. and Noirot, E. (1978). Neonate orientation behavior towards human voice. *Int. J. Behav. Dev.* **1**, 291–312.

Bach-y-Rita, P. (1983). Tactile vision substitution: past and future. *Int. J. Neurosci.* **19**, 29–36.

Baron-Cohen, S. (1994). How to build a baby that can read minds: cognitive mechanisms in mindreading. *Cah. Psychol. Cogn.* **13**, 513–52.

Baron-Cohen, S. (1995). *Mindblindness: an essay on autism and theory of mind.* Cambridge, MA: MIT Press.

Baron-Cohen, S., Jolliffe, T., Mortimore, C. and Robertson, M. (1997). Another advanced test of theory of mind: evidence from very high functioning adults with autism or Asperger syndrome. *J. Child Psychol. Psychiat.* **38**, 813–22.

Bates, E. (1976). *Language and context: the acquisition of pragmatics.* New York: Academic Press.

Bates, E. (1979). On the evolution and development of symbols. In *The emergence of symbols: cognition and communication in infancy* (ed. E. Bates), pp. 1–32. New York: Academic Press.

Blakemore, S.-J. and Decety, J. (2001). From the perception of action to the understanding of intention. *Nature Rev. Neurosci.* **2**, 561–67.

Bonda, E., Petrides, M., Ostry, D. and Evans, A. (1996). Specific involvement of human parietal systems and the amygdala in the perception of biological motion. *J. Neurosci.* **15**, 3737–44.

Boucher, J. and Lewis, V. (1992). Unfamiliar face recognition in relatively able autistic children. *J. Child Psychol. Psychiat.* **33**, 843–59.

Bowler, D. M. (1992). 'Theory of mind' in Asperger's syndrome. *J. Child Psychol. Psychiat.* **33**, 877–93.

Bryant, P. E. (1991). Face to face with babies. *Nature* **354**, 19.

Bushnell, E. W. and Boudreau, J. P. (1993). Motor development and the mind: the potential role of motor abilities as a determinant of aspects of perceptual development. *Child Dev.* **64**, 1005–21.

Bushnell, I. W. R., Sai, F. and Mullin, J. T. (1989). Neonatal recognition of the mother's face. *Br. J. Devl Psychol.* **7**, 3–15.

Celani, G., Battacchi, M. W. and Arcidiacono, L. (1999). The understanding of the emotional meaning of facial expressions in people with autism. *J. Autism Devl Disorders* **29**, 57–66.

Churchland, P. S., Ramachandran, V. S. and Sejnowski, T. J. (1994). A critique of pure vision. In *Large-scale neuronal theories of the brain. Computational neuroscience* (ed. C. Koch and J. L. Davis), pp. 23–60. Cambridge, MA: MIT Press.

Clark, A. (1999). An embodied cognitive science? *Trends Cogn. Sci.* **3**, 345–51.

Dahlgren, S. O. and Trillingsgaard, A. (1996). Theory of mind in non-retarded children with autism and Asperger's syndrome. A research note. *J. Child Psychol. Psychiat.* **37**, 759–63.

Damasio, A. (1999). *The feeling of what happens: body and emotion in the making of consciousness*. New York: Harcourt Brace.

Dawson, G., Meltzoff, A. N., Osterling, J., Rinaldi, J. and Brown, E. (1998). Children with autism fail to orient to naturally occurring social stimuli. *J. Autism Devl Disorders* **28**, 479–85.

Dawson, G., Carver, L., Meltzoff, A. N., Panagiotides, H., McPartland, J. and Webb, S. J. (2002). Neural correlates of face and object recognition in young children with autism spectrum disorder, developmental delay and typical development. *Child Dev.* **73**, 700–17.

Diamond, R. and Carey, S. (1986). Why faces are and are not special: an effect of expertise. *J. Exp. Psychol.* **115**, 107–17.

Dittrich, W. H., Troscianko, T., Lea, S. E. and Morgan, D. (1996). Perception of emotion from dynamic point-light displays represented in dance. *Perception* **25**, 727–38.

Eimas, P., Siqueland, E., Jusczyk, P. and Vigorito, J. (1971). Speech perception in infants. *Science* **171**, 303–06.

Eisenberg, R. and Marmarou, A. (1981). Behavioural reactions of newborns to speech-like sounds and their implications for developmental studies. *J. Infant Mental Hlth* **2**, 129–38.

Engel, A. K., Fries, P. and Singer, W. (2001). Dynamic predictions: oscillations and synchrony in top-down processing. *Nature Rev. Neurosci.* **2**, 704–16.

Fernald, A. (1993). Approval and disapproval: infant responsiveness to vocal affect in familiar and unfamiliar languages. *Child Dev.* **64**, 657–74.

Field, T., Vega-Lahar, N., Scafidi, F. and Goldstein, S. (1986). Effects of maternal unavailability on motion-infant interactions. *Infant Behav. Dev.* **9**, 473–78.

Fox, R. and McDaniel, C. (1982). The perception of biological motion by human infants. *Science* **218**, 486–87.

Frith, C. D. and Frith, U. (1999). Interacting minds: a biological basis. *Science* **286**, 1692–95.

Gaffan, E. A., Gaffan, D. and Harrison, S. (1988). Disconnection of the amygdala from visual association cortex impairs visual-reward association learning in monkeys. *J. Neurosci.* **8**, 3144–50.

Gardner, H. (1985). *The mind's new science: a history of the cognitive revolution*. New York: Basic Books.

Gauthier, I. and Nelson, C. A. (2001). The development of face expertise. *Curr. Opin. Neurobiol.* **11**, 219–24.

Gauthier, I. and Tarr, M. (1997). Becoming a 'greeble' expert: exploring mechanisms for face recognition. *Vis. Res.* **37**, 1673–81.

Gauthier, I., Tarr, M., Anderson, A., Skudlarski, P. and Gore, J. (1999). Activation of the middle fusiform face area increases with expertise in recognizing novel objects. *Nature Neurosci.* **2**, 568–73.

Gergely, G., Nadasdy, Z., Csibra, G. and Biro, S. (1995). Taking the intentional stance at 12 months of age. *Cognition* **56**, 165–93.

Gibson, J. J. (1963). The useful dimension of sensitivity. *Am. Psychol.* **18**, 1–15.

Grelotti, D. J., Klin, A., Volkmar, F. R., Gauthier, I., Skudlarski, P., Cohen, D. J., *et al.* (2003). FMRI activation of the fusiform gyrus and amygdala to cartoon characters but not faces in a boy with autism. (Submitted.)

Grezes, J., Fonlupt, P., Bertenthal, B., Delon-Martin, C., Segebarth, C. and Decety, J. (2001). Does perception of biological motion rely on specific brain regions? *NeuroImage* **13**, 775–85.

Grigorenko, E. L., Klin, A., Pauls, D. L., Senft, R., Hooper, C. and Volkmar, F. R. (2002). A descriptive study of hyperlexia in a clinically referred sample of children with developmental delays. *J. Autism Devl Disorders* **32**, 3–12.

Grossman, E. and Blake, R. (2000). Brain activity evoked by inverted and imagined motion. *Vision Res.* **41**, 1475–82.

Grossman, E., Donnelly, M., Price, R., Pickens, D., Morgan, V., Neighbor, G., *et al.* (2000). Brain areas involved in perception of biological motion. *J. Cogn. Neurosci.* **12**, 711–20.

Gusella, J. L., Muir, D. W. and Tronick, E. Z. (1988). The effect of manipulating maternal behavior during an interaction on 3- and 6-month olds' affect and attention. *Child Dev.* **59**, 1111–24.

Hadwin, J., Baron-Cohen, S., Howlin, P. and Hill, K. (1997). Does teaching theory of mind have an effect on the ability to develop conversation in children with autism? *J. Autism Devl Disorders* **27**, 519–37.

Haith, M. M., Bergman, T. and Moore, M. J. (1979). Eye contact and face scanning in early infancy. *Science* **198**, 853–55.

Happé, F. G. (1994). An advanced test of theory of mind: understanding of story characters' thoughts and feelings by able autistic, mentally handicapped, and normal children and adults. *J. Autism Devl Disorders* **24**, 129–54.

Haviland, J. M. and Lelwica, M. (1987). The induced affect response: 10-week-old infants' responses to three emotional expressions. *Devl Psychol.* **23**, 97–104.

Haxby, J., Ungerleider, L., Clark, V., Schouten, J., Hoffman, E. and Martin, A. (1999). The effect of face inversion on activity in human neural systems for face and object perception. *Neuron* **22**, 189–99.

Heider, F. and Simmel, M. (1944). An experimental study of apparent behavior. *Am. J. Psychol.* **57**, 243–59.

Held, R. (1965). Plasticity in sensory-motor systems. *Sci. Am.* **213**, 84–94.

Held, R. and Hein, A. (1958). Adaptation of disarranged hand-eye coordination contingent upon re-afferent stimulation. *Percept. Motor Skills* **8**, 87–90.

Held, R. and Hein, A. (1963). Movement-produced stimulation in the development of visually guided behavior. *J. Comp. Physiol. Psychol.* **56**, 872–76.

Hobson, R. P., Ouston, J. and Lee, A. (1988). What's in a face? The case of autism. *Br. J. Psychol.* **79**, 441–53.

Howlin, P., Baron-Cohen, S. and Hadwin, J. (1999). *Teaching children with autism to mind-read.* New York: Wiley.

Iacoboni, M. (2000*a*). Attention and sensorimotor integration: mapping the embodied mind. In *Brain mapping: the systems* (ed. A. W. Toga and J. C. Mazziotta), pp. 463–90. San Diego, CA: Academic Press.

Iacoboni, M. (2000*b*). Mapping human cognition: thinking, numerical abilities, theory of mind, consciousness. In *Brain mapping: the systems* (ed. A. W. Toga and J. C. Mazziotta), pp. 523–34. San Diego, CA: Academic Press.

Iriki, A., Tanaka, M. and Iwamura, Y. (1996). Coding of modified body schema during tool use by macaque postcentral neurons. *NeuroReport* **7**, 2325–30.

Jackendoff, R. (1987). *Consciousness and the computational mind.* Cambridge, MA: MIT Press.

Johansson, G. (1973). Visual perception of biological motion and a model for its analysis. *Percept. Psychophys.* **14**, 201–11.

Johnson, M. (1987). *The body in the mind: the bodily basis of meaning.* Chicago, IL: University of Chicago Press.

Johnson, M. (2001). Functional brain development in humans. *Nature Rev. Neurosci.* **2**, 475–83.

Jordan, H., Reiss, J. E., Hoffman, J. E. and Landau, B. (2002). Intact perception of biological motion in the face of profound spatial deficits: Williams syndrome. *Psychol. Sci.* **13**, 162–67.

Kanwisher, N., McDermott, J. and Chun, M. (1997). The fusiform face area: a module in human extrastriate cortex specialized for face perception. *J. Neurosci.* **17**, 4302–11.

Klin, A. (1989). Understanding early infantile autism: an application of G. H. Mead's theory of the emergence of mind. *Lond. School Economics Q.* **3**, 336–56.

Klin, A. (1991). Young autistic children's listening preferences in regard to speech: a possible characterization of the symptom of social withdrawal. *J. Autism Devl Disorders* **21**, 29–42.

Klin, A. (1992). Listening preferences in regard to speech in four children with developmental disabilities. *J. Child Psychol. Psychiat.* **33**, 763–69.

Klin, A. (2000). Attributing social meaning to ambiguous visual stimuli in higher functioning autism and Asperger syndrome: the social attribution task. *J. Child Psychol. Psychiat.* **41**, 831–46.

Klin, A., Sparrow, S. S., de Bildt, A., Cicchetti, D. V., Cohen, D. J. and Volkmar, F. R. (1999). A normed study of face recognition in autism and related disorders. *J. Autism Devl Disorders* **29**, 497–507.

Klin, A., Schultz, R. and Cohen, D. (2000). Theory of mind in action: developmental perspectives on social neuroscience. In *Understanding other minds: perspectives from developmental neuroscience*, 2nd edn (ed. S. Baron-Cohen, H. Tager-Flusberg and D. Cohen), pp. 357–388. Oxford: Oxford University Press.

Klin, A., Jones, W., Schultz, R., Volkmar, F. and Cohen, D. (2002*a*). Defining and quantifying the social phenotype in autism. *Am. J. Psychiat.* **159**, 895–908.

Klin, A., Jones, W., Schultz, R., Volkmar, F. R. and Cohen, D. J. (2002*b*). Visual fixation patterns during viewing of naturalistic social situations as predictors of social competence in individuals with autism. *Arch. Gen. Psychiat.* **59**, 809–16.

Koslowski, L. T. and Cutting, J. E. (1978). Recognizing the sex of a walker from point-lights mounted on ankles: some second thoughts. *Percept. Psychophys.* **23**, 459.

Lakoff, G. and Johnson, M. (1999). *Philosophy in the flesh.* Cambridge, MA: MIT Press.

Langdell, T. (1978). Recognition of faces: an approach to the study of autism. *J. Child Psychol. Psychiat.* **19**, 255–68.

Le Grand, R., Mondloch, C. J., Maurer, D. and Brent, H. P. (2001). Early visual experience and face processing. *Nature* **410**, 890.

LeDoux, J. (2002). *Synaptic self: how our brains become who we are.* New York: Viking Penguin.

Leslie, A. (1987). Pretence and representation: the origins of 'theory of mind'. *Psychol. Rev.* **94**, 412–26.

Lord, C. (1995). Follow-up of two-year olds referred for possible autism. *J. Child Psychol. Psychiat.* **36**, 1365–82.

Lord, C. and Paul, R. (1997). Language and communication in autism. In *Handbook of autism and pervasive developmental disorders* (ed. D. Cohen and F. Volkmar), pp. 195–225. New York: Wiley.

McBeath, M., Shaffer, D. and Kaiser, M. (1995). How baseball outfielders determine where to run to catch fly balls. *Science* **268**, 569–73.

Markman, A. N. and Dietrich, E. (2000). Extending the classical view of representation. *Trends Cogn. Sci.* **4**, 470–75.

Maturana, H. R. and Varela, F. G. (1973). *De máquinas y seres vivos.* Santiago, Chile: Editorial Universitaria.

Maurer, D., Lewis, T. L., Brent, H. P. and Levin, A. V. (1999). Rapid improvement in the acuity of infants after visual input. *Science* **286**, 108–10.

Mead, G. H. (1924). *Mind, self, and society.* Chicago, IL: University of Chicago Press.

Meltzoff, A. N. (1995). Understanding the intention of others: re-enactment of intended acts by 18-month-old children. *Devl Psychol.* **31**, 838–50.

Meltzoff, A. N. and Moore, M. K. (1977). Imitation of facial and manual gestures by human neonates. *Science* **198**, 75–78.

Merleau-Ponty, M. (1962). *Phenomenology of perception.* London: Routledge and Kegan Paul.

Mills, M. and Melhuish, E. (1974). Recognition of mother's voice in early infancy. *Nature* **252**, 123–24.

Mundy, P. and Neal, R. (2000). Neural plasticity, joint attention and autistic developmental pathology. In *International review of research in mental retardation*, vol. 23 (ed. L. Glidden), pp. 141–68. New York: Academic Press.

Nadel, J., Croue, S., Mattlinger, M.-J., Canet, P., Hudelot, C., Lecuyer, C., *et al.* (2000). Do children with autism have expectancies about the social behavior of unfamiliar people? A pilot study using the still face paradigm. *Autism* **4**, 133–46.

Neisser, U. (1997). The future of cognitive science: an ecological approach. In *The future of the cognitive revolution* (ed. D. M. Johnson and C. E. Erneling), pp. 247–60. New York: Oxford University Press.

Neri, P., Morrone, M. C. and Burr, D. C. (1998). Seeing biological motion. *Nature* **395**, 894–96.

Newell, A. (1991). *Unified theories of cognition.* Cambridge, MA: Harvard University Press.

Oram, M. W. and Perrett, D. I. (1994). Response of anterior superior temporal polysensory (STPa) neurons to 'biological motion' stimuli. *J. Cogn. Neurosci.* **6**, 99–116.

Osterling, J. and Dawson, G. (1994). Early recognition of children with autism: a study of first birthday home video tapes. *J. Autism Devl Disorders* **24**, 247–57.

Ozonoff, S. and Miller, J. N. (1995). Teaching theory of mind: a new approach to social skills training for individuals with autism. *J. Autism Devl Disorders* **25**, 415–33.

Piaget, J. (1973). The affective unconscious and the cognitive unconscious. *J. Am. Psychoanal. Assoc.* **21**, 249–61.

Prizant, B. and Duchan, J. (1981). The functions of immediate echolalia in autistic children. *J. Speech Hearing Disorders* **46**, 241–49.

Puce, A., Allison, T., Bentin, S., Gore, J. C. and McCarthy, G. (1998). Temporal cortex activation in humans viewing eye and mouth movements. *J. Neurosci.* **18**, 2188–99.

Regolin, L., Tommasi, L. and Vallortigara, G. (2000). Visual perception of biological motion in newly hatched chicks as revealed by an imprinting procedure. *Anim. Cogn.* **3**, 53–60.

Rogers, S. (1999). An examination of the imitation deficits in autism. In *Imitation in infancy: Cambridge studies in cognitive perceptual development* (ed. J. Nadel and G. Butterworth), pp. 254–83. New York: Cambridge University Press.

Schultz, R. T., Gauthier, I., Klin, A., Fulbright, R., Anderson, A., Volkmar, F. R., *et al.* (2000). Abnormal ventral temporal cortical activity among individuals with autism and Asperger syndrome during face discrimination. *Arch. Gen. Psychiat.* **57**, 331–40.

Searle, J., Kiefer, F. and Bierwisch, M. (1980). *Speech act theory and pragmatics.* Boston, MA: D. Reidel.

Sparrow, S., Balla, D. and Cicchetti, D. (1984). *Vineland adaptive behavior scales,* expanded edn. Circle Pines, MN: American Guidance Service.

Symons, L. A., Hains, S. M. J. and Muir, D. W. (1998). Look at me: five-month-old infants' sensitivity to very small deviations in eye-gaze during social interactions. *Infant Behav. Dev.* **21**, 531–36.

Tager-Flusberg, H. and Sullivan, K. (1994). A second look at second-order belief attribution in autism. *J. Autism Devl Disorders* **24**, 577–86.

Tanaka, J. W., Kay, J. B., Grinnell, E., Stansfield, B. and Szechter, L. (1998). Face recognition in young children: when the whole is greater than the sum of its parts. *Vis. Cogn.* **5**, 479–96.

Tarabulsy, G. M., Tessier, R. and Kappas, A. (1996). Contingency detection and the contingent organization of behavior in interactions: implications for socioemotional development in infancy. *Psychol. Bull.* **120**, 25–41.

Thelen, E. and Smith, L. (1994). *A dynamic systems approach to the development of cognition and action.* Cambridge, MA: MIT Press.

Thelen, E., Schoener, G., Scheier, C. and Smith, L. B. (2001). The dynamics of embodiment: a field theory of infant perseverative reaching. *Behav. Brain Sci.* **24**, 1–86.

Tronick, E., Als, H., Adamson, L., Wise, S. and Brazelton, T. B. (1978). The infant's response to entrapment between contradictory messages in face-to-face interaction. *J. Am. Acad. Child Adolesc. Psychiat.* **17**, 1–13.

Tronick, E. Z., Cohn, J. and Shea, E. (1986). The transfer of affect between mothers and infants. In *Affective development in infancy* (ed. T. B. Brazelton and M. W. Yogman), pp. 11–25. Norwood, NL: Ablex.

Uller, C. and Nichols, S. (2000). Goal attribution in chimpanzees. *Cognition* **76**, B27–34.

van der Geest, J. N., Kemner, C., Verbaten, M. N. and van Engeland, H. (2002). Gaze behavior of children with pervasive developmental disorder toward human faces: a fixation time study. *J. Child Psychol. Psychiat.* **43**, 1–11.

Varela, F., Thompson, E. and Rosch, E. (1991). *The embodied mind: cognitive science and human experience.* Cambridge, MA: MIT Press.

Walker, A. S. (1982). Intermodal perception of expressive behaviors by human infants. *J. Exp. Child Psychol.* **33**, 514–35.

Weeks, S. and Hobson, R. (1987). The salience of facial expression for autistic children. *J. Child Psychol. Psychiat.* **28**, 137–151.

Werner, E., Dawson, G., Osterling, J. and Dinno, H. (2000). Recognition of autism spectrum disorder before one year of age: a retrospective study based on home videotapes. *J. Autism Devl Disorders* **30**, 157–62.

Wetherby, A. M., Prizant, B. M. and Schuler, A. L. (2000). Understanding the nature of communication and language impairments. In *Autism spectrum disorders: a transactional developmental perspective* (ed. A. M. Wetherby and B. M. Prizant), pp. 109–42. Baltimore, MD: Paul H. Brookes Publishing Co.

Winograd, T. and Flores, F. (1986). *Understanding computers and cognition.* Norwood, NJ: Ablex Publications.

Zajonc, R. (1980). Feeling and thinking: preferences need no inferences. *Am. Psychol.* **35**, 151–75.

Glossary

EM: enactive mind
fMRI: functional magnetic resonance imaging
FG: fusiform gyrus

8

The systemizing quotient: an investigation of adults with Asperger syndrome or high-functioning autism, and normal sex differences

Simon Baron-Cohen, Jennifer Richler, Dheraj Bisarya, Nhishanth Gurunathan, and Sally Wheelwright

Systemizing is the drive to analyse systems or construct systems. A recent model of psychological sex differences suggests that this is a major dimension in which the sexes differ, with males being more drawn to systemize than females. Currently, there are no self-report measures to assess this important dimension. A second major dimension of sex differences is empathizing (the drive to identify mental states and respond to these with an appropriate emotion). Previous studies find females score higher on empathy measures. We report a new self-report questionnaire, the Systemizing Quotient (SQ), for use with adults of normal intelligence. It contains 40 systemizing items and 20 control items. On each systemizing item, a person can score 2, 1 or 0, so the SQ has a maximum score of 80 and a minimum of zero. In Study 1, we measured the SQ of $n = 278$ adults (114 males, 164 females) from a general population, to test for predicted sex differences (male superiority) in systemizing. All subjects were also given the Empathy Quotient (EQ) to test if previous reports of female superiority would be replicated. In Study 2 we employed the SQ and the EQ with $n = 47$ adults (33 males, 14 females) with Asperger syndrome (AS) or high-functioning autism (HFA), who are predicted to be either normal or superior at systemizing, but impaired at empathizing. Their scores were compared with $n = 47$ matched adults from the general population in Study 1. In Study 1, as predicted, normal adult males scored significantly higher than females on the SQ and significantly lower on the EQ. In Study 2, again as predicted, adults with AS/HFA scored significantly higher on the SQ than matched controls, and significantly lower on the EQ than matched controls. The SQ reveals both a sex difference in systemizing in the general population and an unusually strong drive to systemize in AS/HFA. These results are discussed in relation to two linked theories: the 'empathizing–systemizing' (E–S) theory of sex differences and the extreme male brain (EMB) theory of autism.

Keywords: Asperger syndrome; sex differences; systemizing; empathizing

8.1 The empathizing–systemizing theory

A recent model of sex differences in the mind proposes that the major dimensions of relevance are empathizing and systemizing (Baron-Cohen 2002). Systemizing is held to be our most powerful way of understanding and predicting the law-governed inanimate universe. Empathizing is held to be our most powerful way of understanding and predicting the social world.

Empathizing is the drive to identify another person's emotions and thoughts, and to respond to these with an appropriate emotion. Empathizing allows you to *predict* a person's behaviour, and to care about how others feel. A large body of evidence suggests that, on average, females spontaneously empathize to a greater degree than do males. Systemizing is the drive to analyse the variables in a system, to derive the underlying rules that govern the behaviour of a system. Systemizing also refers to the drive to construct systems. Systemizing allows you to *predict* the behaviour of a system, and to control it. A growing body of evidence suggests that, on average, males spontaneously systemize to a greater degree than do females.

A system is defined as something that takes inputs, which can then be operated on in *variable* ways, to deliver *different* outputs in a rule-governed way. There are at least six kinds of system: Technical, Natural, Abstract, Social, Organizable, Motoric, but all share this same underlying process which is monitored closely during systemizing:

INPUT → OPERATION→ OUTPUT

Below, an example from each of the six types of system are given:

A. An example of a *technical* system: a sail

INPUT	→	OPERATION	→	OUTPUT
Sail		Angle 10°		Speed slow
Sail		Angle 30°		Speed medium
Sail		Angle 60°		Speed fast

B. An example of a *natural* system: a plant

INPUT	→	OPERATION	→	OUTPUT
Rhododendron		Mildly alkaline soil		Light blue petals
Rhododendron		Strongly alkaline soil		Dark blue petals
Rhododendron		Acidic soil		Pink petals

C. An example of an *abstract* system: mathematics

INPUT	→	OPERATION	→	OUTPUT
3		Squared		9
3		Cubed		27
3		Inverse		0.3

D. An example of a *social* system: a constituency boundary

INPUT	→	OPERATION	→	OUTPUT
New York		Inner city		Small number of voters
New York		Whole city		Medium number of voters
New York		Whole state		Large number of voters

E. An example of an *organizable* system: a CD collection

INPUT	→	OPERATION	→	OUTPUT
CD collection		Alphabetical		Order on shelf: A–Z

| CD collection | Date of release | Order on shelf: 1980–2000 |
| CD collection | Genre | Order on shelf: classical → pop |

F. An example of a *motoric* system: a tennis stroke

INPUT	→	OPERATION	→	OUTPUT
Hit ball		Top spin		Ball bounces left
Hit ball		Back spin		Ball bounces right
Hit ball		No spin		Ball bounces forward

As can be seen in the examples above, the process in systemizing is always the same. One of the three elements (typically the input) is treated as a *fixed* feature (i.e. it is held constant), while another of the three elements (typically the operation) is treated as a *variable* (i.e. it can vary: think of a dimmer on a light switch). Merely observing the consequences of these two elements delivers to you important information: the output changes from Output 1, to Output 2, to Output 3. That is, you learn about the system. Systemizing works for phenomena that are indeed ultimately lawful, finite and deterministic. Note that the other way we systemize is when we are confronted by various outputs, and try to infer *backwards* from the output as to what the operation is that produces this particular output.

Systemizing is practically useless for predicting the moment-by-moment changes in a person's behaviour. To predict human behaviour, empathizing is required. Systemizing and empathizing are very different kinds of process. Empathizing involves attributing mental states to others, and responding with appropriate affect to the other's affective state. Empathizing covers not only what is sometimes called 'theory of mind or 'mentalizing' (Morton *et al.* 1991), but also what is covered by the English words 'empathy' and 'sympathy'.

In order see why you cannot systemize a person's behaviour with much predictive power, consider the next example:

INPUT	→	OPERATION	→	OUTPUT
Jane		Birthday		Relaxes
Jane		Birthday		Withdraws
Jane		Birthday		Laughs
Jane		Birthday		Cries

Why does the same input (Jane) have such different outputs (behaviour) when the same operation (her birthday) is repeated? Someone who relies on systemizing to predict people's behaviour would have to conclude that people are not clearly rule-governed. This is a correct conclusion, but there is nevertheless an alternative way of predicting and making sense of Jane's behaviour: via empathizing. During empathizing, the focus is on the person's *mental state* (including his or her emotion). Furthermore, during empathizing there is an appropriate emotional reaction in the observer to the other person's mental state. Without this extra stage, one could have a very accurate reading of the person's emotion, a very accurate prediction of the other's behaviour, but a psychopathic lack of concern about their mental state.

To complicate matters further, during empathizing, the observer does not expect lawful relationships between the person's mental state and his or her behaviour. The observer only expects that the person's mental state will at least constrain their behaviour.

There are individual differences in both empathizing and systemizing. According to the E–S theory, individuals in whom empathizing is more developed than systemizing are referred to as type E. Individuals in whom systemizing is more developed than empathizing are called type S. Individuals in whom systemizing and empathizing are both equally developed are called type B (to indicate the 'balanced' brain). Individuals whose systemizing is normal or even hyperdeveloped but whose empathizing is hypodeveloped are an extreme of type S. That is, they may be talented systemizers but at the same time, they may be 'mind-blind' (Baron-Cohen 1995). We test if individuals on the autistic spectrum fit the profile of having an extreme of type S. Finally, we postulate the existence of a brain of extreme type E: people who have normal or even hyperdeveloped empathizing skills, whereas their systemizing is hypodeveloped—they may be 'system-blind'.

One final central claim of the E–S theory is that, on average, *more* males than females have a brain of type S, and *more* females than males have a brain of type E. The evidence for female superiority in empathizing is reviewed elsewhere (Baron-Cohen 2002) and includes the finding that women are better at decoding non-verbal communication, picking up subtle nuances from tone of voice or facial expression, or judging a person's character (Hall 1978). The evidence for a male advantage in systemizing is also reviewed elsewhere (Baron-Cohen *et al.* 2002) and includes the findings that maths, physics and engineering (which all require a high degree of systemizing) are largely male in sex ratio. For example, on the Scholastic Aptitude Math Test, the maths part of the test administered nationally to college applicants in the USA males, on average, score 50 points higher than females on this test (Benbow 1988). Among those scoring above 700, the sex ratio is 13 : 1 (men : women) (Geary 1996). A candidate biological factor influencing these sex differences is prenatal testosterone and its action on the developing brain (Geschwind and Galaburda 1985; Lutchmaya *et al.* 2002).

8.2 The extreme male brain theory of autism

The EMB theory of autism was first informally suggested by Hans Asperger (1944). He wrote: 'The autistic personality is an extreme variant of male intelligence. Even within the normal variation, we find typical sex differences in intelligence ... In the autistic individual, the male pattern is exaggerated to the extreme' (Frith 1991). It took 53 years from the date that this controversial hypothesis was raised casually for it to be formally examined (Baron-Cohen and Hammer 1997). We can test the EMB theory empirically, now that we have definitions of the female brain (type E) (Fig. 8.1: narrow diagonal stripes), the

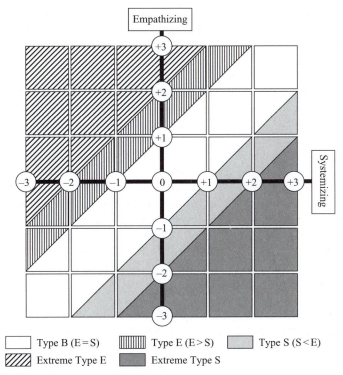

Type B (E = S)   Type E (E > S)   Type S (S < E)
Extreme Type E   Extreme Type S

*Axes show standard deviations from the mean

Fig. 8.1 A model of the E–S theory. Type B (E = S): unshaded; type E (E > S): narrow diagonal stripes; type S (E < S): grey shading; extreme type E: wide diagonal stripes; extreme type S: dark grey shading. Axes show s.d. from mean.

male brain (type S) (Fig. 8.1: light grey zone), and the balanced brain (Fig. 8.1: white zone). According to the EMB theory, people with autism or AS should fall into the dark grey zone: that is, they should have impaired empathizing but intact or superior systemizing, relative to their mental age.

8.3 Evidence for the EMB theory

Initial tests of this theory are providing convergent lines of evidence consistent with the EMB theory of autism. The evidence related to impaired empathizing is reviewed elsewhere (Baron-Cohen *et al.* 2002) and includes the findings from the 'Reading the Mind in the Eyes' Test, that females score higher than males, but people with AS score even lower than males (Baron-Cohen *et al.* 1997). Additionally, on the Faux Pas Test, females are better than males at judging what would be socially insensitive or potentially hurtful and offensive and people with autism or AS have even lower scores on tests of this than males (Baron-Cohen *et al.* 1999*a*).

The evidence in relation to superior systemizing includes the fact that some people with autism spectrum conditions have 'islets of ability' in, for example, mathematical calculation, calendrical calculation, syntax acquisition, music or memory for railway timetable information to a precise degree (Baron-Cohen and Bolton 1993; Hermelin 2002). In high-functioning individuals these abilities can lead to considerable achievement in mathematics, chess, mechanical knowledge and other factual, scientific, technical or rule-based subjects (Baron-Cohen *et al*. 1999*c*). All of these are highly systemizable domains. On the EFT, males score higher than females, and people with AS or HFA score even higher than males. The EFT is a systemizing test, in that each piece of the puzzle (the target shape) is the input, its orientation is the operation, with rules from these that predict if the piece of the puzzle will fit in the target locations (Shah and Frith 1983; Jolliffe and Baron-Cohen 1997). Finally, on the AQ, males in the general population score higher than females, and people with AS or HFA score highest of all (Baron-Cohen *et al*. 2001).

8.4 The systemizing quotient

To test both the E–S theory and the EMB theory further, we designed the SQ. This was to fulfil the need to have an instrument that could assess an individual's interest in systems across the range of different classes of system. In the two studies reported here, we first test for a sex difference in systemizing in the general population, and secondly test for the predicted superiority in systemizing in adults with AS or HFA.

The SQ was designed to be short, easy to complete and easy to score. It is shown in Appendix A. The SQ comprises 60 questions, 40 assessing systemizing and 20 filler (control) items. Approximately half the items were worded to produce a 'disagree' and half an 'agree', for the systemizing response. This was to avoid a response bias either way. Following this, items were randomized. An individual scores two points if they strongly display a systemizing response and one point if they slightly display a systemizing response. There are 20 filler items (items 2, 3, 8, 9, 10, 14, 16, 17, 21, 22, 27, 36, 39, 46, 47, 50, 52, 54, 58, 59), randomly interspersed throughout the SQ, to distract the participant from a relentless focus on systemizing. These questions are not scored at all. The final version of the SQ has a forced-choice format, can be selfadministered and is straightforward to score, since it does not depend on any interpretation in the scoring.

Initially, we had planned to devise the SQ so that it would tap into each of the domain-specific systems described above. However, this proved to be problematical because individuals who were well rounded but not necessarily good systemizers would end up scoring highly, whereas those who were highly systematic but only interested in one domain would receive a low score. Thus, we decided, instead, to use examples from everyday life in which systemizing could be used to varying degrees. The assumption is that a strong systemizer would be drawn to use their systemizing skills across the range of examples more often than a poor systemizer, and would consequently score higher on the SQ.

A pilot study was conducted by distributing the SQ to 20 normal adults to check that the questions were understandable and that the range of results indicated both individual differences across the scale, and avoided ceiling or floor effects. These participants were also able to offer feedback about the questionnaire.

8.5 The empathizing quotient

In the two studies reported below, subjects were not only given the SQ, but also given the EQ (S. Baron-Cohen and S. Wheelwright, in press). This is shown in Appendix B. The EQ has a very similar structure to the SQ, in that it also comprises 60 questions, broken down into two types: 40 questions tapping empathy and 20 filler items (items 2, 3, 5, 7, 9, 13, 16, 17, 20, 23, 24, 30, 31, 33, 40, 45, 47, 51, 53, 56). Each of the empathy items scores one point if the respondent records the empathic behaviour mildly, or two points if strongly (see below for scoring each item). Like the SQ, approximately half the items were worded to produce a 'disagree', and half an 'agree' for the empathic response, to avoid a response bias either way. Also, as with the SQ, the EQ has a forcedchoice format, can be self-administered and is straightforward to score.

8.6 Aims

In the studies reported below, we had four aims.

(i) To test for a female superiority on the EQ, replicating earlier work (Hoffman 1977; Hall 1978; Davis 1980; Davis and Franzoi 1991; S. Baron-Cohen and S. Wheelwright, unpublished data) (Study 1).
(ii) To test for sex differences in systemizing, given the male superiority in many separate systemizable domains reported earlier (Benbow 1988; Kimura 1999).
(iii) To test if adults with HFA or AS scored lower than normal males on the EQ but higher than normal males on the SQ (Study 2).
(iv) To test if the EQ was inversely correlated with the SQ.

8.7 High-functioning autism and asperger syndrome

Autism is diagnosed when an individual shows abnormalities in social and communication development, in the presence of marked repetitive behaviour and limited imagination (American Psychiatric Association 1994). The term HFA is given when an individual meets the criteria for autism in the presence of normal IQ. AS is defined in terms of the individual meeting the same criteria for autism but with no history of cognitive or language delay (ICD-10 1994). Language delay itself is defined as not using single words by two years of age, and/or phrase speech by three years of age. There is growing evidence that autism and AS are of genetic origin. The evidence is strongest for autism, and comes from twin and behavioural genetic family studies (Folstein and Rutter 1977, 1988; Bolton and Rutter 1990; Bailey *et al.* 1995). Furthermore, family pedigrees of AS implicate heritability (Gillberg 1991). There is also an assumption that autism and AS lie on a continuum, with AS as the 'bridge' between autism and normality (Wing 1981, 1988; Frith 1991; Baron-Cohen 1995).

8.8 Subjects

(a) Subjects in Study 1

Study 1 comprised $n = 278$ normal adults (114 males, 164 females) taken from two sources: $n = 103$ were drawn from the general public in the UK and Canada, and represented a mix of occupations, both professional, clerical and manual workers, and $n = 174$ were drawn from undergraduate students currently studying at Cambridge University or a local 'A' level college in Cambridge. Students from a variety of disciplines were targeted. In Study 1, to check if academic/educational attainment influences either SQ or EQ, these sub-groups were analysed separately. The students had a mean age of $x = 20.5$ yr (s.d. $= 6.5$) and the non-students had a mean age of $x = 41.3$ yr (s.d. $= 12.7$).

(b) Subjects in Study 2

Two groups of subjects were tested:

Group 1 comprised $n = 47$ adults with AS/HFA (33 males, 14 females). This sex ratio of $2.4 : 1$ (m : f) is similar to that found in other samples (Klin *et al.* 1995). All subjects in this group had been diagnosed by psychiatrists using established criteria for autism or AS (American Psychiatric Association 1994). They were recruited from several sources, including the National Autistic Society (UK), specialist clinics carrying out diagnostic assessments, and advertisements in newsletters/web pages for adults with AS/HFA. Their mean age was 38.1 yr (s.d. $= 13.3$). They had all attended mainstream schooling and were reported to have an IQ in the normal range (see below for a check of this). Their occupations reflected their mixed socioeconomic status. Because we could not confirm age of onset of language with any precision (due to the considerable passage of time), these individuals are grouped together, rather than attempting to separate them into AS versus HFA.

Group 2 comprised 47 adults selected from the pool of 278 controls in Study 1 based on being matched with Group 1 for age, sex and handedness. The 278 volunteers are described in Study 1. The 47 comparison subjects, as in Group 1, consisted of 32 males and 15 females. Their mean age was 36.5 years (s.d. = 13.2). Their socio-economic status profile was similar to that of Group 1.

8.9 Methods (for studies 1 and 2)

Subjects were sent the SQ and EQ by post. Two versions of the questionnaires were sent out, one in which the SQ appeared first, followed by the EQ, and the other in the reverse order, so as to guard against order effects. The exception to this were a sub-group of subjects in each group, who had already completed the EQ for another study, so these individuals only received the SQ for this study. Subjects were instructed to complete the two questionnaires on their own, as quickly as possible, and to avoid thinking about their responses too long. Subjects in Group 2 had the option to remain anonymous. To confirm the diagnosis of adults in Group 1 being high-functioning, 15 subjects in each of Groups 1 and 2 were randomly selected and invited into the laboratory for intellectual assessment using four sub-tests of the WAIS-R (Wechsler 1958) The four sub-tests of the WAIS-R were Vocabulary, Similarities, Block Design and Picture Completion. On this basis, all of these had a prorated IQ of at least 85, that is, in the normal range (Group 1, $x = 106.5$, s.d. $= 8.0$; Group 2, $x = 105.8$, s.d. $= 6.3$), and these did not differ from each other statistically (t-test, $p > 0.05$).

Subjects in Group 1 were also sent the AQ (Baron-Cohen et al. 2001) by post. Their mean AQ score was 36.4 (s.d. = 7.1). This is in the clinical range on this measure, as our previous study using the AQ shows that more than 80% of people with a diagnosis of AS or HFA score equal to or above 32 (maximum: 50).

8.10 Scoring

(a) The SQ

'Strongly agree' responses score two points, and 'slightly agree' responses score one point, on the following items: 1, 4, 5, 7, 13, 15, 19, 20, 25, 29, 30, 33, 34, 37, 41, 44, 48, 49, 53, 55. 'Strongly disagree' responses score two points, and 'slightly disagree' responses score one point on the following items: 6, 11, 12, 18, 23, 24, 26, 28, 31, 32, 35, 38, 40, 42, 43, 45, 51, 56, 57, 60. The filler (control) questions score no points, irrespective of how the individual answers them. Nevertheless, responses on the filler items were analysed for any systematic bias.

(b) The EQ

'Strongly agree' responses score two points and 'slightly agree' responses score one point, on the following items: 1, 6, 19, 22, 25, 26, 35, 36, 37, 38, 41, 42, 43, 44, 52, 54, 55, 57, 58, 59, 60. 'Strongly disagree' responses score two points, and 'slightly disagree' responses score one point, on the following items: 4, 8, 10, 11, 12, 14, 15, 18, 21, 27, 28, 29, 32, 34, 39, 46, 48, 49, 50.

8.11 Results

(a) Study 1

The response rate was 60%, which is a good response rate in a postal survey research. Mean SQ scores and subscores for these individuals are shown in Table 8.1. This shows that, within this general population sample, males (mean = 30.3, s.d. = 11.5) scored significantly higher than females (mean = 24.1, s.d. = 9.5) on the SQ. A between-subjects ANOVA was performed to test for the main effects of sex and group. In this case, 'group' was used to separate students from workers. Scores by group are also shown in Table 8.1. There was a main effect of sex ($F(1,270) = 18.1$, $p < 0.0001$), as predicted. There was no significant main effect of group ($F(1,270) = 0.18$, $p = 0.67$) and no sex by group interaction ($F(1,270) = 2.05$, $p = 0.15$). Age was treated as a covariate in all analyses.

Mean EQ scores are also shown in Table 8.1. A between-subjects ANOVA was performed to test for the main effects of sex and group. As before, 'group' was used to separate students from workers. There was a main effect of sex ($F(1,269) = 38.6$, $p < 0.0001$), as predicted. There was no significant main effect of group ($F(1, 264) = 1.24$, $p = 0.27$) and no sex by group interaction ($F(1, 269) = 1.43$, $p = 0.23$). Pearson's correlation shows that, as predicted,

Table 8.1 EQ and SQ scores in students versus non-students in Study 1 (maximum score on each: 80).

	males			females		
group	*n*	mean	s.d.	*n*	mean	s.d.
EQ						
students	65	39.4	11.5	109	46.7	10.5
workers	49	38.0	13.6	54	49.6	11.8
combined groups	114	38.8	12.4	164	47.7	11.0
SQ						
students	65	30.0	11.7	109	22.3	8.6
workers	49	30.6	11.2	55	27.7	11.2
combined groups	114	30.3	11.5	164	24.1	9.5

there is a significant negative correlation between the EQ and SQ when all subjects' data were analysed ($r = -0.16$, $p < 0.01$).

Finally, a factor analysis was carried out to investigate whether any meaningful factors in the SQ could be elucidated. The factor analysis was necessarily only explorative in nature as the items on the SQ are ordinal rather than continuous. Following the initial principal component analysis, 11 factors had an eigenvalue of greater than one, and were retained. The data were then subjected to a varimax rotation. An examination of the factors generated suggested that these did not correspond to factors with any psychological significance. Thus, total SQ score was the only measure analysed.

(b) Study 2

The response rate was 50%, which again is a good response rate in a postal survey research. Mean SQ scores of AS/HFA subjects and controls are shown in Table 8.2. These scores show that HFA/AS individuals scored higher (mean = 35.7, s.d. = 15.3) than matched controls (mean = 29.7, s.d. = 10.2). A t-test was used to examine the significance of the difference between the means of the two samples. This indicated that the AS/HFA group scored significantly higher than controls on the SQ ($t = 2.2$, d.f. = 80, $p < 0.03$).

The two subject groups were then compared on their responses to the filler (control) items. A t-test revealed that there was no significant difference in their responses to these questions ($t = 1.496$, d.f. = 323, $p > 0.14$). This suggests the groups only performed differently in their responses to system-based questions. The mean SQ scores of males and females in the AS/HFA sample are also shown in Table 8.2. This shows that males with AS/HFA (mean = 36.3, s.d. = 15.5) do not score significantly higher than females with AS/HFA (mean = 34.1, s.d. = 15.1). A t-test reveals that there is no significant difference between the two means ($t = -0.46$, d.f. = 45, $p > 0.65$). Figure 8.2 shows the distribution of scores from the full population in Study 1 (normal males and females) and the distribution of scores from the AS/HFA group in Study 2. Note that the curve from the AS/HFA group is only based on $n = 47$, whereas the curves from the control males and females are based on $n = 278$.

Table 8.2 Means (and s.d.) of SQ and EQ scores in AS versus matched controls (Study 2) (maximum on each test: 80).

group	n	SQ		EQ	
		mean	s.d.	mean	s.d.
AS/HFA	47	35.7	15.3	20.3	11.4
males	33	36.3	15.5	18.9	9.9
females	14	34.1	15.1	23.4	14.1
controls	47	29.7	10.2	42.2	13.6

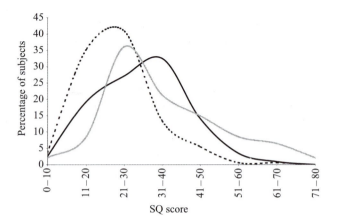

Fig. 8.2 Distribution of scores on the SQ in typical males (solid black line), females (dashed line), and in people with AS (grey line) conditions.

On the EQ, individuals with HFA/AS scored lower than matched controls. A t-test revealed that the difference between means was significant ($t = -8.5$, d.f. $= 92, p < 0.0001$). The mean EQ scores of males and females in the AS/HFA sample are also shown in Table 8.2. A t-test revealed that there was no significant difference between these two means ($t = 1.09$, d.f. $= 18.68, p > 0.22$). It was possible to look at correlations between the EQ, SQ and AQ for the HFA/AS group alone. This showed that whereas the EQ was inversely correlated with the AQ ($r = -0.48, p < 0.001$), the SQ was positively correlated with the AQ ($r = 0.46$, $p < 0.002$), as would be expected. Finally, Cronbach's alpha coefficent on the SQ (for all subjects) was 0.79, which is good, and for the HFA/AS subjects alone, was 0.91, which is very high. This suggests the SQ is tapping a single construct. (Cronbach's alpha coefficient for the EQ is reported elsewhere; S. Baron-Cohen and S. Wheelwright (unpublished data) as 0.92, also very high.)

One possibility, suggested by Fig. 8.2, is that the *mean* for the AS group on the SQ is actually higher than for males in the general population, whereas the *mode* for males in the general population is higher than it is in the AS group. The mean of the AS group may be being pulled up by a sub-group of people with AS who have particularly high scores on the SQ, as suggested by both the skew of the distribution and by the standard deviation for the AS group, which was larger than for the males in the general population.

8.12 Discussion

The two studies report results from a new instrument, the SQ. This was needed to test two linked theories: the E–S theory of sex differences in the mind

(Baron-Cohen 2002) and the EMB theory of autism (Baron-Cohen and Hammer 1997; Baron-Cohen 2000; Baron-Cohen *et al*. 2002).

As predicted, in Study 1, males scored significantly higher than females on the SQ. Replicating our earlier study and those of others who have studied sex differences in empathy (Davis 1994; S. Baron-Cohen and S. Wheelwright, in press) females scored higher than males on the EQ. Unsurprisingly, the SQ and EQ were inversely correlated, but while this was significant, the correlation was small ($r = -0.16$, $p < 0.01$). The strength of this correlation may reflect the fact that systemizing and empathizing are wholly different kinds of process, and that although there is some trade-off between performance on these two instruments, there is no necessary trade-off. This confirms predictions from the E–S theory and the model shown in Fig. 8.1.

Again, as predicted in Study 2, people with AS/HFA scored significantly higher on the SQ, and significantly lower on the EQ, compared with matched controls. The latter result replicates the finding on empathy measures from our earlier study (S. Baron-Cohen and S. Wheelwright, in press) and the former is in line with the EMB model of autism. The fact that the group with AS/HFA actually scored higher on the SQ, rather than at an equivalent level to them, is noteworthy, because the EMB predicts either normal or superior performance on systemizing measures. It also replicates good performance from more specific measures of systemizing such as the Physical Prediction Questionnaire (J. Lawson, S. Baron-Cohen and S. Wheelwright, in press). Figure 8.2 suggests the possibility of a sub-group of people with AS who are particularly high systemizers, which could be tested more thoroughly in future in a larger sample of people with AS.

The results can be interpreted with some confidence, for several reasons. First, if the AS/HFA group were in some way disadvantaged overall, this should have been evident on lower scores on both questionnaires, whereas the pattern of results actually obtained is exactly as predicted by the EMB theory. Second, the analysis of performance on the filler items of both questionnaires shows that the groups did not differ on these, but only on the items of relevance to each questionnaire. Third, the lack of a difference between the students and the non-students in the general population study (Study 1) on either the SQ or EQ suggests that these dimensions are not a function of age or education, but are best predicted on the basis of sex.

It is, of course, important to acknowledge several limitations of the present studies. First, only a proportion of subjects could actually be tested *in vivo*, and it would be beneficial for future studies to validate performance of subjects on these measures with observed test performance on related instruments. Second, it was not possible to include a non-autistic psychiatric control group in Study 2, and this would be of interest to establish if the superior systemizing found in the group with AS/HFA is specific to this clinical condition. Third, the design of the questionnaires makes them mainly suitable for adults of normal intelligence who are capable of completing self-report questionnaires. In the future, it would be valuable to adapt them for parental report of their children. Finally, the AS/HFA group is only $n = 47$, and in future it would be important to increase this sample size.

It is worth emphasizing that the pattern of scores on the SQ and EQ is clearly not one that would be predicted by alternative cognitive theories of autism. The executive dysfunction theory (Ozonoff *et al.* 1994; Russell 1997) would make no clear prediction on the EQ, but might even predict impaired performance on the SQ, as many aspects of systemizing require executive function. Equally, the weak central coherence theory (Frith 1989; Happé 1996) would predict that people with autism should be impaired on both the EQ and the SQ, as both need strong central coherence. In this respect, the E–S theory makes predictions of a highly specific profile (impaired EQ, superior SQ), which were confirmed. It is difficult to maintain that good systemizing is predicted by weak central coherence theory for two reasons: (i) weak central coherence theory was first described in 1989 (Frith 1989) and for the 10 years following this there was no mention by its proponents that good systemizing would be expected; (ii) systemizing requires excellent integration of information using the rule-based structure (input–operation–output), whereas weak central coherence predicts poor integration. Good systemizing in autism was first predicted by the E–S theory (Baron-Cohen 2002), and the data reported here provide good evidence for this. Central coherence theory predicts that integration of information should be impaired in autism, whereas E–S theory predicts that if a domain is systemizable, ability in autism will be in line with mental age, or even superior. Furthermore, central coherence theory predicts 'holistic' processing deficits, whereas E–S theory predicts that both holistic systems (such as astronomy) or particle-based systems (such as particle physics) should be readily grasped, and only non-systemizable domains (such as fiction) will be poorly integrated in autism. These predictions remain to be tested.

An objection to E–S theory might be of circularity, namely, that empathizing deficits and systemizing talents might be expected purely because of how people with autism are diagnosed. Against this criticism, DSM-IV does not gather information about systemizing, and although empathizing deficits might be noted as a diagnostic symptom, neither of these constructs is quantified during diagnostic procedures. The SQ and EQ thus go beyond diagnosis to provide quantitative instruments for measuring individual differences. In addition, some of the behaviours that the E–S theory sees as a result of superior systemizing (such as expertise or detailed perception) are viewed by DSM-IV in rather negative terms (e.g. as restricted or repetitive interests or behaviour, or obsessions). In this way, the E–S theory provides a fresh lens through which to understand these behaviours.

What remains unclear is the nature of the underlying neurocognitive mechanisms that drive empathizing and systemizing. In particular, it is of considerable importance to establish if these reflect independent mechanisms, or one underlying one, such that as one gets better at one, one gets worse at the other.

We suspect that two independent mechanisms are involved, simply because of the existence of few individuals who are superior at both empathizing and systemizing. However, there seems to be a trend for some trade-off between these two domains, suggesting that even if two independent mechanisms are involved, there may be a special relationship between them. The nature of this special relationship needs to be understood both at the level of cognition and neuroscience. In terms of the brain basis of empathizing, several important brain regions have now been identified, specifically the orbito- and medial-frontal cortex, superior temporal sulcus and the amygdala (Baron-Cohen and Ring 1994; Frith and Frith 1999; Baron-Cohen *et al.* 1999*b*, 2000). The brain basis of systemizing remains to be studied.

We conclude by suggesting that the E–S theory of sex differences in the mind, and the EMB theory of autism warrant further biomedical research, as a result of this new evidence of intact or superior systemizing in AS, as measured on the SQ.

S.B.-C., J.R. and S.W. were supported by the Medical Research Council and the James S. McDonnell Foundation, during the development of this work. D.B. and N.G. submitted this work as a final year project in part fulfilment of the BSc in Psychology, Cambridge University. The authors are grateful to Johnny Lawson for help in preparing Fig. 8.1.

Appendix A: The systemizing quotient

1.	When I listen to a piece of music, I always notice the way it's structured.	strongly agree	slightly agree	slightly disagree	strongly disagree
2.	I adhere to common superstitions.	strongly agree	slightly agree	slightly disagree	strongly disagree
3.	I often make resolutions, but find it hard to stick to them.	strongly agree	slightly agree	slightly disagree	strongly disagree
4.	I prefer to read non-fiction than fiction.	strongly agree	slightly agree	slightly disagree	strongly disagree
5.	If I were buying a car, I would want to obtain specific information about its engine capacity.	strongly agree	slightly agree	slightly disagree	strongly disagree
6.	When I look at a painting, I do not usually think about the technique involved in making it.	strongly agree	slightly agree	slightly disagree	strongly disagree
7.	If there was a problem with the electrical wiring in my home, I'd be able to fix it myself.	strongly agree	slightly agree	slightly disagree	strongly disagree
8.	When I have a dream, I find it difficult to remember precise details about the dream the next day.	strongly agree	slightly agree	slightly disagree	strongly disagree
9.	When I watch a film, I prefer to be with a group of friends, rather than alone.	strongly agree	slightly agree	slightly disagree	strongly disagree
10.	I am interested in learning about different religions.	strongly agree	slightly agree	slightly disagree	strongly disagree
11.	I rarely read articles or web pages about new technology.	strongly agree	slightly agree	slightly disagree	strongly disagree
12.	I do not enjoy games that involve a high degree of strategy.	strongly agree	slightly agree	slightly disagree	strongly disagree
13.	I am fascinated by how machines work.	strongly agree	slightly agree	slightly disagree	strongly disagree
14.	I make it a point of listening to the news each morning.	strongly agree	slightly agree	slightly disagree	strongly disagree
15.	In maths, I am intrigued by the rules and patterns governing numbers.	strongly agree	slightly agree	slightly disagree	strongly disagree

	strongly agree	slightly agree	slightly disagree	strongly disagree
16. I am bad about keeping in touch with old friends.	strongly agree	slightly agree	slightly disagree	strongly disagree
17. When I am relating a story, I often leave out details and just give the gist of what happened.	strongly agree	slightly agree	slightly disagree	strongly disagree
18. I find it difficult to understand instruction manuals for putting appliances together.	strongly agree	slightly agree	slightly disagree	strongly disagree
19. When I look at an animal, I like to know the precise species it belongs to.	strongly agree	slightly agree	slightly disagree	strongly disagree
20. If I were buying a computer, I would want to know exact details about its hard drive capacity and processor speed.	strongly agree	slightly agree	slightly disagree	strongly disagree
21. I enjoy participating in sport.	strongly agree	slightly agree	slightly disagree	strongly disagree
22. I try to avoid doing household chores if I can.	strongly agree	slightly agree	slightly disagree	strongly disagree
23. When I cook, I do not think about exactly how different methods and ingredients contribute to the final product.	strongly agree	slightly agree	slightly disagree	strongly disagree
24. I find it difficult to read and understand maps.	strongly agree	slightly agree	slightly disagree	strongly disagree
25. If I had a collection (e.g. CDs, coins, stamps), it would be highly organised.	strongly agree	slightly agree	slightly disagree	strongly disagree
26. When I look at a piece of furniture, I do not notice the details of how it was constructed.	strongly agree	slightly agree	slightly disagree	strongly disagree
27. The idea of engaging in 'risk-taking' activities appeals to me.	strongly agree	slightly agree	slightly disagree	strongly disagree
28. When I learn about historical events, I do not focus on exact dates.	strongly agree	slightly agree	slightly disagree	strongly disagree
29. When I read the newspaper, I am drawn to tables of information, such as football league scores or stock market indices.	strongly agree	slightly agree	slightly disagree	strongly disagree
30. When I learn a language, I become intrigued by its grammatical rules.	strongly agree	slightly agree	slightly disagree	strongly disagree

continued

Appendix A: *continued*

		strongly agree	slightly agree	slightly disagree	strongly disagree
31.	I find it difficult to learn my way around a new city	strongly agree	slightly agree	slightly disagree	strongly disagree
32.	I do not tend to watch science documentaries on television or read articles about science and nature.	strongly agree	slightly agree	slightly disagree	strongly disagree
33.	If I were buying a stereo, I would want to know about its precise technical features.	strongly agree	slightly agree	slightly disagree	strongly disagree
34.	I find it easy to grasp exactly how odds work in betting.	strongly agree	slightly agree	slightly disagree	strongly disagree
35.	I am not very meticulous when I carry out D.I.Y.	strongly agree	slightly agree	slightly disagree	strongly disagree
36.	I find it easy to carry on a conversation with someone I've just met.	strongly agree	slightly agree	slightly disagree	strongly disagree
37.	When I look at a building, I am curious about the precise way it was constructed.	strongly agree	slightly agree	slightly disagree	strongly disagree
38.	When an election is being held, I am not interested in the results for each constituency.	strongly agree	slightly agree	slightly disagree	strongly disagree
39.	When I lend someone money, I expect them to pay me back exactly what they owe me.	strongly agree	slightly agree	slightly disagree	strongly disagree
40.	I find it difficult to understand information the bank sends me on different investment and saving systems.	strongly agree	slightly agree	slightly disagree	strongly disagree
41.	When travelling by train, I often wonder exactly how the rail networks are coordinated.	strongly agree	slightly agree	slightly disagree	strongly disagree
42.	When I buy a new appliance, I do not read the instruction manual very thoroughly.	strongly agree	slightly agree	slightly disagree	strongly disagree
43.	If I were buying a camera, I would not look carefully into the quality of the lens.	strongly agree	slightly agree	slightly disagree	strongly disagree
44.	When I read something, I always notice whether it is grammatically correct.	strongly agree	slightly agree	slightly disagree	strongly disagree

	strongly agree	slightly agree	slightly disagree	strongly disagree
45. When I hear the weather forecast, I am not very interested in the meteorological patterns.	strongly agree	slightly agree	slightly disagree	strongly disagree
46. I often wonder what it would be like to be someone else.	strongly agree	slightly agree	slightly disagree	strongly disagree
47. I find it difficult to do two things at once.	strongly agree	slightly agree	slightly disagree	strongly disagree
48. When I look at a mountain, I think about how precisely it was formed.	strongly agree	slightly agree	slightly disagree	strongly disagree
49. I can easily visualise how the motorways in my region link up.	strongly agree	slightly agree	slightly disagree	strongly disagree
50. When I'm in a restaurant, I often have a hard time deciding what to order.	strongly agree	slightly agree	slightly disagree	strongly disagree
51. When I'm in a plane, I do not think about the aerodynamics.	strongly agree	slightly agree	slightly disagree	strongly disagree
52. I often forget the precise details of conversations I've had.	strongly agree	slightly agree	slightly disagree	strongly disagree
53. When I am walking in the country, I am curious about how the various kinds of trees differ.	strongly agree	slightly agree	slightly disagree	strongly disagree
54. After meeting someone just once or twice, I find it difficult to remember precisely what they look like.	strongly agree	slightly agree	slightly disagree	strongly disagree
55. I am interested in knowing the path a river takes from its source to the sea.	strongly agree	slightly agree	slightly disagree	strongly disagree
56. I do not read legal documents very carefully.	strongly agree	slightly agree	slightly disagree	strongly disagree
57. I am not interested in understanding how wireless communication works.	strongly agree	slightly agree	slightly disagree	strongly disagree
58. I am curious about life on other planets.	strongly agree	slightly agree	slightly disagree	strongly disagree
59. When I travel, I like to learn specific details about the culture of the place I am visiting.	strongly agree	slightly agree	slightly disagree	strongly disagree
60. I do not care to know the names of the plants I see.	strongly agree	slightly agree	slightly disagree	strongly disagree

Appendix B: The Empathizing Quotient

		strongly agree	slightly agree	slightly disagree	strongly disagree
1.	I can easily tell if someone else wants to enter a conversation.	strongly agree	slightly agree	slightly disagree	strongly disagree
2.	I prefer animals to humans.	strongly agree	slightly agree	slightly disagree	strongly disagree
3.	I try to keep up with the current trends and fashions.	strongly agree	slightly agree	slightly disagree	strongly disagree
4.	I find it difficult to explain to others things that I understand easily, when they don't understand it first time.	strongly agree	slightly agree	slightly disagree	strongly disagree
5.	I dream most nights.	strongly agree	slightly agree	slightly disagree	strongly disagree
6.	I really enjoy caring for other people.	strongly agree	slightly agree	slightly disagree	strongly disagree
7.	I try to solve my own problems rather than discussing them with others.	strongly agree	slightly agree	slightly disagree	strongly disagree
8.	I find it hard to know what to do in a social situation.	strongly agree	slightly agree	slightly disagree	strongly disagree
9.	I am at my best first thing in the morning.	strongly agree	slightly agree	slightly disagree	strongly disagree
10.	People often tell me that I went too far in driving my point home in a discussion.	strongly agree	slightly agree	slightly disagree	strongly disagree
11.	It doesn't bother me too much if I am late meeting a friend.	strongly agree	slightly agree	slightly disagree	strongly disagree
12.	Friendships and relationships are just too difficult, so I tend not to bother with them.	strongly agree	slightly agree	slightly disagree	strongly disagree
13.	I would never break a law, no matter how minor.	strongly agree	slightly agree	slightly disagree	strongly disagree
14.	I often find it difficult to judge if something is rude or polite.	strongly agree	slightly agree	slightly disagree	strongly disagree
15.	In a conversation, I tend to focus on my own thoughts rather than on what my listener might be thinking.	strongly agree	slightly agree	slightly disagree	strongly disagree
16.	I prefer practical jokes to verbal humour.	strongly agree	slightly agree	slightly disagree	strongly disagree
17.	I live life for today rather than the future.	strongly agree	slightly agree	slightly disagree	strongly disagree
18.	When I was a child, I enjoyed cutting up worms to see what would happen.	strongly agree	slightly agree	slightly disagree	strongly disagree

		strongly agree	slightly agree	slightly disagree	strongly disagree
19.	I can pick up quickly if someone says one thing but means another.	strongly agree	slightly agree	slightly disagree	strongly disagree
20.	I tend to have very strong opinions about morality.	strongly agree	slightly agree	slightly disagree	strongly disagree
21.	It is hard for me to see why some things upset people so much.	strongly agree	slightly agree	slightly disagree	strongly disagree
22.	I find it easy to put myself in somebody else's shoes.	strongly agree	slightly agree	slightly disagree	strongly disagree
23.	I think that good manners are the most important thing a parent can teach their child.	strongly agree	slightly agree	slightly disagree	strongly disagree
24.	I like to do things on the spur of the moment.	strongly agree	slightly agree	slightly disagree	strongly disagree
25.	I am good at predicting how someone will feel.	strongly agree	slightly agree	slightly disagree	strongly disagree
26.	I am quick to spot when someone in a group is feeling awkward or uncomfortable.	strongly agree	slightly agree	slightly disagree	strongly disagree
27.	If I say something that someone else is offended by, I think that that's their problem, not mine.	strongly agree	slightly agree	slightly disagree	strongly disagree
28.	If anyone asked me if I liked their haircut, I would reply truthfully, even if I didn't like it.	strongly agree	slightly agree	slightly disagree	strongly disagree
29.	I can't always see why someone should have felt offended by a remark.	strongly agree	slightly agree	slightly disagree	strongly disagree
30.	People often tell me that I am very unpredictable.	strongly agree	slightly agree	slightly disagree	strongly disagree
31.	I enjoy being the centre of attention at any social gathering.	strongly agree	slightly agree	slightly disagree	strongly disagree
32.	Seeing people cry doesn't really upset me.	strongly agree	slightly agree	slightly disagree	strongly disagree
33.	I enjoy having discussions about politics.	strongly agree	slightly agree	slightly disagree	strongly disagree
34.	I am very blunt, which some people take to be rudeness, even though this is unintentional.	strongly agree	slightly agree	slightly disagree	strongly disagree
35.	I don't tend to find social situations confusing.	strongly agree	slightly agree	slightly disagree	strongly disagree
36.	Other people tell me I am good at understanding how they are feeling and what they are thinking.	strongly agree	slightly agree	slightly disagree	strongly disagree

continued

Appendix B: *continued*

		strongly agree	slightly agree	slightly disagree	strongly disagree
37.	When I talk to people, I tend to talk about their experiences rather than my own.	strongly agree	slightly agree	slightly disagree	strongly disagree
38.	It upsets me to see an animal in pain.	strongly agree	slightly agree	slightly disagree	strongly disagree
39.	I am able to make decisions without being influenced by people's feelings.	strongly agree	slightly agree	slightly disagree	strongly disagree
40.	I can't relax until I have done everything I had planned to do that day.	strongly agree	slightly agree	slightly disagree	strongly disagree
41.	I can easily tell if someone else is interested or bored with what I am saying.	strongly agree	slightly agree	slightly disagree	strongly disagree
42.	I get upset if I see people suffering on news programmes.	strongly agree	slightly agree	slightly disagree	strongly disagree
43.	Friends usually talk to me about their problems as they say that I am very understanding.	strongly agree	slightly agree	slightly disagree	strongly disagree
44.	I can sense if I am intruding, even if the other person doesn't tell me.	strongly agree	slightly agree	slightly disagree	strongly disagree
45.	I often start new hobbies but quickly become bored with them and move on to something else.	strongly agree	slightly agree	slightly disagree	strongly disagree
46.	People sometimes tell me that I have gone too far with teasing.	strongly agree	slightly agree	slightly disagree	strongly disagree
47.	I would be too nervous to go on a big roller-coaster.	strongly agree	slightly agree	slightly disagree	strongly disagree
48.	Other people often say that I am insensitive, though I don't always see why.	strongly agree	slightly agree	slightly disagree	strongly disagree
49.	If I see a stranger in a group, I think that it is up to them to make an effort to join in.	strongly agree	slightly agree	slightly disagree	strongly disagree
50.	I usually stay emotionally detached when watching a film.	strongly agree	slightly agree	slightly disagree	strongly disagree
51.	I like to be very organised in day to day life and often make lists of the chores I have to do.	strongly agree	slightly agree	slightly disagree	strongly disagree

	strongly agree	slightly agree	slightly disagree	strongly disagree
52. I can tune into how someone else feels rapidly and intuitively.	strongly agree	slightly agree	slightly disagree	strongly disagree
53. I don't like to take risks.	strongly agree	slightly agree	slightly disagree	strongly disagree
54. I can easily work out what another person might want to talk about.	strongly agree	slightly agree	slightly disagree	strongly disagree
55. I can tell if someone is masking their true emotion.	strongly agree	slightly agree	slightly disagree	strongly disagree
56. Before making a decision I always weigh up the pros and cons.	strongly agree	slightly agree	slightly disagree	strongly disagree
57. I don't consciously work out the rules of social situations.	strongly agree	slightly agree	slightly disagree	strongly disagree
58. I am good at predicting what someone will do.	strongly agree	slightly agree	slightly disagree	strongly disagree
59. I tend to get emotionally involved with a friend's problems.	strongly agree	slightly agree	slightly disagree	strongly disagree
60. I can usually appreciate the other person's viewpoint, even if I don't agree with it.	strongly agree	slightly agree	slightly disagree	strongly disagree

© February 1998 C/SJW

References

American Psychiatric Association (1994). *DSM-IV Diagnostic and Statistical Manual of Mental Disorders*, 4th edn. Washington, DC: American Psychiatric Association.

Asperger, H. (1944). Die 'Autistischen Psychopathen' im Kindesalter. *Arch. Psychiat. Nervenkrank.* **117**, 76–136.

Bailey, T., Le Couteur, A., Gottesman, I., Bolton, P., Simonoff, E., Yuzda, E., *et al.* (1995). Autism as a strongly genetic disorder: evidence from a British twin study. *Psychol. Med.* **25**, 63–77.

Baron-Cohen, S. (1995). *Mindblindness: an essay on autism and theory of mind.* Boston, MA: MIT Press/Bradford Books.

Baron-Cohen, S. (2000). Theory of mind and autism: a fifteen year review. In *Understanding other minds*, vol. 2 (ed. S. Baron-Cohen, H. Tager Flusberg and D. Cohen). Oxford: Oxford University Press.

Baron-Cohen, S. (2002). The extreme male brain theory of autism. *Trends Cogn. Sci.* **6**, 248–54.

Baron-Cohen, S. and Bolton, P. (1993). *Autism: the facts.* Oxford: Oxford University Press.

Baron-Cohen, S. and Hammer, J. (1997). Is autism an extreme form of the male brain? *Adv. Infancy Res.* **11**, 193–217.

Baron-Cohen, S. and Ring, H. (1994). A model of the mindreading system: neuropsychological and neurobiological perspectives. In *Origins of an understanding of mind* (ed. P. Mitchell and C. Lewis). Hillsdale, NJ: Lawrence Erlbaum Associates.

Baron-Cohen, S., Jolliffe, T., Mortimore, C. and Robertson, M. (1997). Another advanced test of theory of mind: evidence from very high functioning adults with autism or Asperger Syndrome. *J. Child Psychol. Psychiat.* **38**, 813–22.

Baron-Cohen, S., O'Riordan, M., Jones, R., Stone, V. and Plaisted, K. (1999*a*). A new test of social sensitivity: detection of faux pas in normal children and children with Asperger syndrome. *J. Autism Devl Disorders* **29**, 407–18.

Baron-Cohen, S., Ring, H., Wheelwright, S., Bullmore, E., Brammer, M., Simmons, A., *et al.* (1999*b*). Social intelligence in the normal and autistic brain: an fMRI study. *Eur. J. Neurosci.* **11**, 1891–98.

Baron-Cohen, S., Wheelwright, S., Stone, V. and Rutherford, M. (1999*c*). A mathematician, a physicist, and a computer scientist with Asperger syndrome: performance on folk psychology and folk physics test. *Neurocase* **5**, 475–83.

Baron-Cohen, S., Ring, H., Bullmore, E., Wheelwright, S., Ashwin, C. and Williams, S. (2000). The amygdala theory of autism. *Neurosci. Behav. Rev.* **24**, 355–64.

Baron-Cohen, S., Wheelwright, S., Skinner, R., Martin, J. and Clubley, E. (2001). The autism spectrum quotient (AQ): evidence from Asperger syndrome/high functioning autism, males and females, scientists and mathematicians. *J. Autism Devl Disorders* **31**, 5–17.

Baron-Cohen, S., Wheelwright, S., Griffin, R., Lawson, J. and Hill, J. (2002). The exact mind: empathising and systemising in autism spectrum conditions. In *Handbook of cognitive development* (ed. U. Goswami). Oxford: Blackwell.

Baron-Cohen, S. and Wheelwright, S. (in press). The Empathy Quotient: An investigation of adults with Asperger syndrome or high-functioning autism, and normal sex differences. *J. Autism Devl Disorders.*

Benbow, C. P. (1988). Sex differences in mathematical reasoning ability in intellectually talented preadolescents: their nature, effects, and possible causes. *Behav. Brain Sci.* **11**, 169–232.

Bolton, P. and Rutter, M. (1990). Genetic influences in autism. *Int. Rev. Psychiat.* **2**, 67–80.

Davis, M. H. (1980). A multidimensional approach to individual differences in empathy. *JSAS Cat. Select. Docs Psychol.* **10**, 85.

Davis, M. H. (1994). *Empathy: a social psychological approach.* Boulder, CO: Westview Press.

Davis, M. H. and Franzoi, S. L. (1991). Stability and change in adolescent self-consciousness and empathy. *J. Res. Personality* **25**, 70–87.

Folstein, S. and Rutter, M. (1977). Infantile autism: a genetic study of 21 twin pairs. *J. Child Psychol. Psychiat.* **18**, 297–321.

Folstein, S. and Rutter, M. (1988). Autism: familial aggregation and genetic implications. *J. Autism Devl Disorders* **18**, 3–30.

Frith, C.D. and Frith, U. (1999). Interacting minds—a biological basis. *Science* **286**, 1692–95.

Frith, U. (1989). *Autism: explaining the enigma.* Oxford: Basil Blackwell.

Frith, U. (1991). *Autism and Asperger's syndrome.* Cambridge: Cambridge University Press.

Geary, D. (1996). Sexual selection and sex differences in mathematical abilities. *Behav. Brain Sci.* **19**, 229–84.

Geschwind, N. and Galaburda, A. M. (1985). Cerebral lateralization. biological mechanisms, associations, and pathology: I. A hypothesis and a program for research. *Arch. Neurol.* **42**, 428–59.

Gillberg, C. (1991). Clinical and neurobiological aspects of Asperger syndrome in six family studies. In *Autism and Asperger syndrome* (ed. U. Frith). Cambridge: Cambridge University Press.

Hall, J. A. (1978). Gender effects in decoding nonverbal cues. *Psychol. Bull.* **85**, 845–58.

Happé, F. (1996). Studying weak central coherence at low levels: children with autism do not succumb to visual illusions. A research note. *J. Child Psychol. Psychiat.* **37**, 873–77.

Hermelin, B. (2002). *Bright splinters of the mind: a personal story of research with autistic savants.* London: Jessica Kingsley.

Hoffman, M. L. (1977). Sex differences in empathy and related behaviors. *Psychol. Bull.* **84**, 712–22.

ICD-10 (1994). *International Classification of Diseases*, 10th edn. Geneva: World Health Organization.

Jolliffe, T. and Baron-Cohen, S. (1997). Are people with autism or Asperger's syndrome faster than normal on the embedded figures task? *J. Child Psychol. Psychiat.* **38**, 527–34.

Kimura, D. (1999). *Sex and cognition.* Cambridge, MA: MIT Press.

Klin, A., Volkmar, F., Sparrow, S., Cicchetti, D. and Rourke, B. (1995). Validity and neuropsychological characterization of Asperger syndrome: convergence with nonverbal learning disabilities syndrome. *J. Child Psychol. Psychiat.* **36**, 1127–40.

Lawson, J., Baron-Cohen, S., and Wheelwright, S. (in press). Empathizing and systemizing in adults with and without Asperger syndrome. *J. Autism Devl Disorders.*

Lutchmaya, S., Baron-Cohen, S. and Raggett, P. (2002). Foetal testosterone and eye contact in 12 month old infants. *Infant Behav. Dev.* **25**, 327–35.

Morton, J., Frith, U. and Leslie, A. (1991). The cognitive basis of a biological disorder: autism. *Trends Neurosci.* **14**, 434–38.

Ozonoff, S., Strayer, L., McMahon, A. and Filloux, F. (1994). Executive function abilities in autism and Tourette syndrome: an information processing approach. *J. Child Psychol. Psychiat.* **35**, 1015–32.

Russell, J. (1997). How executive disorders can bring about an inadequate theory of mind. In *Autism as an executive disorder* (ed. J. Russell). Oxford: Oxford University Press.

Shah, A. and Frith, U. (1983). An islet of ability in autism: a research note. *J. Child Psychol. Psychiat.* **24**, 613–20.

Wechsler, D. (1958). *Sex differences in intelligence: the measurement and appraisal of adult intelligence.* Baltimore, OH: Williams and Wilking.

Wing, L. (1981). Asperger syndrome: a clinical account. *Psychol. Med.* **11**, 115–30.

Wing, L. (1988). The autistic continuum. In *Aspects of autism: biological research* (ed. L. Wing). London: Gaskell/Royal College of Psychiatrists.

Glossary

AQ: autism spectrum quotient
AS: Asperger syndrome
EFT: embedded figures task
EMB: extreme male brain
EQ: empathy quotient
E–S: empathizing–systemizing
HFA: high-functioning autism
SQ: systemizing quotient
WAIS-R: Weschler Adult Intelligence Scale—Revised

9

Towards an understanding of the mechanisms of weak central coherence effects: experiments in visual configural learning and auditory perception

Kate Plaisted, Lisa Saksida, José Alcántara, and Emma Weisblatt

The weak central coherence hypothesis of Frith is one of the most prominent theories concerning the abnormal performance of individuals with autism on tasks that involve local and global processing. Individuals with autism often out-perform matched nonautistic individuals on tasks in which success depends upon processing of local features, and underperform on tasks that require global processing. We review those studies that have been unable to identify the locus of the mechanisms that may be responsible for weak central coherence effects and those that show that local processing is enhanced in autism but not at the expense of global processing. In the light of these studies, we propose that the mechanisms which can give rise to 'weak central coherence' effects may be perceptual. More specifically, we propose that perception operates to enhance the representation of individual perceptual features but that this does not impact adversely on representations that involve integration of features. This proposal was supported in the two experiments we report on configural and feature dis-crimination learning in high-functioning children with autism. We also exam-ined processes of perception directly, in an auditory filtering task which measured the width of auditory filters in individuals with autism and found that the width of auditory filters in autism were abnormally broad. We consider the implications of these findings for perceptual theories of the mechanisms under-pinning weak central coherence effects.

Keywords: perception; configuration; local; global; integration

9.1 Introduction

Throughout the history of experimental research in autism, there has been an interest in the perceptual and attentional abnormalities that have been widely reported by clinicians, parents of children with autism and individuals with the disorder themselves (Kanner 1943; Grandin and Scariano 1986; Myles *et al.* 2000;

Sainsbury 2000). Early research focused on possible sensory differences in the autistic population (Goldfarb 1961; Ornitz 1969), while later research examined possible differences in selective attention (Lovaas *et al.* 1979). More recently, research on perceptual and attentional aspects of autism has been inspired by the conceptualization by Frith (1989) of these abnormalities as 'weak central coherence'. Her hypothesis postulates a weakness in the operation of central systems that are normally responsible for drawing together or integrating individual pieces of information to establish meaning, resulting in a cognitive bias towards processing local parts of information rather than the overall context.

It has been argued that weak central coherence can be seen at both 'low' and 'high' levels (Happé 1996, 1997). An example of 'low' level weak central coherence that has been cited is the exceptionally good performance of individuals with autism on the embedded figures task and the block design subtest of the Wechsler intelligence scales (Shah and Frith 1983, 1993; Happé *et al.* 2001), as success on these tasks requires the participant to process the local parts of the stimuli and to ignore the visual context in which the stimuli are presented. The term 'high' level weak central coherence has been used to describe studies of contextual processing, such as mispronunciation of homographs in sentence context and drawing incorrect bridging inferences between two sentences by individuals with autism (Happé 1997; Jolliffe and Baron-Cohen 1999). Thus, 'low' level weak central coherence has been used to refer to processes such as perception, learning and attention whilst 'high' level weak central coherence has been used to refer to linguistic and semantic processes.

The idea of weak central coherence clearly and neatly characterizes the style of stimulus processing that could give rise to this pattern of responding—a piecemeal approach that results in superior performance on some tasks and poor performance on others. However, what is less clear is the nature of the mechanisms of weak central coherence that give rise to these effects and, furthermore, what single cognitive mechanism could give rise to both 'low' and 'high' level weak central coherence. Attempts to address this question have so far been limited to searching for a mechanism of 'low' level weak central coherence. For example, some researchers have indicated that the mechanism might be a 'narrow' spotlight of attention, which normally serves to enhance processing at a particular location in attentional space and operates to bind together or integrate separate features (Townsend and Courchesne 1994). However, in one type of test of the spotlight of attention, the conjunctive visual search task, a series of studies has generally found that children with autism *outperform* typical children (Plaisted *et al.* 1998a; O'Riordan and Plaisted 2001). Another proposal has been that right-hemisphere attentional processes which may serve to process the overall form of a visual stimulus (Lamb *et al.* 1990) may be compromised in autism and thus constitute the locus of the 'low' level weak central coherence mechanism. These studies have employed hierarchical stimuli (such as a large triangle comprised of small squares) and participants are required to respond to the overall form of the stimulus (referred to as the global level) or the constituent features (referred to as the local level). In typical individuals, a common effect is that the global level of the stimulus dominates responding, with slower and less accurate responding to the local level (Navon 1977). The literature comparing individuals with and without autism has produced mixed results. Nonetheless, two findings have been replicated across studies. The first is that individuals with autism can respond to the global level of a hierarchical stimulus in the same way as comparison individuals (Mottron and Belleville 1993; Ozonoff *et al*. 1994; Plaisted *et al*. 1999). The second is that, under some circumstances, individuals with autism show faster and more accurate responding to the local level than comparison individuals (Mottron and Belleville 1993; Plaisted *et al*. 1999). Furthermore, although most of these studies have been conducted in the visual domain, an analogous finding has been reported in the auditory domain (Mottron *et al*. 2000). The fact that individuals with autism can process the global level of a stimulus normally is clear evidence that those attentional mechanisms responsible for global processing are not deficient in autism and thus cannot be the locus of 'low' level weak central coherence. However, the fact that individuals with autism can show enhanced local processing as well as normal global processing challenges the central idea of the weak central coherence hypothesis, that a local-level processing bias results from a deficit in global-level processing.

These challenges to the weak central coherence hypothesis have led to alternative proposals for the mechanism that underpins enhanced local processing in autism on tasks such as the embedded figures and block design. One suggestion has been that their performance may result from abnormal perceptual processing in autism, which serves to enhance the salience of individual stimulus features and allows greater acuity in their representation but does not compromise processing of global configurations. We have offered this possibility as an explanation for enhanced discrimination effects in autism that we have observed in a difficult perceptual learning discrimination task and conjunctive search tasks in which there is high perceptual similarity between targets and accompanying distracters (Plaisted *et al*. 1998*b*; O'Riordan and Plaisted 2001; Plaisted 2001). Thus, differences in perception that enhance feature processing may constitute an alternative hypothesis to 'low' level weak central coherence. As this hypothesis is limited to perception, it makes no prediction (unlike weak central coherence) that processing the global level of a stimulus would be abnormal, since processing at that level would rely on post-perceptual mechanisms such as grouping and integration (see Palmer and Rock (1994), for a theory of the mechanisms involved in the processing of complex stimuli). We begin this paper by comparing the two hypotheses in configural and elemental learning tasks in the visual domain. In the second part of the paper, we directly examine the possibility that auditory perception in autism is abnormal using an auditory filtering task.

9.2 Configural and feature processing

At the heart of the weak central coherence hypothesis is the idea that individuals with autism have deficits in the ability to integrate disparate features in order to derive the overall global configuration of the stimulus. This kind of deficit has clear implications for the way in which the meaning or significance of stimuli can be interpreted: the significance of a stimulus is rarely determined by a single distinctive feature but rather a particular configuration of features. Furthermore, some features of one stimulus can also configure with other features in a second stimulus, defining a different significance. An example that may be of relevance in autism is recognizing the emotional significance of a facial expression: different expressions share some features, but their particular configurations denote particular emotional expressions. For example, a down-turned mouth configured with a frown denotes sadness, a frown configured with narrowed eyes denotes a cross expression and a down-turned mouth with narrowed eyes indicates disgust.

This configural problem can be stated more formally as follows: features AB = expression X, features BC = Y and AC = Z. Models of configural learning indicate that when the significance of a stimulus is determined only by the combination of two or more features, those features are unified in a single representation as a configuration, and this configural representation is qualitatively different from the separate representations of each individual feature (Pearce 1994; Bussey and Saksida 2002). Thus, these models would identify abnormalities in configural representations as the locus of weak central coherence in autism. By contrast, the perceptual hypothesis predicts no deficit in configural processing; however, because this hypothesis states that features are more salient and acutely represented, it predicts that the significance of stimuli that are defined solely by the presence of particular features, rather than the configuration of features, would be easily acquired by an individual with autism, and perhaps more easily than individuals without autism. We tested these predictions in two tests of configural and feature processing, comparing high-functioning children with autism with normally developing children, matched for mental age.

9.3 Experiment 1: the biconditional configural discrimination

Children were presented with two discrimination tasks—one which required configural processing for its solution and another in which the solution could be derived from the simple association between individual features and a left or right key press action. The configural task was a biconditional discrimination involving stimuli composed of two features. In this task, no single feature defined the left or right key press action. The stimuli and associated actions can be represented as follows: Features A and B → press left, features B and C → press right, features C and D → press left, features A and D → press right. Hence, each individual feature A, B, C or D is equally associated with both left and right key presses, and the solution to the problem can be solved only by considering the configuration of the two features combined. The feature discrimination had the following structure: features S and T → left, U and V → right, WX → left, YZ → right. Thus, each feature diagnosed the appropriate key press action.

(a) Methods

(i) Participants

A group of nine high-functioning children with autism and a group of nine typically developing children participated. All children in the group with autism had received a diagnosis of autism by trained clinicians using instruments such as the Autism Diagnostic Interview (Le Couteur *et al.* 1989) and met established criteria for autism, such as those specified in DSM-IV (American Psychiatric Association 1994). None of the children in either group had received any other psychiatric diagnosis. Each child in the autistic group was pairwise matched with a child in the typically developing group for CA and nonverbal IQ using the RSPMs (Raven 1958). Details of the CAs and RSPM scores for each group are provided in the top half of Table 9.1.

(ii) Apparatus and stimuli

The stimuli were generated by a Dell Latitude LM portable PC and displayed in the centre of a 14 inch monitor. Participants responded on each trial by pressing either the '.' key or the 'x' key on the keyboard. Coloured geometric shapes were used for both the biconditional configural discrimination and the feature discrimination. For the biconditional discrimination, four stimuli were

Table 9.1 Participant characteristics.

group	age (yrs : mths)	RSPM scores
experiment 1		
autistic ($N = 9$)		
mean	10 : 6	29.0
s.d.	1 : 1	7.77
typical ($N = 9$)		
mean	10 : 2	30.44
s.d.	1 : 1	7.6
experiment 2		
autistic ($N = 12$)		
mean	9 : 6	31.83
s.d.	1 : 2	8.59
typical ($N = 12$)		
mean	9 : 6	30.33
s.d.	1 : 2	7.5

used, each comprising a colour feature and a shape feature. Stimulus AB was a blue bar, stimulus BC was a red bar, stimulus CD was a red circle and stimulus AD was a blue circle. For the four stimuli used in the feature task, stimulus ST was a pink star, stimulus UV was an orange square, stimulus WX was a yellow triangle and stimulus YZ was a purple cross. In both tasks, the children sat 140 cm in front of the computer display.

(iii) Design and procedure
Each child was given two testing sessions, separated by an interval of not less than 2 days. During the first session, the RSPM was administered, followed by either the biconditional or the feature discrimination. In order to counterbalance for practice or fatigue effects, four of the children in each group received the biconditional discrimination first and the feature discrimination second and the remaining children received the two tasks in reverse order.

For both discriminations, the child's task was to learn which stimuli were associated a left key press (by pressing the 'x' key) and which were associated with a right key press (by pressing the '.' key). In the biconditional task, stimuli AB and CD were associated with the left key and stimuli BC and DA were associated with the right key. This ensured that each feature (colour or shape) was equally associated with both left and right key presses, so that the task could be solved only by reference to the configuration of two features. In the feature discrimination, stimuli ST and UV were associated with the left key, and stimuli WX and YZ were associated with the right key.

At the start of each test, the children were shown each stimulus separately and told that their task was to find which of the two keys they should press after each type of stimulus. They were shown that if they pressed the 'correct' key, the computer would display a large tick in the centre of the screen and make a chirping sound whereas if they pressed the 'incorrect' key, the computer would display a cross and make an 'uh-oh' sound. Once children had indicated that they understood the task, the test trials began. In each task on each trial, a stimulus was presented in the centre of the screen until a response had been made. The feedback for that trial was then immediately presented for 500 ms, followed by a blank screen for 500 ms. After this intertrial interval, the next stimulus was presented. The computer was programmed to present a minimum of 32 trials and a maximum of 128 trials and calculated the percentage correct score within every 16-trial block. If children had reached a criterion of 12 out of 16 trials correct in any 16-trial block (following the first 16 trials) the programme terminated. Within every 16-trial block, each of the four stimulus types appeared on four trials. Stimulus trial types were randomly intermixed in each 16-trial block. Error data were recorded on each trial.

(b) Results

The average percentage of correct trials for each group are presented in Fig. 9.1. The graph indicates that there was no difference between the two groups on

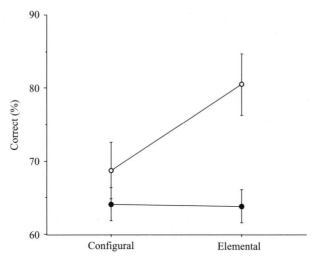

Fig. 9.1 Average per cent correct for each group in the biconditional configural discrimination and the feature discrimination in experiment 1. The error bars represent s.e.m. White circles, autistic; black circles, control.

the biconditional discrimination task but that the group with autism performed better on the feature discrimination task compared with the typically developing group. These data were analysed by mixed ANOVA, with group (autistic and typical) and order (biconditional task first followed by feature task and vice versa) as between-participants factors and discrimination type (biconditional and feature) as a within-participants factor. There was a significant main effect of group ($F_{1,14} = 6.24$, $p < 0.03$) and discrimination type ($F_{1,14} = 12.63$, $p < 0.004$) and a significant interaction between group and discrimination type ($F_{1,14} = 20.23$, $p < 0.0006$). There were no other significant main effects or interactions. The main effect of group was due to the fact that, overall, the group with autism performed better than the typically developing group and the effect of discrimination type showed that the feature task was easier than the configural task. However, the interaction between group and discrimination type indicated that this was the case for the group with autism only. This was confirmed by simple effects analysis of the interaction: there was a significant effect of group on the feature task ($F_{1,16} = 5.83$, $p < 0.03$) but not on the biconditional task, and a significant difference for the autistic group between their performance on the two tasks ($F_{1,16} = 39.19$, $p < 0.0001$) but no difference for the typically developing group.

(c) Discussion

The finding that the children with autism performed better than the typically developing children on the feature task and found this task easier than the biconditional discrimination is consistent with the idea that individual features are processed extremely efficiently in autism and the hypothesis that perception of features is highly acute. Furthermore, the lack of difference between the two groups of children on the biconditional discrimination task indicates that children with autism do not have a deficit in learning about the significance of configurations of features. Nonetheless, it is a possibility (which we explore further following the next experiment) that the superior processing of the individual features of shape and colour in the biconditional discrimination may have interfered with learning the configurations in that task and that the performance of the group with autism on the biconditional task might otherwise have been better than observed. The question is whether this constitutes evidence for the weak central coherence hypothesis: possibly, except that weak central coherence would predict that the interference from the features should be sufficiently great to impair performance substantially on the biconditional task relative to the typically developing group.

9.4 Experiment 2: the feature–configuration patterning task

It could be argued that the biconditional discrimination task in the previous experiment in Section 9.3 was too simple to challenge any deficiency in configural processing in autism. In order to examine configural processing further, we presented another type of configural discrimination task that included both feature and configural trials. In the feature–configuration patterning task, on feature trials a stimulus, either A or B, is presented and each is followed by the same outcome (i.e. A → left press, B → left press). On configural trials, stimuli A and B are presented together followed by a difference outcome (i.e. AB → press right). A feature solution to this task is therefore not possible since learning that the individual features A and B are associated with the left key press would signify (even more strongly) a left key press when the features A and B are presented together. Instead, the configural association (AB → right key) must be learned separately from the individual feature-action associations.

(a) Methods

(i) Participants
A group of 12 high-functioning children with autism and a group of 12 typically developing children participated. As before, all children in the group with autism met established criteria for autism, such as those specified in DSM-IV (American Psychiatric Association 1994) and had received a diagnosis of autism by trained clinicians. None of the children in either group had received any other psychiatric diagnosis. The children were pairwise matched across groups for CA and RSPM scores. Details of the CAs and RSPM scores for each group are provided in the bottom half of Table 9.1.

(ii) Apparatus and stimuli

The stimuli were generated by a Macintosh PowerBook G3 portable computer and displayed in the centre of a 14 inch monitor. Participants responded on each trial by pressing either the '.' key or the 'x' key on the keyboard. Each stimulus was composed of a set of coloured dots randomly located on the screen. For the feature trials, one type of trial consisted of pink dots and the other type consisted of blue dots. The configural trials consisted of a mixture of pink and blue dots. For any trial (feature and configural), the total number of dots varied from a minimum of 6 to a maximum of 20 and the spatial position of the dots varied from trial to trial. Thus, the task could not be solved by incidental factors of number or spatial position of dots. In addition, a small proportion of yellow and green dots were added to each stimulus, for both the feature and configural trials. These were added after a pilot study revealed ceiling performance in both children with and without autism using pink and blue dots only. The yellow and green dots were therefore added as distracters in order to increase the overall difficulty of the task, to allow the observation of any differences that might exist between the two groups. The numbers of yellow and green distracter dots added to each stimulus varied between two and eight (examples of the stimuli used are presented in Fig. 9.2).

(iii) Design and procedure

Each child in each group was first administered the RSPM followed by the computerized feature–configuration patterning task. Children were shown each trial type (A, B and AB) separately and it was explained that they had to find out which of two keys ('x' or '.') they must press for each stimulus. For each trial type, they were shown that if they pressed the 'correct' key, the computer would display a large tick in the centre of the screen and make a chirping sound, whereas if they pressed the 'incorrect' key, the computer would display a cross and make an 'uh-oh' sound. The children were then given eight practice trials, two trials of A, two of B and four of AB, randomly intermixed. After a short pause (the length depending on the child saying that they were ready) the test

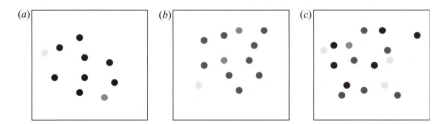

Fig. 9.2 Illustrations of the stimuli presented in feature trials (*a,b*) and in configural trials (*c*) in experiment 2. The absolute numbers of dots and their positions on the computer screen were varied across trials. A random number of green and yellow dots were added to each stimulus to increase the overall difficulty of the discrimination. (See Plate 1 of the Plate Section, at the centre of this book.)

trials began. There were 88 trials in total, 44 configural AB trials and 22 feature
trials of A and 22 trials of B. Trial types were randomly intermixed. Children
were required to complete all 88 trials. For each trial, the stimulus remained on
the screen until a response had been made or 6 s had elapsed, whichever was the
sooner. Following stimulus offset, feedback was presented in the centre of the
screen for 500 ms followed by a 500 ms intertrial interval during which a blank
screen was presented. Error data were recorded on each trial.

(b) Results

For each child, the average per cent correct for the feature trials was separately
calculated from that for the configural trials. The graph in Fig. 9.3 shows the
average per cent correct scores for the feature and configural trials for the
group with autism and typically developing children. The graph indicates that
the typically developing children responded more accurately on the configural
trials, whereas the children with autism responded more accurately on the
feature trials. A mixed ANOVA was conducted on the data, with group as a
between-participants factor and trial type (configural and feature) as a within-
participants factor. There were no significant main effects but a significant
interaction between group and trial type ($F_{1,22} = 16.9$, $p < 0.0006$). Simple
effects of this interaction revealed a significant effect of trial type for the typically developing group ($F_{1,22} = 10.75$, $p < 0.003$), confirming that these children performed better on configural than feature trials, and a significant effect

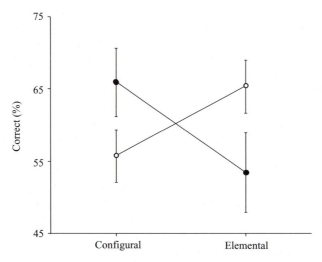

Fig. 9.3 Average per cent correct for each group for configural trials and for
feature trials in the feature–configural patterning task in experiment 2. The error bars
represent s.e.m. White circles, autistic; black circles, control.

of trial type for the group with autism ($F_{1,22} = 6.39$, $p < 0.02$), showing that autistic children performed better on the feature than the configural trials. The difference between the groups on the feature trials marginally failed to reach significance at the 0.05 level ($F_{1,30} = 3.6$, $p = 0.069$). Finally, there was no difference between groups on the configural trials.

(c) Discussion

The pattern of results on the feature–configural patterning task is broadly consistent with that observed in the previous experiment: performance by the group with autism on the feature trials was better than their performance on the configural trials and the two groups did not differ on the configural trials. Rather different from the pattern of results of the previous experiment was the fact that the typically developing group responded more accurately on the configural than on the feature trials. Thus, it might be said that while the group with autism showed a bias towards feature processing, the typically developing group showed a bias towards configural processing. This bias in the typically developing children is not unexpected: the same has been shown in several studies with typical adults (Williams *et al.* 1994; Shanks *et al.* 1998). The weak central coherence hypothesis might account for these patterns by arguing that, while in normal individuals there is a drive for coherence which interfered with performance on feature trials, the lack of this drive in autism resulted in a bias for feature processing, which interfered with processing the configuration of the features on configural trials. The difficulty with this argument is that no difference was observed between groups on the configural trials, indicating that configural processing is not compromised in autism. Instead, the enhanced performance on the feature trials might be accounted for by the hypothesis that the perception of features is particularly acute in autism, but that this perceptual advantage does not interfere with the processing of configurations of features.

The results of the experiments presented so far raise the possibility that some of the effects seen in visual–spatial tasks in autism, such as the superior performance on the embedded figures task, could result from abnormal perceptual processes that enhance the salience of feature representations, rather than the deficient integration processes proposed by the weak central coherence hypothesis. However, in order to fully assess the suggestion that the locus of 'low' level weak central coherence is perceptual processing, we need to conduct studies that assess perception from the very earliest perceptual processes. Very little research has been conducted to assess early visual perceptual processes in autism, such as spatial resolution. However, there have been some preliminary suggestions of enhanced pitch perception in autism (Bonnel 2003). Two of us (J. Alcántara and E. Weisblatt) have begun a programme of experiments systematically to investigate peripheral auditory processing in autism, and one of these studies, on auditory filters, is presented here.

9.5 Auditory-filter shapes in high-functioning individuals with autism or asperger syndrome

There have long been suggestions that abnormalities of sensory processing might be primary in autism but relatively little formal work has been carried out in the auditory domain. In an early study, Goldfarb (1961) studied 'schizophrenic' children, many of whom would now probably be diagnosed with autism. The children had normal auditory thresholds but showed either extreme distress or lack of response to a tone that normal children found noticeable but not aversive. More recently, Myles *et al.* (2000) conducted a survey of 42 children with AS and showed that 71% of the children showed some difficulties with auditory perception, such as hypersensitivity to specific auditory signals.

One of the most commonly reported auditory problems in individuals with autism is an inability to understand speech when background sounds are present. The problems often quantified in the laboratory by measuring the SNR required to achieve 50% correct identification of speech, referred to as the SRT. In a recent study, Alcántara *et al.* (2003) measured the SRTs of a group of HFA or AS. Participants were required to identify sentences presented in five different background sounds, including a steady speech-shaped noise, a single competing talker, and noises with spectral or temporal dips. The temporal dips arise because there are moments, during brief pauses in speech, for example, when the overall level of the competing speech is low. The spectral dips arise because the spectrum of the target speech is often quite different from that of the background speech, at least over the short term. The individuals with HFA–AS were found to have significantly lower (i.e. worse) SRTs than the age and IQ-matched control participants, particularly for those background sounds that contained temporal dips.

The speech perception problem may be understood in terms of both deficits in central and peripheral levels of processing. For example, the process of detecting speech in background sounds may be viewed as an example of 'auditory scene analysis', whereby information arising from several simultaneous sources is perceptually grouped into separate 'auditory objects' or perceptual streams (Bregman 1990). In other words, the complex sound is analysed into several streams and we choose to attend to one stream at a time. This 'attended' stream then stands out perceptually, while the rest of the sound is less prominent. This is an example of what the Gestalt psychologists called the 'figure–ground phenomenon' (Koffka 1935). Deficits in the perception of speech in noise, as the weak central coherence hypothesis would argue, may therefore result from problems in combining information from the constituent parts to form the 'whole', or using nonauditory information, such as contextual cues, to facilitate speech recognition.

Alternatively, at the peripheral processing level, the process of detecting speech in background sounds may be understood in terms of the 'frequency selectivity' of the auditory system. Frequency selectivity is one of the most basic properties of hearing and refers to our ability to separate or resolve, at least to a limited extent, the components in a complex sound, such as speech. It depends on the filtering that takes place in the cochlea. Specifically, sounds undergo an initial frequency analysis at the level of the BM in which they are decomposed into their constituent frequency components. The BM behaves as if it contained a bank of continuously overlapping bandpass filters, called 'auditory filters'. Each filter is tuned to a particular centre frequency, with the BM responding maximally to that frequency and responding progressively less to frequencies away from the centre frequency. The relative response of the filter, as a function of frequency, is known as the *auditory filter shape*. Thus, masking only occurs when the masking sound produces responses in the auditory filters tuned close to the signal frequency.

The frequency tuning properties of the BM are quantified by measuring the 'shape' of the auditory filter (Patterson and Moore 1986). This is a physically defined measure of the sharpness of tuning at a given BM location and describes the frequency selectivity of the peripheral auditory system. In normal hearing individuals, the action of a physiological 'active process' (Ruggero 1992) markedly influences the degree of frequency selectivity present. Thus, in normal hearing participants the auditory filters are relatively sharp, and have BWs of *around* 10–12% of the centre frequency of the filter (Moore and Glasberg 1981). In hearing-impaired individuals, the active process is often reduced or absent, resulting in frequency tuning properties that are significantly worse than those measured in individuals with normal hearing (Ruggero *et al*. 1996): auditory filters are often two to three times as wide as normal (Glasberg and Moore 1986).

The role of frequency selectivity in speech-in-noise perception is best illustrated by studies using hearing-impaired individuals who also report particular difficulty understanding speech in the presence of background sounds. This is the case even when the speech is presented at a high level, so that it is above their absolute hearing threshold and audibility is not a factor. The relatively poor performance of hearing-impaired people appears to arise partly from a decrease in frequency selectivity. One of the perceptual consequences of a decrease in frequency selectivity is a greater susceptibility to masking by interfering sounds: when we try to detect a sinusoidal signal in a noisy background, we use the auditory filter that gives the best SNR. When the auditory filters are relatively narrow, as is the case for normal hearing individuals, most of the background noise is attenuated as it falls outside the pass-band of the auditory filter centred on the signal frequency. In an impaired ear, this same filter passes much more of the noise, as it is wider, especially on its low-frequency side, making it harder to hear the signal. This is generally known as 'upward spread of masking', and results in a marked susceptibility to masking by low-frequency sounds, such as car noise and air-conditioning noise.

Accordingly, the aim of the current study was to measure frequency selectivity for a group of individuals with HFA or AS. This was done in order to determine whether abnormalities in the peripheral processing of auditory stimuli are responsible for the observed difficulties in speech-in-noise perception, or whether, as predicted by the weak central coherence hypothesis, they result from post-perceptual processes such as grouping and integration. We measured the auditory filter shapes of eight individuals using a masking experimental paradigm. Masking experiments may be used to explore the limitations in frequency selectivity of the auditory system in the following way: it is a matter of everyday experience that one sound may be rendered inaudible in the presence of other sounds. For example, if a signal to be detected and a masking sound are widely different in frequency, then the signal will generally be heard. If the signal and masker are close in frequency, then masking is more likely to occur. Thus, masking reflects the limits of frequency selectivity: if the selectivity of the ear is insufficient to separate the signal and the masker, then masking occurs.

In order to determine the auditory filter shape, we measured the threshold for a 2 kHz sinusoidal tone signal in the presence of a masker whose frequency content is varied in a systematic way. We used the notched-noise method of Patterson (1976), which ensures that the listener always listened through the auditory filter centred at the signal frequency. The experiment is illustrated schematically in Fig. 9.4 (taken from Moore 1997). The masker is a noise whose spectrum has a notch centred at the signal frequency. The deviation of each edge of the notch from the centre frequency is denoted by Δf. The width of the notch is varied, and the threshold of the signal is determined as a function of the notch width. For a signal symmetrically placed in the notched

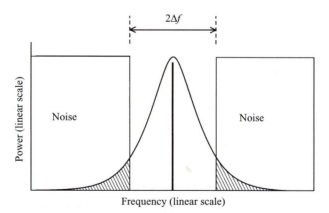

Fig. 9.4 Schematic illustration of the notched-noise technique used by Patterson (1976) to derive the shape of the auditory filter. The threshold of the sinusoidal signal is measured as a function of the width of the spectral notch in the noise masker, which has an overall width of $2\Delta f$. The amount of noise passing through a filter centred at the signal frequency is proportional to the area of the shaded regions (taken from Moore 1997).

noise, the highest signal-to-masker ratio will be achieved with the auditory filter centred at the signal frequency, as illustrated in Fig. 9.4. As the width of
the notch in the noise is increased, less and less noise will pass through the
auditory filter. Thus, the threshold of the signal will drop. The amount of noise
passing through the auditory filter is proportional to the area under the filter
covered by the noise. This is shown as the shaded areas in Fig. 9.4. If we
assume that threshold corresponds to a constant signal-to-masker ratio at the
output of the auditory filter, then the change in signal threshold with notch
width tells us how the area under the filter varies with Δf. By differentiating
the function-relating threshold to Δf, the shape of the auditory filter is
obtained. In other words, the slope of the function-relating threshold to Δf for
a given deviation Δf is equal to the 'height' of the auditory filter, at that value
of Δf. If the threshold decreases rapidly with increasing notch width, this indicates a sharply tuned filter. If the threshold decreases slowly with increasing
notch width, this indicates a broadly tuned filter. An example of an auditory
filter shape obtained using this method is shown in Fig. 9.5. It should be
noted, however, that although the derivation is based on the use of linear power
units, the relative response of the filter is usually plotted on a decibel scale, as
in Fig. 9.5. The response of the filter at its centre frequency is arbitrarily

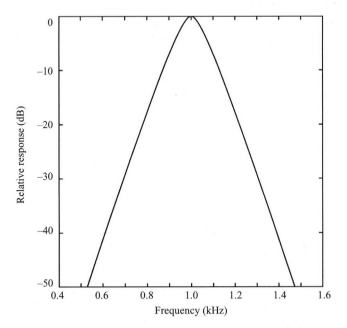

Fig. 9.5 An example of an auditory filter shape obtained using the notched-noise
method. The filter has a centre frequency of 1 kHz. The filter response is plotted
relative to the response at the tip, which is arbitrarily defined as 0 dB.

defined as 0 dB, meaning that the output magnitude is equal to the input magnitude for a signal at the centre of the frequency. For signals with frequencies above and below the centre frequency of the filter, the output magnitude is less than the input magnitude, hence the negative decibel value, meaning that the signal level is attenuated when it is filtered.

(a) Methods

(i) Stimuli

The masker comprised two noise bands symmetrically placed about the signal frequency of 2 kHz. The spectrum level of the noise was 40 dB SPL. Each noise band was 800 Hz wide at the 3 dB down points (equivalent to a 50% reduction in power). The deviation from the signal frequency (f_0) to the edges of the notch of each noise band, expressed as $\Delta f/f_0$, was 0.0, 0.1, 0.2 or 0.3. That is, notch widths (Δf) of 0, 200, 400 or 600 Hz were used to separate the two noise bands. On each trial, two bursts of noise were presented, separated by a silent interval of 500 ms. The noise burst had a 200 ms steady-state portion and 10 ms cosine-shaped rise–fall times. The signal was turned on at the same time as either the first or second of the noise bursts, the choice being selected at random. The stimuli were generated exactly as described in Glasberg *et al.* (1984) and were recorded onto a CD. They were replayed through a Marantz CD player attached to a NAD (New Acoustic Dimension) power amplifier, and the left earphone of a Sennheiser HD414 headset.

(ii) Participants

Eight HFA–AS took part in the study. All had normal hearing thresholds (<20 dB hearing loss) across the audiometric frequencies (0.25–8 kHz) and middle-ear function within normal limits, and were paid for their services. Participants were clinically diagnosed according to the criteria specified by DSM-IV (American Psychiatric Association 1994). The mean age of the participants was 18 years 3 months (range 13–28 years).

(iii) Procedure

Signal thresholds, determined using a two-interval forced-choice task, were used to estimate the psychometric functions for each notch width. Participants were required to mark on a score sheet whether the signal occurred in the first or second interval of each test trial. Feedback was not provided. The 2 kHz signal was presented at four levels covering a 12 dB range in 4 dB steps for each notch width. The highest levels used were 71, 68, 55 and 46 dB SPL, for notch widths of 0.0, 0.1, 0.2 and 0.3, respectively. Participants were first given practice on the task, using between 40 and 80 trials, at a notch width of 0.0, before the formal testing began. Forty trials were then presented at each signal level. They were given a brief rest between each block of 40 trials. Thresholds, defined as the signal levels corresponding to 75% correct, were determined by interpolation. Testing was carried out in a quiet but not sound-attenuating room. Thresholds in the notched noise were at least 20 dB above the threshold that would be imposed by the background noise in the room.

(iv) Analysis

It has been found empirically that the shape of the auditory filter can be well approximated by a simple expression, based on the form of a exponential with a rounded top (i.e. the 'roex' model of Patterson *et al.* 1982). In this expression, frequency is described relative to the centre frequency of the filter, by introducing the variable g, which is defined as the deviation from the centre frequency of the filter, divided by the centre frequency (i.e. $g = \Delta f/f$). The shape of the auditory filter, as a function of g, that is, $W(g)$, is therefore approximated by

$$W(g) = (1 + pg)\, e^{-pg}, \tag{5.1}$$

where the variable p is a parameter that determines the degree of frequency selectivity, or sharpness, of the filter. The value of p, which varies from one individual to another, was derived by fitting the integral of equation (5.1) to the data-relating threshold to notch width (see Patterson *et al.* (1982) for full details). The fitting procedure also gives values for the parameter K, which is a measure of the 'efficiency' of the detection process following the auditory filter. Here, K is expressed in terms of the SNR at the output of the auditory filter required to achieve the threshold criterion.

A bandpass filter is often characterized by its BW, which is a measure of the effective range of frequencies passed by the filter. The filter BW is often defined as the difference between the two frequencies at which the response of the filter has fallen by half in power units (i.e. by 3 dB) relative to the peak response. This is commonly known as the *half-power* BW or *3 dB down* BW. For example, if a filter has its peak response at 2000 Hz, and the response at 1900 and 2100 Hz is 3 dB less than the response at 2000 Hz, then it is said to have a BW of 200 Hz. In general, the smaller the BW value, the sharper the filters and the better the frequency selectivity. An alternative measure of BW commonly used is the ERB. The ERB of a filter is equal to the BW of a rectangular filter (i.e. a filter with a flat top and vertical edges) that has been scaled to have the same maximum height and area as that of the specified filter. The ERB of the auditory filter may be easily determined from the results of the notched-noise data as it is equal to $4/p$ multiplied by the centre frequency of the filter.

(b) Results

The roex (p) model gave reasonable fits to the data collected: averaged across the eight participants, the root-mean-square deviation of the data from the fitted values was 4.1 dB. The mean value of p was 22.6 with a s.d. of 4.1. The mean value of the ERB was 365 Hz with a s.d. of 72 Hz. The value of K, the

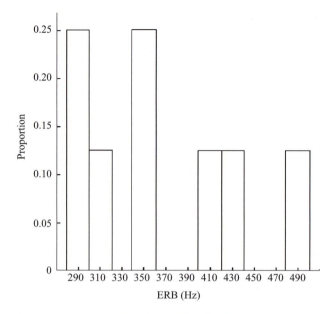

Fig. 9.6 The distribution of auditory filter BWs (ERBs) measured for the individuals with autism. The ERBs have been grouped into bins 20 Hz wide, and the figure shows the proportion of ERBs falling in each bin.

'efficiency' parameter, has a mean of -1.6 dB and a s.d. of 2.3 dB. According to the model, the mean signal threshold for a notch width of 0.0 should be equal to the sum of the noise spectrum level (40 dB), 10 log (ERB) (25.5 dB) and K (-1.6 dB), that is, 63.9 dB. The actual measured value of 62.9 dB (s.d. $= 1.4$ dB) was in close agreement with the predicted value. Figure 6 shows the distribution of auditory filter BWs (ERBs) measured for the eight HFA–AS subjects. The ERBs have been grouped into bins 20 Hz wide, and the figure shows the proportion of ERBs falling in each bin.

The results for the HFA–AS subjects were compared with those of normal hearing subjects without autism, measured previously by Moore (1987). The subjects used in Moore (1987) were 93 undergraduates at Cambridge University, aged 19–21. No attempt was made to match our subjects with those of Moore (1987), on the basis of IQ or age; therefore, the subjects cannot strictly be treated as controls, and comparisons with our data should be treated with due caution. However, exactly the same procedure was used for both subject groups for the measurement of the auditory filter shapes, and testing was carried out under very similar conditions. Therefore, we believe there is some value in comparing the results of both groups. The mean ERB for the subjects of Moore (1987) was 308 Hz, with a s.d. of 32 Hz. The mean value of K was -0.7 dB with a s.d. of 1.9 dB. A nonparametric analogue of the one-way ANOVA (i.e. the Kruskal–Wallis test) was performed in order to determine if the ERBs measured for the HFA–AS subjects were significantly higher than those of Moore (1987). This test was used as it was not reasonable to assume a particular form of the distribution for the subject populations; however, the data are quantitative and therefore could be ranked. The value of the H statistic was 6.88, so we can reject the null hypothesis that there is no significant difference in the ERB values of both subject groups with a probability level of $p = 0.009$.

(c) Discussion

The objective of the current study was to determine the frequency selectivity abilities of a group of HFA or AS. This was achieved by measuring the width of the auditory filter centred at 2 kHz, specifically the ERB, specified in hertz. The mean ERB, as calculated using the roex (p) model of Patterson (1976), was 365 Hz (s.d. = 72 Hz). The mean SNR required for signal detection (K) was –1.6 dB (s.d. = 2.3 dB). As only data for a centre frequency of 2 kHz are reported, and there was a relatively large degree of inter-subject variability in our ERB estimates (s.d. = 72 Hz; see also Fig. 9.6), the results of the current study should be treated as preliminary data only.

The mean ERB for our eight subjects was significantly larger than that reported by Moore (1987), for normal hearing university students. In other words, the frequency selectivity of the HFA–AS individuals was worse than for individuals without autism. It is unlikely that the difference in ERBs measured for our participants and those of Moore (1987) was due to a lack of concentration or an inability to perform the psychophysical task on the part of the HFA–AS participants. This is because the value of K measured for our participants was quite small (-1.6 dB), indicating an efficient detection process following auditory filtering, and that the participants were concentrating during the task. In the fitting process, K is an additive constant that adjusts the mean of the fitted values to the mean of the threshold data, both in decibels. Therefore, if our participants' threshold data were, at every point, say 3 dB higher than those of control participants, indicating a lack of concentration or application to the task, the value of K for the autistic participants would be 3 dB higher than that of the controls. In fact, the value of K was negative and very similar to that estimated for control participants who were highly motivated (Patterson et al. 1982).

One of the perceptual consequences of having wider than normal auditory filters is a greater susceptibility to masking by interfering sounds, as the auditory filters, centred on a signal, also pass a relatively large amount of noise along with the signal. This may explain why subjects with autism or AS commonly report problems understanding speech when there is background noise also present, as described in Section 9.1. The current results are also consistent with the findings of Alcántara et al. (2003), who found that subjects with autism performed significantly worse on speech recognition tasks when there was background noise simultaneously present, than did age- and IQ-matched control subjects. However, Alcántara *et al.* (2003) also found that the subjects with autism were significantly worse at making use of temporal dips present in the background noise. This may indicate that there is also a problem in the integration of information presented over successive time intervals, and consequently a failure to perceptually group information from several simultaneously presented sources into separate 'auditory objects' (e.g. speech and noise). However, the results of the current study indicate that the difficulty encountered by individuals with autism or AS, to perceive speech in noise, can be at least partially explained on the basis of deficits occurring in processing at the level of the auditory periphery.

9.6 General discussion

The general aim of the experiments reported here was to investigate the possible locus of apparent weak central coherence in individuals with autism. With respect to visual processing, it was proposed that individuals with autism might experience difficulty in the formation of a configuration of features, the significance of which differs from when its constituent features are presented alone or in another configuration with other features. However, on the basis of previous experiments that indicate enhanced feature processing but not at the expense of global processing, it was also suggested that the formation of configural representations in autism may be normal, but that their performance on tasks based on feature information may be superior. This was confirmed in two experiments comparing configural and feature processing. These findings are consistent with the proposal that perceptual processing in autism is abnormal in such a way as to enhance the salience of individual perceptual features, but that this does not impact on post-perceptual processes responsible for integrating perceptual information to form a configural representation.

This raises the question of how perceptual processing might result in the abnormally acute representation of feature information. The most rational approach to this question would be to assess perceptual processing in its very earliest stages. This was accomplished here by measuring the auditory filter shapes of individuals with autism, an assessment of peripheral auditory processing on the BM. Contrary to the perceptual hypothesis that we have proposed, which predicts that autistic individuals might show greater than normal auditory frequency selectivity, the auditory filters of individuals with autism were found to be broader than has been found for typical individuals. It seems more than reasonable to suppose that such early auditory analysis in the cochlea would have an important impact on later stages of auditory perception. Indeed, the abnormally broad auditory filters observed here could account for the difficulty of detecting speech in noise observed in individuals with autism by Alcántara *et al.* (2003).

However, at first glance, such a finding does not appear to be consistent with the proposal that perceptual processing results in particularly acute representations of stimulus features. At this point, we can only speculate about why. One possibility is that acute feature representation may be specific to the visual modality. This seems highly unlikely, since there are studies that show enhanced feature processing in the auditory domain (Heaton *et al.* 1998; Mottron *et al.* 2000). A second possibility is that abnormalities in the earliest stages of perceptual processing, such as those observed here, do not impact adversely on all later perceptual processes. Intriguingly, although hearing-impaired individuals show auditory filters two to three times as wide as those of the normally hearing population (and have difficulties hearing speech in noise), these individuals do not necessarily show deficits in pitch perception and frequency discrimination (Moore *et al.* 1995). A third possibility is that the abnormalities that produce the enhancement of feature processing in autism may occur later in the formation of perceptual representations. This possibility assumes that the relationship between the product of peripheral perceptual processing and the nature of the consequent perceptual representation is not straightforward.

Alternatively, we may need to appeal to abnormalities in post-perceptual stimulus processes to explain enhanced feature processing in autism. There are, for example, cortical mechanisms that could modify the salience of perceptual representations by changes in the SNR. For example, it is known that the anticholinergic drug, scopolamine, impairs visual and auditory signal detection (Warburton 1977), and cortical cholinergic lesions impair the detection of feature stimuli in the environment (Robbins *et al.* 1989). These findings indicate that one important function of the central cholinergic system is the enhancement of stimulus processing at the cortical level, in effect a cortical system that modulates attention to feature stimuli. These studies therefore raise the possibility that enhanced feature processing in autism may be a consequence of abnormal cortical arousal systems, such as enhanced cholinergic activity which increases feature detectability, and suggest new avenues of investigation of abnormal stimulus processing in autism at the neural level.

Finally, the possibility that the salience of perceptual representations of features can be altered would be usefully investigated in connectionist models that could attempt to model data such as those obtained in the configural learning experiments presented here by modifying different parameters that have the effect of raising the salience of features in an information processing task. It is hoped that further studies of peripheral perceptual processes, central cortical processes and computational studies will allow us to identify the mechanisms underlying the abnormalities in stimulus processing associated with autism spectrum disorders.

Part of this research was funded by an MRC Career Establishment Grant awarded to K.P.

References

Alcántara, J. I., Weisblatt, E. J., Moore, B. C. J. and Bolton, P. F. (2003). Speech-in-noise perception in high-functioning individuals with autism or Asperger's syndrome. *J. Child Psychol. Psychiat.* (In preparation.)

American Psychiatric Association (1994). *Diagnostic and statistical manual of mental disorders, DSM-IV*, 4th edn. Washington, DC: APA.

Bonnel, A. C., Mottron, L., Peretz, I., Trudel, M., Gallun, E. J. and Bonnel, A. M. (2003). Enhanced pitch sensitivity in individuals with autism: a signal detection analysis. *J. Autism Devl. Disord.* (Submitted.)

Bregman, A. S. (1990). *Auditory scene analysis: the perceptual organization of sound.* Cambridge, MA: Bradford Books, MIT Press.

Bussey, T. J. and Saksida, L. M. (2002). The organisation of visual object representations: a connectionist model of effects lesions in perirhinal cortex. *Eur. J. Neurosci.* **15**, 355–64.

Frith, U. (1989). *Autism: explaining the enigma.* Oxford: Blackwell.

Glasberg, B. R. and Moore, B. C. J. (1986). Auditory filter shapes in participants with unilateral and bilateral cochlear impairments. *J. Acoust. Soc. Am.* **79**, 1020–33.

Glasberg, B. R., Moore, B. C. J., Patterson, R. D. and Nimmo-Smith, I. (1984). Dynamic range and asymmetry of the auditory filter. *J. Acoust. Soc. Am.* **76**, 419–27.

Goldfarb, W. (1961). *Childhood schizophrenia.* Cambridge, MA: Harvard University Press.

Grandin, T. and Scariano, M. M. (1986). *Emergence: labeled autistic.* New York: Arena Press.

Happé, F. G. E. (1996). Studying weak central coherence at low levels: children with autism do not succumb to visual illusions. A research note. *J. Child Psychol. Psychiat.* **37**, 873–77.

Happé, F. G. E. (1997). Central coherence and theory of mind in autism: reading homographs in context. *Br. J. Dev. Psychol.* **15**, 1–12.

Happé, F., Briskman, J. and Frith, U. (2001). Exploring the cognitive phenotype of autism: 'weak central coherence' in parents and siblings of children with autism: 1. Experimental tests. *J. Child Psychol. Psychiat.* **42**, 299–307.

Heaton, P., Hermelin, B. and Pring, L. (1998). Autism and pitch processing: a precursor for savant musical ability? *Music Percept.* **15**, 291–305.

Jolliffe, T. and Baron-Cohen, S. (1999). Linguistic processing in high-functioning adults with autism or Asperger's syndrome: is local soherence impaired? *Cognition* **71**, 149–85.

Kanner, L. (1943). Autistic disturbance of affective contact. *Nervous Child* **2**, 217–50.

Koffka, K. (1935). *Principles of Gestalt psychology.* New York: Harcourt Brace.

Lamb, M. R., Robertson, L. C. and Knight, R. T. (1990). Component mechanisms underlying the processing of hierarchically organised patterns: inferences from patients with unilateral cortical lesions. *J. Exp. Psychol. Learning Memory Cogn.* **16**, 471–83.

Le Couteur, A., Rutter, M., Lord, C., Rios, P., Robertson, S., Holdgrafer, M., *et al.* (1989). Autism Diagnostic Interview: a semi-structured interview for parents and caregivers of autistic persons. *J. Autism Dev. Disord.* **19**, 363–87.

Lovaas, O. I., Koegel, R. L. and Shreibman, L. (1979). Stimulus overselectivity in autism: a review of research. *Psychol. Bull.* **86**, 1236–54.

Moore, B. C. J. (1987). Distribution of auditory-filter bandwidths at 2 kHz in young normal listeners. *J. Acoust. Soc. Am.* **81**, 1633–35.

Moore, B. C. J. (1997). *An introduction to the psychology of hearing*, 4th edn. San Diego, CA: Academic.

Moore, B. C. J. and Glasberg, B. R. (1981). Auditory filter shapes derived in simultaneous and forward masking. *J. Acoust. Soc. Am.* **70**, 1003–14.

Moore, B. C. J., Glasberg, B. R. and Vickers, D. A. (1995). Simulation of the effects of loudness recruitment on the intelligibility of speech in noise. *Br. J. Audiol.* **29**, 131–43.

Mottron, L. and Belleville, S. (1993). A study of perceptual analysis in a high-level autistic subject with exceptional graphic abilities. *Brain Cogn.* **23**, 279–309.

Mottron, L., Peretz, I. and Ménard, E. (2000). Local and global processing of music in high-functioning persons with autism: beyond Central Coherence? *J. Child Psychol. Psychiat.* **41**, 1057–65.

Myles, B. S., Cook, K. T., Miller, N. E., Rinner, L. and Robbins, L. A. (2000). *Asperger Syndrome and sensory issues.* Shawnee Mission, KS: Autism Asperger.

Navon, D. (1977). Forest before trees: the precedence of global features in visual perception. *Cogn. Psychol.* **9**, 353–383.

O'Riordan, M. A. F. and Plaisted, K. C. (2001). Enhanced discrimination in autism. *Q. J. Exp. Psychol.* A **54**, 961–79.

Ornitz, E. M. (1969). Disorder of perception common to early infantile autism and schizophrenia. *Compreh. Psychiat.* **10**, 259–74.

Ozonoff, S., Strayer, D. L., McMahon, W. M. and Filloux, F. (1994). Executive function abilities in autism and Tourette's syndrome: an information processing approach. *J. Child Psychol. Psychiat.* **35**, 1015–32.

Palmer, S. E. and Rock, I. (1994). Rethinking perceptual organization: the role of uniform connectedness. *Psychonomic Bull. Rev.* **1**, 9–55.

Patterson, R. D. (1976). Auditory filter shapes derived with noise stimuli. *J. Acoust. Soc. Am.* **59**, 640–54.

Patterson, R. D. and Moore, B. C. J. (1986). Auditory filters and excitation patterns as representations of frequency resolution. In *Frequency selectivity in hearing* (ed. B. C. J. Moore), pp. 123–77. London: Academic Press.

Patterson, R. D., Nimmo-Smith, I., Weber, D. L. and Milroy, R. (1982). The deterioration of hearing with age: frequency selectivity, the critical ratio, the audiogram, and speech threshold. *J. Acoust. Soc. Am.* **72**, 1788–803.

Pearce, J. M. (1994). Similarity and discrimination: a selective review and a connectionist model. *Psychol. Rev.* **101**, 587–607.

Plaisted, K. C. (2001). Reduced generalisation in autism: an alternative to weak central coherence. In *Development and autism: perspectives from theory and research* (ed. J. A. Burack, A. Charman, N. Yirmiya and P. R. Zelazo). Hillsdale, NJ: Lawrence Erlbaum Associates.

Plaisted, K. C., O'Riordan, M. A. and Baron-Cohen, S. (1998*a*). Enhanced visual search for a conjunctive target in autism: a research note. *J. Child Psychol. Psychiat.* **39**, 777–83.

Plaisted, K. C., O'Riordan, M. A. and Baron-Cohen, S. (1998*b*). Enhanced discrimination of novel, highly similar stimuli by adults with autism during a perceptual learning task. *J. Child Psychol. Psychiat.* **39**, 765–75.

Plaisted, K. C., Swettenham, J. and Rees, L. (1999). Children with autism show local precedence in a divided attention task and global precedence in a selective attention task. *J. Child Psychol. Psychiat.* **40**, 733–42.

Raven, D. (1958). *Standard progressive matrices*. London: H. K. Lewis.

Robbins, T. W., Everitt, B. J., Marston, H. M., Wilkinson, J., Jones, G. H. and Page, K. J. (1989). Comparative effects of ibotenic acid and quisqualic acid induced lesions of the substantia innominata on attentional functions in the rat: further implications for the role of the cholinergic system of the nucleus basalis in cognitive processes. *Behav. Brain Opin.* **35**, 221–240.

Ruggero, M. A. (1992). Responses to sound of the basilar membrane of the mammalian cochlea. *Curr. Opin. Neurobiol.* **2**, 449–56.

Ruggero, M. A., Rich, N. C., Robles, L. and Recio, A. (1996). The effects of acoustic trauma, other cochlea injury and death on basilar membrane responses to sound. In *Scientific basis of noise-induced hearing loss* (ed. A. Axelsson, H. Borchgrevink, R. P. Hamernik, P. A. Hellstrom, D. Henderson and R. J. Salvi), pp. 23–35. New York: Georg Thieme.

Sainsbury, C. (2000). *Martian in the playground*. Bristol: Lucky Duck.

Shah, A. and Frith, U. (1983). An islet of ability in autistic children: a research note. *J. Child Psychol. Psychiat.* **24**, 613–620.

Shah, A. and Frith, U. (1993). Why do autistic individuals show superior performance on the block design task? *J. Child Psychol. Psychiat.* **34**, 1351–64.

Shanks, D. R., Charles, D., Darby, R. J. and Azmi, A. (1998). Configural processes in human associative learning. *J. Exp. Psychol. Learning Memory Cogn.* **24**, 1353–78.

Townsend, J. and Courchesne, E. (1994). Parietal damage and narrow 'spotlight' spatial attention. *J. Cogn. Neurosci.* **6**, 220–32.

Warburton, D. M. (1977). Stimulus detection and behavioural inhibition. In *Handbook of psychopharmacology*, vol. 8 (ed. L. L. Iverson, S. D. Iverson and S. H. Snyder), pp. 385–431. New York: Plenum.

Williams, D. A., Sagness, K. E. and McPhee, J. E. (1994). Configural and elemental strategies in predictive learning. *J. Exp. Psychol. Learning Memory Cogn.* **20**, 694–709.

Glossary

ANOVA: analysis of variance
AS: Asperger syndrome
BM: basilar membrane
BW: bandwidth
CA: chronological age
ERB: equivalent rectangular bandwidth
HFA: high-functioning individuals with autism
RSPM: Raven's Standard Progressive Matrix
SNR: signal-to-noise ratio
SPL: sound pressure level
SRT: speech reception threshold

10

Disentangling weak coherence and executive dysfunction: planning drawing in autism and attention-deficit/hyperactivity disorder

Rhonda Booth, Rebecca Charlton, Claire Hughes, and Francesca Happé

A tendency to focus on details at the expense of configural information, 'weak coherence', has been proposed as a cognitive style in autism. In the present study we tested whether weak coherence might be the result of executive dysfunction, by testing clinical groups known to show deficits on tests of executive control. Boys with autism spectrum disorders (ASD) were compared with age- and intelligence quotient (IQ)-matched boys with attention-deficit/hyperactivity disorder (ADHD), and typically developing (TD) boys, on a drawing task requiring planning for the inclusion of a new element. Weak coherence was measured through analysis of drawing style. In line with the predictions made, the ASD group was more detail-focused in their drawings than were either ADHD or TD boys. The ASD and ADHD groups both showed planning impairments, which were more severe in the former group. Poor planning did not, however, predict detail-focus, and scores on the two aspects of the task were unrelated in the clinical groups. These findings indicate that weak coherence may indeed be a cognitive style specific to autism and unrelated to cognitive deficits in frontal functions.

Keywords: autism; coherence; executive function; cognitive style; drawing; planning

10.1 Introduction

Autism has attracted a number of psychological theories and accounts that focus on the deficits in social and communicative development and the inflexibility of behaviour and interests. Prominent among these accounts are the 'theory of mind' deficit account and the executive dysfunction theory. The former posits a failure of an innate system for attending to and representing the mental states of others, and explains well some of the social and communication difficulties (Baron-Cohen *et al.* 2000). The latter attempts to explain the non-social difficulties in autism, such as repetitive behaviour and poorly controlled novel goal-directed action, in terms of deficits in frontal functions such as planning, inhibition and set-shifting, covered by the umbrella term 'executive functions' (Russell 1997).

These accounts explain well some of the deficits in autism, but cannot, on the face of it, explain the areas of preserved or even superior skill seen in people with ASDs. These include the high rate of savant skills (in, for example, music, mathematics and art), the 'islets of ability' (in, for example, rote memory and visuo-spatial puzzles) and the perception of small details (often leading to distress at small changes in the familiar environment). One psychological account that does attempt to explain these assets, along with certain areas of difficulty in autism, is the 'central coherence' account. This term was first introduced by Frith (1989) to refer to the normal tendency for global, configural processing, which integrates information in context to give meaning. People with autism, by contrast, appear to show a processing bias for parts versus wholes, surface form versus gist, and are able to process information in a relatively context-independent fashion (see Happé (1999) for a review of this account and recent evidence). This bias for 'weak coherence' is hypothesized to be a cognitive style rather than a deficit, because it leads to assets on tasks that benefit from detail focus (e.g. the embedded figures test; Shah and Frith 1983) and because people with autism appear to be capable of processing information globally when directed to do so.

The relationship between the postulated cognitive style of weak coherence and the deficits seen in theory of mind and executive function has been little explored (but see Jarrold *et al.* (2000) for work on coherence and theory of mind). In particular, it seems possible that executive dysfunction and weak coherence may be overlapping or even redundant notions. In particular, it might be argued that the processing of information in context for global meaning is an executive skill and that the findings currently attributed to weak coherence might be explained by executive dysfunction. Even savant skills have recently been suggested to result from 'disinhibition', or release from top-down frontal control (e.g. Snyder and Thomas 1997). Failure to process information globally might be argued to follow from problems in shifting between local and global processing, if local processing is considered to be the default. Limitations of working memory might bias performance towards smaller fragments of information. Similarly, poor planning might result in piecemeal approaches to novel tasks. Harris and Leevers (2000), for example, have argued that inability to draw imaginary objects might be due to planning problems in autism.

The present study aimed to disentangle coherence and executive dysfunction by comparing two clinical groups. Executive problems are by no means specific to autism, and can be found in several other developmental disorders, most notably ADHD (see Sergeant *et al.* (2002) for a review). We hypothesized that, while children with ASD and those with ADHD might share some executive impairments, only the former group would show a detail-focused processing bias, that is 'weak coherence'. Thus we hypothesized that poor executive functions would not necessarily lead to or accompany weak coherence, and that individuals with ADHD would show normal global processing despite their executive impairments. To this end, we developed a task with both executive and coherence components, to examine the effect of one aspect of executive dysfunction (poor planning) on local–global processing. Our planning drawing task was inspired by an original test by Henderson and Thomas (1990), and required children to copy a drawing (e.g. a snowman), and then to make a new drawing including an additional feature (e.g. teeth). Addition of the new feature required planning in advance, to allow space and adjust the size of the relevant elements (e.g. the head). Thus the second drawings could be compared with the first to assess the degree of planning (an executive function). In addition, the drawing style was analysed for global or local processing bias. We attempted to make the task as naturalistic and open-ended as possible, because it appears to be in such non-directive tasks that the bias for local processing is most clearly seen in ASD (e.g. Plaisted *et al.* 1999). Our prediction was that (i) the ASD group, but not the ADHD or control groups, would show a tendency for detail-focused drawing; (ii) both the ASD and ADHD groups would show poor planning compared with the control group; and (iii) detailed drawing style would not be related to poor planning.

10.2 Methods

(a) Subjects

The ASD group comprised 30 boys with a formal diagnosis of either high-functioning autism ($n = 5$) or Asperger syndrome ($n = 25$) who were recruited through specialist units and parent group contacts. In each case, it was confirmed that a psychiatrist or paediatrician had made the diagnosis according to established criteria. Children were excluded if they had co-morbid ADHD, ADD, hyperkinetic disorder or Tourette syndrome.

The ADHD group comprised 30 boys with a formal diagnosis of either ADHD (DSM-IV (American Psychiatric Association 1994); $n = 20$) or hyperkinetic disorder (ICD-10 (World Health Organization 1992); $n = 10$) who were recruited through specialist referral centres. Children were excluded if they had additional disorders such as PDD, Tourette syndrome or obsessive compulsive disorder. Furthermore, children with a diagnosis of ADD without the hyperactivity component were not included. The majority of boys ($n = 27$) had been prescribed medication for the management of their ADHD. All were required not to take medication for at least 24 h prior to the administration of the experimental tasks. One exception occurred where a boy could only be taken off medication 17 h prior to assessment owing to family constraints. Data from this child were included, after analysis of group data excluding this participant showed no resulting change in the pattern or significance of the results. Following clinical advice, IQ assessments were conducted with

Table 10.1 Participant characteristics: means (s.d.).

group	n	age (yr)	FIQ	VIQ	PIQ
ASD	30	10.7 (2.2)	100.0 (19.3)	102.8 (18.6)	96.8 (18.3)
ADHD	30	11.7 (1.7)	99.1 (17.7)	99.7 (18.6)	97.7 (14.7)
TD	31	11.3 (2.0)	107.1 (13.5)	110.3 (11.9)	101.7 (18.5)

children on medication, as this is considered to result in a more fair assessment of intellectual level.

A TD comparison group was included, comprising 31 boys recruited through schools, family friends of participants in the clinical groups and personal contacts. Boys were excluded from this group if they had any clinically significant impairment or diagnosis, or family history of social- or attention-related problems (i.e. ADHD or PDD).

Across all groups, no child was excluded on the basis of comorbid epilepsy, reading (five ADHD, one ASD, one TD), conduct (five ADHD) or anxiety disorder (one ADHD, two ASD). All participants were aged between 8 and 16 years and had a minimum FIQ of 69 or above as assessed by the WISC-III (Wechsler 1992). Owing to time constraints, 15 boys in the control group were administered a shortened version of the WISC-III (based on four subtests: information, vocabulary, picture completion and block design). The IQ estimate calculated from this short form of the test is reported to have high reliability (Sattler 1992). Participant characteristics for each group are presented in Table 10.1. Statistical comparisons showed that groups did not differ significantly in age, FIQ or PIQ, although the ADHD group had lower VIQ than the TD group ($F_{(2,88)} = 3.31$, $p = 0.04$; Tukey's HSD: $p = 0.04$) perhaps reflecting the literacy difficulties commonly found to accompany this disorder.

(b) Materials

For the planning drawing task, seven picture stimuli were created and piloted with a group of 63 children aged from 8 to 16 years. Four of these pictures were then selected as appropriate for the present age and ability range. The drawings were as shown in Fig. 10.1: a snowman (add teeth), a clock (add numbers), a house (add four windows) and a ship (add people at the portholes). The drawings were chosen to have clear local and global elements, as well as necessitating planning ahead to increase the size of key parts (snowman's head, clock's face, house, portholes) in order to incorporate the additional detail. Participants were provided with a crayon and blank sheets of A4 paper. A crayon was used after piloting suggested that fine pens allowed children to fit in the additional detail without needing to plan ahead, and to make drawing parts bigger.

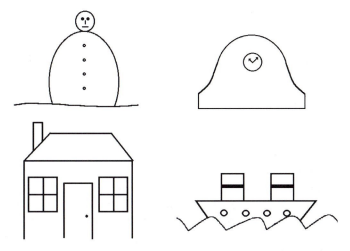

Fig. 10.1   Drawing stimuli.

(c) Procedure

Testing took place within the context of a larger study that consisted of two sessions of around 2 h. Because the data from the four drawings were combined, a set order of presentation was used; the house, the snowman, then after around 60 min, the clock and then the ship. In each case, the children were shown a picture and told: 'this is a picture of a (house) that I drew earlier. I want you to draw a picture of a (house) like mine'. The picture was left in view while the children used it as a model for their own drawing. When it was clear that the drawing was complete, both the original and copy were removed from view. A further blank sheet of paper was provided and the experimenter told the participant: 'now I want you to draw another picture of a (house), but this time draw it with (four windows)'. Each picture was presented in the same manner with the instructions to add a feature as appropriate to the picture. The drawing process was videotaped for later analysis, and the experimenter noted the order in which features were drawn.

(d) Scoring

(i) For central coherence
Three aspects of the drawings were rated for detail-focused style. First, the *initial features* drawn were noted: were the first two elements that were drawn local elements or details, rather than global aspects such as the outline? This was scored on a three-point scale, with two points being given where local features were drawn first, one point where local features were the second thing to be drawn, or where undefined features (e.g. the roof on the house) were drawn

first, and zero points where global aspects were drawn first. Because for the second drawing in each pair the child was explicitly directed to add an extra detail, initial feature was rated from the first drawing only, where the child's natural approach could be fairly judged.

The second dimension rated for central coherence scoring was *fragmentation*; did the drawing proceed in a piecemeal fashion? This too was rated on a three-point scale from highly fragmented (two points) to not at all fragmented (zero points). Fragmentation was defined by the degree of disjointed appearance, separation of parts or drawing style that was not sequential in the usual manner (e.g. breaking off from incomplete lines in order to move to another part of the drawing; drawing four individual window panes rather than drawing two lines dissecting the square that represented the window).

The third and last dimension rated was the degree of *configural violation*; did the drawing include parts that were placed wrongly in relation to other parts, with distorted or omitted outline, or abnormal in overall shape? This rating related to the finished drawing only and was scored on a three-point scale according to the degree of change in the overall configuration of the object to be copied.

Fragmentation and configural violation were scored for all (first and second) drawings. The three aspects rated for coherence were, in principle, independent of one another, that is, a child could start a drawing with a detail but draw in a cohesive fashion without fragmentation and produce a fully 'coherent' drawing at the end. Similarly, a child could begin with the house outline, for example, then draw the windows piece by piece (i.e. pane by pane: an example of fragmentation), and still produce a coherent finished drawing. Lastly, a child could start with the outline, draw each part as a whole, yet violate the configuration by drawing a fractured outline.

(ii) For planning

An *allowance score* was given based on the degree of advance planning evident in the changes that were made to accommodate the new feature. This was judged by comparing the first and second pictures in a pair, for example to assess how much larger the head of the second snowman had been made in order to fit in the mouth with teeth.

An enlarged picture did not necessarily indicate good allowance, but there must be evidence that a modification was made to take into account the additional feature (e.g. drawing the windows of the house smaller in order to fit in four windows, in preference to increasing the size of the house). Two points were given when a clear and effective allowance was made, one point for some allowance but not enough to prevent the drawing from seeming squashed, and zero points for no allowance.

(iii) Reliability

Thirty per cent of the pictures, taken equally from the three participant groups, were scored by a second rater blind to diagnosis. Inter-rater agreement was good, with Kappa values in every case above 0.75, ranging from 0.77 to 0.95 across the different types of score. Disagreements were resolved between the two coders.

10.3 Results

Mean scores for each of the coherence variables were low, and so a summed score was created combining the independent ratings for initial feature, fragmentation and configuration violation. Higher scores indicated weaker coherence. The mean score for this measure showed a significant effect of group: mean = 0.9 (s.d. = 0.88) for ASD; 0.47 (0.78) for ADHD; and 0.26 (0.44) in the TD group ($F_{(2,88)} = 6.22$, $p = 0.003$). This group difference was due to higher scores in the ASD group (versus TD: $p = 0.002$; versus ADHD: $p = 0.058$; Tukey's HSD). However, analysis in terms of frequencies appeared more appropriate in view of the small absolute number of instances of fragmentation and so forth, and the possibility that means reflected high scores by a small proportion of the participants.

Table 10.2 shows the numbers (and percentages) of children in each group who showed weak coherence as measured by the initial feature, fragmentation and configuration violation scores. Figure 10.2 shows examples of drawings scoring two points for each of these variables. Significantly more of the ASD participants started at least one of their (first) drawings with a detail, compared with the ADHD and TD groups ($\chi^2 = 7.10$, d.f. = 2, $p = 0.03$). More of the ASD group drew at least one of their drawings in a fragmented style ($\chi^2 = 4.53$, d.f. = 2, $p = 0.10$), and this reached significance for the comparison with the TD group ($\chi^2 = 4.55$, d.f. = 1, $p = 0.03$). Significantly more of the ASD children broke configuration (scoring two on configuration violation) on at least one drawing, compared with the ADHD and TD groups ($\chi^2 = 6.18$, d.f. = 2, $p = 0.04$). Across these three types of rating, 60% of the ASD group showed weak coherence (scoring one or two for one or more drawings) on at least one of these ratings, versus 33% of the ADHD and 26% of the TD group ($\chi^2 = 8.18$, d.f. = 2, $p = 0.02$ for ASD, versus

Table 10.2   Frequency data for coherence scores.

group	number (%) ever scoring two for initial feature	number (%) ever scoring one or two for fragmentation	number (%) ever scoringtwo for configural violation
ASD ($n = 30$)	8[a] (26.7)	8 (26.7)	10[a] (33.3)
ADHD ($n = 30$)	2 (6.67)	5 (16.7)	4 (13.3)
TD ($n = 31$)	2 (6.45)	2 (6.45)	3 (9.67)

[a] ASD > ADHD, TD, $p > 0.05$.

(a)

(b)

(c)

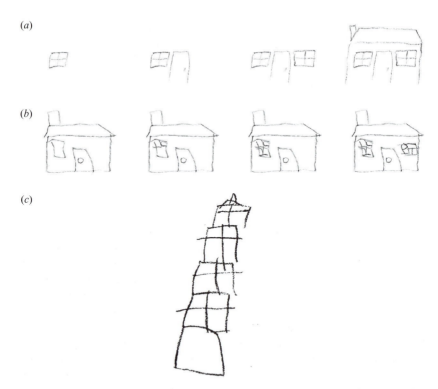

Fig. 10.2   Examples of drawings scoring two for each of the weak coherence ratings: (*a*) initial feature, (*b*) fragmentation, and (*c*) configural violation.

ADHD: $\chi^2 = 4.29$, d.f. = 1, $p = 0.04$). The boys in the ASD and ADHD groups who showed weak coherence on this task did not differ from the other boys in their diagnostic group in either age or IQ (all $p > 0.2$). However, among the TD boys, the eight who showed some degree of weak coherence were significantly lower than the rest of the group in FIQ (mean 99 versus 110; $F_{(1,29)} = 4.14, p = 0.05$) and PIQ (89 versus 106; $F_{(1,29)} = 6.27, p = 0.02$).

Figure 10.3 shows an example of good planning. A frequency analysis of the planning measure was carried out, looking at the numbers of children who ever scored zero on the allowance measure (showing no planning). Eighty per cent of the ASD group showed some lack of planning by this standard, as did 70% of the ADHD group and 52% of the TD group. A chi square test showed a marginally significant difference between the three groups ($\chi^2 = 5.74$, d.f. = 2, $p = 0.057$), but the two clinical groups did not differ from one another. The 'poor planners' by this criterion did not differ from the remainder of their groups in age or IQ (all $p > 0.1$).

A key question for the present study was whether weak coherence might be a result of executive dysfunction, so the relationship between planning and

Fig. 10.3   Example of good planning.

detail-focused drawing style was examined. The correlation between the total allowance score and the summed coherence score was 0.15 in the ASD group and 0.16 in the ADHD group ($p > 0.4$). By contrast, the correlation in the TD group was significant ($r = 0.36$, $p = 0.04$). Bearing in mind the relationship between weak coherence and PIQ in this group, the correlation was repeated partialling out PIQ, resulting in a correlation of 0.34, which fell below significance ($p = 0.07$). It should be noted that the positive correlations show that children in the TD group who obtained high allowance scores scored more highly on the weak coherence composite also: that is, good planners showed *more* detail focus. This is also seen when the planning and coherence measures are compared in terms of frequencies of children showing good versus poor planning, and weak versus normal coherence of drawing style (using the divisions described above). Chi square analysis showed a significant relationship between these categorizations in the TD group only ($\chi^2 = 6.61$, d.f. $= 1$, $p = 0.01$). The TD children classed as 'good planners' ($n = 15$) divided equally into those showing weak coherence ($n = 7$) and those not doing so ($n = 8$), while the 'poor planners' ($n = 16$) were predominantly classed as *not* showing weak coherence ($n = 15$). There was a trend towards a very similar distribution in the ADHD group, but the relationship between the two measures did not reach significance in this group ($p = 0.09$). In the ASD group, by contrast, there appeared to be no relationship between the two measures ($p = 0.58$).

10.4 Discussion

This study explored the relationship between weak coherence and executive dysfunction through comparison of contrasting clinical groups performing a specially designed drawing task. The results largely confirmed the predictions that (i) boys with ASD but not those with ADHD tended to show a detail-focused drawing style; (ii) boys from both clinical groups showed planning deficits, but these were particularly noticeable in the ASD group; and (iii) measures of detail focus were not related to poor planning. These findings indicate that weak coherence is independent of executive dysfunction and is not common to other groups with difficulties of executive control. Below we briefly discuss each of these findings, and their relevance for our understanding of autism.

The ASD group in this study was more likely to begin drawing with a detail, to draw in a piecemeal fashion and to create a drawing in which configuration was violated than were TD boys and those with ADHD. This fits with previous findings in the literature. Fein *et al.* (1990) also explored fragmentation in drawing, as well as overlap of drawn parts. They found more evidence of these signs of failure to integrate the whole in a group of 5- to 17-year-olds with autism compared with developmental-level-matched TD children when asked to draw a child. Mottron and colleagues have studied drawing style in a savant artist with Asperger syndrome (Mottron and Belleville 1993) and a group of adolescents and adults with autism (Mottron *et al.* 1999). In both studies, the ASD participants tended to begin drawing with a local feature.

While the ASD group as a whole was significantly different from the ADHD and TD groups in drawing style, it is important to note that not every child with ASD in this study showed detail focus on our task. Forty per cent of the ASD group did not show evidence of preference for featural processing, at least as measured by this task and scoring system. These boys did not appear to be different in age or IQ from the boys showing detail focus, but it remains to be seen whether they differ in other respects (such as clinical features) or whether they might show weak coherence on other types of tasks. We are currently exploring the nature of weak coherence in TD and ASD groups to attempt to establish whether detail focus in the visual domain is related to detail focus in, for example, auditory tasks. It is also worth mentioning that our scoring system for the drawings deliberately distinguished between focus on detail and inability to capture the configuration. While many of the classic tests of coherence cannot measure separately the ability to process parts and the (in)ability to process wholes, it seems important to distinguish these processes. It may well be that children with autism are not poor at configural processing but rather excel at featural processing, or it is possible that different subgroups within the autism spectrum have a facility for details or a difficulty with configurations.

The second prediction supported by this study was that both the ASD and ADHD groups would show planning deficits. The most commonly used tests of planning in the literature are probably the Tower of Hanoi and Tower of London, which require participants to plan ahead a sequence of moves. These are considerably more challenging, and also more directed, than the task employed in the present study. In their useful review of recent work on executive functions, Sergeant *et al.* (2002) summarize findings from 12 studies using the Towers tasks with ADHD and/or ASD groups. Three of the five studies with

ADHD participants found significant impairment compared with control participants, as did all five of the studies comparing ASD with control groups. Two studies directly comparing the two clinical groups found significantly worse performance in the ASD group than the ADHD and control groups (Ozonoff *et al.* 1991; Ozonoff and Jensen 1999). The present finding using a much simpler and more naturalistic test of planning ability also indicates that planning is more severely impaired in children with ASD than in those with ADHD.

The third finding was that impairments of planning did not account for the tendency for detail focus in the drawing task; allowance scores did not correlate significantly with coherence scores in the clinical groups, and in the TD group it appeared that poor planners were, if anything, *less* likely to be detail focused. This, along with the lack of detail focus in the ADHD group—a disorder strongly associated with deficits in at least some executive functions—argues against an executive dysfunction explanation of weak coherence in autism. This is important because it might well have been that children with autism start their drawings with details, draw in a piecemeal fashion and create less coherent drawings because they do not plan ahead and fail to use 'top-down' strategies such as sketching in outline before filling in details. Instead, the present results indicate that detail focus is a characteristic of autism unrelated to impairments in executive skills such as planning, and also unrelated to age or IQ. Further work is needed to clarify the nature and mechanism of weak coherence, but findings from this drawing task support the characterization of weak coherence as a cognitive *style* rather than deficit.

This work was funded by a Wellcome Trust project grant to F.H. Our sincere thanks go to the boys who participated in this research, as well as to their families and schools. We are extremely grateful to the following for their generous help with recruitment: Eric Taylor, Jodie Warner-Rogers and the ADHD team at the Institute of Psychiatry; Mima Simic; Gillian Baird; Marilyn Hammill; Janet Poole; St Anthony's RC Primary School; Ernest Bevin College; Stewart Flemming Primary School; Fircroft Primary School; Langley Park School for Boys; and Alderbrook Primary School. John Rogers gave invaluable help with coding.

References

American Psychiatric Association (1994). *Diagnostic and statistical manual of mental disorders*, 4th Edition (DSM-IV). Washington, DC: American Psychiatric Association.

Baron-Cohen, S. Tager-Flusberg, H. and Cohen, D. J. (eds) (2000). *Understanding other minds: perspectives from autism and developmental cognitive neuroscience*, 2nd edn. Oxford: Oxford University Press.

Fein, D., Lucci, D. and Waterhouse, L. (1990). Brief report: fragmented drawings in autistic children. *J. Autism Devl Disorders* **20**, 263–69.

Frith, U. (1989). *Autism: explaining the enigma*. Oxford: Blackwell.

Happé, F. (1999). Understanding assets and deficits in autism: why success is more interesting than failure. *Psychologist* **12**, 540–46.

Harris, P. L. and Leevers, H. J. (2000). Pretending, imagery and self-awareness in autism. In *Understanding other minds: perspectives from autism and developmental cognitive neuroscience*, 2nd edn (ed. S. Baron-Cohen, H. Tager-Flusberg and D. J. Cohen), pp. 182–202. Oxford: Oxford University Press.

Henderson, J. A. and Thomas, G. V. (1990). Looking ahead: planning for the inclusion of detail affects relative sizes of head and trunk in children's human figure drawings. *Br. J. Devl Psychol.* **8**, 383–91.

Jarrold, C., Butler, D. W., Cottington, E. M. and Jimenez, F. (2000). Linking theory of mind and central coherence bias in autism and in the general population. *Devl Psychol.* **36**, 126–38.

Mottron, L. and Belleville, S. (1993). A study of perceptual analysis in a high-level autistic subject with exceptional graphic abilities. *Brain Cogn* **23**, 279–309.

Mottron, L., Belleville, S. and Menard, E. (1999). Local bias in autistic subjects as evidenced by graphic tasks: perceptual hierarchization or working memory deficit? *J. Child Psychol. Psychiatry* **40**, 743–55.

Ozonoff, S. and Jensen, J. (1999). Brief report: specific executive function profiles in three neurodevelopmental disorders. *J. Autism Devl Disorders* **29**, 171–77.

Ozonoff, S., Pennington, B. F. and Rogers, S. J. (1991). Executive function deficits in high-functioning autistic individuals: relationship to theory of mind. *J. Child Psychol. Psychiatry* **32**, 1081–105.

Plaisted, K., Swettenham, J. and Rees, L. (1999). Children with autism show local precedence in a divided attention task and global precedence in a selective attention task. *J. Child Psychol. Psychiatry* **40**, 733–42.

Russell, J. (ed.) (1997). *Autism as an executive disorder*. New York: Oxford University Press.

Sattler, J. M. (1992). *Assessment of children*, 3rd edn. San Diego, CA: J. M. Sattler.

Sergeant, J. A., Geurts, H. and Oosterlaan, J. (2002). How specific is a deficit in executive functioning for attentiondeficit/hyperactivity disorder? *Behav. Brain Res.* **130**, 3–28.

Shah, A. and Frith, U. (1983). An islet of ability in autistic children: a research note. *J. Child Psychol. Psychiatry* **24**, 613–20.

Snyder, A. W. and Thomas, M. (1997). Autistic artists give clues to cognition. *Perception* **26**, 93–96.

Wechsler, D. (1992). *Manual for the Wechsler intelligence scale for children*, 3rd edn. London: The Psychological Corporation.

World Health Organization (1992). *The ICD-10 classification for mental and behavioural disorders: clinical descriptions and diagnostic guidelines*. Geneva, Switzerland: World Health Organization.

Glossary

ADD: attention deficit disorder
ADHD: attention-deficit/hyperactivity disorder
ASD: autism spectrum disorders

FIQ: full-scale IQ
HSD: honestly significant difference test
IQ: intelligence quotient
PDD: pervasive developmental disorder
PIQ: performance IQ
TD: typically developing
VIQ: verbal IQ
WISC: Wechsler intelligence scale for children

11

Autism and movement disturbance

*Morena Mari, Deborah Marks, Catherine Marraffa,
Margot Prior, and Umberto Castiello*

Autism is associated with a wide and complex array of neurobehavioural symptoms. Examination of the motor system offers a particularly appealing method for studying autism by providing information about this syndrome that is relatively immune to experimental influence. In this article, we considered the relationship between possible movement disturbance and symptoms of autism and introduced an experimental model that may be useful for rehabilitation and diagnostic purposes: the reach-to-grasp movement. Research is reviewed that characterizes kinematically the reach-to-grasp movement in children with autism compared with age-matched 'controls'. Unlike the age-matched children, autistic children showed differences in movement planning and execution, supporting the view that movement disturbances may play a part in the phenomenon of autism.

Keywords: autism; reach-to-grasp; human; motor control; human development; movement disorders

11.1 Autism and movement

Autism is a developmental disorder of largely unknown etiology. It is characterized by abnormalities in language, social relationships and reactions to the environment (Happé and Frith 1996; Happé 1999). Despite autistic children having been described as delayed from a developmental perspective, little emphasis has been placed on the development of motor function, which has often been thought to be intact. However, a growing number of descriptions and observations indicate that this may not be the case (Damasio and Maurer 1978; Vilensky *et al*. 1981; Bauman 1992; Hallett *et al*. 1993; Manjiviona and Prior 1995; Hughes 1996; Teitelbaum *et al*. 1998; Brasič 1999; Table 11.1).

As described by Bauman (1992), people with autism exhibit a large collection of motor symptoms. These include delays in the attainment of motor milestones, such as clumsiness (i.e. awkwardness and difficulty in carrying out organized movements and actions in parallel), hyperactivity and hand flapping. These signs are particularly evident in stressful and/or stimulating conditions.

Neurological 'soft signs' have also been observed, the most common being choreoform movement of extremities, poor balance, poor coordination and

Table 11.1 Summations of previously conducted research on the development of motor function in autistic children.

study authors	number of subjects	task	significant findings
Vilensky *et al.* (1981)	21 children with autism (ages 3.3–10.0), 15 normal children (ages 3.9–11.3), five non-autistic hyperactive-aggressive children (ages 5.1–13.1)	following an IQ test, to walk (barefoot, whilst wearing shorts) at their normal rate along a rubber track	Kinesiologic gait analysis revealed that the autistic patients had: (i) reduced stride lengths; (ii) increased stance times; (iii) increased hip flexion at 'toe-off'; and (iv) decreased knee extension and ankle dorsiflexion at ground contact. In many respects, the gait differences between the autistic and normal subjects resembled differences between the gaits of Parkinsonian patients and of normal adults. The results are compatible with the view that the autistic syndrome may be associated with specific dysfunction of the motor system affecting, among other structures, the basal ganglia.
Hallett *et al.* (1993)	five adults with autism (four male, one female; ages 25–38), five healthy, age-matched controls (three male, two female; ages 25–36)	following an IQ test, to walk (barefoot, whilst wearing shorts) at a self-determined pace	Clinical assessment showed mild clumsiness in four patients and upper limb posturing during walking in three patients. The velocity of gait, step length, cadence, step width, stance time and vertical ground reaction forces were normal in all patients. The only significant abnormality was a decreased range of motion of the ankle. Some patients exhibited slightly decreased knee flexion in early stance. Clinically, the gait appeared to be irregular in three patients, but the variability was not significantly increased.
Manjiviona and Prior (1995)	12 children with AS (ages 7–17), nine children	IQ test followed by assessments of manual dexterity (speed and accuracy	The two groups did not differ on either total or subscale impairment scores. The results offer no

	with HFA (ages 10–15)	of hand movements, eye–hand coordination, coordination of both hands for a single task), ball skills (aim and catch a ball using both hands) and balance (static ability to hold a position and dynamic ability to be able to make spatially precise movements slowly, and with control of momentum)	support for clumsiness as a diagnostically differentiating feature of these disorders.
Hughes (1996)	36 children with DSM-III-R (American Psychiatric Association 1987) diagnosis of autism (22 male, 14 female), 24 non-autistic children with moderate LDs (11 male, 13 female), 28 young, normally developing, controls (12 male, 16 female)	following assessment of non-verbal mental age the subjects were instructed to insert an (experimenter-specified) end of a wooden rod (painted half black, half white) within either a red or a blue (again experimenter-specified) disc (each with a central well) such that it stood upright	The results obtained make clear that even very simple activities, such as this, depend upon several different processes of 'executive control': anticipatory monitoring, adjustment of an act in response to external feedback and coordination of separate elements into a goal-directed sequence. The performance of the normally developing pre-schoolers indicates that significant gains in executive control occur between the ages of 2 and 4 years. The performances of the other two groups indicate that although the development of executive control is delayed in both clinical groups, subjects with autism show an independent and marked impairment in this domain.

continued

Table 11.1 *continued*

study authors	number of subjects	task	significant findings
Miyahara *et al.* (1997)	26 children with AS (22 male, four female; ages 6–15), 16 children with LD (14 male, two female; ages 6–15)	following an IQ test, tests consisting of eight subtests in three sections: manual dexterity (two manipulative tasks and one drawing or cutting task); ball skills (one throwing and one catching task); and balance skills (one static and two dynamic balance tasks)	No relationship was found between intellectual and motor function; both groups demonstrated a high incidence of motor delay on the total test scores. A statistically significant difference was found between the two groups only on the manual dexterity subscore. Although the difference between the AS and LD groups did not reach an alpha level of 0.05, one particularly noteworthy result was the poorer ball skills exhibited by the children with AS.
Teitelbaum *et al.* (1998)	17 autistic infants (subsequently diagnosed by conventional methods at *ca.* 3 years or older), 15 normal infants	no specific task. Videos of the autistic children (recorded when they were infants) and normal infants were used to compare their patterns of lying (prone and supine), righting from their back to their stomach, sitting, crawling, standing and walking	Disturbances of movement were clearly detected in the autistic infants at the age of four to six months, long before they had been diagnosed as autistic. Specifically, disturbances were revealed in the shape of the mouth and in some or all of the milestones of development, including, lying, righting, sitting, crawling and walking.

impaired finger–thumb opposition. Muscle tone and reflex abnormalities are also common. In particular, the persistence of newborn reflexes and increased or decreased muscle tone have been found in children with autism. In fact, as infants, many autistic children have been noted to stiffen when held, or have been described as hypotonic.

Probably the most characteristic abnormal motor behaviour exhibited by people with autism is the repetitive and stereotypical movement of the body, limbs and fingers.

Of particular interest are the unusual gait patterns that have been linked to those observed for extrapyramidal motor disorders. These patterns include poorly coordinated limb movements and shortened steps, as well as 'toe walking'. For example, Damasio and Maurer (1978) and Vilensky *et al.* (1981) reported that autistic children between the ages of 3 and 10 years exhibited walking patterns similar to those observed for patients with Parkinson's disease (see also Woodward 2001). They walked more slowly and with shorter steps than non-autistic children. However, the existence of such a Parkinsonian-type disturbance is disputed by Hallett *et al.* (1993) who found normal gait velocities and step lengths in patients with autism. Nevertheless, they identified movement abnormalities such as a decreased range of motion of the ankle, slightly decreased knee flexion in early stance and gait irregularity. They thus proposed that this clinical picture is suggestive of a disturbance of the cerebellum. Other symptoms that may resemble extrapyramidal impairments include delays in the initiation, change or arrest of a motor sequence. Expressionless faces with little spontaneous movements were also described.

Poor performance of motor imitation tasks and the failure to use gestures for communicative purposes have been largely addressed (Smith and Bryson 1994). Several deficits have been proposed that aimed to explain how the learning of expressive gestures is negatively affected. Such deficits include: the lack of imitative skills, motor dyspraxia and basic perceptual and attentional impairments.

Leary and Hill (1996) have recently adopted a radical point of view about the presence of movement disturbance symptoms in individuals with autism. These authors provide an explanatory analysis of the bibliography on movement impairments in autism, based on the modified Rogers scale (i.e. a checklist of movement disturbance symptoms for individuals with developmental or psychiatric disorders). Their review lists several papers that describe movement disturbance in autism. Instead of dismissing these symptoms as peripheral to the syndrome, they propose that motor disorder symptoms may have a significant impact on the core characteristics of autism. In particular, their aim was to show how some of the socially referenced characteristics of autism might be based on neurological symptoms of movement disturbance. Following the categories adopted by the motor checklist, they grouped the symptoms into three levels of disturbance. The first includes disturbances of motor function, which affect posture, muscle tone, movements that normally accompany other actions, and extraneous, non-purposeful movements such as tics. The second category lists impairments in volitional movements (e.g. motor planning difficulties, repetitive spontaneous movements, language difficulties, etc.). The third level of motor disturbance affects overall behaviour and activity, and symptoms were considered to be pervasive, uncontrollable behaviours. It follows that it is possible to connect social descriptions such as 'a failure to cuddle', 'socially inappropriate gestures' and 'an indifference to affection' to neurological motor symptoms like 'abnormal posture and tone', 'dyskinesia' and 'marked underactivity'. The authors stress that the application of a social context to the observed behaviours may divert attention from an appreciation of the possible neurological explanations for the same behaviours. They propose that a shift in focus to a movement perspective may provide new insights, which could result in the development of useful tools for future diagnosis and rehabilitation. The specificity of movement disturbance may be of particular research interest with a view to addressing diagnostic issues. In fact, movement symptoms may define specific subgroups of the autism spectrum. If movement symptoms are found to be present in any individual with autism, this may lead to new ways of perceiving and addressing existing difficulties (Leary and Hill 1996).

Along these lines, Manjiviona and Prior (1995) and Miyahara *et al.* (1997) investigated the usefulness of motor impairment as a diagnostic feature aimed at differentiating groups within the autistic population. Both studies assessed motor clumsiness by administering behavioural tests that addressed both fine and gross motor skills (e.g. manual dexterity, ball skills and balance). Manjiviona and Prior (1995) tested the assumption that motor impairment differentiates people with AS from people with HFA. The DSMIV (American Psychiatric Association 1994) classifies both disorders as PDDs[1]. As no significant group differences were found for any measure on the behavioural motor test that they adopted (TOMI-H), the notion of clumsiness as a distinctive diagnostic feature between AS and HFA was refuted. For the sake of our discussion, the interesting finding of this study is that half of the subjects in both groups exhibited motor impairments and low-level performances when compared with normative data. In particular, children who exhibit motor impairment are not likely to have an isolated symptom, but show more pervasive movement disturbances that affect both fine and gross motor skills.

Miyahara *et al.* (1997) administered a standardized test of movement impairment, movement—ABC, which is a revision of the TOMI-H used by Manjiviona and Prior (1995), to both AS children and to children with LDs. This test assesses manual dexterity, ball skills and balance (as did the test employed by Manjiviona and Prior (1995)). They found a higher rate of AS children with motor incoordination (85%) than did Manjiviona and Prior (50%). Even though not directly explored by the author, the subscores obtained by AS subjects and the LD children for each subcategory on the movement test were almost identical. These results may provide further support for the hypothesis of a general, pervasive motor impairment in people with PDD, as proposed by Manjiviona and Prior (1995). Both studies sustain the need for future research to clarify the pattern of motor impairments within the autistic spectrum disorders, its specificity to the syndrome and its possible utility in the diagnosis and characterization of the syndrome itself.

A recent paper about motor control in autism addresses planning problems (Hughes 1996). The author administers a simple 'reach, grasp and place' task, which encourages a particular hand posture. The task leads to either comfortable or awkward final hand positions depending upon the subjects' planning abilities. Subjects with autism were significantly more likely to return their hand to an uncomfortable position. This result allows us to conclude that autistic children exhibit planning deficits for simple goal-directed sequences.

In line with the idea of using natural, non-arbitrary action sequencing to investigate a possible impairment in goal-directed activity in autism, the research described here is aimed at assessing one of the major motor milestones in the development of children, the reach-to-grasp movement. The reasons why the reach-to-grasp movement can be considered a motor milestone are various. For example, the high degree of development of the hand is paralleled by the development of a remarkable neural apparatus. The amount of cortical surface devoted to innervation of the hand testifies to its functional importance. This includes not only the large areas devoted to the hand in primary somatosensory and motor cortices, but also in the posterior parietal cortex and the premotor cortex. Further, it requires the coordination and the parallel processing of information streams concerned with *where* and *what* an object is together with *how* to deal with it.

In the following sections, we shall first describe the main kinematical features of the adult reach-to-grasp movement with particular emphasis on kinematic scaling with respect to object size and distance. We shall then describe the behavioural steps that underlie the development of a mature reach-to-grasp action. Next, we shall compare the reach-to-grasp pattern observed in autistic children with that of age-matched non-autistic children. Finally, we shall highlight features of the autistic reach-to-grasp kinematics, which may allow a (previously unidentified) association between IQ level and movement disorders in autism to be made.

11.2 The reach-to-grasp movement

The reach-to-Grasp movement is performed normally and routinely within the familiar context of living activities. It is also a movement that has been well characterized experimentally (reviewed in Bennett and Castiello 1994). In particular, this experimental model has been used to characterize disturbances in various neurologically compromised populations and at different age levels, including infants and children (Bennett and Castiello 1994).

The everyday action of reaching to grasp an object is commonly described in terms of a proximodistal distinction. The reaching and positioning actions, affected by upper arm and forearm musculature, are subserved by central nervous system visuomotor mechanisms that are largely independent from mechanisms subserving the grasping action, i.e. hand opening and subsequent closing (upon the object). With this description, the two neural channels, reaching and grasping, are said to be activated simultaneously and in parallel (the 'channel' hypothesis of Jeannerod (1981, 1984)), being coupled functionally for the goal-directed action by a higher-order coordinative structure (Jeannerod 1981, 1984). The 'reaching' channel is said to extract information about the spatial location of the object for transformation into motor patterns that bring the hand appropriately towards the object. The 'grasp' channel extracts information about the intrinsic properties of the object (such as size and shape) for the determination of a suitable grasping pattern.

Many behavioural studies of the kinematics of the human reach-to-grasp movement have tested the hypothesis that the two modules, reaching and grasping, are implemented through separate neural channels (Marteniuk *et al.* 1990; Gentilucci *et al.* 1991; Jakobson and Goodale 1992; Castiello 1996). An approach common to many of these studies is that of attempting to choose experimental conditions that exert effects upon only one visuomotor channel. However, although the two components can be considered as distinct, they seem to be coupled functionally. Hence, although arm reaching serves the function of bringing the hand to the target object, and because therefore it may be postulated that its neural channel will be primarily affected by changing the object's spatial location, the object's size will also modify this component. For example, the peak velocity of the reaching arm is generally lower and the duration of its deceleration time longer for objects that are perceived to require greater precision (i.e. small and/or delicate etc.) than for objects requiring less precise handling (reviewed in Weir (1994)). Similarly, although hand posture serves the function of grasping the target object, and because therefore it may be postulated that its neural channel will be primarily affected by changing the object's size, the object's spatial location will also modify this component. For example, the time of maximum grip aperture is generally earlier for objects that are positioned near to the subject than for those positioned further away (Weir 1994).

Figure 11.1 depicts some kinematic features of the reach-to-grasp action that are sensitive to object size and distance. For the reaching component, these features are movement duration, the velocity amplitudes with which the movement unfolds and the time from peak velocity to the end of the movement (deceleration time). In particular, movement duration is longer, the amplitude of peak velocity is lower and deceleration time is more prolonged for smaller than for larger stimuli and for far than near stimuli (e.g. Gentilucci *et al.* 1991).

For the grasping component, these landmarks are the amplitude and the time of maximum grip aperture. In particular, the amplitude of maximum grip aperture is lower and it is reached earlier for smaller than for larger stimuli and

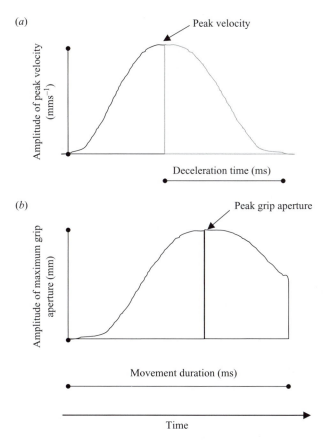

(a)

Peak velocity

Amplitude of peak velocity (mms^{-1})

Deceleration time (ms)

(b)

Peak grip aperture

Amplitude of maximum grip aperture (mm)

Movement duration (ms)

Time

Fig. 11.1 A graphical description of the kinematical variables analysed. Grey lines indicate the deceleration phase of the movement.

for far than for near stimuli (e.g. Gentilucci *et al.* 1991). As can be seen in Section 11.3, these parameters play a key part during the development of a mature reach-to-grasp pattern.

11.3 The development of the reach-to-grasp movement

In humans, reaching and grasping movements are not present at birth. Their development occurs as a series of steps during ontogeny. Reaching serves to bring the hand to a desired location in space. Thus grasping objects requires appropriate goal-directed reaching. Grasping involves digit coordination according to the intrinsic properties of the object (e.g. size and shape). Newborn infants do not grasp the objects they reach for. As observed in some of the newborn reflexes, as the arm extends forward, the hand has a tendency to open, and conversely, as the arm is flexed towards the body, the hand has a tendency to close (von Hofsten 1984). It is at around two months of age that the synergy described above begins to break up. von Hofsten (1984) found that, instead of opening the hand during the extension of the arm, two-month-old infants typically fisted the hand in the extended phase of the arm movement. At around three months of age, the infants started to open the hand again when extending the arm, but this time only when fixating upon a target. The significance of this change lies in the fact that the opening of the hand can no longer be described simply as a part of an extension synergy, but as a preparation for grasping the object. At approximately four to five months of age, both the distance and the direction of the reach improve, but the hand orientation and finger closure are still rather limited.

It is by nine months of age that the hand begins to be shaped according to object size. von Hofsten and Rönnqvist (1988) monitored the distance between the thumb and index finger in reaches performed by five- to six-month-old, nine- and 13-month-old infants. They found that the infants in the two older age groups did adjust the opening of the hand to the size of the target, but this was not evident for the youngest age group. The reason for this difference is that infants of five to six months of age do not predominantly use the thumb and the index finger when grasping objects, but the medial part of the hand and the palm. Further, although the older infants would adjust the opening of the hand to the size of the object, their pattern is still very different from the adult pattern where the hand fully opened during the approach to targets of different sizes (von Hofsten and Rönnqvist 1988). A possible interpretation of this behaviour is that a fully opened hand optimizes the possibility of grasping the object if the movement is not spatially precise.

The natural question is, therefore, when do children start to exhibit correct hand-preshaping (as a function of time and amplitude) with respect to object size and distance? Unfortunately, while the kinematics of the reach-to-grasp movement have been widely investigated in adults, and to some extent in infants, there are not many data available for the intermediate age level. Some evidence, however, is provided by Kuhtz-Buschbeck *et al.* (1998), who studied the kinematics of the reach-to-grasp action in children of 6–7 years of age, and from our pilot study (Mari *et al.* 1999) where children ranging from 8 to 12 years of age were tested. These children typically showed a patterning (with respect to object size and distance) that was similar to that of adults. These results are particularly relevant given that they provide a baseline for the comparison with autistic children of similar ages described in the following section.

11.4 The reach-to-grasp movement in autistic children

Our investigation of the reach-to-grasp movement in autistic children relies on kinematic measures (Mari *et al.* 1999)[2]. We used a three-dimensional kinematic system to compare the reach-to-grasp movements of autistic children and age-matched 'controls'.

Given reports of awkwardness and difficulty in planning actions, together with the common finding of problems when executing goal-directed actions, it was hypothesized that the movement of children with autism might not show appropriate scaling for the size and distance functions. The choice of object size enables the manipulation of accuracy planning, a small object requiring a more precise grasp (precision grip) than a large object (whole-hand prehension). The choice of object distance enables assessment of the ability to scale appropriately the reaching velocity and acceleration for near and far objects. Further, based on reports stating that autistic children show difficulty in the activation of movement components (reviewed in Leary and Hill 1996), it is also hypothesized that a lack of coordination between the individual components might characterize the 'autistic' reach-to-grasp synergy. We tested 20 participants with either ASD or AS. Children were assessed for movement disorders that are common in a population with developmental disabilities and that would confound any interpretation of the results (e.g. tics, tremors and cerebral palsy). The children with such movement disorders and developmental disabilities were excluded from the study group ($n = 2$). Individual characteristics are shown in Table 11.2. IQ was measured with the Weschler intelligence scale for children (WISC-R). The score for 10 of the autistic children was in the range of 70–79 and we labelled these children as 'low ability'. The IQ score for six of the autistic children was in the range of 80–89 and we labelled the children in this group as 'average ability'. The IQ score for the remaining four autistic children was in the range of 90–109 and we labelled these children as 'high ability'. We also tested 20 sex-and age-matched 'control' participants who reported no neurological or skeletomotor dysfunctions and were assessed to have an IQ in the normal range.

Figure 11.2 represents the experimental set-up and the stimuli used by Mari *et al.* (1999) and for collecting the data presented here. The participant was seated in a height-adjustable chair such that their feet and back were supported, and their forearms rested on the table surface (see Fig. 11.2*a*). The starting position of the arm and hand to be observed (either right or left, dependent upon the handedness of the participant), was with the shoulder slightly flexed and internally rotated (at about 45°), the elbow flexed (at about 90°), the forearm in mid-pronation and the ulnar border of the hand resting upon a yellow pad 10 cm anterior to the thorax. The thumb and index finger were held in a relaxed position of opposition. The objects to be grasped were highly translucent blocks of clear Perspex (see Fig. 11.2*a*) that were either small (1 cm × 1 cm × 1 cm) or large (4 cm × 4 cm × 4 cm) in size (independent variable = object size) and positioned vertically in the midline at either 18 cm or 28 cm (independent variable = object distance) from the starting position. Computer-controlled LEDs embedded within the working surface were used to illuminate the objects. Three LEDs were placed below the large object and

Table 11.2 Characteristics of the autistic and 'control' subjects.

				autistic group			control group			
subject	diagnosis	age	sex	hand	IQ range	IQ score	subject	age	sex	hand
1	ASD	11.3	M	RH	low ability	(70–79)	21	11	F	RH
2	ASD	9.3	M	LH	low ability	(70–79)	22	12.1	M	LH
3	AS	12.7	M	RH	low ability	(70–79)	23	10.4	M	RH
4	ASD	10.2	F	LH	low ability	(70–79)	24	10.2	M	RH
5	AS	10	F	RH	low ability	(70–79)	25	10	F	RH
6	AS	12.3	F	RH	low ability	(70–79)	26	12	F	RH
7	ASD	12.1	M	RH	low ability	(70–79)	27	12.5	M	RH
8	AS	9.6	M	RH	low ability	(70–79)	28	10	M	RH
9	ASD	10	F	RH	low ability	(70–79)	29	10	F	RH
10	ASD	12	F	RH	low ability	(70–79)	30	11.8	F	RH
11	ASD	9.6	F	RH	average ability	(80–89)	31	11.7	F	RH
12	AS	10.1	M	RH	average ability	(80–89)	32	8.9	M	RH
13	AS	9	M	RH	average ability	(80–89)	33	8.8	M	RH
14	AS	12.3	M	LH	average ability	(80–89)	34	12	M	LH
15	AS	11	F	RH	average ability	(80–89)	35	11	F	RH
16	ASD	9	F	RH	average ability	(80–89)	36	9.4	F	RH
17	ASD	9.8	M	RH	high ability	(90–109)	37	8	F	RH
18	ASD	13.1	F	RH	high ability	(90–109)	38	8.5	M	RH
19	ASD	7.4	M	RH	high ability	(90–109)	39	8.9	M	RH
20	ASD	9.5	M	RH	high ability	(90–109)	40	11.5	F	RH

one LED was placed below the small one (see Fig. 11.2c,d, respectively). The number of LEDs illuminated depended upon the object in question. Upon the illumination of an object, the participant was required to reach towards and then grasp and lift it. A specific movement speed was not stipulated, but each participant was instructed to perform the movement as they would normally do when reaching to grasp an object at home. The experiment lasted around 30 minutes and comprised about 60 reaches divided into four blocks. Pauses were allowed between the blocks to avoid fatigue. For each target size/distance combination, the participants performed five practice trials and then a block of 10 'real' trials. To distribute practice effects across conditions (size and distance), the block order was counterbalanced across participants.

Movements were recorded using an ELITE motion analysis system, which consisted of two infrared cameras (sampling rate 100 Hz) inclined at an angle

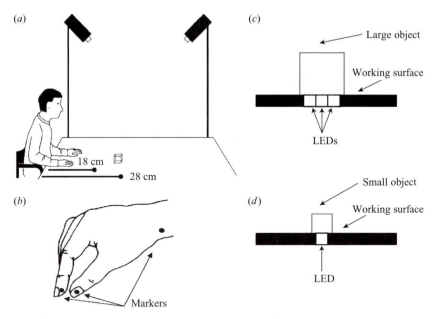

Fig. 11.2 A schematic depiction of the experimental set-up. (*a*) The position of the subject and the two ELITE cameras. (*b*) The three marker positions. (*c*), (*d*) The method by which the target objects were illuminated.

of 30° to the vertical and placed 2 m from the side of the table and 2 m apart (see Fig. 11.2*a*). These recorded the reflections of passive markers (0.25 cm diameter) attached to the following points of either the right or left upper limb (again dependent upon the handedness of the participant): (i) the wrist–radial aspect of the distal styloid process of the radius; (ii) the index finger–radial side of the nail; and (iii) the thumb–ulnar side of the nail (see Fig. 11.2*b*). Each experiment was also recorded on videotape. The polar orientation of each subject (and the table, which was able to rotate) was dependent upon their handedness, thus allowing the (fixed-position) cameras to have the same relative perspective of all subjects.

The reaching component was assessed by analysing the trajectory and velocity profiles of the wrist marker. The grasping component was assessed by analysing the distance between the thumb and index finger markers as a function of time. Movement duration was calculated as the time between movement onset (defined as the time at which the wrist first began to move) and the end of the action (defined as the time at which the index finger and thumb closed upon the target and there was no further change in the distance between them). The period following this, during which the target was lifted, was not assessed. The dependent variables were chosen on the basis of having demonstrated size and distance functions in previous research (Jakobson and Goodale 1992; see Fig. 11.1). The difference between the onset of the reaching component (as defined above) and the onset of the grasping component (defined as the time at which the index finger and thumb first began to open), i.e. the onset 'delay', was also calculated. For each participant in the two groups, mean values for each of the dependent measures were calculated for each size/distance combination. An ANOVA has been conducted with 'group' as the between-subjects factor (autistic and 'control') and 'object size' (small, large) and 'object distance' (near, far) as within-subjects factors. Prior to the ANOVA, normal distribution of the data was verified. Post-hoc comparisons were performed with the Newman–Keuls procedure (alpha level = 0.05).

A global view of the results obtained by comparing the 20 autistic children with the 20 'control' children indicates that the autistic children show a generalized slowness that, as explained in the following section, has to be ascribed to the autistic children belonging to the 'low ability' group. Apart from this, the disorder appears to have little influence on the size and distance functions addressed in this study. In general, the results obtained for both the autistic and 'control' participants mirrored those from previous studies of adults and children (Gentilucci *et al.* 1991; Jakobson and Goodale 1992; Castiello 1996; Kuhtz-Buschbeck *et al.* 1998). Autistic children were thus able to regulate these measured movement parameters correctly. The manipulation of object size and distance had predictable effects on the reaching and grasping components for the two groups. Consistent results within the reach-to-grasp literature reveal a longer movement duration, a prolonged arm deceleration time and a lower amplitude of arm peak velocity for smaller than for larger stimuli and for near than for far stimuli. Further, they reveal that the amplitude of maximum grip aperture is usually lower and it occurs earlier for smaller than for larger stimuli (Marteniuk *et al.* 1990; Gentilucci *et al.* 1991; Jakobson and Goodale 1992; Castiello 1996). As shown in Table 11.3, movement duration for the two groups was longer for the small than for the large object and for the objects positioned at the far than at the near distance. The peak velocity was higher and occurred earlier for the large than for the small object and for objects positioned at the greater distance. The time from peak velocity to the end of the movement (deceleration time) was longer for the small than for the large object and for the objects positioned at the far than at the near distance. For the grasping component, autistic children showed neither a greater proportional opening of the hand nor a larger absolute hand opening than that found for the 'control' group. For both groups, the timing of the peak aperture was earlier for the small than for the large object and for the objects positioned at the near than at the far distance.

In addition, the autistic children exhibited no inability to activate the required and appropriate motor components. Further, this study illustrates that autistic

Table 11.3 Kinematic parameters for the autistic and 'control' groups with respect to object size (small, large) and distance (near, far), and statistical values for the main factors group, size and distance; s.d. (standard deviation) in parentheses.

size function	kinematic parameters				statistical values	
	autistic group		control group			
	small	large	small	large	main factor group	main factor size
movement duration (ms)	1010 (427)	900 (347)	845 (84)	786 (84)	$F_{(1,19)} = 20.01$, $p < 0.0001$	$F_{(1,19)} = 46.21$, $p < 0.0001$
deceleration time (ms)	623 (289)	520 (173)	532 (64)	476 (54)	$F_{(1,19)} = 37.45$, $p < 0.0001$	$F_{(1,19)} = 24.11$, $p < 0.0001$
amplitude of peak velocity (mm s^{-1})	600 (187)	681 (133)	638 (76)	732 (76)	$F_{(1,19)} = 28.41$, $p < 0.0001$	$F_{(1,19)} = 33.87$, $p < 0.0001$
time of maximum grip aperture (ms)	625 (308)	700 (295)	405 (61)	473 (58)	$F_{(1,19)} = 76.32$, $p < 0.0001$	$F_{(1,19)} = 42.25$, $p < 0.0001$
amplitude of maximum grip aperture (mm)	41 (5)	75 (4)	41 (4)	75 (5)	n.s.	$F_{(1,19)} = 56.52$, $p < 0.0001$

distance function						
	near	far	near	far	main factor group	main factor distance
movement duration (ms)	867 (301)	952 (282)	777 (100)	848 (121)	$F_{(1,19)} = 58.32$, $p < 0.0001$	$F_{(1,19)} = 53.49$, $p < 0.0001$
deceleration time (ms)	549 (195)	645 (240)	467 (65)	543 (71)	$F_{(1,19)} = 41.06$, $p < 0.0001$	$F_{(1,19)} = 35.72$, $p < 0.0001$
amplitude of peak velocity (mm s^{-1})	603 (175)	707 (226)	655 (78)	754 (86)	$F_{(1,19)} = 17.31$, $p < 0.0001$	$F_{(1,19)} = 40.31$, $p < 0.0001$
time of maximum grip aperture (ms)	609 (290)	680 (195)	400 (54)	482 (60)	$F_{(1,19)} = 63.25$, $p < 0.0001$	$F_{(1,19)} = 46.37$, $p < 0.0001$
amplitude of maximum grip aperture (mm)	61 (5)	60 (6)	59 (6)	60 (5)	n.s.	n.s.

participants showed that the timing of the peak hand opening changing as a function of movement duration demonstrates how aspects of one component are sensitive to changes in the other (Gentilucci *et al.* 1991). The autistic children showed no dysfunction in this sensitivity. The overall form of the motor programme of autistic participants thus appears to be maintained. The selection of muscles and the timing of their activation enable the correct relative timing of all movement parameters of the reach-to-grasp components. A suitable number of neuronal sets are mobilized and the temporal arrangement of these sets is maintained.

Despite this patterning remaining intact, the following section highlights several differences between the autistic groups that may serve as a first step towards identifying specific areas that are worthy of future investigation.

11.5 The relationship between IQ and movement patterning

As judged from examination of the video recordings, the movements of the autistic children with IQs indicating 'low ability' were substantially different from those of the autistic children with 'high' and 'average' ability (for examples of these movements please refer to www.pc.rhbnc.ac.uk/staff/ucastiello/autism. html). The results presented below refer to the comparison between the 'low ability' autistic children, the 'average/high ability' autistic children and the 'control' children (see Table 11.2). The children belonging to the 'high ability' and the 'average ability' groups were grouped together because preliminary analyses showed no difference in their respective performances. To examine possible differences in the kinematics, an ANOVA with 'group' ('low ability', 'average/high ability' and 'control') as a between-subjects factor and 'object size' (small, large) and 'object distance' (near, far) as within-subjects factors was conducted.

A question of interest associated with the autistic syndrome is whether motor assessment alone is able to provide a means of differentiating objectively between the putative subgroups. The kinematical assessment of the present study reveals differences between the 'average/high ability' and 'low ability' autistic subjects. Interestingly, the main difference between the two groups lies in the speeds with which the movement unfolds. As shown in Figs. 11.3*a–d*, both movement duration and deceleration time were significantly longer, the amplitude of peak velocity was significantly lower, and the time of maximum grip aperture was significantly later for the 'low ability' group than for the other two groups. For the 'average/high ability' group, both movement duration and deceleration time were significantly shorter, the amplitude of peak velocity was higher and the time of maximum grip aperture was reached earlier than for the other two groups. For the same parameters, the 'control' group showed intermediate values.

The slowness of the 'low ability' group shows a strong resemblance to Parkinsonian-type bradykinesia. The parallelism between autistic and

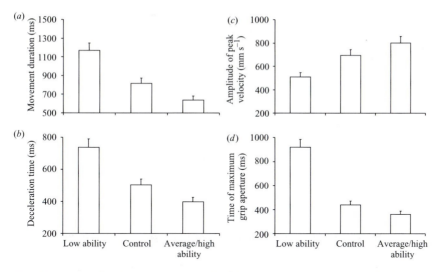

Fig. 11.3 A graphical representation of the differences between the 'low ability', 'average/ high ability' and 'control' groups for the parameters: (*a*) movement duration; (*b*) deceleration time; (*c*) amplitude of peak velocity; and (*d*) time of maximum grip aperture, collapsed for object size and distance. Error bars reflect the standard error.

Parkinsonian movement has already been proposed by a few authors who found abnormalities in gait (Vilensky *et al.* 1981; Hallett *et al.* 1993; Teitelbaum *et al.* 1998).

The slowness with which the autistic 'low ability' group unfolds the kinematic patterning of the reach-to-grasp action seems similar to the Parkinsonian-type pattern (Castiello *et al.* 1994). Although the performance was slow, there were no deficits in the 'low ability' groups' ability to modify the spatiotemporal characteristics of the reach-to-grasp pattern in response to experimentally imposed changes in either the distance of the object from the subject and/or the size of the object. The 'low ability' autistic participants were thus deemed able to regulate the movement parameters correctly. For the participants of this group, however, it was the relative activations of the reach and grasp components that revealed abnormalities: the onset of the grasp component was delayed with respect to the onset of the reaching component ($F_{(2,18)} = 21.06$, $p < 0.0001$; Fig. 11.4). The 'low ability' autistic children, as already found for Parkinson's disease patients (Castiello *et al.* 1994), were not able to initiate the two components in a near-simultaneous manner. As depicted in Fig. 11.4, the 'low ability' autistic children show a difference when the onset time of the grasping component is compared with that of the reaching component. For the 'average/high ability' group, the onset of grasping occurred, on average, 110 ms after the onset of the reaching. By contrast, the 'low ability' group

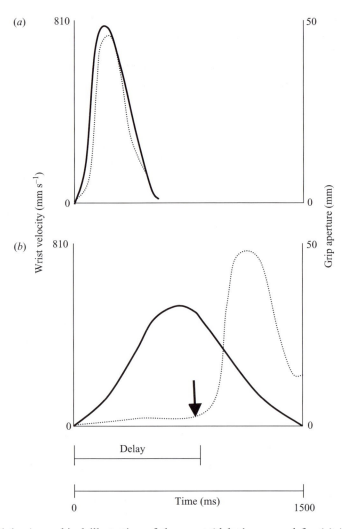

Fig. 11.4 A graphical illustration of the onset 'delay' measured for (*a*) 'average/ high ability' and (*b*) 'low ability' groups. Solid line, wrist velocity; dotted line, grip aperture. The arrow indicates the onset of finger opening with respect to the onset of arm movement, as measured from the wrist velocity profile.

began grasping, on average, 802 ms after reaching. This result could be attributed to the slower movement duration measured for the 'low ability' group. However, to give additional confirmation of this result, the onset of grasping was expressed as a percentage of movement duration. The opening of the index finger and thumb thus began at 72% of movement duration for the 'low ability' group, but at only 15% for the 'average/high ability' group ($F_{(2,18)} = 41.32, p < 0.0001$). A regression analysis was performed comparing the onset of grasping (using both absolute and relative values) and movement duration. The fact that no correlations were found indicates that the later onset of grasping measured for the 'low ability' group was not due to a relationship between movement duration and grasping onset. However, despite the fact that the bradykinesia and the delayed finger opening seem to be independent effects, it might well be that both of them could result from a generally low speed of information processing. An interesting feature of this delay in the onset of grasping found for the 'low ability' group is the difference in grasping times measured for the small and the large objects (interaction group by size, $F_{(2,18)} = 9.32$, $p < 0.001$, $p_s < 0.05$). For this group, grasping began, on average, 812 ms after reaching when a movement towards the small object was performed. However, when reaching for the large object, grasping began, on average, 748 ms after reaching. For the 'average/high ability' group, the parameter delay was similar for both the small and the large objects (110 ms and 112 ms, respectively). Further, as a result of this delay, it was found that the grip opening and closing phases exhibited by the 'low ability' participants were performed much faster than for the other groups.

These results might indicate that the near-concurrent activation of the reach and grasp components is desynchronized by a specific impairment in the management of synchronous motor programmes in the 'low ability' autistic participants. Theoretically, this result is interesting since several researchers have attributed the deficit in the initiation of motor sequences and the poor coordination of separate elements into a goal-directed sequence to the autistic syndrome (reviewed in Leary and Hill (1996) and Hughes (1996)). This delay in the near-concurrent activation of the two components could also reflect the dysfunction in autistic children of the central mechanisms that process the superimposition of the two motor programmes. In the case of the reach-to-grasp movement, the control channels for reaching are most probably distinct from those required for manipulation (Jeannerod 1984). Thus, the deficit in the 'low ability' autistic children applies to the simultaneous activation of motor programmes that are largely independent, but show functional coordination. Interestingly, the delay between the activation of the two components is related to the size of the object to be grasped. With the more accurate precision task (i.e. reaching-to-grasp the small object), 'low ability' autistic children show a greater delay than for the more gross type of grasp (i.e. reaching-to-grasp the large object). This adds support for a central neural processing origin for the lag in activation of the distal motor pattern. This 'dysfunction' may be more pronounced in the performance of more precise tasks that require more complex neural programming, i.e. a greater problem for less cognitively able children.

In contrast to the 'low ability' autistic group, the children of the 'average/high ability' autistic group seem to adopt a strategy that might be the product of a feed-forward system that defines both the initial state of the limb and the ultimate goal, and then determines a movement towards the appropriate target location. The very rapid actions executed by this group indicate that once the action planning has been finalized, it must be performed very quickly to avoid any disruptive feedback mechanisms. In this regard, Masterton and Biederman (1983) indicated that children with autism were unable to visually control reaching movements very efficiently. Hence, the pattern exhibited by the 'average/high ability' autistic children might be related to the difficulties experienced when attempting to use external feedback to guide behaviour. Further, we add to this conclusion by suggesting that this deficiency may be different with respect to different autistic groups. Another possible explanation is that the children of the 'average/high ability' group demonstrate both hyperagility and hyperdexterity, being thus able to unfold the reach-to-grasp pattern very quickly and efficiently.

11.6 Conclusion

In conclusion, our findings support the view that movement disturbances may play an intrinsic part in the phenomenon of autism, that they are present during childhood and that they can be used to subdivide autism into specific groups. Further, given that the reach-to-grasp movement is one of the major motor milestones in child development, it might well be that movement analysis could be used as an early indicator of potential autism.

On the basis of the evidence provided above, it can thus be suggested that differences in the reach-to-grasp patterning exhibited by autistic people confirm their dysfunctioning ability to initiate, switch, efficiently perform or continue any ongoing action including those involved in communicating, interacting socially or performing useful daily living activities. Consequently, it follows that a shift in focus to a movement perspective may reveal a new route for investigating autistic behaviour that might be useful for rehabilitation and diagnostic purposes.

The autistic and 'control' subjects who participated in this study are gratefully acknowledged. Dr Claudia Bonfiglioli and Dr James Taylor are thanked for helping with various aspects of this research.

Endnotes

1 This classification is no longer inherent in the APA DSM-IV, although it was in previous editions and when the Manjiviona and Prior study was conducted.
2 This reference is concerned with an abstract publication describing data from only 10 of the 20 autistic children presented here.

References

American Psychiatric Association (1987). *Diagnostic and statistical manual of mental disorders*, 3rd edn. Washington, DC: American Psychiatric Association.

American Psychiatric Association (1994). *Diagnostic and statistical manual of mental disorders*, 4th edn. Washington, DC: American Psychiatric Association.

Bauman, M. L. (1992). Motor dysfunction in autism. In *Movement disorders in neurology and neuropsychiatry* (ed. A. B. Joseph and R. R. Young), pp. 658–61. Boston, MA: Blackwell Scientific.

Bennett, K. M. B. and Castiello, U. (eds) (1994). *Insights into the reach to grasp movement*. Amsterdam: Elsevier.

Brasiĉ, J. R. (1999). Movements in autistic disorder. *Med. Hypoth.* **53**, 48–49.

Castiello, U. (1996). Grasping a fruit: selection for action. *J. Exp. Psychol. Hum. Percept. Perf.* **22**, 582–603.

Castiello, U., Bennett, K. M. B. and Scarpa, M. (1994). The reach to grasp movement of Parkinson's disease patients. In *Insights into the reach to grasp movement* (ed. K. M. B. Bennett and U. Castiello), pp. 215–37. Amsterdam: Elsevier.

Damasio, A. R. and Maurer, R. G. (1978). A neurological model for childhood autism. *Arch. Neurol.* **35**, 777–86.

Gentilucci, M., Castiello, U., Corradini, M. L., Scarpa, M., Umiltá, C. and Rizzolatti, G. (1991). Influence of different types of grasping on the transport component of prehension movements. *Neuropyschologia* **29**, 361–78.

Hallett, M., Lebiedowska, M. K., Thomas, S. L., Stanhope, S. J., Denckla, M. B. and Rumsey, J. (1993). Locomotion of autistic adults. *Arch. Neurol.* **50**, 1304–08.

Happé, F. (1999). Autism: cognitive defect or cognitive style? *Trends Cog. Sci.* **6**, 216–22.

Happé, F. and Frith, U. (1996). The neuropsychology of autism. *Brain* **119**, 1377–400.

Hughes, C. (1996). Brief report: planning problems in autism at the level of motor control. *J. Autism Devl Disorders* **26**, 99–107.

Jakobson, L. S. and Goodale, M. A. (1992). Factors affecting higher-order movement planning: a kinematic analysis of human prehension. *Exp. Brain Res.* **86**, 199–208.

Jeannerod, M. (1981). Intersegmental coordination during reaching at natural visual objects. In *Attention and performance IX* (ed. J. Long and A. Baddeley), pp. 153–68. Hillsdale, NJ: Lawrence Erlbaum Associates.

Jeannerod, M. (1984). The timing of natural prehension movements. *J. Mot. Behav.* **16**, 235–54.

Kuhtz-Bushbeck, J. P., Stolze, H., Boczek-Funcke, A., Johnk, K., Heinrichs, H. and Ilert, M. (1998). Kinematic analysis of prehension movements in children. *Behav. Brain Res.* **93**, 131–41.

Leary, M. R. and Hill, D. A. (1996). Moving on: autism and movement disturbance. *Mental Retard.* **34**, 39–53.

Manjiviona, J. and Prior, M. (1995). Comparison of Asperger syndrome and high-functioning autistic children on a test of motor impairment. *J. Autism Devl Disorders* **25**, 23–39.

Mari, M., Castiello, U., Marks, D., Marraffa, C. and Prior, M. (1999). The reach-to-grasp movement in children with autism spectrum disorder. European Congress on Autism, Glasgow, UK.

Marteniuk, R. G., Leavitt, J. L., MacKenzie, C. L. and Athenes, S. (1990). Functional relationships between the grasp and transport components in a prehension task. *Hum. Mov. Sci.* **9**, 149–76.

Masterton, B. A. and Biederman, G. B. (1983). Proprioceptive versus visual control in autistic children. *J. Autism Devl Disorders* **13**, 141–52.

Miyahara, M., Tsujii, M., Hori, M., Nakanishi, K., Kageyama, H. and Sugiyama, T. (1997). Brief report: motor incoordination in children with Asperger syndrome and learning disabilities. *J. Autism Devl Disorders* **27**, 595–603.

Smith, I. M. and Bryson, S. E. (1994). Imitation and action in autism: a critical review. *Psychol. Bull.* **116**, 259–73.

Teitelbaum, P., Teitelbaum, O., Nye, J., Fryman, J. and Maurer, R. G. (1998). Movement analysis in infancy may be useful for early diagnosis of autism. *Proc. Natl Acad. Sci. USA* **95**, 13 982–987.

Vilensky, J. A., Damasio, A. R. and Maurer, R. G. (1981). Gait disturbances in patients with autistic behaviour. *Arch. Neurol.* **38**, 646–49.

von Hofsten, C. (1984). Developmental changes in the organization of prereaching movements. *Devl Psychol.* **20**, 378–88.

von Hofsten, C. and Rönnqvist, L. (1988). Preparation for grasping an object: a developmental study. *J. Exp. Psychol. Hum. Percept. Perf.* **14**, 610–21.

Weir, P. L. (1994). Object property and task effects on prehension. In *Insights into the reach to grasp movement* (ed. K. M. B. Bennett and U. Castiello), pp. 129–50. Amsterdam: Elsevier.

Woodward, G. (2001). Autism and Parkinson's disease. *Med. Hypoth.* **56**, 246–49.

Glossary

AS: Asperger syndrome
ASD: autism spectrum disorder
DSM: diagnostic and statistical manual
HFA: high-functioning autism
IQ: intelligence quotient
LD: learning disability
LED: light-emitting diode
PDD: pervasive developmental disorder
TOMI-H: test of motor impairment—Henderson revision

12

Investigating individual differences in brain abnormalities in autism

*C. H. Salmond, M. de Haan, K. J. Friston,
D. G. Gadian, and F. Vargha-Khadem*

Autism is a psychiatric syndrome characterized by impairments in three domains: social interaction, communication, and restricted and repetitive behaviours and interests. Recent findings implicate the amygdala in the neurobiology of autism. In this paper, we report the results of a series of novel experimental investigations focusing on the structure and function of the amygdala in a group of children with autism. The first section attempts to determine if abnormality of the amygdala can be identified in an individual using magnetic resonance imaging *in vivo*. Using single-case voxel-based morphometric analyses, abnormality in the amygdala was detected in half the children with autism. Abnormalities in other regions were also found. In the second section, emotional modulation of the startle response was investigated in the group of autistic children. Surprisingly, there were no significant differences between the patterns of emotional modulation of the startle response in the autistic group compared with the controls.

Keywords: autism; neurobiological basis; magnetic resonance imaging; voxel-based morphometry; startle response; amygdala

12.1 Introduction

Current understanding of the neurobiological basis of autism is limited. The diagnosis of autism is commonly made based on the child's historical and current behavioural symptomatology. The clinician is often required to make qualitative judgements about the significance of the child's difficulties. Diagnosis can therefore be highly subjective and may vary among clinicians (Howlin and Asgharian 1999).

Recently, there has been increasing evidence for the role of the amygdala in the neurobiology of autism (Baron-Cohen *et al.* 2000; Howard *et al.* 2000). For example, post-mortem studies have revealed increased cell density and abnormally small cells in the amygdala (Bauman and Kemper 1985, 1994; Raymond *et al.* 1989; Bauman 1991; Bailey *et al.* 1998). Structural imaging studies have identified abnormalities in amygdala volume (although some studies have found increased volume and others decreased volume; Aylward *et al.* 1999; Howard *et al.* 2000; Pierce *et al.* 2001). Magnetic resonance spectroscopy studies have suggested neuronal loss or damage in the amygdala–hippocampal region (Otsuka *et al.* 1999). In a recent imaging study, Baron-Cohen *et al.* (1999) reported that a group of individuals with autism did not activate the amygdala when it was activated in the controls.

We report the results of a study investigating the integrity of the amygdala in a group of children with autism. The first section addresses the issue of individual neuropathological profiles, and attempts to determine if it is possible to detect a structural abnormality in the amygdala in an autistic individual, as opposed to averaged data from a control group. Detection of such an abnormality might be a first step towards establishing a quantitative and objective measure for diagnostic purposes.

The second section reports on the use of a psychophysiological measure (i.e. emotional modulation of the startle response) to assess amygdala function in the group of children with autism. This independent measure of amygdala function may be useful in assessing the impact of abnormality in this brain region on emotional modulation.

12.2 Participants

Fourteen children with autism (aged between 8 and 18 years) were recruited through parental support groups (including the National Autistic Society) and from schools specializing in the education of children with autism. Each child had been diagnosed with HFA or AS by independent clinicians (including paediatricians, clinical psychologists and psychiatrists). Children were excluded from the study if they had additional neurological or psychiatric diagnoses (e.g. fragile X, epilepsy and attention deficit hyperactivity disorder), if they were taking medication or had a history consistent with a diagnosis of secondary autism (such as rubella).

Normally developing control children (aged between 8 and 18 years) were recruited from local London schools. These children were required to meet the same inclusionary and exclusionary criteria as the children with autism, with the additional requirement that there was no family history of autism. Further details of the groups are provided in Table 12.1. Although the control and autistic groups were not matched on sex, the results remained unchanged when analyses were restricted to males only.

(a) Intelligence

The age-appropriate Wechsler Intelligence Test (Wechsler 1991, 1997) was administered to provide verbal, performance and full-scale IQs. All autistic children and controls investigated in this study had verbal IQs within a standard deviation of the normal mean (85–115).

Table 12.1   Characteristics of the HFA and AS groups.

group	size	mean age (years)	diagnosis	sex
control	18	12.6	N/A	12 female; 6 male
autistic	14	12.9	3 HFA; 11 AS	1 female; 13 male

12.3 Individual neuropathological measures

This section attempts to detect a pattern of neural abnormality that is characteristic of autism, utilizing the prior hypothesis of bilateral neural abnormality as being causal. The underlying rationale is that autism is a neuro-developmental disorder with selective and chronic cognitive deficits. It is well established that in adult humans, unilateral brain damage is sufficient to produce selective cognitive impairments that are severe and chronic. By contrast, in children, bilateral lesions of a brain system appear to be necessary to produce chronic syndromes (e.g. amnesia; Gadian *et al.* 2000). The absence of such selective impairments in the face of early unilateral damage is presumed to reflect the plasticity of the immature brain, and its capacity for reorganization of a developing function to a homologous region in the undamaged hemisphere.

VBM is a technique that has been developed to characterize cerebral grey and white matter differences with uniform sensitivity throughout the entire brain. Although typically used to assess group differences, VBM has recently been validated for use in individual subjects (see Salmond *et al.* 2002). Using this technique, the presence or absence of abnormalities in the amygdala was determined for each individual. In addition, other neural areas (including the hippocampal formation, the cerebellum, the STG and the OFC) found to be abnormal in a group analysis of individuals with autism (see Salmond 2001) were investigated.

A second MRI technique, T_2 relaxometry, was used to provide a quantitative method of detecting abnormalities that are more conventionally evaluated by visual inspection of T_2-weighted images. T_2 relaxation times have been shown to detect lesions or abnormalities that may not be identified in standard clinical imaging (Van Paesschen *et al.* 1996). T_2 relaxation times were therefore determined for each of the participants in this study.

12.4 Methods: individual neuropathological measures

(a) MRI acquisition

All the children underwent non-sedated MRI scans in a 1.5 T Siemens Vision System. A 3D FLASH sequence was collected (TR: 16.8 ms; TE: 5.7 ms; flip angle: 21°; voxel size 0.8 mm × 0.8 mm × 1 mm) for use in the individual VBM analyses. HCT2 and AT2 maps were obtained using a 16-echo sequence as previously described (Van Paesschen *et al.* 1996, 1997; TR: 2400 ms, TE: 22–262 ms; one slice, 5 mm thick). The HCT2 map was oriented in a tilted coronal plane along the anterior border of the brainstem, perpendicular to, and at the level of, the body of the hippocampal formation. The AT2 was oriented in a tilted axial plane parallel to and above the long axis of the hippocampal formation.

(b) Individual VBM

The scans were analysed using VBM, according to the bilateral method described by Salmond *et al.* (2000). Briefly, the data were normalized and segmented into grey and white matter images. The grey matter images were then smoothed with 4 and 12 mm isotropic Gaussian kernels. This smoothing renders the voxel values into an index of the amount of grey matter per unit volume under the smoothing kernel. The term 'grey matter density' is generally used to refer to this probabilistic measure. Smoothing parameters of 4 and 12 mm were chosen as these correspond roughly to the cross-sectional dimensions of the hippocampal formation and amygdala, respectively, and, by the matched filter theorem, sensitized the analysis to differences at these spatial scales. Age and sex were included as covariates.

Each child in the autistic group was compared with the entire control group, searching for bilateral deficits in grey matter density using a conjunction analysis as described previously. Salmond *et al.* (2002) have reported that single-subject versus group comparisons can be subject to violations of normality assumptions at very low degrees of smoothing. This violation can render the Gaussian field correction for multiple comparisons inexact. We therefore eschewed the multiple comparisons correction by restricting our inferences to prespecified anatomical regions. These regions, which included the hippocampal formation, amygdala, OFC, STG and cerebellum, were identified on the basis of a review of the literature (Bachevalier 1994; Carper and Courchesne 2000). The exact locations of the regions were determined by a group analysis of pilot data (Salmond 2001). As a control, we also investigated an area of the visual cortex thought not to be involved in the neuropathogenesis of autism. We used an uncorrected threshold of $p = 0.001$, which corresponds roughly to a corrected p value of 0.05 having accounted for the small volume and the number of structures involved.

(c) T_2 maps

HCT2 and AT2 were measured by placing the largest possible circle as a region of interest within the hippocampal formation and amygdala (respectively) while avoiding boundaries where partial volume effects within cerebrospinal fluid might occur. HCT2 and AT2 values are expressed in milliseconds.

12.5 Results: individual neuropathological measures

(a) VBM

Results from the individual VBM analyses are shown in Tables 12.2 and 12.3. The individual VBM analyses revealed that most children in the autistic group showed evidence of abnormality in the OFC, STG and the cerebellum. Fewer individuals showed evidence of medial temporal lobe abnormality. Representative results are shown in Fig. 12.1. Similar analyses comparing each child in the control group with the remaining controls revealed no evidence of neural abnormality.

The significance of these differing patterns of neural abnormality in relation to cognitive and behavioural function in the children with autism was explored using tests commonly thought to be associated with the functions of

Table 12.2 Results from individual VBM analyses. (Y indicates presence of abnormality at threshold uncorrected $p < 0.001$, N indicates no significant abnormality at threshold.)

autistic subject no.	hippocampal formation	amygdala	OFC	STG	cerebellum	visual cortex (V1)
1	Y	N	Y	N	Y	N
2	Y	Y	Y	Y	Y	N
3	N	N	N	Y	Y	N
4	Y	Y	Y	Y	Y	N
5	Y	Y	Y	Y	Y	N
6	N	N	Y	N	Y	N
7	Y	Y	Y	Y	Y	N
8	N	Y	Y	Y	Y	N
9	N	N	Y	N	N	N
10	N	N	Y	Y	N	N
11	N	N	Y	Y	Y	N
12	N	N	Y	Y	N	N
13	Y	Y	Y	Y	Y	N
14	Y	Y	Y	N	Y	N

Table 12.3 Summary of group variation according to VBM analyses.

area	number of individuals showing abnormality
hippocampal formation	7
amygdala	7
OFC	13
STG	10
cerebellum	11

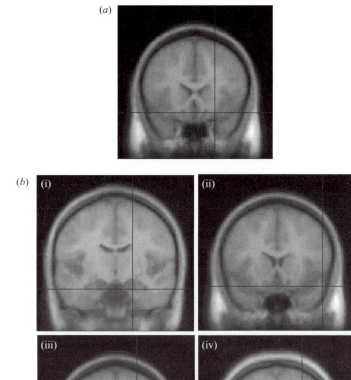

Fig. 12.1 Representative results. (*a*) Child 9, abnormality in OFC; child 8, abnormality in (i) amygdala, (ii) STG, (iii) OFC and (iv) cerebellum. All figures shown at uncorrected $p < 0.01$ for display purposes. Displayed in neurological convention (left is left).

these areas (Salmond 2001). These included measures of episodic memory (Rivermead Behavioural Memory Test; Wilson *et al.* 1991), orbitofrontal function (number of correct responses; i.e. failure to maintain set; Stuss *et al.* 1983, 2000; Nagahama *et al.* 1996) on the Wisconsin Card Sorting Test (Heaton 1981), and motor coordination (Movement Assessment Battery for Children Checklist; Henderson and Sugden 1992) as well as ratings on the Autistic Behaviour Checklist (Krug *et al.* 1993). The behavioural and cognitive profiles did not distinguish between autistic children with significant

Table 12.4 Performance scores according to presence of detected abnormality on individual VBM.

area of abnormality (performance measure)	range of raw scores and no. of children in the autistic group showing significant abnormality	range of scores and no. of children in the autistic group showing no significant abnormality
hippocampal formation (Rivermead)	13–19 ($n = 7$)	13–22 ($n = 7$)
OFC (number of correct responses)	6–50 ($n = 13$)	44 ($n = 1$)
cerebellum (Movement Assessment Battery for Children)	3–84 ($n = 11$)	0–53 ($n = 13$)

Table 12.5 Symptom severity according to presence of detected abnormality on individual VBM.

area of abnormality	range of scores on autistic behaviour checklist of children in autism group with no significant detected abnormality in this region	range of scores on autistic behaviour checklist of children in autism group with no significant detected abnormality in this region
hippocampal formation	10–76	35–94
OFC	10–94	35[a]
cerebellum	10–94	46–74

[a] $n = 1$.

abnormality in individual VBM analyses and those without significant abnormality (see Tables 12.4 and 12.5).

(b) T_2 maps

There were no significant differences between the AT2 and HCT2 values of the two groups (AT2: $F_{1,21} = 0.7$, $p = 0.4$; HCT2: $F_{1,23} = 1.6$, $p = 0.2$). There were no effects of side, or significant interactions between side and group ($p > 0.2$). Figure 12.2 shows the range of T_2 values obtained for (a) the amygdala and (b) the hippocampal formation.

12.6 Discussion: individual neuropathological measures

The individual VBM analyses revealed abnormality in the amygdala in only half the autistic children. This is consistent with reports of hetereogeneity in

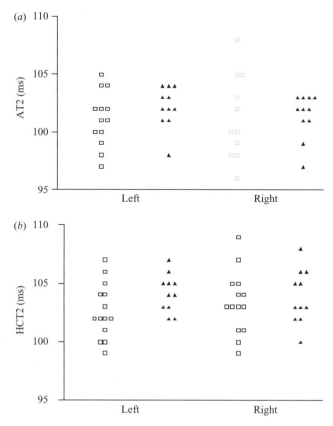

Fig. 12.2   Scattergraph of T_2 values of (*a*) the amygdala (AT2); (*b*) the hippocampal formation (HCT2). Squares represent control group and triangles represent autistic group.

individuals with autism (Aylward *et al.* 1999; Howard *et al.* 2000). By contrast, the OFC abnormality was found in all but one of the autistic children, highlighting the possibility that this area is important in the pathogenesis of autism.

However, the neuropsychological tests purporting to pinpoint orbitofrontal function that we used in this study did not reflect this abnormality. Further research is required to reveal the significance of abnormality in this region in relation to other brain areas implicated in autism. Importantly, no evidence of abnormality was found in the visual cortex, suggesting that neural abnormalities are not present in every region of the autistic brain.

No neural area was found to be significantly abnormal in all of the autistic children. Additionally, there was no association between a specific area of abnormality and a selective deficit in a particular domain of cognitive or behavioural function. This suggests that autism is unlikely to be associated with abnormality in one particular location alone. Instead, the autistic phenotype may reflect abnormalities within a particular neural system or, indeed, multiple systems. Five highly interconnected regions have been implicated in the neural pattern characteristic of autism: the OFC, the cerebellum, the hippocampal formation, the amygdala and the STG (Heath and Harper 1974; Heath *et al.* 1978; Sasaki *et al.* 1979; Barbas and De Olmos 1990; Middleton and Strick 1994; Barbas and Blatt 1995; Schmahmann and Pandya 1997). However, the combination of areas detected as abnormal have shown wide individual variation.

The results from the T_2 maps revealed no group differences in either the amygdala or the hippocampal formation. Furthermore, there was no relation between an individual's T_2 values and VBM results. However, this is compatible with the VBM findings, as it is quite possible to detect a change in the volume of a structure with no change in its T_2 relaxation time. For example, cases of abnormal hippocampal volume and normal HCT2 have been reported in the literature (Van Paesschen *et al.* 1997; Gadian *et al.* 2000). The null result of the T_2 data emphasizes the difficulties inherent in detecting abnormalities in an individual using the methods currently available in clinical practice.

Our results suggest that VBM can reveal abnormalities in the amygdala, as well as in other brain regions, in particular OFC, in at least some of the autistic individuals. This raises the possibility that different etiologies may be identifiable in different individuals with autism. In the future, it may be appropriate to use cluster analyses in a larger sample of children with autism to investigate factors contributing to the homogeneity and heterogeneity of the disorder.

It is clearly premature to suggest that the results of this study have definitively determined the neural pattern characteristic of autism. First, this study investigated only five sites of anatomical abnormality. Whilst these areas are the most frequently reported sites associated with abnormality in autism, other areas may also be affected. Second, this study investigated only autistic children with verbal IQs within the normal range. It is possible that lower functioning children with autism may show more extensive neural abnormalities or may show a different pattern. Third, this study has not demonstrated specificity of the pattern of neural abnormality: children with other developmental disorders may show a similar pattern (e.g. amygdala abnormalities have also been reported in anxious and depressed children; De-Bellis *et al.* 2000; Thomas *et al.* 2001).

12.7 Emotional modulation of the startle response

An independent behavioural measure of the amygdala is the emotional modulation of the startle response. The startle response is a brainstem-mediated motor response that occurs following the presentation of a sudden and intense stimulus. The vigour of the startle response varies systematically with the emotional state of the individual (Lang *et al*. 1990). This emotional modulation of the startle response has been shown to be dependent on the amygdala (e.g. Rosen *et al*. 1996; Davis *et al*. 1999).

In humans, the fastest and most stable element of the startle response is the sudden closure of the eyelids (Anthony 1985). This is the traditional experimental measure of the startle response in humans. The vigour of the startle response varies systematically with the affective status of the individual (Lang *et al*. 1990). In adult humans, the startle response is facilitated by unpleasant arousal and inhibited by pleasant arousal (e.g. Davis 1989; Lang *et al*. 1990, 1992). Studies of the normative development of emotional modulation of the startle response have produced mixed results. Two studies with school-aged children have reported non-significant trends *opposite* to those reported in adults: smaller responses to fearful than pleasant stimuli (Cook *et al*. (1995) for boys and girls; McManis *et al*. (1995) for boys). These results cannot be due to delayed maturation of the emotional modulation of the startle response, since infants in the first year of life show enhanced startle to angry, compared with happy, faces (Balaban 1995) and to a stranger approaching compared with baseline (Schmidt and Fox 1998).

One possible explanation for the negative findings in school-aged children is that these studies used fearful and pleasant stimuli that were categorized as such according to adult normative ratings. Children may not perceive the valence of the stimuli in the same way as adults, and individual differences in perception of fear may be particularly evident during childhood. One way to address this problem, adopted in the present study, is to have children themselves rate pictures as fearful or pleasant, and tailor the analysis of emotional modulation of response to their individual responses. This individual tailoring maximizes the possibility of detecting emotional modulation, which might otherwise be masked by inclusion of pleasant stimuli in the fearful category, and vice versa. This approach also prevents 'false' findings of abnormal response patterns merely due to any idiosyncratic fears or preferences of children with autism.

12.8 Methods: emotional modulation of the startle response

(a) Stimuli

More than 50 pictures were chosen from a variety of websites and rated as pleasant or unpleasant by 10 adults. From these, the 15 pictures rated as most pleasant and the 15 pictures rated as most unpleasant were selected. An additional nine pictures were selected with varying ratings for use as filler stimuli in non-probed trials.

A pilot study with adults using these stimuli demonstrated the expected pattern of augmented startle to the unpleasant compared with the pleasant pictures.

The pictures were deliberately selected to exclude facial stimuli. Children with autism have been shown to have impaired recognition of facial expression (Hobson *et al.* 1988; Teunisse and Gelder 2001). This impairment is therefore likely to confound any intended affective modulation in the paradigm (i.e. if the child does not recognize a fearful expression, such a face cannot be assumed to engender a fearful emotional response).

An acoustic startle probe (consisting of a 50 ms burst of white noise with instantaneous rise time) was presented binaurally over headphones. The intensity of the probe was chosen to be within a comfortable range for the children (at around 70 dB, sound pressure level).

(b) Paradigm

Each picture was presented for 7 s and startle probes were presented at 1300 ms after slide picture onset. The pictures were presented on a Dell 1500 FP computer screen. Picture offset was followed by a blank screen.

The child was instructed that a series of slides would be presented and that each slide should be viewed for the whole time it was on the screen. Each child was encouraged to pay attention by being told that questions would be asked about the pictures at the end of the assessment. The child was told that occasional noises would be heard over the headphones that could be ignored.

After the startle probe series had been completed, the child was shown each picture again and asked to rate it as 'nice' or 'scary'. In order to check comprehension of these concepts, the child was asked to give an example of something 'nice' and 'scary' on a previous assessment day. These ratings were used to produce individual categorizations of the stimuli (pleasant and unpleasant) for each child.

(c) Data recording

Unilateral right blink magnitude was measured by vEOG measurements using a pair of bipolar AgCl electrodes placed just above and below the orbit in a vertical line through the pupil. Sampling rate was 500 Hz and the data were recorded with a 50 Hz notch filter. Impedances were kept below 10 kΩ. Although it is more traditional to measure blink magnitude from EMG, when both EMG and vEOG were recorded they yielded highly similar results (Sugawara *et al.* 1994). The raw vEOG signal was epoched and baseline corrected (interval: 200 to 0 ms).

(d) Data analysis

The peak of the blink was defined as the point of maximum deflection before a return towards baseline that continued for 5 ms. Latency of response was defined as the latency of peak amplitude. When multiple blinks occurred, the response whose latency was closest to the mean latency for that condition was scored. Trials were deemed non-scorable (and therefore rejected) if a blink was in progress at reflex stimulus onset or if the blink did not recover within the sampling period of 250 ms (return to at least 25% of peak amplitude).

12.9 Results: emotional modulation of the startle response

All the children were able to give appropriate examples of items or events that were scary or nice. Responses given included going on holiday, pets and chocolate (nice), and spiders, the dark and horror films (scary). There was no qualitative difference between the responses of the two groups.

The children's individual ratings of the pictures were used to determine the categorization of visual stimuli. There was no group difference in the number of stimuli labelled as scary ($F_{1,29} = 0.1$, $p = 0.7$). As table 6 shows, there was a large number of trials that did not elicit a blink response, but there was no significant difference in the number of no-response trials between the groups ($F_{1,29} = 0.4$, $p = 0.5$). Trials with no blink response were also evenly distributed across the 'nice' and 'scary' categories. There was no significant difference between the groups on the number of trials rejected ($F_{1,29} = 2$, $p = 0.2$).

(a) Control group

In order to characterize the pattern of responses elicited by this paradigm in control children, prior to the group analysis the results from the control group were explored. Statistical analysis was carried out with a paired *t*-test.

Analysis of the results from the control group showed that there was a significant difference between the blink amplitudes to the two picture categories ($t = -3$, d.f. = 15, $p = 0.006$). This was due to increased amplitude responses to pictures categorized as 'nice' (see Fig. 12.3). There was no significant difference between blink latencies to the two picture categories (nice–scary: paired *t*-test: $t = 1$, d.f. = 15, $p = 0.3$) (see Fig. 12.4).

(b) Group analysis

To compare responses of the control group with those of the autistic group, a mixed ANOVA was computed with Group (autism, control) as the

Table 12.6   Numbers of trials with no blink response and numbers of rejected trials (means ± s.e.m.; total number of trials: 30).

group	no. of trials with no response	no. of trials rejected
control	14.2 ± 2.1	1.7 ± 0.5
autistic	12.1 ± 2.7	2.9 ± 0.6

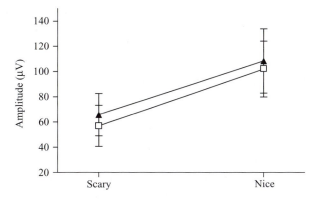

Fig. 12.3 Blink response according to individual child's picture categorization (mean ± s.e.m.). Squares represent control group and triangles represent autistic group.

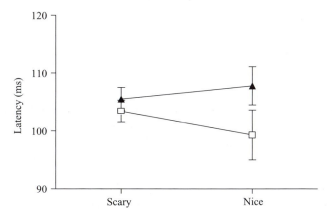

Fig. 12.4 Mean latency of blink response by picture category (mean ± s.e.m.). Squares represent control group and triangles represent autistic group.

between-subjects factor and Picture Type (scary, nice) as the within-subjects factor. The amplitude analysis revealed a main effect of Picture Type, ($F_{1,26} = 9.79$, $p < 0.01$), which occurred because the response to 'nice' pictures was larger than for 'scary' pictures in both groups (autism: scary = 65.7 μV, nice = 108.5 μV; control scary = 56.8 μV, nice = 102.06 μV). There was no main effect of Group or Group by Picture Type interaction (see Fig. 12.3). There were no group differences in latency responses (see Fig. 12.4).

There was no relationship between the amplitude of the startle response and the detection of amygdala structural abnormality in the autistic group.

12.10 Discussion: emotional modulation of the startle response

In this study, both the autistic and the control groups showed a greater startle response to pleasant compared with unpleasant stimuli. To the extent that modulation of the startle response is regulated by the amygdala, the present results provide no evidence to suggest functional abnormality of this structure in the autistic group.

The results are consistent with those of two prior studies reporting trends towards larger startle responses to pleasant compared with unpleasant stimuli in school-aged children (Cook *et al.* 1995; McManis *et al.* 1995). Neither of the two previous studies used the children's individual ratings of the stimuli, which might explain why the trends were not statistically significant in those studies. This pattern of emotional modulation of the startle response is opposite to the one reported in adults and adolescents, who show fear potentiation of the response. It is not well understood why children show a reverse pattern of modulation of the startle response when visual stimuli are used to alter emotional state (Cook *et al.* 1995; McManis *et al.* 1995). In our study, this cannot be a peculiarity of the stimuli used, because adults tested with the same procedure showed the typical pattern of larger startle response to scary stimuli. Further research on the normative development of emotional modulation of the startle response will help to address this question and to understand abnormalities of the startle response in clinical populations.

One possible explanation for the reverse pattern of modulation seen in the children compared with the adult data involves attentional resource allocation. It has been previously reported that the modulation of the startle response in humans can reflect differing attentional processes (Bradley *et al.* 1993). When more attention is paid to arousing stimuli, less attention is paid to the startle probe and the response to the latter is therefore reduced. With respect to the current study, it is possible that the 'scary' stimuli were more arousing than 'nice' stimuli. This theory could be tested by having children rate stimuli on arousal, as has been done with adults (e.g. the International Affective Picture System; Lang *et al.* 1995). Measurement of galvanic skin responses may also help address this question.

One consideration in interpreting the results of our study is that only about half of the children with autism showed evidence of amygdala abnormalities in the MRI analysis. It is thus possible that modulation of the startle response would differ for children with and without autism if we restricted our analysis to include only the subgroup children with autism who had evidence of amygdala abnormalities. However, this explanation can be ruled out because the results of the analysis with only this subgroup were the same as those for the whole group. Another consideration when interpreting the results of our study is the low response rate in both groups. Although it is reported that up to 10% of subjects fail to show the startle response to even very intense stimuli (Ornitz 1999), the response rate in this study fell below this level. This may, at least in part, be due to the low decibel level of the startle probe (see Berg and Balaban 1999). This was chosen to minimize subjects failing to complete the paradigm due to discomfort or dislike of the probe.

In conclusion, affective modulation of the startle response was not found to be different in controls and in the autistic group. We cannot rule out that emotional modulation of the startle response differs for autistic children compared with controls either early or later in the development of this response. This possibility is worth pursuing, because the non-verbal nature of the paradigm potentially lends itself to the study of all individuals with autism, regardless of their intellectual abilities.

12.11 Summary

This paper has explored both structural and functional approaches in an attempt to uncover the role of the amygdala in autism. Individual VBM analyses revealed abnormality in a number of different regions of the brain and substantial heterogeneity in the pattern of abnormality. Only half the group showed structural abnormalities in the amygdala. The startle response paradigm thought to reflect aspects of amygdala function was used for the first time with autistic children. Unexpectedly, the emotional modulation of the startle response was not found to differ significantly between the two groups. The results suggest that abnormality in the amygdala may not be a core feature of autism. These results need to be confirmed in a larger sample of autistic children and extended to investigate the precise combinations and extents of abnormalities associated with the disorder.

Many thanks to all the children and their families who took part in this study and to the National Autistic Society (UK) for help with recruitment. This research was supported by the Wellcome Trust and the Medical Research Council. Research at the Institute of Child Health and Great Ormond Street Hospital for Children NHS Trust benefits from Research and Development Funding from the NHS Executive.

References

Anthony, B. J. (1985). In the blink of an eye: implications of reflex modification for information processing. In *Advances in psychophysiology* (ed. P. K. Ackles, J. R. Jennings and M. G. H. Coles), pp. 167–218. Greenwich, CT: JAI Press.

Aylward, E. H., Minshew, N. J., Goldstein, G., Honeycutt, N. A., Augustine, A. M., Yates, K. O., *et al.* (1999). MRI volumes of amygdala and hippocampus in non-mentally retarded autistic adolescents and adults. *Neurology* **52**, 2145–50.

Bachevalier, J. (1994). Medial temporal lobe structures and autism: a review of clinical and experimental findings. *Neuropsychologia* **32**, 627–48.

Bailey, A., Luthert, P., Dean, A., Harding, B., Janola, I., Montgomery, M., *et al.* (1998). A clinicopathological study of autism. *Brain* **121**, 889–905.

Balaban, M. T. (1995). Affective influences on startle in five-month-old infants: reactions to facial expressions of emotions. *Child Dev.* **66**, 28–36.

Barbas, H. and Blatt, G. J. (1995). Topographically specific hippocampal projections target functionally distinct prefrontal areas in the rhesus monkey. *Hippocampus* **5**, 511–33.

Barbas, H. and De Olmos, J. (1990). Projections from the amygdala to basoventral and mediodorsal prefrontal regions in the rhesus monkey. *J. Comp. Neurol.* **334**, 1–18.

Baron-Cohen, S., Ring, H. A., Wheelwright, S., Bullmore, E. T., Brammer, M. J., Simmons, A., *et al.* (1999). Social intelligence in the normal and autistic brain: an fMRI study. *Eur. J. Neurosci.* **11**, 1891–98.

Baron-Cohen, S., Ring, H. A., Bullmore, E. T., Wheelwright, S., Ashwin, C. and Williams, S. C. (2000). The amygdala theory of autism. *Neurosci. Biobehav. Rev.* **24**, 355–64.

Bauman, M. L. (1991). Microscopic neuroanatomic abnormalities in autism. *Pediatrics* **87**, 791–96.

Bauman, M. and Kemper, T. L. (1985). Histoanatomic observations of the brain in early infantile autism. *Neurology* **35**, 866–74.

Bauman, M. and Kemper, T. L. (1994). Neuroanatomic observations of the brain in autism. In *The neurobiology of autism* (ed. M. Bauman and T. L. Kemper), pp. 119–145. Baltimore, MD: Johns Hopkins University Press.

Berg, W. K. and Balaban, M. T. (1999). Startle elicitation: stimulus parameters, recording techniques and quantification. In *Startle modification: implications for neuroscience, cognitive science and clinical science* (ed. M. E. Dawson, A. M. Schell and A. H. Bohmelt), pp. 21–50. Cambridge: Cambridge University Press.

Bradley, M. M., Cuthbert, B. N. and Lang, P. J. (1993). Pictures as prepulse: attention and emotion in startle modification. *Psychophysiology* **30**, 541–45.

Carper, R. A. and Courchesne, E. (2000). Inverse correlation between frontal lobe and cerebellum sizes in children with autism. *Brain* **123**, 836–44.

Cook, E. W., Hawk, L. W., Hawk, T. M. and Hummer, K. (1995). Affective modulation of startle in children. *Psychophysiology* **32**, S25.

Davis, M. (1989). The role of the amygdala and its efferent projections in fear and anxiety. In *Psychopharmacology of anxiety* (ed. P. Tyrer), pp. 52–79. Oxford: Oxford University Press.

Davis, M., Walker, D. L. and Lee, Y. (1999). Neurophysiology and neuorpharmacology of startle and its affective modification. In *Startle modification: implications for neuroscience, cognitive science and clinical science* (ed. M. E. Dawson, A. M. Schell and A. H. Bohmelt), pp. 114–36. Cambridge: Cambridge University Press.

De-Bellis, M. D., Casey, B. J., Dahl, R. E., Williamson, D. E., Thomas, K. M., Axelson, D. A., *et al.* (2000). A pilot study of amygdala volumes in pediatric generalized anxiety disorder. *Biol. Psychiat.* **48**, 51–7.

Gadian, D. G., Aicardi, J., Watkins, K. E., Porter, D. A., Mishkin, M. and Vargha-Khadem, F. (2000). Developmental amnesia associated with early hypoxic-ischaemic injury. *Brain* **123**, 499–507.

Heath, R. G. and Harper, J. W. (1974). Ascending projections of the cerebellar fastigial nucleus to the hippocampus, amygdala, and other temporal lobe sites: evoked potential and histological studies in monkeys and cats. *Exp. Neurol.* **45**, 268–87.

Heath, R. G., Dempesy, C. W., Fontana, C. J. and Myers, W. A. (1978). Cerebellar stimulation: effects on septal region, hippocampus and amygdala of cats and rats. *Biol. Psychiat.* **13**, 501–29.

Heaton, R. K. (1981). *Wisconsin card sorting test*. Odessa: Psychological Assessment Resources.

Henderson, S. E. and Sugden, D. A. (1992). *Movement assessment battery for children*. Sidcup, UK: The Psychological Corporation.

Hobson, R. P., Ouston, J. and Lee, A. (1988). What's in a face? The case of autism. *Br. J. Psychol.* **79**, 441–53.

Howard, M. A., Cowell, P. E., Boucher, J., Broks, P., Mayes, A., Farrant, A., *et al.* (2000). Convergent neuroanatomical and behavioural evidence of an amygdala hypothesis of autism. *Neuroreport* **11**, 2931–35.

Howlin, P. and Asgharian, A. (1999). The diagnosis of autism and Asperger syndrome: findings from a survey of 770 families. *Dev. Med. Child Neurol.* **41**, 834–39.

Krug, D. A., Arick, J. R. and Almond, P. J. (1993). *Autism screening instrument for educational planning: an assessment and educational planning system for autism and developmental disabilities*. Austin, TX: Pro-Ed.

Lang, P. J., Bradley, M. M. and Cuthbert, B. N. (1990). Emotion, attention, and the startle reflex. *Psychol. Rev.* **97**, 377–95.

Lang, P. J., Bradley, M. M. and Cuthbert, B. N. (1992). A motivational analysis of emotion: reflex–cortex connections. *Psychol. Sci.* **3**, 44–49.

Lang, P. J., Bradley, M. M. and Cuthbert, B. N. (1995). *International affective picture system (IAPS): technical manual and affective manual*. Gainesville, FL: The Center for Research In Psychophysiology, University of Florida.

McManis, M. H., Bradley, M. M., Cuthbert, B. N. and Lang, P. J. (1995). Kids have feelings too: children's physiological responses to affective pictures. *Psychophysiology* **33**, S53.

Middleton, F. A. and Strick, P. L. (1994). Anatomical evidence for cerebellar and basal ganglia involvement in higher cognitive function. *Science* **266**, 458–61.

Nagahama, Y., Fukuyama, H., Yamauchi, H., Matsuzaki, S., Konishi, J., Shibasaki, H., *et al.* (1996). Cerebral activation during performance of a card sorting test. *Brain* **119**, 1667–75.

Ornitz, E. M. (1999). Startle modification in children and developmental effects. In *Startle modification: implications for neuroscience, cognitive science and clinical science* (ed. M. E. Dawson, A. M. Schell and A. H. Bohmelt), pp. 245–68. Cambridge: Cambridge University Press.

Otsuka, H., Harada, M., Mori, K., Hisaoka, S. and Nishitani, H. (1999). Brain metabolites in the hippocampus–amygdala region and cerebellum in autism: an ^{1}H-MR spectroscopy study. *Neuroradiology* **41**, 517–19.

Pierce, K., Muller, R. A., Ambrose, J., Allen, G. and Courchesne, E. (2001). Face processing occurs outside the fusiform 'face area' in autism: evidence from functional MRI. *Brain* **124**, 2059–73.

Raymond, G. V., Bauman, M. and Kemper, T. L. (1989). The hippocampus in autism: Golgi analysis. *Ann. Neurol.* **26**, 483–84.

Rosen, J. B., Hamerman, E., Sitcoske, M., Glowa, J. R. and Schulkin, J. (1996). Hyperexcitability: exaggerated fear-potentiated startle produced by partial amygdala kindling. *Behav. Neurosci.* **110**, 43–50.

Salmond, C. H. (2001). Investigations into the role of the medial temporal lobes in autism. PhD thesis, University of London.

Salmond, C. H., Ashburner, J., Vargha-Khadem, F., Gadian, D. G. and Friston, K. J. (2000). Detecting bilateral abnormalities with voxel-based morphometry. *Hum. Brain Map.* **11**, 223–32.

Salmond, C. H., Ashburner, J., Vargha-Khadem, F., Connelly, A., Gadian, D. G. and Friston, K. J. (2002). Distributional assumptions in voxel-based morphometry. *NeuroImage* **17**, 1027–30.

Sasaki, M., Jinnai, K., Gemba, H., Hashimoto, S. and Mizuno, N. (1979). Projection of the cerebellar dentate nucleus onto the frontal association cortex in monkeys. *Exp. Brain Res.* **37**, 193–98.

Schmahmann, J. D. and Pandya, D. N. (1997). Anatomic organization of the basilar pontine projections from prefrontal cortices in rhesus monkey. *J. Neurosci.* **17**, 438–458.

Schmidt, L. A. and Fox, N. A. (1998). Fear-potentiated startle responses in temperamentally different human infants. *Dev. Psychobiol.* **32**, 113–20.

Stuss, D. T., Benson, D. F., Kaplan, E. F., Weir, W. S., Naeser, M. A., Lieberman, I., *et al.* (1983). The involvement of orbitofrontal cerebrum in cognitive tasks. *Neuropsychologia* **21**, 235–48.

Stuss, D. T., Levine, B., Alexander, M. P., Hong, J., Palumbo, C., Hamer, L., *et al.* (2000). Wisconsin card sorting test performance in patients with focal frontal and posterior brain damage: effects of lesion location and test structure on separable cognitive processes. *Neuropsychologia* **38**, 388–402.

Sugawara, M., Sadeghpour, M., Traversay, J. D. and Ornitz, E. M. (1994). Prestimulation induced modulation of the P300 component of event related potentials accompanying startle in children. *Electroenceph. Clin. Neurophysiol.* **90**, 201–13.

Teunisse, J. and Gelder, B. D. (2001). Impaired categorical perception of facial expressions in high-functioning adolescents with autism. *Neuropsychol. Dev. Cogn. Sect. C Child Neuropsychol.* **7**, 1–14.

Thomas, K. M., Drevets, W. C., Dahl, R. E., Ryan, N. D., Birmaher, B., Eccard, C. H., *et al.* (2001). Amygdala response to fearful faces in anxious and depressed children. *Arch. Gen. Psychiat.* **58**, 1057–63.

Van Paesschen, W., Connelly, A., Johnson, C. L. and Duncan, J. S. (1996). The amygdala and intractable temporal lobe epilepsy: a quantitative magnetic resonance imaging study. *Neurology* **47**, 1021–31. (Published erratum appears in *Neurology* 1997 **48**, 1751.)

Van Paesschen, W., Connelly, A., King, M. D., Jackson, G. D. and Duncan, J. S. (1997). The spectrum of hippocampal sclerosis: a quantitative magnetic resonance imaging study. *Ann. Neurol.* **41**, 41–51.

Wechsler, D. (1991). *Wechsler intelligence scale for children.* Sidcup, UK: The Psychological Corporation.

Wechsler, D. (1997). *Wechsler adult intelligence scale.* London: The Psychological Corporation.

Wilson, B., Cockburn, J. and Baddeley, A. D. (1991). *The Rivermead behavioural memory test.* Bury St Edmonds: Thames Valley Test Company.

Glossary

AT2: amygdala T_2
AS: Asperger syndrome
HCT2: hippocampal T_2
HFA: high-functioning autism
IQ: intelligence quotient
MRI: magnetic resonance imaging
OFC: orbitofrontal cortex
STG: superior temporal gyrus
TE: echo time
TR: repetition time
VBM: voxel-based morphometry
vEOG: vertical electro-oculogram

13

The role of the fusiform face area in social cognition: implications for the pathobiology of autism

Robert T. Schultz, David J. Grelotti, Ami Klin,
Jamie Kleinman, Christiaan Van der Gaag,
René Marois, and Pawel Skudlarski

A region in the lateral aspect of the fusiform gyrus (FG) is more engaged by human faces than any other category of image. It has come to be known as the 'fusiform face area' (FFA). The origin and extent of this specialization is currently a topic of great interest and debate. This is of special relevance to autism, because recent studies have shown that the FFA is hypoactive to faces in this disorder. In two linked functional magnetic resonance imaging (fMRI) studies of healthy young adults, we show here that the FFA is engaged by a social attribution task (SAT) involving perception of human-like interactions among three simple geometric shapes. The amygdala, temporal pole, medial prefrontal cortex, inferolateral frontal cortex and superior temporal sulci were also significantly engaged. Activation of the FFA to a task without faces challenges the received view that the FFA is restricted in its activities to the perception of faces. We speculate that abstract semantic information associated with faces is encoded in the FG region and retrieved for social computations. From this perspective, the literature on hypoactivation of the FFA in autism may be interpreted as a reflection of a core social cognitive mechanism underlying the disorder.

Keywords: amygdala; autism; fusiform face area; medial prefrontal cortex; social cognition; superior temporal sulcus

13.1 Introduction

For the first time, the field of autism has a replicated neurofunctional marker of the disorder—hypoactivation of the FFA. The FFA is that region of the middle aspect of the right FG that is selectively engaged by faces (when contrasted with object perception tasks) (Puce *et al.* 1995; Kanwisher *et al.* 1997; Kanwisher 2000). Anatomically, the middle portion of the FG is split along its rostral–caudal extent by a shallow mid-fusiform sulcus, (MFS). In fMRI, the centre of activation in face perception tasks is typically offset towards the lateral aspect of the FG, in the right hemisphere (Haxby *et al.* 1999). Whereas individual subjects may or may not also show left FG activation during face perception, group composites always show right-side activations to be larger. At least five fMRI studies have shown that older children, adolescents and adults with autism spectrum disorders have reduced levels of activity to images of the human face in this specialized face region of the right hemisphere (Critchley *et al.* 2000; Dierks *et al.* 2001; Pierce *et al.* 2001; Schultz *et al.* 2000*a*, 2001). These data are consistent with an older, and more extensive, psychology literature documenting performance deficits in face perception (Langdell 1978; Klin *et al.* 1999), and facial expression recognition in autism (e.g. Hobson *et al.* 1988*a,b*; MacDonald *et al.* 1989; Yirmiya *et al.* 1992). They seem to provide an important clue as to the neural ontogeny and pathobiology of autism.

Whereas the consistency of these findings is encouraging, what it means to have an under-responsive FFA remains unclear. Our initial interpretation of this finding focused on the role of experience for shaping the visual cortices (Schultz *et al.* 2000*a,b*; Grelotti *et al.* 2001). It is known that the ventral temporal visual areas are quite plastic and can be moulded by early experiences (Gaffan *et al.* 1988; Webster *et al.* 1991; Fujita *et al.* 1992; Löwel and Singer 1992). Persons with autism pay much less attention to the face (Osterling and Dawson 1994; Klin *et al.* 2002) and this may be why they fail to acquire normal perceptual skill in this domain. Inadequate attention to faces during critical periods of cortical development should affect the maturation of these areas, and presumably lead to underactivation of the FFA during face perception.

This interpretation fits nicely into the perceptual expertise model of the FFA, first championed by Gauthier and colleagues (Gauthier *et al.* 1999, 2000). Gauthier has shown, in two elegant fMRI studies, that the FFA responds preferentially to any class of object for which a person is perceptually 'expert'. For example, she found that bird experts engage the FFA more strongly when viewing birds than cars, but the reverse is true for car experts (Gauthier *et al.* 2000). Moreover, normal young adults can enhance their FFA activity to a class of novel objects through extensive perceptual training (Gauthier *et al.* 1999). Interpreting the hypoactivation of the FFA in autism from an expertise model, however, argues that this finding is an outcome of having autism rather than part of the cause. In other words, the hypoactivation of the FFA is merely a reflection of the social disability, the culmination of a set of developmental experiences across many years whereby the person has reduced interest in other people and pays inadequate attention to their faces. In this regard, the under-responsiveness of the FFA is a biological marker. Identifying an endophenotype such as this is extremely important and takes the field one significant step closer to understanding the underlying biological mechanisms, but it falls short of providing a snapshot of the brain mechanisms that actually cause autism.

An alternative view would be that the FFA is a core component of the 'social brain'. Data emerging over recent years from neuroimaging studies, human lesion studies and animal studies suggest a working model of the social brain that comprises a diverse set of frontal, limbic and temporal lobe circuitry. Select aspects of the orbital and medial prefrontal cortices, the amygdala and lateral aspects of the temporal cortex involving the STS have each been implicated in social functioning (Brothers 1990; Fletcher *et al*. 1995; Baron-Cohen *et al*. 1999; Frith and Frith 1999; Allison *et al*. 2000; Castelli *et al*. 2000, 2002; Schultz *et al*. 2000*b*). The frontal and temporal cortices have dense, and often reciprocal, connections to the amygdala (Carmichael and Price 1995; Price *et al*. 1996). The amygdala is centrally positioned, and capable of modulating and interpreting the emotional significance of data processed in the perceptual cortices, as well as assisting with the integration of emotion and cognition for decision making and action in the frontal cortices (Amaral *et al*. 1992; Schultz *et al*. 2000*b*). Collectively, this system defines a heuristic model of the social brain, with the precise functions of each node only understood in an, as yet, superficial manner.

But is there a role for the FFA in this social circuitry? Whereas the role of the FG in face perception is undisputed, only one prior study has implicated the FFA in social cognition. Castelli *et al*. (2000) used social animations involving interacting geometric shapes to probe the social brain. These animations were based on the classic study of Heider and Simmel (1944) that showed how certain movements by inanimate objects could strongly and automatically suggest personal agency, and that a group of interacting geometric forms will naturally suggest social interactions. All but one of the 34 female college students in Heider and Simmel's study described the animations through a social lens and in human terms (e.g. shapes chase one another, fight, entrap, play, get frightened, elated, etc.). It seems that the contingent nature of the shape movements and the fact that their movements violate the rules of simple physics (i.e. the shapes seem to have 'agency' or will) naturally invoke social cognitive and social perceptual ideation. Using PET in six healthy young adults, Castelli *et al*. showed that interpreting this type of animation engaged the medial prefrontal cortices, the TP, the STS and the right FG. Although the localization of the fusiform activations in their study is in the area generally reported to be the FFA, it is not clear whether this region of activation would have overlapped with the FFA in these subjects, as location of the FFA can vary from person to person. Nevertheless, engagement of the right FG by a social cognitive task that does not involve images of the face suggests that this FG region may have a broader, more important set of functions, extending beyond simple face perception. As such, it provides a basis to argue that the hypoactivation of the FFA to faces in autism might be illuminating part of a causal mechanism, as opposed to a developmental consequence of having autism.

The current study also used an adaptation of the procedure of Heider and Simmel (1944), involving what Klin (2000) called the SAT. Klin (2000) used the SAT to show how persons with autism fail to spontaneously impose social meaning on these types of movements. Other investigators have also reported a paucity of theory of mind ideation among persons with autism to other renditions of the Heider–Simmel procedure (Abell *et al.* 2000; Bowler and Thommen 2000). Use of simple shapes to display human social interactions without perceptual representations of real people strips the social event down to the essential elements needed to convey social meanings. In this regard, the SAT is an ideal neuroimaging probe for assessing social cognitive and social perceptual processes in a way that is not confounded by perceptual processes that would be provoked if actual images of faces or people were used. The original SAT from Klin (2000) is a 50 s silent film in which three moving geometric shapes (a circle, a small triangle and a larger triangle) interact with each other in a social manner. Interestingly, in Klin's study, some attributions by those with an autism spectrum disorder were given in terms of physical meaning (e.g. magnetic forces), not social meaning. We took note of this observation in developing the following fMRI experiments, and created a control task for the SAT that involves judgements of object mass.

In two fMRI studies of the same group of normal control subjects, we show that the FG is robustly engaged by an adaptation of the SAT suitable for a block design fMRI study. Engagement of the right FG by non-face stimuli suggests that this region has functions beyond static face perception. To test the exact location of the fusiform activations during the SAT, nine of the 12 participants consented to return for a fMRI study of face perception. Results from this second study found the location of the FFA to be highly overlapping with the FG activations to the SAT. Thus, making social judgements on non-face geometric figures, and making identity judgements on grey-scale pictures of human faces, draws upon a similar neural substrate in the FG. This result challenges the specificity of the middle portion of the FG for faces, and raises the possibility that the FFA is part of the primary circuitry for social cognition. As such, it has important implications for the hypoactivation of the FFA in autism, and more generally, for specifying a distributed social network whose dysfunction might cause autism.

13.2 Methods

(a) Participants

Twelve participants were recruited for this study from the staff and student populations at Yale University. The sample included six men (three left-handed) and six women (one left-handed), ranging in age from 20 to 31 years (mean $\pm$ s.d. $= 24.2 \pm 3.1$). Participants were screened for neurological and DSM IV Axis I psychiatric disorders. Estimated full-scale IQ, as measured by four subtests of the Wechsler Adult Intelligence Scale, 3rd edition (Wechsler 1997) averaged 128.8 ($\pm$ 10.4) (Information, Vocabulary, Picture Completion and Block Design). All subjects scored in the normal range on the Benton Test of Facial Recognition (Benton 1994) (raw score range: 41–50;

mean $\pm$ s.d. $= 46.8 \pm 2.6$). There were no significant differences between the sexes on any of these variables.

Nine of the twelve agreed to participate in a follow-up fMRI study of face perception conducted so that localization of the FFA could be compared with SAT activations in the middle FG area in the right hemisphere. Five were male (one left-handed) and four were female (one left-handed); mean age was 23.6 ± 2.6 years. All subjects gave written informed consent for both studies in accordance with procedures and protocols approved by the Institutional Review Board of the Yale University School of Medicine.

(b) Experimental tasks

We adapted the SAT for use in a fMRI block-design study by programming 16 new SAT QuickTime film skits using Director published by Macromedia (600 Townsend Ave, San Francisco, CA; www.macromedia.com). From these, a final set of eight were chosen for use in the fMRI study on the basis of ratings by project staff of the film's realism and ability to capture one's social attention (these films can be downloaded from http://info.med.yale.edu/chldstdy/neuroimg/sat_movies.htm). Each film lasted 15.1 s and was designed like the original SAT with movements intended to suggest a sense of personal agency, and reciprocal and contingent interactions that were meant to be easily interpreted as social. Each film contained three types of white geometric figures (a triangle, diamond and circle) that moved against a black background. In common with the original SAT, there was a box in the centre of the field, with one wall that opened as if on a hinge, allowing the shapes to open and shut the door, and to enter, chase or drag other shapes inside. Each film was scripted to follow a social story, for example, hide-andseek, a fight, a love triangle, etc. The participants were asked to decide, by pushing a button, if all three of the shapes were 'friends' or not. Half of the films were intended to have 'all friends' as the correct answer (correct answer was determined by a consensus-rating process among the developers of the tasks, with each final film version judged to have a clear answer). The films were scripted such that any adversarial interactions occurred in the final few seconds of the film, to force the participant to attend throughout to derive the correct answer. In creating our control task for contrast to the SAT, we reasoned that each SAT film requires three important processes:

(i) monitoring the movements and physical interactions between the shapes;
(ii) pretending that the shapes represent something else, i.e. people; and
(iii) an inferential, social reasoning process based on the nature of the interactions (judging whether the movements represent friendly or non-friendly interactions).

A 'bumper car' control task was created that contained all of the elements of the SAT films, with the exception of the social reasoning process. This task also entailed eight 15.1 s films depicting the same geometric shapes moving about a black field with the same centrally positioned white box. The participant's task was to pretend that these figures were 'bumper cars'—small racing cars found at amusement parks that are encapsulated by rubber bumpers to allow safe, playful collisions. Participants monitored the car's movements and interactions, and decided on the basis of the car's trajectories and speed after each collision if the three shapes were all equally 'heavy' or not, for example, upon collision, if one car shot off more rapidly than another, then the two were not equally heavy. Key collisions that gave away the correct answer always occurred in the final seconds of the film. Collisions early in the 15.1 s skit were often mere grazes that failed to provide definitive information about relative mass. Thus, the control task contained the first two elements, but instead of a social decision, participants were required to make a decision about a physical property. The bumper car and SAT films were designed to be equivalent with respect to movement quantity and location, so that the comparison between the two tasks would reveal the location of brain processes that are distinctly involved in social perceptual and social cognitive processes. It is interesting to note that we piloted a version of the control task that involved physical judgements on the SAT films (as opposed to the bumper car films), but participants reported that they were not able to consciously stop seeing the films as social stories. Thus, it did not seem possible to use the exact same stimuli in both tasks as might otherwise be desirable, because social perceptual and cognitive processes would probably be engaged to a greater or lesser extent in both the experimental and control tasks. Two other lower level control conditions were also included in each experimental run in the block design, and were intended to further pull apart the three distinct processes outlined above. However, the results of these contrasts were generally uninformative and thus are not reported here. Between each film was a 12 s rest period with a black screen. All participants underwent practice, using films that did not make the final group of eight, in order to become completely familiar with the tasks before fMRI scanning. During the fMRI experiment, each film was preceded by a 3 s cue: 'BUMPER CARS, SAME WEIGHT?' or 'PEOPLE, ALL FRIENDS?' Subjects responded by pressing a button upon completion of each film, both as a measure of reaction time and accuracy, and to ensure that the subjects watched the entire film.

In the follow-up study (hereafter, 'Study 2') side-by-side grey-scale faces, objects or patterns were presented in a same/different task, in a block-design experiment to localize the FFA. We have previously used this task to localize the FFA in a large group of normal controls (Schultz *et al.* 2000*b*, 2001). Image pairs were presented for 2.8 s, with a 0.5 s inter-stimulus interval. The person identity task employed same-gender pairs of neutral (non expressive) faces on a black background. Pictures were taken from standard sources and were edited to remove hair, ears and shirt collars, so as to force subjects to focus on features of the face with central relevance to non-verbal social communication, i.e. the eyes, nose, mouth and face geometry. Objects were pictures of spectacles taken from an online retail catalogue that were contrast inverted to make the background black and the spectacles shades of grey, to match the faces. Patterns were distorted versions of the faces or spectacles. Results from contrasts with patterns were not used to localize the FFA, and thus are not reported here. As is conventional, the face versus subordinate-level object-discrimination contrast defined the FFA. Each task block lasted 16.5 s, and was separated by a 10.5 s rest period during which cross hairs (+ +) centred in the same position as the image pairs flashed with the same presentation rate.

(c) Data acquisition

SAT and face perception fMRI data were collected on different occasions, averaging approximately 2.5 months apart (range: 3 weeks to 6 months). Only after the original 12 subjects completed the SAT fMRI study was the decision made to rescan subjects with the face-localization protocol. Changes in BOLD contrast were measured as subjects performed the SAT, bumper car, face-discrimination and object-discrimination tasks. The stimuli were run as QuickTime films in Study 1, and as PICT image files in Study 2. Studies were programmed in PSYSCOPE 1.2.5 PPC (Carnegie Mellon University, Pittsburgh, PA, USA) and run on a MacIntosh G3 computer. Images were back-projected onto a translucent screen mounted near the end of the MRI gantry, and were viewed through a periscopic prism system on the head coil. Behavioural response data were collected with a fibre-optic button box, with two response alternatives (Yes or No for 'all friends?', 'same weight?', 'same person?' and 'same object?'). The participant's head was immobilized using foam wedges, and tape across the forehead.

T2* weighted images sensitive to BOLD contrast were acquired on a GE Signa 1.5 Tesla scanner with a standard quadrature head coil, using a gradient echo, single-shot echo planar sequence and a coronal orientation perpendicular to the plane through the AC–PC. The pulse sequence for both studies was TR = 1500 ms, TE = 60, flip angle = 60, NEX = 1, in-plane voxel size = 3.125 mm × 3.125 mm. In the SAT study, we collected 14 coronal slices, 10 mm thick (skip 1 mm) starting at the anterior-most aspect of the frontal lobe, and covering all of the brain except the caudal-most aspect of the occipital lobe. Data were collected in four runs of an ABCD block design (block = one 15.1 s film), with blocks of each type presented twice per run in a pseudo-random order. Across runs, a total of 80 echo planar images were collected per slice, per task condition. In the face-perception study, we also collected 14 coronal slices perpendicular to the AC–PC, starting from the posterior aspect of the occipital cortex up through the rostral-most aspect of the cingulate gyrus. Slice thickness was 9 mm (skip 1 mm) to be compatible with a separate face-perception study ongoing at that time. Data were collected in a block design with a pseudorandom order across six separate runs, with three blocks of each task per run, for 180 echo planar images per slice, per task condition. Functional data in both studies were co-registered to T1- weighted structural images of the same thickness collected in the same session (TR = 500, TE = 14, field of view = 200 mm, 256 mm × 192 mm matrix, 2 NEX).

(d) Data analysis

Data were corrected for motion using SPM99 for three translation directions and for the three possible rotations (Wellcome Department of Cognitive Neurology, London, UK). Image volumes with centre of mass (*x, y* or *z*) movement of more than 1.5 mm within a run were discarded. Image analyses and tests of statistical significance were done using locally developed software (Skudlarski; http://mri.med.yale.edu/members_framed.html). Motion corrected images were spatially smoothed with a Gaussian filter with a full-width half-maximum value of 6.25 mm. The specific effects of each task were evaluated by creating *t*-maps for each imaging series, incorporating a correction for linear drift (Skudlarski *et al.* 1999), of specific task contrasts: social versus bumper car in Study 1, and face versus object in Study 2; *t*-maps were averaged across imaging series and co-registered with the higher resolution anatomical images for display and localization. These maps were then transformed, by in-plane registration and slice interpolation, into a proportional three-dimensional grid defined by Talairach and Tournoux (1988), and averaged across all subjects to create composite *t*-maps, with the acquired data in 14 slices interpolated to 18 slices (N.B. 16 slices are shown in Fig. 13.1, as fMRI activations on the first and last slice are corrupted by motion correction). The SAT versus bumper car maps are displayed in the figures using a significance level of $p < 0.0005$ (uncorrected). Face versus object *t*-maps were created and displayed at $p < 0.05$ (uncorrected) with the *a priori* hypothesis that the right lateral FG would define the FFA. No other brain areas are examined in the second study, thus avoiding any multiple comparison problem.

ROI analyses were conducted in the SAT study by tracing significant pixels on the group composite activation map (Fig. 13.1) in the following regions: the right FG, the right and left STS and STG, the right TP, the right amygdala, and right and left dorsal MPFC. To more thoroughly assess activity in the FG, medial and lateral FG ROIs (and the combined whole FG) were defined anatomically and traced across the two coronal slices where there was significant SAT activation. The activated SAT ROI for the FG is 33% of the size of the entire anatomically defined FG at those two slices. Individual subject data were interrogated using the ROIs to obtain the mean per cent signal change for each person for each region, and Talairach centre of mass coordinates (the centre of ROI activation, weighted by the amplitude of activation across the region). Mean per cent signal change data were used in correlational analyses to estimate the consistency of conjoint activity between ROIs, across subjects.

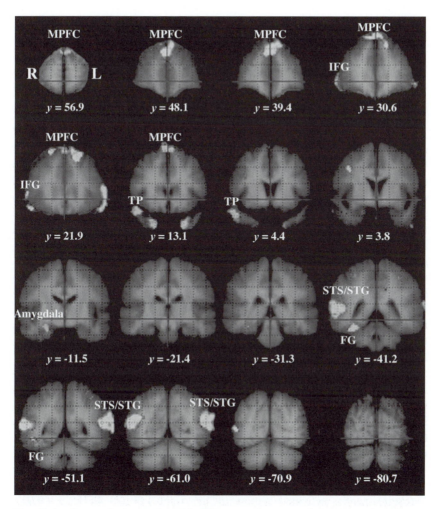

Fig. 13.1 Composite *t*-map for 12 healthy controls, contrasting the social attribution (yellow/red) and the bumper car (blue/purple) tasks ($p < 0.0005$). Right and left are reversed by convention. Abbreviations: BA, Brodman area; FG, fusiform gyrus; IFG, inferior frontal gyrus; MPFC, medial prefrontal cortex; STG, superior temporal gyrus; *Y*-coordinates are from the system of Talairach and Tournoux (1988). (See Plate 2 of the Plate Section, at the centre of this book.)

13.3 Results

(a) Behavioural performance

There were no significant differences between the social and bumper car tasks in performance accuracy ($t_{1,22} = 1.63$, $p > 0.10$; social $= 86 \pm 16\%$ correct; bumper $= 74 \pm 16\%$ correct) or reaction time ($t_{1,22} = 0.62$, $p > 0.60$). There were no significant differences in task accuracy between males and females or left-handers and right-handers. In addition, there were no significant correlations between task performance and age, Full Scale Intelligence Quotient or Benton Face Recognition performance.

(b) Brain activity associated with the social attribution task

As shown in Fig. 13.1, comparison of the SAT with the bumper car control condition resulted in a widely distributed set of significant activations. There was very little significant activation for the bumper car task, with the one region shown clearly in Fig. 13.1 being bilateral activation of the dorsal bank of the intra-parietal sulcus. The SAT network included a region within the right and left dorsal MPFC, the right and left inferior frontal gyrus, pars orbitalis and the lateral orbital gyrus, the right TP, the right amygdala, the right and left STS and STG, and the right FG. It is important to note that at lower thresholds (e.g. $p < 0.01$) there was also left amygdala activation, and a ROI analysis of the per cent signal change failed to find significantly more right than left amygdala activation. It is also worth noting that the FG activations seem quite specific to the SAT task, in the sense that reducing the threshold down to $p < 0.05$ failed to show additional ventral pathway activation. More widespread activations might have indicated a general SAT effect on arousal or attention that was manifested throughout the ventral stream, but this was not the case.

The largest areas of activation were the STG (especially on the right) and MPFC. Direct comparison of the right versus left MPFC mean per cent signal change failed to find significant differences (paired $t_{11} = 0.45$, $p > 0.50$). However, the right STG was significantly more activated than the left STG (paired $t_{11} = 2.64$, $p = 0.02$). Table 13.1 presents the Talairach coordinates for the centre of activation mass for each ROI. Table 13.2 presents a correlational matrix showing the consistency of conjoint activity between regions. The strongest correlation is between the right amygdala and the ROI that defines the significantly activated region of the right FG ($r = 0.71$, $p = 0.01$). Interestingly, this correlation is nominally larger than that of the entire FG and

Table 13.1 ROI centres of mass coordinates.

ROI	mean Talairach coordinates (X, Y, Z)		Brodmann areas
	right hemisphere	left hemisphere	
MPFC	4.9, 34.9, 43.6	$-7.4, 36.1, 43.4$	6, 8, 9
TP	46.3, 13.8, -12.8	—	38
amygdala	22.8, $-10.9, -12.4$	—	—
FG (SAT)	34.4, $-46.8, -9.0$	—	37
FG (face)	37.4, $-48.0, -12.6$	—	37
STG	50.7, $-57.1, 15.2$	$-56.5, -60.8, 19.4$	22, 39

Table 13.2 ROI correlation matrix (Correlations are based on mean per cent signal change from each ROI (see Section 2 for ROI procedures). SAT accuracy data represent the percentage of films that each participant correctly).

	activated right FG	whole right FG	right amygdala	left amygdala	left MPFC	right MPFC	left STG	right STG	right TP
whole right FG	0.69***								
right amygdala	0.71***	0.32							
left amygdala	0.56*	0.19	0.70***						
left MPFC	0.21	0.13	0.32	0.11					
right MPFC	−0.18	−0.08	0.21	0.19	0.48				
left STG	0.21	0.29	0.19	0.05	0.56*	0.18			
right STG	0.54*	0.69***	0.22	0.25	0.09	−0.16	0.60**		
right TP	−0.07	−0.11	0.40	0.33	0.48	0.34	0.38	−0.10	
SAT % accuracy	0.45	0.65**	−0.12	0.09	0.13	−0.17	−0.1	0.22	−0.34

$***p \leq 0.01$ ($r \geq 0.69$); $**p \leq 0.05$ ($r \geq 0.57$); $*p \leq 0.10$.

the smaller, subcomponent FG ROI defined by the SAT activated pixels ($r = 0.69$, $p = 0.013$). Since some correlation would be expected between these overlapping ROIs, especially since the data were spatially smoothed, the robust correlation to the amygdala is even more impressive. Other notable results from the correlation matrix include the lack of correlation between the MPFC and either the amygdala or temporal lobe ROIs. Within the temporal lobes, however, the right STG is significantly correlated with the left STG and with both definitions of the right FG.

Accuracy of performance on the SAT correlates with the amount of activity in the anatomically defined right FG ($r = 0.65$, $p = 0.02$) but not with any other node in the SAT network. Females showed significantly more right STG activation than males ($t_{10} = 2.34$, $p = 0.04$). Males, however, showed significantly more right TP activation ($t_{10} = 2.53$, $p = 0.03$). There were no other significant sex differences, and no significant associations with handedness or age.

(c) Comparison of activity in the right fusiform gyrus during social attribution task and face perception

At the time Study 1 data were collected, finding significant right FG activation to the SAT was unexpected. To clarify whether the FG activation was in the precise location of the FFA, we compared it with the result of the face versus object discrimination contrast (the standard means of identifying the FFA in the literature). Both the FFA and the SAT activations of the FG were confined to two coronal slices, in highly overlapping locations. These two sets of group composite maps are shown in Fig. 13.2. The FG activations were stronger in the SAT versus bumper contrast than the face versus object contrast, but this may have had as much do with the baseline as the experimental task. The Talairach coordinates for the SAT and FFA activations show that their centre of mass differs by less than one voxel. The SAT activation is 3 mm more medial than that of the FFA, straddling the MFS that delineates the lateral and medial aspects of the FG. The FFA, on the other hand, is clearly positioned in the lateral FG, as expected (Haxby *et al.* 1999). The SAT activation is also centred 3.6 mm more superior and about 1 mm more anteriorly than the FFA. A count of the overlapping significant pixels showed that 50% of the SAT activation falls within the FFA. This provides a good approximation of how these regions overlap. However, there is no definitive way to measure the percent overlap in this study, because it would change with the use of different control tasks in either condition or different significance levels for thresholding the *t*-maps.

Two of the participants (one male, one female) were also part of a reproducibility study of the FFA, and had both undergone the face discrimination protocol on two occasions. Figure 13.3 presents *t*-maps of their FG for each face perception study and the SAT. The female participant shows reversed asymmetry, as sometimes happens, with the left FG showing greater face activation

(a) SAT versus bumber car: FFA activation

(b) Enlargement and alignment of FFA

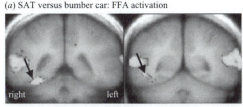

right   left

(c) Face versus object discrimination: FFA activation

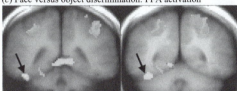

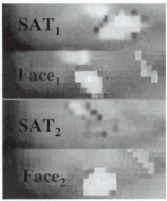

Fig. 13.2 (*a*) Composite (*n* = 12) *t*-map at two slices showing significant (*p* < 0.0005) activation for the SAT contrast (yellow/red) with the bumper car control task (blue/purple). (*b*) Composite (*n* = 9) *t*-map at two slices showing significant (*p* < 0.05) activation for the face (yellow/red) versus object discrimination (blue/purple). This contrast defines the FFA. (*c*) Subregions of composite *t*-maps shown in (*a*) and (*b*) are enlarged and aligned to demonstrate the overlap of activation in the FG for the SAT and face discrimination activations. Subscripts 1 and 2 refer to the first (more anterior) and second coronal slices with significant activation. (See Plate 3 of the Plate Section, at the centre of this book.)

than the right. Nevertheless, her SAT activations track her FFA and are more left-sided than typical. These results show that the FFA activation is reproducible, so that the less than perfect overlap between the FFA and the SAT FG activation is probably not a measurement or reliability issue.

13.4 Discussion

(a) The social brain network

The current study required participants to observe the movements of geometric figures, and to interpret these with regard to a conceptual template about what constitutes a friendly or unfriendly social interaction. It required close attention to the contingent nature of a sequence of movements, and inferences about mental states of each character to explain their actions. Perception of the movements of these simple shapes as wilful seems to be automatic and effortless for healthy controls, but not for persons with autism (Klin 2000). As shown in Fig. 13.1, the network engaged by the social attribution process (in contrast to the physical attribution control task) included nearly all of the brain areas implicated by past research on the social brain (Brothers 1990), including cognitive aspects, such as theory of mind (Castelli *et al.* 2000), as well as

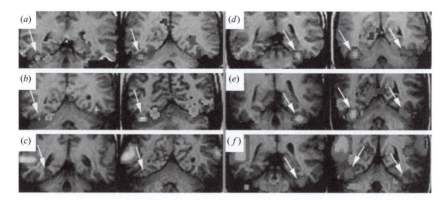

Fig. 13.3 Scans of two individuals across three different occasions showing the reproducibility of FFA activations at two timepoints, and relationship to SAT activations. (*a–c*) are from a 23-year-old male; (*d–f*) are from a 24-year-old female. Panels are arranged chronologically. (*a,d*) The first face versus object experiment. (*b,e*) The second face versus object scan. (*c,f*) SAT versus bumper car contrast. Both coronal slices are shown where there was FFA ($t \geqslant 1.5$ in yellow/red) or SAT activation ($t \geqslant 3.0$ in yellow/red). Arrows point to FG activity (right and left are reversed by convention). As in the group results (Fig. 13.2), the SAT activation is centred slightly more medially along the MFS. Left FG activation shown in these two subjects does not survive thresholding in the group composite (Fig. 13.2). Control tasks (object discrimination, bumper car) are shown in purple/blue. (See Plate 4 of the Plate Section, at the centre of this book.)

perceptual aspects, such as the perception of social displays and biological movement (Allison *et al.* 2000). We found significant activation of the bilateral MPFC, superior STG and STS, and inferior FG, pars orbitalis extending into the lateral orbital gyri. In addition, there were significant activations on the right side only for the amygdala, TP and the FG. The predominance of right-side activations is consistent with the notion that the right hemisphere is more concerned than the left with social processes (Siegal *et al.* 1996; Winner *et al.* 2002). Our results differ from some past research by finding significant right FG activation, and by failing to find orbito-MPFC activation.

Several earlier neuroimaging studies have shown that the dorsal MPFC (i.e. that cortex anterior and superior to the anterior cingulate gyrus) is a critical substrate for social judgements, including empathizing and thinking about other's thoughts and intentions (Fletcher *et al.* 1995; Goel *et al.* 1995; Happé *et al.* 1996; Castelli *et al.* 2000, 2002; Gallagher *et al.* 2000). Our findings are consistent with these imaging studies and with non-human primate studies that have documented social failures and loss of social position within the group following lesions to orbital prefrontal cortices and MPFC (Butter *et al.* 1969; Myers *et al.* 1973; Bachevalier and Mishkin 1986). The important role for the MPFC in social cognition is further suggested by studies of autism spectrum disorders that find functional abnormalities in this area (Happé *et al.* 1996;

Ernst *et al.* 1997; Haznedar *et al.* 1997; Castelli *et al.* 2002). Gusnard *et al.* (2001) suggest that the dorsal MPFC is involved in any kind of thought that uses the self as a referent. Thus, the SAT activations in this area may have been driven by theorizing about others' minds, but with explicit reference to the participant's own frame of reference as to how they would feel in a similar situation.

The orbital prefrontal cortex and to a lesser extent the dorsal MPFC have dense reciprocal connections with medial temporal areas (Carmichael and Price 1995; Price *et al.* 1996), providing the anatomical bases for a system that regulates emotional processes. Damasio and colleagues (Damasio *et al.* 1990; Bechara *et al.* 1996) have argued that the orbito-MPFC have a primary function of integrating information about rewards and punishments to bias future behaviour (Rolls 1995; Dias *et al.* 1996; Hornak *et al.* 1996; Lane *et al.* 1997; Reiman *et al.* 1997). A functional circuitry such as this would seem especially important in the development and acquisition of social behaviour. However, even acquired lesions to these regions in adulthood can result in abnormalities of social conduct (Damasio *et al.* 1990). Brothers (1990) highlighted the orbital prefrontal cortex as one of the three principal brain regions involved in social cognition. We observed poor signal in this region (these areas are notoriously prone to fMRI signal drop-out and distortion), and thus we cannot know if the orbital prefrontal region was engaged by the SAT or not. However, using a similar psychological task but with PET, where signal acquisition in this region is not degraded, Castelli *et al.* (2000, 2002) failed to find activation of the orbital prefrontal cortex. Collectively, these results call into question the importance of the orbital prefrontal cortex in social cognition, and instead shift the focus on anterior cortices toward the dorsal MPFC.

The SAT also generated robust activations of the right amygdala, and nearby cortex of the right TP. The amygdala is often given a central role in theories of social perception and cognition (Brothers 1990; Bachevalier 1994; Adolphs *et al.* 1998; Baron-Cohen *et al.* 2000; Schultz *et al.* 2000*b*). The amygdala has a critical role in emotional arousal, assigning significance to environmental stimuli and mediating the formation of visual-reward associations, that is, 'emotional' learning (Gaffan *et al.* 1988; LeDoux 1996; Anderson and Phelps 2001). It is reliably engaged during judgements of personality characteristics from pictures of the face or part of the face (Adolphs *et al.* 1998; Baron-Cohen *et al.* 1999; Winston *et al.* 2002). Activation of the amygdala appears to be automatic and stimulus driven, as it can be engaged by images of facial expressions in conscious awareness, as well as by subliminal presentations of faces displaying affect (Morris *et al.* 1998; Whalen *et al.* 1998; Critchley *et al.* 2000). Thus, the amygdala's engagement by the SAT could stem from the general emotional arousal evoked by the animations, or it could represent its computational role in some more specific social perceptual process.

The amygdala has dense reciprocal connections with the ventral visual processing stream (Amaral and Price 1984). The strong correlation observed in this study between the right amygdala and the right FG could indicate that emotional inputs from the amygdala to the FG are necessary for engaging the social computational processes of the FG. Brothers (1995) has speculated that the amygdala generates 'social feelings' that are of importance in cutting through the complexities of social situations and guiding behaviour by simpler, learned contingencies. Social events are complex because their meaning often comes from specific combinations of features that do not add up in a linear manner, making it more difficult to decompose the events by cognitive analysis. Effective social engagement requires *integration* of context, historical relationships and current social–emotional communications expressed through prosodic tone as well as facial expressions, posture and gesture. They are made more complex by the rapid pace of social transactions. This would necessitate some fast response system based on general principles from past social–emotional experiences, a role for which the amygdala would seem ideally suited. In other words, the amygdala might drive intuition or 'gut feelings' to guide rapid non-verbal social interactions involving facial expressions, gesture, etc. Thus, the strong amygdala–FG correlation observed here could be interpreted as the amygdala informing the FG of the relevance of a social event, and also of the outcome of its quick and dirty social perceptual analyses, thereby guiding the FG (and other social nodes) in their finer grained computations.

Perhaps the largest and strongest activations to the SAT were those of the posterior aspects of the STS, spreading into the adjacent STG. This area has been implicated as a specific site for perception of biological motion (Bonda *et al.* 1996; Allison *et al.* 2000; Grèzes *et al.* 2001; Vaina *et al.* 2001). Biological motion is a broad construct that seems to encompass the perception of static images of events that could move, or did move, such as facial expressions, as well as actual movement by animate objects. This region of the STS–STG is also critical for the decoding visual displays of social action or intention (e.g. gaze direction, gesture and facial displays of emotion) (Critchley *et al.* 2000; Hoffman and Haxby 2000). In this regard, the SAT activations here are completely expected, and a testament to the effectiveness of these animations in inducing the desired illusion of anthropomorphic action. The majority of the STS–STG activations were anterior to location of the V5/MT, as defined in other recent fMRI studies (Culham *et al.* 2001), but they also extended posteriorly into these more general movement sensitive cortices. Unlike the amygdala, some evidence suggests that activity of the STS is mediated by explicit attention to social characteristics of the face, and that STS engagement it is not automatic or stimulus driven (Winston *et al.* 2002). We surmise, therefore, that activation of the STS by the SAT was due to explicit task instructions to judge the social interactions.

(b) Role of the fusiform face area in social cognition

We also found significant SAT activation of the right FG. When compared directly in a subset of participants to their FFA gleaned from a separate scanning session with a perceptual discrimination task of person versus object identity, we found that both ROIs were confined to the right side, on the same two coronal slices. There was about 50% overlap between the SAT, FG and FFA activations, and the centre of the two activations differed by less than 1 voxel. The FFA activation was offset to the lateral prominence of the FG, whereas the SAT activated a region of the FG that was closer to the centre of the FG, but still largely in the lateral aspect. Because the SAT does not contain any face representations, the FFA engagement was unexpected, as this region is thought of as selective for faces (Kanwisher *et al.* 1997) or to other classes of complex objects for which one is perceptually expert (Gauthier *et al.* 2000).

These results have important implications for the possible role of the fusiform in social brain circuitry and autism. Interestingly, the magnitude of the FG activation predicted SAT task accuracy; no other ROI correlated significantly with task accuracy. This would seem to argue against any interpretation that the FFA activation is inconsequential to the SAT; that it is activated simply because it is well connected to other areas that are directly involved in the social attribution process. Using a task that is similar to the SAT, Castelli *et al.* (2000) also reported significant right FG activation using PET. However, in their follow-up PET study comparing autism and normal controls (Castelli *et al.* 2002), they failed to find significant FG activation in either group. The failure of their second study to find right FG activations may be due to the more stringent random effects model used in the data analyses. However, because we find right FG activation with fMRI, which is more sensitive than PET and because Castelli *et al.* (2000) found it with what amounts to a lower threshold, it seems quite probable that the effect is real. In fact, we have preliminary evidence from an ongoing fMRI study that reproduces the SAT FG activations in healthy controls (Schultz *et al.* 2001). In addition, there may be some task attributes that differ between our studies and Castelli *et al.*'s that might impact on the strength with which FG computational processes are evoked.

The key question, then, is why is the FG engaged by the SAT and what role does the right FG have in social cognition and perception? Currently, there are three competing theories of the functional organization of the FG and related ventral visual perceptual areas. One model, put forth by Haxby, Chao, Martin and colleagues, specifies that objects are encoded in a distributed fashion across a wide expanse of the ventral temporal-occipital cortex (Haxby *et al.* 2001). They call this the 'object form typology' model (Ishai *et al.* 1999). Their data indicate that object category specificity is achieved by unique spatial patterns of activation across this extrastriate visual cortex. They show that the pattern of activations across this cortex is diagnostic of object category membership, more so than any localized activation maxima (Haxby *et al.* 2001). They also argue that object category perception involves retrieval of category-related information about specific features and attributes of the object category (Chao *et al.* 2002). They admit that the 'nature of the information about objects that is represented in the ventral temporal cortex is a great puzzle' (Haxby *et al.* 2000, p. 4), but open the possibility that semantic information may be important.

A second view championed by Kanwisher *et al.* holds that several select perceptual categories, including faces, bodies and spatial layout of places are encoded in highly specific locations, in a modular fashion (Kanwisher *et al.* 1997; Epstein and Kanwisher 1998; Downing *et al.* 2001; Spiridon and Kanwisher 2002). The FFA is thought to be most concerned with discriminating among individual identities, and not with discriminating images at the categorical level. In fact, lesions to the FFA cause a specific deficit in recognizing individual identities, but not in recognizing the general category of face versus non-face (Wada and Yamamoto 2001). Spiridon and Kanwisher (2002) provide a partial replication of Haxby *et al.*'s (2001) object form typology model. They show that patterns of ventral visual cortical activation can distinguish object categories. Nevertheless, their data show category specificity for select areas, such as the FFA, and they argue the ventral visual cortex is not equipotential.

Gauthier *et al.*, however, have argued that the ventral occipital temporal pathway is organized by the nature of the perceptual computations, and that these processing biases are acquired through experience (Gauthier *et al.* 2000; Tarr and Gauthier 2000). For example, the parahippocampal place area is a function of a bias towards processing landscapes in terms of their spatial layout, because we have learned through repeated experiences that this is very useful information to extract when perceiving landscapes and related visual images. Similarly, we learn quite early in life that it is important to discriminate faces on an individual level, for example, discriminating mother from others. This bias towards individual identification, according to Gauthier, accounts for the FFA's apparent modularity (Gauthier *et al.* 1997, 2000; Tarr and Gauthier 2000). According to this third model, the type of information needed and our cumulative experience in processing that information organizes the ventral occipital–temporal pathway into regional centres with preferred modes of processing.

All three models seem to agree that the functional organization of the ventral visual cortices is driven by the need to categorize perceptions into object classes. We believe that our findings showing FFA activation by nonface objects are consistent with aspects of both the processing map model of Gauthier and the object form typology model of Haxby *et al.* First, consistent with Haxby *et al.*, we suggest that semantic information is important to the ventral visual pathway for object categorization. Second, consistent with Gauthier *et al.*, we believe that repeated perceptual experience with faces biases the type of information that FG finds important. We propose that the middle FG area encodes semantic attributes of people because of repeated perceptual experiences with faces that occur during social interactions. In fact, we would guess that most perceptual experiences with faces occur during social situations, and these social situations often involve repeated social judgements. Thus, information about the social nature of people might be stored in the FG (though not exclusively).

The nature of the semantic information stored in the FG might be restricted to anything that would be helpful in defining faces as a distinct category of object, because making such distinctions appears to be the primary charge of the ventral visual pathway. This would include knowledge of people as having personal agency and of having the capability to disturb each other's emotional homeostasis (e.g. to act friendly or unfriendly). By pretending that the three shapes in the SAT are people, stored knowledge about people in social interactions might be retrieved, causing the observed activations in the FG. There would be a measure of efficiency from this arrangement, that is, having representations and computations of more abstract attributes of people inter-digitated with front-end perceptual processes about physical attributes. Gauthier's claim is that the same group of neurons can be engaged by perceptually different categories of objects; it is the type of processing, rather than the visual details, that are important. Extrapolating from this, we would argue that the SAT engages a region of the FG, overlapping with the FFA, because it demands computational processes to classify the SAT geometric figures as people or person-like. Chao *et al.* (1999) reach a similar conclusion. They argued that activity in the ventral pathway reflects stored information about an object category, not just physical features. They point out that this arrangement could explain why lesion patients with category specific perceptual deficits also have trouble retrieving general information about that visual category. Thus, we would add that the FFA must store general information about people, or some meta-representation of 'peopleness'.

(c) Implications for the pathobiology of autism

The SAT used in this current study appears to be an effective neurobehavioural probe for engaging a distributed network of brain regions involved in different aspects of social perception and cognition. It will be important to use this and similar procedures in persons with autism to better define the nature of brain functions in this disorder. Castelli *et al.* (2002) have already taken the first step in this process, and they describe a pattern of hypoactivation in the MPFC, STS and TPs in autism. In an ongoing study of autism spectrum disorders, we have presented preliminary data using the SAT showing that we too find hypoactivation of these regions, and in the amygdala and FG (Schultz *et al.* 2001). Thus, we predict that future work in this area will show that the entire social brain network is underactive in autism during tasks requiring social perceptual and social cognitive processing.

There are already sufficient data to argue strongly for a role of the FG in the pathobiology of autism. No less than five previous fMRI studies have shown the FFA region to be significantly less engaged among persons with autism compared with controls during face perception tasks (Critchley *et al.* 2000; Dierks *et al.* 2001; Pierce *et al.* 2001; Schultz *et al.* 2000*a*, 2001). Activation of the FG by the social judgements in the current study adds an important piece of evidence in favour of a causal role for the FG in the pathobiology of autism. This conclusion, however, must remain tentative, until additional studies more precisely define the factors leading to FG activation during social attribution and gather better data to prove its computational role in social cognition. In addition, the effect of FG lesions for social functioning must be clarified. If the FG is involved in social computations, one would expect to find social cognitive deficits in persons with lesions to this area. However, social deficits in prosopagnosics have not been widely reported. It might be that prosopagnosic patients have not been carefully tested on this dimension. In this regard, using our behavioural version of the SAT (Klin 2000) to test social perception among prosopagnosics would be quite interesting. The parallels, however, between autism and prosopagnosia are incomplete, because autism is clearly a developmental disorder, whereas the research literature on prosopagnosia is mostly confined to lesions acquired in adolescence or adulthood. Among the few cases of developmental prosopagnosia reported in the literature, there is indeed one that highlights severe social impairments (Kracke 1994). It may be that the role of the FG in the development of autistic symptoms is different from the role of the FG in the maintenance of social cognitive functions after brain maturity.

It is also possible that the role of the FG in social processes is dependent on its functional relationships with other nodes in the social brain, and that it is the collective action and interaction of the network that is of primary importance for social behaviours. For example, we found a strong correlation across participants in the amount of FG and amygdala activation. A strictly modular view of these areas may be inappropriate, as the functions of each node could be quite dependent on one another, and when only considered in isolation, quite insufficient to support social processes. Thus, whereas a lesion to the FG may impair visual perception, it might not have a large impact on social functioning if this depends on an extended network that is dynamic and capable of compensatory adjustments. Dysfunction of the FG may be necessary but not sufficient to produce social deficits. Indeed our reliance on modular models of brain functioning may be leading us astray in our search for causal mechanisms in autism. Instead, it may be the collective action of a distributed system that is critical to the pathobiology of autism. The FG region may be a key partner in this distributed system, but nevertheless just one node, and insufficient by itself to support in any substantive manner social cognitive processes, or to explain social cognitive deficits seen in autism.

13.5 Conclusion and future directions

Using the SAT, we isolated a distributed network of activations that conform to the emerging model of the social brain. Most important, we found significant activation of the central aspect of the FG, thus adding this region to the expanding list of structures involved in social processes. The FG region activated by the SAT overlaps in its spatial extent with the FFA, with centres of mass differing by less than 1 voxel. We speculate that these SAT activations represent computational processes associated with more abstract attributes of people.

It is an open question as to whether the substantial overlap between the FFA and SAT FG activation is due to an overlapping or shared set of neuronal assemblies. This will need to be clarified by future work. Electrophysiological studies show that there are small face-specific patches in the FG cortex (Allison *et al.* 1999). In the current study, small patches of face cells and SAT cells could be intermingled, but distinct and not drawing on any of the same neuronal assemblies. The spatial resolution of fMRI has limitations that may preclude any definitive answer to this question, but there are strategies that can be used to address the issue. For example, the current study design did not contain SAT and face discriminations in the same experimental fMRI series. Doing so would enable direct comparisons of the computational demands placed on the common area of the FFA. It also would be informative if follow-up studies superimposed faces within the geometric figures of the SAT without changing the film scripts in any way. We could then determine if the computations of the common area of the FFA increase in a predictable fashion— would the activation be a linear summation of the original SAT plus face discrimination? Any significant deviation from an additive model would suggest that there is some sharing of neuronal assemblies with the SAT and face discrimination tasks when presented alone.

This work was supported by grants from the National Institutes of Child Health and Human Development (grants PO1 HD 03008 and PO1 HD/DC35482) and the Korczak Foundation. The authors thank the anonymous reviewers for their helpful comments, Michael Lee for programming the fMRI tasks, Hedy Serofin and Terry Hickey for their assistance in acquiring the fMRI data, John Herrington for his valuable assistance in data analyses of preliminary studies, and members of the Yale Developmental Neuroimaging Program for their helpful comments on this manuscript. A special acknowledgement of appreciation is given to Donald Cohen, who passed away in October of 2001, for his outstanding mentorship in all aspects of this program of work.

References

Abell, F., Happé, F. and Frith, U. (2000). Do triangles play tricks? Attribution of mental states to animated shapes in normal and abnormal development *J. Cogn. Dev.* **15**, 1–20.

Adolphs, R., Tranel, D. and Damasio, A. R. (1998). The human amygdala in social judgement. *Nature* **393**, 470–74.

Allison, T., Puce, A., Spencer, D. D. and McCarthy, G. (1999). Electrophysiological studies of human face perception. I: potentials generated in occipitotemporal cortex by face and non-face stimuli. *Cerebr. Cortex* **9**, 415–30.

Allison, T., Puce, A. and McCarthy, G. (2000). Social perception from visual cues: role of the STS region. *Trends Cogn. Sci.* **4**, 267–78.

Amaral, D. G. and Price, J. L. (1984). Amygdalo-cortical projections in the monkey (*Macaca fascicularis*). *J. Comp. Neurol.* **230**, 465–96.

Amaral, D. G., Price, J. L., Pitkanen, A. and Carmichael, S. T. (1992). Anatomical organization of the primate amygdaloid complex. In *The amygdala: neurobiological aspects of emotion, memory and mental dysfunction* (ed. J. Aggleton), pp. 1–66. New York: Wiley-Liss.

Anderson, A. K. and Phelps, E. A. (2001). Lesions of the human amygdala impair enhanced perception of emotionally salient events. *Nature* **411**, 305–09.

Bachevalier, J. (1994). Medial temporal lobe structures and autism: a review of clinical and experimental findings. *Neuropsychologia* **32**, 627–48.

Bachevalier, J. and Mishkin, M. (1986). Visual recognition impairment follows ventromedial but not dorsolateral prefrontal lesions in monkeys. *Behav. Brain Res.* **20**, 249–61.

Baron-Cohen, S., Ring, H. A., Wheelwright, S., Bullmore, E. T., Brammer, M. J., Simmons, A., *et al.* (1999). Social intelligence in the normal and autistic brain: an fMRI study. *Eur. J. Neurosci.* **11**, 1891–98.

Baron-Cohen, S., Ring, H. A., Bullmore, E. T., Wheelwright, S., Ashwina, C. and Williams, S. C. R. (2000). The amygdala theory of autism. *Neurosci. Biobehav. Rev.* **24**, 355–64.

Bechara, A., Tranel, D., Damasio, H. and Damasio, A. R. (1996). Failure to respond autonomically to anticipated future outcomes following damage to prefrontal cortex. *Cerebr. Cortex* **6**, 215–25.

Benton, A. (1994). *Face recognition*. Los Angeles, CA: Western Psychological Services.

Bonda, E., Petrides, M., Ostry, D. and Evans, A. (1996). Specific involvement of human parietal systems and the amygdala in the perception of biological motion. *J. Neurosci.* **16**, 3737–44.

Bowler, D. M. and Thommen, E. (2000). Attribution of mechanical and social causality to animated displays by children with autism. *Autism* **4**, 147–71.

Brothers, L. (1990). The social brain: a project for integrating primate behavior and neurophysiology in a new domain. *Concepts Neurosci.* **1**, 27–151.

Brothers, L. (1995). Neurophysiology of the perception of intention by primates. In *The cognitive neurosciences*, 2nd edn (ed. M. S. Gazzaniga), pp. 1107–15. Cambridge, MA: MIT Press.

Butter, C. M., McDonald, J. A. and Snyder, D. R. (1969). Orality, preference behavior, and reinforcement value of nonfood object in monkeys with orbital frontal lesions. *Science* **164**, 1306–07.

Carmichael, S. T. and Price, J. L. (1995). Limbic connections of the orbital and medial prefrontal cortex in macaque monkeys. *J. Comp. Neurol.* **363**, 615–41.

Castelli, F., Happé, F., Frith, U. and Frith, C. (2000). Movement and mind: a functional imaging study of perception and interpretation of complex intentional movement patterns. *NeuroImage* **12**, 314–25.

Castelli, F., Frith, C., Happé, F. and Frith, U. (2002). Autism, Asperger syndrome and brain mechanisms for the attribution of mental states to animated shapes. *Brain* **125**, 1839–49.

Chao, L. L., Haxby, J. V. and Martin, A. (1999). Attribute-based neural substrates in posterior temporal cortex for perceiving and knowing about objects. *Nat. Neurosci.* **2**, 913–19.

Chao, L. L., Weisberg, J. and Martin, A. (2002). Experiencedependent modulation of category-related cortical activity. *Cerebr. Cortex* **12**, 545–51.

Critchley, H. D., Daly, E. M., Bullmore, E. T., Williams, S. C., Van Amelsvoort, T., Robertson, D. M., *et al.* (2000). The functional neuroanatomy of social behaviour: changes in cerebral blood flow when people with autistic disorder process facial expressions. *Brain* **123**, 2203–12.

Culham, J. C., Cavanagh, P. and Kanwisher, N. G. (2001). Attention response functions: characterizing brain areas using fMRI activation during parametric variations of attentional load. *Neuron* **32**, 737–45.

Damasio, A. R., Tranel, D. and Damasio, H. (1990). Individuals with sociopathic behavior caused by frontal damage fail to respond autonomically to social stimuli. *Behav. Brain Res.* **41**, 81–94.

Dierks, T., Bolte, S., Huble, D., Lanfermannm, H. and Poustka, F. (2001). Alterations of face processing strategies in autism (a fMRI study). Presented at the 6th Annual Meeting of the Organization for Human Brain Mapping, Brighton, UK, 10–14 June 2001.

Dias, R., Robbins, T. W. and Roberts, A. C. (1996). Dissociation in prefrontal cortex of affective and attentional shifts. *Nature* **380**, 69–72.

Downing, P. E., Jiang, Y., Shuman, M. and Kanwisher, N. (2001). A cortical area selective for visual processing of the human body. *Science* **293**, 2470–73.

Epstein, R. and Kanwisher, N. (1998). A cortical representation of the local visual environment. *Nature* **392**, 598–601.

Ernst, M., Zametkin, A. J., Matochik, J. A., Pascualvaca, D. and Cohen, R. M. (1997). Reduced medial prefrontal dopaminergic activity in autistic children. *Lancet* **350**, 638.

Fletcher, P. C., Happé, F., Frith, U., Baker, S. C., Dolan, R. J., Frackowiak, R. S., *et al.* (1995). Other minds in the brain: a functional imaging study of 'theory of mind' in story comprehension. *Cognition* **57**, 109–28.

Frith, C. D. and Frith, U. (1999). Interacting minds: a biological basis. *Science* **286**, 1692–95.

Fujita, I., Tanaka, K., Ito, M. and Cheng, K. (1992). Columns for visual features of objects in monkey inferotemporal cortex. *Nature* **360**, 343–46.

Gaffan, E. A., Gaffan, D. and Harrison, S. (1988). Disconnection of the amygdala from visual association cortex impairs visual- reward association learning in monkeys. *J. Neurosci.* **8**, 3144–50.

Gallagher, H. L., Happé, F., Brunswick, N., Fletcher, P. C., Frith, U. and Frith, C. D. (2000). Reading the mind in cartoons and stories: an fMRI study of 'theory of mind' in verbal and nonverbal tasks. *Neuropsychologia* **38**, 11–21.

Gauthier, I., Anderson, A. W., Tarr, M. J., Skudlarski, P. and Gore, J. C. (1997). Levels of categorization in visual recognition studied using functional magnetic resonance imaging. *Curr. Biol.* **7**, 645–51.

Gauthier, I., Tarr, M. J., Anderson, A. W., Skudlarski, P. and Gore, J. C. (1999). Activation of the middle fusiform face area increases with expertise in recognizing novel objects. *Nature Neurosci.* **2**, 568–73.

Gauthier, I., Skudlarski, P., Gore, J. C. and Anderson, A. W. (2000). Expertise for cars and birds recruits brain areas involved in face recognition. *Nature Neurosci.* **3**, 191–97.

Goel, V., Grafman, J., Sadato, N. and Hallett, M. (1995). Modeling other minds. *Neuroreport* **6**, 1741–46.

Grelotti, D., Gauthier, I. and Schultz, R. T. (2001). Social interest and the development of cortical face specialization: what autism teaches us about face processing. *Devl Psychobiol.* **40**, 213–25.

Grèzes, J., Fonlupt, P., Bertenthal, B. and Delon-Martin, C. (2001). Does perception of biological motion rely on specific brain regions? *NeuroImage* **13**, 775–85.

Gusnard, D. A., Akbudak, E., Shulman, G. L. and Raichle, M. E. (2001). Medial pre-frontal cortex and self-referential mental activity: relation to a default mode of brain function. *Proc. Natl Acad. Sci. USA* **98**, 4259–64.

Happé, F., Ehlers, S., Fletcher, P., Frith, U., Johansson, M., Gillberg, C., *et al.* (1996). 'Theory of mind' in the brain. Evidence from a PET scan study of Asperger syndrome. *Neuroreport* **8**, 197–201.

Haxby, J. V., Ungerleider, L. G., Clark, V. P., Schouten, J. L., Hoffman, E. A. and Martin, A. (1999). The effect of face inversion on activity in human neural systems for face and object perception. *Neuron* **22**, 189–99.

Haxby, J. V., Isahai, A., Chao, L. L., Ungerleider, L. G. and Martin, A. (2000). Object-form topology in the ventral temporal lobe: response to I. Gauthier (2000). *Trends Cogn. Sci.* **4**, 3–4.

Haxby, J. V., Gobbini, M. I., Furey, M. L., Ishai, A., Schouten, J. L. and Pietrini, P. (2001). Distributed and overlapping representations of faces and objects in ventral temporal cortex. *Science* **293**, 2425–30.

Haznedar, M. M., Buchsbaum, M. S., Metzger, M., Solimando, A., Spiegel-Cohen, J. and Hollander, E. (1997). Anterior cingulate gyrus volume and glucose metabolism in autistic disorder. *Am. J. Psychiat.* **154**, 1047–50.

Heider, F. and Simmel, M. (1944). An experimental study of apparent behavior. *Am. J. Psychol.* **57**, 243–59.

Hobson, R. P., Ouston, J. and Lee, A. (1988*a*). What's in a face? The case of autism *Br. J. Psychol.* **79**, 441–53.

Hobson, R. P., Ouston, J. and Lee, A. (1988*b*). Emotion recognition in autism: coordinating faces and voices. *Psychol. Med.* **18**, 911–23.

Hoffman, E. A. and Haxby, J. V. (2000). Distinct representations of eye gaze and identity in the distributed human neural system for face perception. *Nature Neurosci.* **3**, 80–84.

Hornak, J., Rolls, E. T. and Wade, D. (1996). Face and voice expression identification in patients with emotional and behavioural changes following ventral frontal lobe damage. *Neuropsychologia* **34**, 247–61.

Ishai, A., Ungerleider, L. G., Martin, A., Schouten, J. L. and Haxby, J. V. (1999). Distributed representation of objects in the human ventral visual pathway. *Proc. Natl Acad. Sci. USA* **96**, 9379–84.

Kanwisher, N. (2000). Domain specificity in face perception. *Nature Neurosci.* **3**, 759–63.

Kanwisher, N., McDermott, J. and Chun, M. M. (1997). The fusiform face area: a module of extrastriate cortex specialized for face perception. *J. Neurosci.* **17**, 4302–11.

Klin, A. (2000). Attributing social meaning to ambiguous visual stimuli in higher functioning autism and Asperger syndrome: the social attribution task. *J. Child Psychol. Psychiat.* **41**, 831–46.

Klin, A., Sparrow, S. S., de Bildt, A., Cicchetti, D. V., Cohen, D. J. and Volkmar, F. R. (1999). A normed study of face recognition in autism and related disorders. *J. Autism Devl Disorders* **29**, 499–508.

Klin, A., Jones, W., Schultz, R. T., Volkmar, F. and Cohen, D. J. (2002). Visual fixation patterns during viewing of naturalistic social situations as predictors of social competence in individuals with autism. *Arch. Gen. Psychiat.* **59**, 809–16.

Kracke, I. (1994). Developmental prosopagnosia in Asperger syndrome: presentation and discussion of an individual case. *Devl Med. Child Neurol.* **36**, 873–86.

Lane, R. D., Reiman, E. M., Ahern, G. L., Schwartz, G. E. and Davidson, R. J. (1997). Neuroanatomical correlates of happiness, sadness, and disgust. *Am. J. Psychiat.* **154**, 926–33.

Langdell, T. (1978). Recognition of faces: an approach for the study of autism. *J. Child Psychol. Psychiat.* **19**, 255–68.

LeDoux, J. E. (1996). *The emotional brain.* New York: Simon and Shuster.

Löwel, S. and Singer, W. (1992). Selection of intrinsic horizontal connections in the visual cortex by correlated neuronal activity. *Science* **255**, 209–12.

Macdonald, H., Rutter, M., Howlin, P., Rios, P., Le Conteur, A., Evered, C., *et al.* (1989). Recognition and expression of emotional cues by autistic and normal adults. *J. Child Psychol. Psychiat.* **30**, 865–77.

Morris, J. S., Ohman, A. and Dolan, R. J. (1998). Conscious and unconscious emotional learning in the human amygdala. *Nature* **393**, 467–70.

Myers, R. E., Swett, C. and Miller, M. (1973). Loss of social group affinity following prefrontal lesions in free-ranging macaques. *Brain Res.* **64**, 257–69.

Osterling, J. and Dawson, G. (1994). Early recognition of children with autism: a study of first birthday home video tapes. *J. Autism Devl Disorders* **24**, 247–57.

Pierce, K., Muller, R. A., Ambrose, J., Allen, G. and Courchesne, E. (2001). Face processing occurs outside the fusiform 'face area' in autism: evidence from functional MRI. *Brain* **124**, 2059–73.

Price, J. L., Carmichael, S. T. and Drevets, W. C. (1996). Networks related to the orbital and medial prefrontal cortex; a substrate for emotional behavior? *Prog. Brain Res.* **107**, 523–36.

Puce, A., Allison, T., Gore, J. C. and McCarthy, G. (1995). Facesensitive regions in human extrastriate cortex studied by functional MRI. *J. Neurophysiol.* **74**, 1192–99.

Reiman, E. M., Lane, R. D., Ahern, G. L., Schwartz, G. E., Davidson, R. J., Friston, K. J., *et al.* (1997). Neuroanatomical correlates of externally and internally generated human emotion. *Am. J. Psychiat.* **154**, 918–25.

Rolls, E. T. (1995). A theory of emotion and consciousness, and its application to understanding the neural basis of emotion. In *The cognitive neurosciences* (ed. M. S. Gazzaniga), pp. 1091–1106. Cambridge, MA: MIT Press.

Schultz, R. T., Gauthier, I., Klin, A., Fulbright, R. K., Anderson, A. W., Volkmar, F., *et al.* (2000*a*). Abnormal ventral temporal cortical activity during face discriminations among individuals with autism and Asperger syndrome. *Arch. Gen. Psychiat.* **37**, 331–40.

Schultz, R. T., Romanski, L. M. and Tsatsanis, K. D. (2000*b*). Neurofunctional models of autistic disorder and Asperger syndrome. In *Asperger syndrome* (ed. A. Klin, F. R. Volkmar and S. S. Sparrow), pp. 172–209. New York: The Guilford Press.

Schultz, R. T., Grelotti, D. J., Klin, A., Levitan, E., Cantey, T., Skudlarski, P., *et al.* (2001). An fMRI study of face recognition, facial expression detection, and social judgment in autism spectrum conditions. Presented at the International Meeting for Autism Research, San Diego, CA, 9–10 November 2001.

Siegal, M., Carrington, J. and Radel, M. (1996). Theory of mind and pragmatic understanding following right hemisphere damage. *Brain Lang.* **53**, 40–50.

Skudlarski, P., Constable, R. T. and Gore, J. C. (1999). ROC analysis of statistical methods used in functional MRI: individual subjects. *Neuroimage* **9**, 311–29.

Spiridon, M. and Kanwisher, N. (2002). How distributed is visual category information in human occipito-temporal cortex? An fMRI study *Neuron* **35**, 1157–65.

Talairach, J. and Tournoux, P. (1988). *Co-planar stereotaxic atlas of the human brain. 3-Dimensional proportional system: an approach to cerebral imaging.* New York: Thieme.

Tarr, M. J. and Gauthier, I. (2000). FFA: a flexible fusiform area for subordinate level visual processing automatized by expertise. *Nature Neurosci.* **3**, 764–69.

Vaina, L. M., Solomoni, J., Chowdhury, S., Sinha, P. and Belliveau, J. W. (2001). Functional neuroanatomy of biological motion perception in humans. *Proc. Natl Acad. Sci.* **98**, 11656–661.

Wada, Y. and Yamamoto, T. (2001). Selective impairment of facial recognition due to a haematoma restricted to the right fusiform and lateral occipital region. *J. Neurol. Neurosurg. Psychiat.* **71**, 254–57.

Webster, M. J., Ungerleider, L. G. and Bachlevalier, J. (1991). Lesions of the inferior temporal area TE in infant monkeys alter cortico-amygdalar projections. *Neuroreport* **2**, 769–72.

Wechsler, D. (1997). *Wechsler Adult Intelligence Scale*, 3rd edn. San Antonio, TX: Psychological Corp.

Whalen, P. J., Rauch, S. L., Etcoff, N. L., McInerney, S. C., Lee, M. B. and Jenike, M. A. (1998). Masked presentations of emotional facial expressions modulate amygdala activity without explicit knowledge. *J. Neurosci.* **18**, 411–18.

Winner, E., Brownell, H., Happé, F., Blum, A. and Pincus, D. (2002). Distinguishing lies from jokes: theory of mind deficits and discourse interpretation in right hemisphere brain-damaged patients. *Brain Lang.* **62**, 89–106.

Winston, J. S., Strange, B. A., O'Doherty, J. and Dolan, R. J. (2002). Automatic and intentional brain responses during evaluation of trustworthiness of faces. *Nature Neurosci.* **5**, 277–83.

Yirmiya, N., Sigman, M. D., Kasari, C. and Mundy, P. (1992). Empathy and cognition in high-functioning children with autism. *Child Dev.* **63**, 150–60.

Glossary

AC–PC: anterior commissure–posterior commissure
BOLD: blood oxygen level dependent
FFA: fusiform face area
FG: fusiform gyrus
fMRI: functional magnetic resonance imaging
IQ: intelligence quotient

MFS: mid-fusiform sulcus
MPFC: medial prefrontal cortex
NEX: number of excitations
PET: positron emission tomography
ROI: region of interest
SAT: social attribution task
STG: superior temporal gyrus
STS: superior temporal sulcus
TE: echo time
TP: temporal pole
TR: repetition time

Index

(page numbers in **bold** type refer to tables)

ability, islets 166, *see also* savant skills
amygdala
    social attribution task (SAT) activations 281
    startle response: emotional modulation
        255–61
    structure/function in autistic subjects
        247–64
    and ventral visual processing stream 281–2
Asperger syndrome (AS)
    auditory perception 198
    definitions 2, 22–3
    differentiation from high-functioning autism
        (HFA) 230
    epidemiology 2
    history, data from Asperger (Vienna) 21–42
        behavioural difficulties **34**
        diagnostic labels **29**
        family background 31–2
        ICD-10 symptom count **36**
        reasons for referral **28**
        sampling methods 24–5
        speech and language characteristics **35**
    see also high-functioning autism (HFA);
        systemizing quotient (SQ)
attention-deficit/hyperactivity disorder *see*
    drawing planning
attentional resource allocation 260
attentional/perceptual impairment 90–2
    see also reflexive visual orienting
auditory perception
    scopolamine 207
    speech-in-noise perception, frequency
        selectivity 199–205
auditory-filter shapes, in HFA or AS 198–206
autism
    causes 3–12, 110–12
    definitions 2, 22–3
    epidemiology 2–3
    non-social features 8–9
    pathogenesis 109–26, 285–6
    phenotypes 13–14
    signs and symptoms 5–12, 70, 74
    spectrum disorders (ASD) *see* Asperger
        syndrome (AS); high-functioning
        autism (HFA)

    typical vs atypical 111–12
Autism Diagnostic Interview – Revised
    (ADI-R) 53, 74, 191
Autism Diagnostic Observation Schedule
    (ADOS) 53, **54**

basilar membrane (BM) 199–200
biconditional configural discrimination 190–4
blindness, congenital 112–26
brain
    asymmetry, language impairment 50–2
    extreme male brain theory 164–7
    volume, V–NV (verbal–non-verbal)
        discrepancies 58–9
brain abnormalities 4–5, 247–64
    amygdala structure/function in autistic
        subjects 248–55
    frontal lobes 11
    fusiform face area (FFA) 148–9, 267–93
    large head circumference 56–8
    limbic system 4

central coherence 8–10
    and executive dysfunction 10–12, 211–23
'channel' hypothesis 232
Checklist for autism in toddlers (CHAT) 70–1
childhood autism rating scale (CARS) 118–21
clinical evaluation of language fundamentals
    (CELF) test 47, 48
cognition, and action, animal model 141
cognitive profiles 52–9
    symptom severity 53–6
    V–NV (verbal–non-verbal) discrepancies
        and brain volume 58–9
coherence 215–16
    see also weak central coherence hypothesis
configural and feature processing 190
    see also visual configural learning and
        auditory perception
conjunctive visual search task 188
contextual elements, mental representations
    140–4

definitions
    Asperger syndrome 2, 22–3
    autism 2

detail-focussed processing bias, embedded
      figures task (EFT) 166, 188, 212
'disinhibition', and savant skills 2–3, 212
drawing planning (ASD vs ADHD) 211–23

echolalia, echopraxia 140
embedded figures task (EFT) 166, 188, 212
embodied cognitive science 127
embodied vision 144–7
empathizing quotient (EQ) 167–75, **180–3**
empathizing–systemizing theory 161–4, 172–5
enactive mind (EM) (acquisition of social
      cognition) approach 133–59
    contextual elements in emergence of mental
        representations 140–4
    developmental elements in emergence of
        mental representations 137–40
    social cognition as social action 147–52
    social functioning, explicit vs naturalistic
        situations 127–34
    social world as open domain task 134–7
    temporal constraints on models of social
        adaptation 144–7
epidemiology of autism 2–3
executive dysfunction theory 10, 12, 211–12
    separation from weak central coherence
        hypothesis 10–12, 211–23
extreme male brain (EMB) theory 164–7
eye-tracking studies 128–34, 136–7
    see also gaze

face scanning, eye-tracking studies 128–34
facial signals, still-face pardigm 139–40
Faux Pas test 165
feature–configuration patterning task,
      configural learning 194–7
females, empathizing–systemizing theory
      161–4
frequency selectivity, auditory perception
      199–205
frontal lobes, damage, disorders 11
fusiform gyrus: face area (FFA) 148–9,
      267–93
    comparison of right fusiform gyrus during
        social attribution task and face
        perception 278–9
    implications for pathobiology of autism
        285–6
    role in social cognition 279–86
    social brain network 279–82

gaze processing
    chimpanzees 90

eye-tracking studies 128–34, 136–7
    impairment in autism 90
    see also reflexive visual orienting
gaze-switching, joint attention 73, 78, 102–4
genetics
    7q31 region 52
    13q region 52
    FOXP2 52
    twin studies 3–4
global processing vs local processing 187, 189
Goldman–Fristoe Test, phonology 46, 47
grammatical deficits, language impairment
      48–50
Griffiths Scale of Infant Development 71–2

head circumference, cognitive correlates 56–8
heritability see genetics
high-functioning autism (HFA) 167–8
    differentiation from Asperger syndrome
        (AS) 230
    see also Asperger syndrome (AS)
hyperactivity see attention-
        deficit/hyperactivity disorder
hyperlexia 140

intellectual function (IQ)
    and movement patterning, relationship 240–4
    Wechsler scales 115, 188
interpersonal aspects of autism 110–12,
      127–34
'islets of ability', and savant skills 166, 212

joint attention 67, 87, 90
    affective vs cognitive 90
    early development of autism 69–71
    activated toy tasks 73
    blocking 73
    gaze-switching/ goal-detection tasks 73, 78
    imitation 73–4
    spontaneous play task 72–3
    symptom severity at 20 and 42 months 71,
        74, 76
    teasing 73
    pointing skills 130–3

Kanner syndrome 22, 24, 25–6

language impairment 45–52
    grammatical deficits 48–50
    language profiles 45–8
    morphometric analysis of brain asymmetry
        50–2
    SLI (specific language impairment) 48–51

local processing vs global processing 187, 189

macrocephaly, cognitive correlates 56–8
males
    empathizing–systemizing theory 161–4
    extreme male brain (EMB) theory 164–7
maths, Scholastic Aptitude Math Test 164
mental representations
    contextual elements 140–4
    developmental elements 137–40
    as proxies for actions 147–8
mental retardation/impairment, association
        with autism 2
mentalizing
    deficit in mentalizing hypothesis 5–8
    theory of mind 5–8, 110, 211
metaphoric language 140
motor function, previous research in
        ASD **226–8**
Movement Assessment Battery for Children
        Checklist 252
movement disturbance 225–46
    IQ and movement patterning
        relationship 240–4
    reach-to-grasp 231–40
MRI
    amygdala structure/function in autistic
        subjects 249–50
    individual VBM (voxel-based
        morphometry) 250–3
    fMRI activations
        cartoon characters 149
        faces as objects 149–52
        role of fusiform face area (FFA) 285–6
    morphometric analysis of brain
        asymmetry 50–2

neurocognitive phenotypes 43–66
    cognitive profiles 52–9
    language impairment 45–52
neuronal pruning 5

parents of autistic children, fathers 13
Parkinsonian-type bradykinesia 229, 240–1
pathogenesis of autism 109–26
    and congenital blindness 112–26
    role of fusiform face area (FFA) 285–6
Peabody picture vocabulary test (PPVT) 46, 47
perception-for-action systems 141–3
perceptual impairment 90–2
    see also reflexive visual orienting
perseveration 11–12

pervasive developmental disorder (PDDNOS)
        44, 53
phonology, Goldman–Fristoe Test 46, 47
planning 211–23
    Towers tests 220–1
point-light animations 142–3
prompt-dependent social gestures 140
psychological theory, joint attention 67–9

reach-to-grasp movement 231–40
reflexive visual orienting 89–107
repeat nonsense words (RNW) test 47
Rett syndrome 44
Reynell Developmental Language Scales 72
Rivermead Behavioural Memory Test 252
Rogers scale, movement disturbance 229

savant skills 2–3
    and 'islets of ability' 166, 212
'schizoid' children 40
scopolamine, auditory perception 207
sensory processing, deficits 10
signs and symptoms 5–12
    executive dysfunction 10–12
    failure to acquire intuitive theory of
        mind 5–8
    severity, and joint attention 71, 74
    weak central coherence and variants 8–10
social adaptation models, temporal constraints
        144–7
social attribution task (SAT) 269–79
    brain activity 276–8
    QuickTime film skits 271
social cognition
    ambiguous visual stimuli experiment 150–2
    disembodied cognition 139
    enactive mind (acquisition of social
        cognition) approach 133–59
    functioning in explicit vs naturalistic
        situations 127–34
    infants' reactions to human sounds/
        faces 138
    interpersonal aspects of autism 110–12,
        127–34
    role of fusiform face area (FFA) 279–86
    as social action 147–52
    see also enactive mind
social orienting model 80–1
social worlds, as open domain tasks 134–7
startle response: emotional modulation 255–61
still-face paradigm 139–40
superior temporal gyrus/sulcus (STG/STS),
        activation 280

systemizing quotient (SQ) 161–75, **176–9**
    empathizing–systemizing theory 161–4
    extreme male brain theory 164–7
    high-functioning autism and Asperger
        syndrome 167–8

theory of mind deficit 5–8, 110
'toe-walking' 229
Towers tests, planning (drawings) 220–1
twin studies 3–4

vertical electro-oculogram (vEOG) 257
visual configural learning and auditory
        perception 187–210
    auditory-filter shapes 198–206

biconditional configural discrimination
        (expt. one) 190–4
configural and feature processing 190
feature–configuration patterning task
        (expt. two) 194–7
voxel-based morphometry (VBM) 250–3

weak central coherence hypothesis 187–210
    configural and feature processing 190
    separation from executive dysfunction
        10–12, 211–23
    variants 8–10
Wechsler scales 115, 188
    block design subtest 188
    embedded figures task (EFT) 166, 188, 212